# FAMILY THERAPY AS AN ALTERNATIVE TO MEDICATION

# FAMILY THERAPY AS AN ALTERNATIVE TO MEDICATION:

## AN APPRAISAL OF PHARMLAND

Phoebe S. Prosky, MSW and David V. Keith, MD, Editors

BRUNNER-ROUTLEDGE

NEW YORK AND HOVE

Published in 2003 by
Brunner-Routledge
29 West 35th Street
New York, NY 10001
www.brunner-routledge.com

Published in Great Britain by
Brunner-Routledge
27 Church Road
Hove, East Sussex
BN3 2FA
www.brunner-routledge.co.uk

Printed in the United States of America on acid-free paper.

"When My Sorrow Was Born," from *The Madman,* by Kahlil Gibran, is reprinted with permission from Dover Publications © copyright 2001.

Cover design by Mark Lerner
Cover photo © Corbis

Library of Congress Cataloging-in-Publication Data
Prosky, Phoebe.
   Family therapy as an alternative to medication : an appraisal
   of pharmland / Phoebe Prosky and David Keith.
      p. cm.
Includes bibliographical references and index.
   ISBN 0-415-93398-6 (hardcover)
   1. Family therapy. 2. Mental illness—Chemotherapy. 3.
Psychotherapy.
   [DNLM: 1.   Family Therapy—methods. 2.   Mental
Disorders—drug therapy. 3.   Psychotherapy—methods. WM 430.5.F2 P966f 2002]
I. Keith, David V. II. Title.

RC488.5 .P75 2002
616.89'156—dc21

2002014093

# Dedication

We would like to dedicate our book to three people who were, and continue to be, guiding spirits in our work, practitioners whose careers were characterized by a spirit of exploration and steady attention to human growth and the deepening of experience in therapeutic work with families: Nathan W. Ackerman, M.D., Edgar H. (Dick) Auerswald, M.D., and Carl A. Whitaker, M.D.

# Contents

# Acknowledgments

The editors acknowledge with great appreciation the contributions of people whose generosity helped to make this book possible. Patricia Dyer shared her editorial insightfulness, created two of the images for the book, and provided invaluable technical assistance in preparing the manuscript for the publisher; her patience throughout the process of the work on this book is greatly appreciated. Noel Keith provided help with sampling and shaping ideas, along with an abundance of encouragement and inspiration when needed. Sarah Auerswald assisted in gaining the permission to republish two of her father's papers in this volume. Barbara Anthonson contributed generously of her time and computer knowledgeability in helping to ready the manuscript for publication. Editor George Zimmar, Assistant Editors Shannon Vargo and Luciana Cassano, and Production Editor Richard Rothschild did a superior job of editing our work and supporting us through its production. We wish to thank Mr. Zimmar and the staff at Brunner-Routledge for being willing to take on the publication of this book in light of its counter-cultural bent.

# Introduction

*"All right," said the Cat; and this time it vanished quite slowly, beginning with the end of the tail, and ending with the grin, which remained some time after the rest of it had gone. "Well! I've often seen a cat without a grin," thought Alice; "but a grin without a cat! It's the most curious thing I ever saw in all my life!*

Lewis Carroll, *Alice's Adventures in Wonderland*

This book explores the *interface* between two different ways of thinking about the world of mental health: family systems-based therapy and modern "biological" psychiatry. Biological psychiatry, with its armamentarium of medications, has largely eclipsed the family systems or ecosystemic model of psychotherapy, which has as its focus context and relationships. Routinely patients are being placed on medication in response to emotional or mental symptoms, not only by psychiatrists, but also by physicians in all specialties, often on the recommendation of nonmedical therapists and teachers. This rush to medicate, with its side effects of dependency and the redefinition of experience as disease, has begun to draw the skepticism of practitioners and a public that senses its possible costs as well as the importance of arriving at self-mastery in life. The powerful potential of the ecosystemic approach of family systems therapy, so much in tune with larger ecological concerns today, responds to this situation. In the 50 years since the ecosystemic approach began to be articulated, its usefulness has become overwhelmingly evident, yet its potential has barely begun to be mined. We are developing this book in an attempt to awaken broader awareness of the vision of systems-oriented psychotherapy in hopes of keeping it from being disappeared by the strong forces of the medical profession and the pharmaceutical industry.

Our book acknowledges the usefulness of medication, but expresses skepticism about the way the medication model has been embraced by practitioners and patients. Our skepticism is based on our experience in working with families as systems in which psychiatric medications are often irrelevant and sometimes harmful. Both editors have practiced and taught family therapy for close to 30 years. Phoebe Prosky, ACSW is a family therapist licensed in social work. David Keith, MD is a family therapist, board certified in general and child and adolescent psychiatry. More than half of the professionals who have agreed to contribute essays to the book are physicians with a view different from the one that prevails in their profession. Many have national reputations in the world of family therapy and related disciplines.

We want to say a word about the book's title. The title was the end product of careful negotiation. The negotiation was among the editors and the publishers who were willing to take the risk of creating a book out of our assembled ideas. We had spiced our manuscript with quotations from Lewis Carroll and we all wanted to keep our neologism "Pharmland" in the title. Finding a title seemed a delicate matter in this issue of being skeptical about medications. It is a matter that evokes strong opinions in surprising situations. And the potential for misunderstanding is ever-present. There is an amusing precedent for our title negotiations in *Through the Looking Glass*, when Alice meets the White Knight. In the course of the interaction he offers to sing her a song. When she inquires about the name of the song, the following amusing and confusing dialogue occurs:

"You are sad," the Knight said in an anxious tone: "let me sing you a song to comfort you."

"Is it very long?" Alice asked, for she had heard a good deal of poetry that day.

"It's long," said the Knight, but it's very, *very* beautiful....The name of the song is called 'Haddock's Eyes.'"

"Oh, that's the name of the song, is it?" Alice said, trying to feel interested.

"No, you don't understand," the Knight said, looking a little vexed. "That's what the song is *called*. The name really *is* 'The Aged, Aged Man.'"

"Then I ought to have said 'That's what the *song* is called'?" Alice corrected herself.

"No, you oughtn't: that's quite another thing! The *song* is called 'Ways And Means,' but that's only what it's *called*, you know!"

"Well, what *is* the song, then?" said Alice, who was by this time completely bewildered.

"I was coming to that," the Knight said. "The song really is 'A Sitting On A Gate,' and the tune's my own invention."

You have substantial reason to believe that the name of this book is *Family Therapy as an Alternative to Medication: An Appraisal of Pharmland* for that is the name on the cover. But in fact, that's what the name is *called*. In two years of musing about the book and then two years of working on the book, our working title was *Family Therapy in Pharmland: Through a Looking Glass (of Sheep in Boats and Other Such)*. And that's what the name *is*. We love that title because it is playful and slightly obscure. And it's our own invention.

The reason we worked with a playful title was to avoid the polarizing that inevitably accompanies skepticism about medications. We added the Alice quotation, "of sheep in boats and other such," because it has to do with the odd juxtapositions and reality distortions, which perplex Alice, implying that what is considered "truth" is changeable and a function of socio–political context. While we are deeply serious in our intentions, the freedom to be playful is important lest the issue become uselessly polarized. There are many ways to consider the relationship between pharmacological psychiatry and systems-oriented psychotherapy. One position is radical and reactive, tending to reject the use of medication without offering creative, viable alternatives. Another position is to combine pharmacology-based psychiatry and family systems work, without consideration of the considerable areas of difficulty and incongruity that arise. Our position is that the two systems are related, but in ways that, to use Alice's words, are "curioser and curioser" and require much more discussion before their relationship is well understood. We hope this book, whatever you might choose to call it, will make a useful contribution to the conversation.

We are, in this book, putting forth the idea that systems-based therapy is an available and alternative approach to human distress that deals with illness and supports health. The book examines the problem by looking at it from multiple perspectives: the theoretical, the political, the client's view, and the clinical.

## A WALKING GUIDE TO PHARMLAND

This book was not written to be read straight through, but rather to allow readers to wander about its pages at their discretion. We suggest certain trails for walkers of different background and inclination (see map, p. xiv). You may want to set out through the first two pieces by the editors, which set the scene for what follows. If you already know something about systems theory, you might want to go right on to Auerswald's challenging and all-encompassing chapter "Family Healing and Planetary Healing: Three Paradigms in Search of a Culture." If you want to be fired up by the political aspects of this issue, try turning to one of the two chapters in that part. If you are a layperson who is unacquainted with the issues

# Map of Pharmland

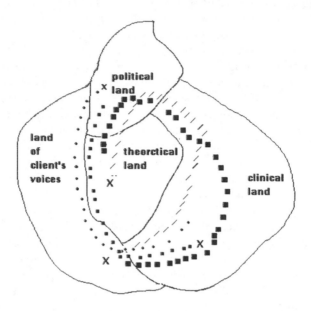

Theorist's walk / / / / /
Political walk • • • • •
Clinician's walk ▪ ▪ ▪ ▪ ▪
Layperson's walk ▪ ▪ ▪ ▪ ▪

under discussion, you might want to start with the articles by people in treatment in the Client's Voice part. From there you may want to saunter on to the policital chapters mentioned above or to look in on the issues from the therapist's point of view in the clinical part, then go on to the theoretical part. And if you are a clinician, you may want to start with the clinical chapters and then move on to one of the other sections according to your bent. No matter who you are, don't forget the Auerswald essay (Chapter 3). You may find it most interesting to read one piece in each of your chosen sections, coming back for seconds afterward, rather than reading any one section straight through. This pattern of peripatetic perambulation may increase digestion!

The family systems perspective does not attempt to make the unknowable knowable. It acknowledges the mystery inherent in human experience. Our goal is that this book will do what the ecosystemic perspective does: help readers fully appreciate the complexity of their living, and make the ambiguity and pain of human experience more bearable, more intriguing, and more productive of creative and enduring change.

We hope your walk opens up new vistas to enrich your understanding of the terrain.

# Part 1

# Introduction:
# Setting the Stage for
# an Exploration of the
# Interface of Family
# Therapy and Medication

Chapter 1

# Biometaphorical Psychiatry: Family Therapy and the Poetics of Experience

David V. Keith, MD

*"But I don't want to go among mad people," Alice remarked.*
*"Oh, you can't help that," said the Cat, "we're all mad here. I'm mad. You're mad."*

Lewis Carroll, *Alice's Adventures in Wonderland*

The way we act, the way we balance the complexities of freedom and responsibility, these depend on what answer we give to an ancient riddle, 'What is man?'... A major difficulty is that the answer we give ... is partly a *product* of the answers that we have already given to the riddle. ... Kurt Vonnegut gives us wry advice—that we should be careful what we pretend because we become what we pretend. And something like that, some sort of self-fulfillment, occurs in all organizations and human cultures. What people presume to be "human" is what they build in as premises of their social arrangements, and what they build in is sure to be learned, is sure to become part of the character of those who participate (Bateson & Bateson, 1987).

The extensive use of psychotropic medication in our culture has altered the language for talking about human experience and emotional pain in the

3

clinical disciplines that attend to mental health. Altering language changes the consciousness of our culture and thereby limits alternatives for problem solving. The use of medications redefines symptoms by making an authoritative, nonverbal proclamation in a language that pretends there is no relation between the symptoms and interpersonal or subjective experience. The problem is placed *inside* the patient and is therefore assumed to be correctable by a medication.

On the other hand, family therapy has the view that pathology is located in relationships and in family patterns (multigenerational patterns of relationships) until proven otherwise. Thus, experience is part of the genesis of a problem, and experience is vital in repair. The practitioner works to promote change in relationships as a way to improve health. This process depends upon the thoughtfulness and creativity of practitioners and of those involved.

The language of modern psychiatry is powerful, probably because of the way it defines reality: It creates the illusion that human experience can be quantified. This quantification illusion is somehow pleasing because it reduces ambiguity about our relationships and our selves. When we can measure experience, we feel smarter and more self-assured. Modern psychiatric language is a language that does not so much reflect human experience as recreate and simplify it. It is a conservative viewpoint that says the unknown, the mystery of being, is to be found in the brain, the synapses, or the genes. Medications provide an apparent solution to the inevitable distress that comes from the deep loneliness of being human, from the struggles with loving; they provide protection against the ever-present, almost-invisible haunt of madness. The locus of control and relief is in the hands of the person having the license to write prescriptions. My point is that we are using psychotropic medications to balance the complexities of freedom and responsibility. We are building something into our social arrangements that is becoming part of our character.

I am skeptical about the way pharmacological language defines experience. I find myself wondering how cultural patterns of psychotropic medication use affect intimate relationships such as family and marriage. How do they interfere with growing and creativity, with freedom and responsibility? How do they affect the expansion of our consciousness? It is not a problem if medications are given to Robert, to Mary, to Heather, to Larry, and to Matt. The problem is that giving medication to large populations interferes with conversations about the world we live in (context) and the relationships in which we are involved. The medications interfere with the frustration and bafflement that deepens conversation, with self and others. Medications interfere with our ability to understand our limitations. Conversations about what it means to be human are inevitably clumsy and awkward and often end in ambiguous questions. In our culture ambiguity in personal experience is often experienced as pain. It is uncaring for a practitioner to allow pain. Practitioners in all disciplines are under tremendous pressure to do *something*.

Although the conversation is clumsy, it is important to talk about medication and its place among our responses to those variations of human experience we call psychopathology. I happen to be a psychiatrist, well trained in the early seventies at the beginning of the "remedicalization of psychiatry," but I have never been very interested in medication. It seems to me to be of secondary importance. Although medication is sometimes necessary, it is rarely sufficient; a therapeutic relationship is always necessary and sometimes sufficient (Marron, 1997).

When I began my psychiatry residency in 1971, the specialty was in full bloom. There was little to be certain about, but much to be fascinated with. Ecosystemic theory and family therapy were important components of psychiatric thinking, which dealt openly with the ancient riddle. What I have learned and observed and experienced from working with families has left me perpetually skeptical about the certainties that characterize modern psychiatry. The ecosystemic way of thinking does not *reduce* ambiguity about our selves and our relationships to others; it provides a way to *tolerate* ambiguity and, ultimately, *to relish it.*

As the deep interest in natural systems and family therapy was developing, another movement, the "remedicalization of psychiatry" movement, was beginning. In natural system/ecosystemic thinking, cause and effect disappear in circular reasoning, and the observer has an effect on the phenomenon he observes. The bioscientific thinking pattern behind the remedicalization creates the fantasy that the observer looks at things "out there" as an expert, objectively. It became the dominant thinking pattern in mental health practice, a thinking pattern that tends to reduce ambiguity and for that reason quickly won over the minds of the many people who find black-white dichotomies more comfortable, and ecosystemic thinking patterns were eclipsed. As this movement became more muscular, it began to refer to itself as "biological psychiatry." In our current cultural language, psychotropic medications appear protective, like anesthesia, an anesthesia that makes life better. Why would anyone withhold anesthesia? Practitioners are almost obliged to use some psychotropic medication for anyone who is upset. However, it is interesting to me that psychotropic medication use is a one-way street. Once a physician makes a diagnosis and starts a psychotropic medication, she very seldom considers stopping the medication; rather, she replaces it with another, or adds another. The language of her conversation accompanying the medication evaluates target symptoms and side effects and offers less emphasis on changes in thoughts, actions, and relationships. The semantics of psychiatric practice enables her to characterize symptoms as a problem with chemical imbalance and makes it most reasonable that she would "try" a different medication.

My skepticism about medication has a powerful and perplexing effect on me. My skepticism induces a wondering that often leaves me feeling disconnected, as though I am living in a parallel universe. The claims of psychotropic psychiatrists and the pharmaceutical industry simply do not match my experience. I know that if the family is available for family therapy sessions, and if they are able to assume some responsibility for what is happening to the member with symptoms, medications are less necessary.

What captured my interest in the ecosystemic thinking behind family therapy, and what continues to hold my interest, is how well natural systems theories embrace human experience in its fullness and how useful the application of these ideas is in clinical settings. I have a way of working with families that is difficult to describe and to teach because it is intended to address the complexity and ambiguity of human experience that language is ill-equipped to describe. This therapeutic pattern embraces experience and looks at the limits of experience. I work with a model for a healthy family, usually different from that of the family in the clinic, and the model induces them to think about their family model. It plays with language and it plays with experience. In this specific pattern of working with families, medication does not seem relevant. You see, I think medication is useful within a set of coordinates different from the ones I use in navigating my clinical work. Inevitably, we therapists become wedded to the coordinate system that has helped us to sail safely, but within Western reductionistic logic, it is hard to keep in mind that there can be more than one coordinate system. Further, it is hard to understand the concept that there can be no competition for ignorance out on the broad ocean where we do our work. It is the ocean of human pain.

## DISEASE AND ILLNESS

In common usage no difference is acknowledged between "disease" and "illness." They are synonymous, and we go to a medical doctor when we have a disease or illness that produces pain or discomfort. However, in his work, Arthur Kleinman (1988) makes a useful distinction between disease and illness that is relevant here as a way toward an understanding of the world of human suffering. But, additionally, it helps to understand the pressure to provide pain relief that is put on practitioners in our culture. What follows is based on Kleiman's distinction, with my elaboration.

## Disease

Disease is a disruption of biological structure or function, which the practitioner, with superior specialized knowledge, can diagnose, that is, measure and name. A disease can be objectively defined in unambiguous, nonmetaphorical language. Examples are pneumonia, diabetes, fractured tibia, lymphoma. The practitioner institutes treatment that mitigates or eradicates the symptoms and signs. Treatment leads to a reduction of pain and ambiguity. Treatment does not demand attention to the whole person. Bioscientific medicine studies, diagnoses, and treats disease.

## Illness

Illness refers to a much more ambiguous territory and is harder to understand, for good reason. Illness, in Kleinman's system, refers to the cultural or interpersonal manifestation of a disease. Illness is shared by all involved with the afflicted—by patient, family, and practitioner. Thus, illness exists between persons; it is multipersonal. Illness is a problem of the whole person, not of a single organ or organ system. Because I think an individual, in my review, is always a fragment of a family, illness is a problem of the whole family. Illness has to do with meaning and therefore is subjectively defined. Illness is not treated; it is contextualized—that is, it is placed in a context of relationships and events. Illness, because it is dynamic and unpredictable, is not nameable. Because illness is not nameable it is easy not to acknowledge or attend to it. Illness represents the *totality* of a family's concerns. These concerns are inevitably aroused by a disease or other sources of distress. By totality of concerns, I refer to the apprehension stimulated by the distress, which awakens all other areas of apprehension in the family's emotional realm (Have I been gone too often? Should I say something about my spouse's drinking? I don't think I love her any longer). Although it is not possible to have a disease without an accompanying illness, it is possible to have an illness without a disease (persistent symptoms with no signs of disease).

Illnesses without disease find their way into the offices of medical practitioners in great numbers. The practitioner finds no disease and may say there is nothing to be done. However, patients are not grateful for this response; they become upset. As a way to repair the upset, to maintain the relationship, the practitioner provides a name (diagnosis), then does *something*. The practitioner may give a medication, order an X ray, get more lab studies, or seek additional consultation from the rheumatologist, endocrinologist, neurologist, or allergist. This behavior matches cultural expectations, but may be unrelated to the reality of the situation, and even be in conflict with the integrity of a practitioner's beliefs. Illness, that unnameable something, is treated with whatever drugs are currently popular. In the 1960s and 1970s Librium and Valium were given freely. We believed they were nonaddictive then. These days we physicians use a variety of serotonin selective reuptake inhibitors (SSRIs) and other psychopharmacological agents to treat the unnameable.

Psychiatry is a medical specialty that deals almost exclusively with illness, that is, with the cultural manifestation of disease or other distress. But because of the cultural discomfort with the uncertainty that goes with ambiguous symptoms, psychiatrists follow the bioscientific paradigm and, recast psychiatric symptoms as diseases. For example, we describe depression as a disease "like diabetes." It is the result of a "chemical imbalance." Now, in fact, there is no measurable chemical imbalance, as there is in diabetes. But in the logic of modern psychiatry, because some symptoms of depression respond to treatment with chemicals, the illness is defined as a chemical imbalance. This formulation reduces the ambiguity that goes with feeling depressed. It seals off the totality of a family's concerns. This pattern of converting an illness into a disease can sometimes appear very useful, as in the treatment of alcoholism. However, with many of the symptoms of illness it produces only a Band-Aid for the distress when it fails to attend to the contextual components. Then the contextual aspects of the problem are likely to deteriorate.

For example, medications are often given to children who are upset with their families but who have no voice; they can protest only through their being, actions, and emotions. The child's behavior is viewed not as a problem *of* the family, but as a problem *for* the family. In our culture there is unlimited freedom to talk about and pathologize children, but there is little language (especially in the clinic) for talking about parents and parenting. In this context the person who is in pain in, or distressed about, a relationship and who has the least power, is often medicated. The subtle, barely conscious patterns of family living, which are the context for the pain, continue.

When I began in psychiatry, we discriminated between reactive and endogenous depression. The term *biological depression* has replaced them in the current cultural semantics. My belief is that these terms, *reactive* and *endogenous,* refer to different styles of history taking. In my style, both reactive and endogenous depression can be found to be responses to the social fabric. Both are therefore illnesses. The reactive depression is the by-product of an event. The endogenous depression, although it appears to bear no relationship to outside experience, can be seen to arise from the almost unconscious patterns of family living: the nonverbal behavior and subjective experiences of family members (Keith, 2001). Modern psychiatry tends on the other hand to have little interest in history, only phenomenological target symptoms, which are assumed to be by-products of molecular events. Therefore it finds most depression to be endogenous and considers it a disease.

## THE PRACTITIONER'S RESPONSE

In our culture today there is astounding pressure on practitioners to respond to any patient's pain with a solution that resolves the pain. In our cultural ambiguity about life or body experience is viewed as pain, or is translated into pain. And constant, ambiguous, difficult-to-describe systemic pressure from family, marriage, or work world produces distress. That persistent distress produces muscle tension, which can result in chronic pain, which then may receive a name like fibromyalgia. If there is a diagnosis and a treatment, the ambiguity about identity and meaning finds resolution.

Many patients who come into a physician's office with symptoms have no detectable disease. In a culture heavily saturated and deeply influenced by technological solutions, persistent ambiguity is viewed as pathological. Bioscientific medicine creates the cultural illusion that if there are questions, there must be answers. Patients and families feel impotent when they cannot define or resolve their distress, and often the impotence is projected onto the practitioner, who feels himself an incompetent imposter when he cannot interfere with their distress. In these situations medications, with moderate efficacy but few side effects, become vessels of hope. The patient feels he has an answer; ambiguity is reduced. The practitioner who provides the answer feels competent. The disquieting pain of persistent ambiguity has been relieved on both sides of the healer-sufferer relationship. Thus, disease also refers to the way that physicians recast ambiguous symptoms to fit their theoretical models. Examples of how ambiguous symptoms might be recast include fibromyalgia, ADHD, chronic fatigue syndrome, panic disorder, and depression. These are illnesses that are recast as diseases. They are by-products of biopsychosystemic stress, but they are treated as though they are primary problems.

The bioscientific practitioner's role in the diagnosis and treatment of disease is active and based on specialized, superior knowledge. The thought processes are convergent: there is an attempt to focus the data on a specific diagnosis. The practitioner may give an antidepressant or antianxiety agent, in that way recasting the symptoms so that they match one of the categories that fits his theory. Medication is a prominent modality in this scenario. But psychotherapeutic methods, psychoeducational, supportive, or behavioral therapies organized around first-order change, also fit this model. Any psychotherapy with specific goals is organized for pain relief as opposed to change. This pattern of treatment, almost inevitably, establishes a healthy/sick dichotomy by designating a patient (one who is afflicted) and others who are healthy (those who are not included in the examination).

A prominent characteristic of the bioscientific model is that the doctor takes over the problem while the patient goes away and waits for the doctor to provide solutions. To go a little further, it reifies or concretizes a process. As a by-product, it is in danger of creating a false hope that can interfere with the family's initiative to take care of a problem. Whatever anxiety the parents may have had about their family fades away when they learn their daughter has a biological depression. What is hidden in their heart of hearts may remain hidden.

In attending to the problem as an illness rather than a disease, the practitioner's response is critical, but it is more difficult to characterize this response. I am going to attempt to invent another kind of model: the Biometaphorical Experiential Family Systems model (I will refer to it as the biometaphorical model and the therapy I use inside it as Symbolic Experiential Family Therapy), with a different kind of practitioner. The biometaphorical practitioner interviews the family that surrounds the symptom, guiding the process in which the story is told, evoking talk about the group and not just the individuals in it, evoking talk about subjective experiences in depth, pointing out nonverbal behavior or communications and including his own subjective experience of them. No individual is more important than any other. A 3 year old may have a comment that makes as much difference as the father's comment. During the interview the practitioner comments on the story, empathically, ironically, and free-associatively. Sometimes the comments are interactive and joining. Sometimes they are parallel and differentiating. In order to escape linear thinking it is necessary for the practitioner to avoid overvaluing the narrative. Rather than acting on the problem, he provides a crucible, the practitioner-patient relationship, through which he is able to simultaneously hold and raise the heat on the family and its pain. In the biometaphorical model the problem stays with the family. The practitioner's role is something like that of a coach who wants the players to win but does not himself play in the game.

One pattern—biological psychiatry—values relief of pain (ambiguity) caused by disruption of biological structure or function. The second pattern—biometaphorical medicine—believes that pain (anxiety induced by ambiguity) is important to emotional growth and creates a context in which pain can lead to change. Here medication has little relevance, especially when the family is therapeutically available. This second model is focused on the person within the relationship system, and the pain is regarded as a symptom of impeded growth and relationship problems. The symptoms belong to the family; thus the healthy/sick dichotomy is collapsed.

Instead of relieving pain, the process puts heat on it so that the healing and growth capacities of the whole family can be brought into action. What happens in this region is not well defined. It is a shadowy region and those who live in the more brightly lighted bioscientific region see only darkness when they look at it. I need to add that the family therapy process is organized around working with illness, the relationship system. The specific disease is relatively unimportant. What I believe to be crucial in family therapy is that the whole family and its various groupings be included. The presence of the family and family subgroups changes the quality of relationships and determines how much therapeutic voltage will be available for needed change.

As a symbolic experiential family therapist, I begin my work with the belief that all psychopathology is related to interpersonal experience *until proven otherwise*. If there is a "chemical imbalance," it is the result of long-term patterns of distress or intergenerational patterning. It is a process that can be modulated by addressing those unarticulated questions and concerns that lie behind illness in the realm I referred to as the "totality of the family's concerns." In most situations, it can be sufficiently rebalanced with biometaphorical "medicine." When these patterns are apparently not reversible, it is usually because the way out appears as painful as the way in.

These two patterns of treatment, biomedical and biometaphorical, are like different sports, say, basketball and baseball. One can play them both, but not at the same time. The rules are different, the equipment is different, the required skills are different, the playing field is different, and the games are scored differently.

In the remainder of the essay, I will attempt, within the limits of linear language, to describe more fully the biometaphorical model.

## AMBIGUITY AND GROWTH

One problem in dealing with illness is the question of what language to use. The God of Delphi (also known as the Oracle), as described by Norman O. Brown (1966), provides a model for communication in the richly ambiguous region of illness. "The God of Delphi, who always spoke the truth, never gave a straight answer . . . (i.e., in contrast with the unambiguous language of science or cost-effective morality). . . . He always spoke in riddles, in parables; ambiguities, temptations; that hearing they might hear and not understand. . . . The real deceivers are the literalists, who say, I cannot tell a lie, or, *hypothesis non fingo* (I only deal with the facts)." This God of Delphi was not much good at public relations. But speaking as this God did provided a catalyst for change.

"The real deceivers are the literalists." In the modern medical clinic that sounds not only blasphemous, but preposterous. So I will deceive you by attempting to explain the value of this kind of communication. Our minds feed on ambiguity. Our minds are enriched by ambiguity. Ambiguity brings us into the present. Ordinarily our souls are cornered, entombed by concreteness. This concreteness forces us into the past with its failures and glories or into the future with it fantasies of failure and glory. Safety and security can be deadening. Straight clear answers are useful in dealing with disease, but they can be deadening when dealing with illness. Children know this intuitively and become defiant, warning of dangerous, but not obvious, hazards. In another context (Keith, 2000; Keith, Connell, G.M. & Connell, L.C. 2001) I described two kinds of psychotherapy: first, a psychotherapy that teaches social adaptation, and second, a psychotherapy that raises consciousness or expands personhood. The first is aligned with the aims of the biomedical model and pain relief and describes most of what is called psychotherapy in our culture. The second includes the biometaphorical model and represents an alternative to pharmacological treatment of "mental disorders" using pain or distress to promote growth. (The disappointing news is that the difference between the two is not always so clear in practice—we sometimes encounter the biomedical model masquerading as a biometaphorical approach.)

When I read this commentary on the God of Delphi, I began to think of illness as an "unstraight" response to as yet unarticulated questions about our families and ourselves, about how we belong and how we are separate. These questions and ideas live within our heart of hearts.

## CASE ILLUSTRATION

This illustration gives a picture of how the use of a psychiatric diagnosis and treatment with medication can affect a family's living over a long range of experience. It demonstrates the cost to the family of characterizing behavior as disease and ignoring the broader, unnamed illness of the family.

The Mahers were referred because Trish, 18, a high school senior, was "completely out of control." Four months earlier, she quit taking her medications, Tegretol and Prozac. She had started taking medications at age 4 when she was diagnosed with bipolar disorder. When the family called for an appointment, I told them that I wasn't much of a medication man and that they would need to bring the whole family. They decided to come in. Based on my phone conversation with the father, I had expected a very disturbed, probably manic, young woman. I greeted a different Trish. Instead of being disturbed and chaotic, she was composed and thoughtful in an appealing way. She was a self-owning young woman who agreed she had been difficult of late. She was annoyed with what she viewed as her parents' overreactions. The pediatric neurologist who had taken care of Trish for 14 years sent the clinical records, which began with her diagnosis at age 4. The notes included the initial evaluation by a child psychiatrist that ended with an indefinite conclusion: Trish "might" have bipolar disorder. This diagnosis had been made at a time when the child psychiatry researchers were newly interested in the possibility of bipolar disorder in children and articles about it were appearing in child psychiatry journals. In keeping with the new standard of practice at the time, the psychiatrist thought she "deserved" a trial of lithium. However, the trial never ended. Trish was later changed to Tegretol and Prozac by the neurologist. Those were the medications she had quit taking, fourteen years later, in October 1998, four months before the family came to see me, in February 1999. A month before she quit taking the medications, her father, an executive in a large corporation, was downsized. He was let go and given a six-month severance package. He acted as if it were not a big deal (only a business decision). He felt certain he would soon find a new executive-level position. The mother, on the other hand, was upset by the father's nonchalance. She felt that the ship of the family had been torpedoed and was slowly sinking. The parents' overconcrete views were shaped by their long experience with the biomedical model. They were polite suburbanites with little capacity or language for self-observation. But they were clear about Trish and what was wrong with her. Father was conservative and repressed. Mother, who was very hesitant when she spoke about her own life, was very articulate about her daughter. There were times when she was sadistic and smirking when it came to describing Trish. I thought of Trish as having been an unnaturally compliant child most of her life. At 18 she had become mildly, but appropriately, rebellious. She was trying to figure out a way to be more than her mother's little girl.

I saw the family; Mother, Father, Trish & Rob, 15, for six visits. I did not view Trish's medication as necessary.

At one point the parents felt as though I should see Trish alone. I did, for two visits. Trish was thoughtful about herself. Of her friends she said, "I like these people, I am having fun; I never knew how to have fun before. I can see my parents have never been happy. I don't want to turn out like them." She was concerned that her mother was trapped and didn't have any friends. She was trying to get her mother connected to the mother of one of her girlfriends who lived on a farm. The friend's mother had a wonderful sense of humor and seemed to enjoy her life. She thought this mother could be a good influence on her own mother. Trish was worried about her parents. She was trying to help her mother grow up a little, to become more of a person. Trish graduated from high school in June 1999 and went away to college in the fall.

Just one month after Trish left for college, her mother, Carol Marie, called me. I was surprised because she wanted to be a patient and come in to see what she could learn about herself. I saw her biweekly for six months, twelve visits. Father, Arthur, would not participate because he was busy hunting for another permanent job (he never found one) while working as furniture salesman. Carol Marie was upset with him. He would not come to the sessions. Carol Marie was a deeply repressed woman. She felt cornered by her marriage. She told stories of their life, which sounded pain-filled, and explained the distance between herself and her husband. In my work with them about Trish's problems, she had become enticed by the thought that she might find a way to love herself. Much to my surprise, she enjoyed being in therapy and became very enlivened. She would arrive for an interview feeling surprised about something she had done. Occasionally the subject of Trish arose. She was away at college and sometimes her poor judgment made her a source of distress. She did have the college freshman's way of doing dumb things. Carol Marie saw these things as symptoms of her bipolar disorder. But bad judgment in a college freshman is not yet a diagnostic category. In her case the troubles she got into were more symptomatic of naïveté and an unusually soft heart.

At first Carol Marie was a careful patient. But she liked the idea of being a patient and liked to come to the sessions. Much of her life had been characterized by apprehension. A fear of an undefined catastrophe fueled her apprehension. She began to do new things. In fact, she was a little like Trish had been. She decided to drop "Marie" and become a less prissy Carol. By her report, the family was surprised and sometimes upset by this new version of Carol Marie. She went for a walk alone one Sunday in the rural area where she lived and got lost. She was gone for four hours. The family was scared by her long absence, but she was exhilarated by the experience. She began looking into the possibility of buying a café in a small town near her home. In January she developed a protracted upper respiratory infection. In February she had an unexplained, extended seizure-like spell, which resulted in a trip to an emergency room. There was no diagnosis; she never lost consciousness. It sounded like a pseudoseizure to me. She had a series of medical evaluations with no clear conclusions. From a metaphorical point of view, I had the impression she was trying to regain herself, to become a somebody. She was energized by the process on the one hand, but on the other, this new self she was becoming had new feelings, and those new feelings were creating distress not only at home, but also inside herself. My working assumption was that the emergence of her new self created a mixture of feelings and the effort to deal with her new self was a partial explanation of her somatic problems: As I indicated earlier, the language inside this biometaphorical model tends to be vague. At the end of the six months she left therapy because she was feeling better about herself and because she felt she had learned enough for the time being. When Carol became a patient on her own, her struggles were implicitly parallel to her daughter's. Her getting lost and being gone overlong was a milder replication of Trish's staying out all night long. Her plan to buy the café was typical of behavior her husband and her old self would regard as unrealistic in Trish.

I chose this case because it represents on one level a long-term study of a family in which the daughter was treated in the bioscientific model, as if she had a disease. The child psychiatrist who saw her initially did not have any language for considering the silent distress in the marriage that had its origins in the families in which Arthur and Carol grew up. This silent distress was covered by polite, orderly suburban success.

What follows may be characterized as me blaming the parents, though I don't see it that way. I found the parents to be naïve about relationships and emotionally hungry people who disguised their hunger in different ways.Their naïveté and emotional hunger were part of the reason Trish was diagnosed with bipolar disorder. Rank has its privileges, but rank also has its responsibilities. The parents did not do anything morally wrong, and so they should not be blamed. The problem with the parents was that while they were successful in their social roles, they were immature personally.

In the biometaphorical family systems model, the family includes at least three generations. All Trish's grandparents were deceased. Arthur came from a family in which his father was successful in a small auto parts business. His mother was portrayed as domineering, harsh, and emotionally unpredictable, the Queen of Hearts incarnate. As a result of his mother's emotional unpredictability, Arthur hated emotion and acted to quell emotion in himself, his spouse, and his children. His demeanor was angry and his behavior repressive, but his hidden motive was fear. Emotion made him feel like an overwhelmed little boy. Arthur didn't take the severance from his job personally. However, he took nothing personally. He was emotionally distant, humorless. His personal style is what I refer to as "culturally invisible pathology."

Carol Marie came from a timid, frightened family. Her father seemed invisible in her memory. Her mother protected the father but was herself fearful and depended on religion and her daughter for emotional sustenance. She had an older brother who was explosive and uncontrollable. He was hospitalized at age 13 and remained in institutions for 12 years.

In the first ten years of the Mahers' marriage there were infertility problems. Carol resigned herself to having no children. Then, like a miracle, Trish appeared. Carol discovered an intimacy with her baby she had never known before. The experience was a deep comfort and soothed much of her pain. But babies are unfaithful. They inevitably disappoint us and grow up; they individuate, say no, become defiant, even at age two. Then there was another baby, born when Trish was three. So the family naturally became emotionally chaotic. Arthur became more distant, more repressive, and more demanding. "You keep quiet. You know I hate it when you get so emotional. And keep those kids quiet. Dammit! Can't you see that Billy needs changing. You didn't iron my shirt. I told you I needed that shirt this morning." Carol felt overwhelmed. If only her 4-year-old Trish was not so difficult, things would be better.

Thus, they went to see a child psychiatrist. The point here, easily lost, is that the problem did not belong to one person; it belonged to the family. When the diagnosis was made, it offered an explanation for why Carol felt so overwhelmed: her daughter had a mental illness. Their anxiety now had an explanation that they were hesitant to disrupt.

Our culture gives parents and professionals unlimited freedom to talk about children. Thus it was easy for Trish to be defined as the problem. Our culture grants us little freedom to talk about parents, and the language for talking about parents is very limited, partly because any discussion of their participation in family problems has come to be (incorrectly) understood as blame. In my clinical work I assume that if a person has a problem, it is a manifestation of a group problem. This example shows how the diagnosis and medical treatment of a family problem as an individual problem, organizes a family. My not encouraging the medication to be restarted had a profound effect on the reality organization of the family. It frightened and exasperated them, but simultaneously, in the mother's case, it stimulated her curiosity about herself and her relationships, and led to change, which was both gratifying and painful.

## BIOMETAPHORICAL FAMILY PSYCHOTHERAPY: THE POETICS OF EXPERIENCE

If I choose to talk about psychotherapy in conventional terms, the discussion tends to end up inside the medical model coordinates. If instead I choose a language inspired by the Oracle, psychotherapy ends up inside the poetics of experience. Poetics gives a framework that says what is possible. The lesson of poetics is an implicit definition of the experiential situation (Eco, 1995).

Are we "afraid" to talk about subjective experience? No, only hesitant. Why are we hesitant? Because there are surprises, and surprises create confusion. True poetry does not have a planned end. It is an experience of spontaneity and creativity. My work is not based on research, but on clinical experience and reflection. The semantics of this process is different from the semantics of research-based methods that are closer to bioscientific medicine.

Novel experiences that break from expected routines have an unusual effect on our relationship to familiar reality, our sense of who we are, the meaning of our perceptions, and our sense of values. Novel language or behavior by a therapist may briefly alter how a family structures reality. In fact, getting an entire family together for the first interview is a novel experience. However, families are so stable that only rarely does a single novel event produce an avalanche of change. It is more likely that the effect of therapeutic action is cumulative and reciprocal. We all have a way of being attached to the world we call reality. In adulthood our patterns of behavior and patterns of perceiving become stable. Unusual, unexpected experiences change the way we are connected to the world. The algorithms of family living make outcome predictable, but these patterns may be nonadaptive or pathological in some way. And even when a family wants to disrupt them, they often cannot.

The way I practice family therapy is different from what popular language refers to as the "talking therapies." There is a blend of power and interaction in the therapist's placement of herself that is crucial and implies much more than simply talking. For me, family therapy means convening the whole family under the direction of the family therapist. The therapist joins the family, consciously and unconsciously. In this way a new variation of the family is developed: a therapeutic family. It is advisable for the therapist to place herself in a parental role, one generation older than the oldest member. Once the therapist has joined, she can feel free to break family rules without losing her honorary membership.

### Case Illustration. A Novel Experience

The 13-year-old daughter was angry and depressed. After a dispute with her parents about dying her hair, she became furious and took a small overdose. The emergency room doctor referred the family to me. When they came in, two days later, she had decided she did not want to go to school. Mother and father were committed to a moralistic rule system, which had no uncertainty in it, no room for self-doubt. The girl said she would go to see the "shrink," but she would not talk. She had been sick the day before the interview and her mother had let her stay home from school. Mother: "Is she getting the best of me here?" Therapist: "Could be. Don't forget, though, she would kill herself to make sure you don't compromise her dignity. I think she should stay home and flunk this semester. She can make it up next year." Girl (breaking out of her silence): "But I don't want to flunk the semester." Therapist: "So just flunk one course. I think it would be good for the family to have somebody flunk." The parents became restless. They had a pattern of living that was firm and moralistic, so as to be assured not only that they will all pass to the next grade, but also get into heaven. Father (bemused): "You are not being helpful here. Are you telling her it's okay to flunk?" Therapist: "Sure. Flunking global studies is a lot different from dying. If she dies, you will have to have a funeral. If she flunks, you will just have to go and meet with the guidance counselor for an hour. And who knows, your daughter might get all of you over the fear of flunking, and you could end up having a real life, instead of the weird overly correct life you have now." This is an example of a novel experience. It sent a little shiver through their reality attachment.

## Case Illustration

Chuck was 43 years old. He had experienced debilitating mental distress since he entered adulthood. He fell into the diagnostic category schizo-affective disorder, that complicated and disabling blend of mood and thought problems, so he was on lithium, Risperdol, Thorazine, and Zoloft. He had been in the state hospital for seven years. A psychiatrist who was interested in my work with families with chronic illness had formed a therapeutic relationship with him. That is, she had a transference to something healthy in him, and he responded. She invited me to see his family, which was coming to visit from their home in another state. In attendance at our first session were his parents, in their early seventies, his older brother, a contractor, his younger sister, a very kind and engaging teacher, and his maternal aunt and her husband, who were his guardians in the local area for a reason I do not recall. The aunt and uncle were active in the National Alliance for the Mentally Ill (NAMI). The family was well schooled in the chemical imbalance theory (disease model) of mental illness. The interview began with attention to what the psychiatrist (my colleague) would like to accomplish. Then I interviewed the family about the family. The interview wandered into how the parents fell in love with each other and what kind of families they had grown up in. Thus the interview included ghosts, their accomplishments, and failures. We talked about Chuck's nuclear family and the adult children when they were kids. They recalled a young and healthy Chuck before his series of breakdowns. Then Chuck talked about what he wanted to do, how he looked upon what he had done. I don't recall anything specific from his self-narrative, but I do recall sensing a Christ-like grandiosity about him. I interrupted a short soliloquy and asked, "Did it ever occur to you that you might be just another schmuck?" I paused. He looked at me, mildly startled. "Just like the rest of us schmucks," I added. Then he chuckled as he said, "Yeah, I guess I'm just another schmuck. I never thought of that, maybe I'm just another schmuck." In the context of a psychiatric interview in a psychiatric hospital, that was a novel experience. It did something to his and their reality. Over the next six months the instability of his moods decreased. His visits away from the hospital were less likely to end in disruption. He would often comment to my friend, his psychiatrist, "It's like that guy said, I guess I'm just another schmuck."

Idiosyncratic, novel behavior by a therapist, or, later, by a family member under the spell of the therapeutic relationship, disrupts a family's way of organizing reality. Novel language or ideas soften concrete thinking and alter the way reality and values are organized. Thus options are increased and the grip of the family's reality system eased. When symptoms become more desperate, families are pressured to change how they look at behavior and life. Biometaphorical therapists work on ways to disrupt routine patterns of thinking and behaving. Biomedical therapists seek stability. In the biometaphorical model there is a level of danger, risk, and outrageousness that is necessary to activate what is needed most: spontaneity. The risk is minimized by the experience, the clinical competence and caring of the practitioner.

For some this language leads to the impression that, under the guise of therapy, "anything goes," which is not so. Of course, novel behavior or ideas by a therapist can be sadistic or capricious. This danger to therapeutic work can be reduced in several ways. The first is that the therapist must have extensive professional training and experience. Novel or idiosyncratic experience in a context of caring is not dangerous. However, when the therapist is too anxious or does not care, novel language or behavior can be dangerous. These therapeutic novel behaviors perturb the family system. This perturbation has unpredictable outcomes. Thus, the therapist must be prepared to deal with whatever responses are produced by the novel experiences. But most often the freed-up family system tends, of its own accord, to reorganize in healthier ways.

The second way in which danger in this therapeutic work is reduced is that the therapist's action is guided by an awareness of morality. Morality is rooted in the fact that I, as therapist, take responsibility for what I do.

Third, the therapist's actions are guided by an underlying sense of beauty, by an awareness of the aesthetics of experience. In the biometaphorical model the therapist's behavior, including language, is aimed at integrating the pathological symptoms and behavior into the living context of the family in a way that promotes change. Integration of disparate parts is a partial definition of the sense of beauty. The intimacy of the caring and the sense of beauty differentiate this work from counseling or psychoeducation. Counseling and psychoeducation are more easily blended with the bioscientific model. In bioscientific psychiatry, on the other hand, morality and sense of beauty are subsumed by the concept of "standard of practice," which can be simplified into an indication of what kind of medication to give based on rumors about what colleagues are doing.

In psychotherapeutic work with families, we practitioners constantly and inevitably encounter patterns of experience that have an aesthetic quality, a sense of beauty. In the poetics of experience these patterns result in a therapeutic epiphany, a glimpse of a kind of wholeness among the disparate parts of life experience. (In the preceding examples the fact that flunking and dying are not the same, and the fact that Chuck was just another schmuck, are examples of somewhat mundane epiphanies.) In my experience these are therapeutic moments. They are never activated by intent. We stumble into these moments. They may be marked by sudden tears or laughter. These moments affect a person's or a family's relationship to reality. Novel comments or behaviors—irony, humor, or free associative non sequiturs—often activate these epiphanies. It is important to note again that their effect is cumulative. The therapist by his behavior establishes a new possibility, then, by commenting on his behavior later, fits it into the family pattern.

This way of thinking about therapy has led me to the conclusion that psychotherapy is an art, not a science. It is not an art like painting or sculpting that produces something that can be held onto and reexamined. It is a performance art, like theater or music. It produces an experience in the moment that results in a changed relationship to the experience of life. As I indicated above, it induces a kind of epiphany, a changeful way of seeing, that deepens our engagement with human experience.

A fundamental requirement for the one who guides the exploration of the mystery of being is the (therapist's) search for her own self. This searching, a lifelong process, requires honesty, ruthlessness, amusement, tenderness, cunning, patience, and persistence (Castaneda, 1987). When the one with power in the hierarchy seeks her own self and takes responsibility for what she does, the result is a therapeutic hierarchy, a hierarchy that simultaneously provides security and allows for growth.

This search for the self or the soul is not a science. It cannot be quantified and handed on. It is a process enshrouded in wonder and mystery. The process of searching for the self deals with something important but elusive. We can refer to that something as the "unknown," the "spiritual world," "abstract reality," or "systemic awareness." However, despite the absence of a clear name, this something is what is most important in my world of alternative psychiatry.

I am paraphrasing bell hooks, an evocative, wide-ranging social commentator, best known as a feminist thinker: Paradox and contradiction are essential mysteries of the soul. In this world the weird and the uncanny are sources of knowledge. In order to know the self we constantly seek but can neither grasp nor define; we must open the heart wide and search every part. We must face the weird, the perverse, the sick, the strange, even the sadistic. Without embracing this metaphysical complexity, we cannot understand the soul. Sometimes deviation from the usual is a special revelation of experiential truth. When normality explodes or breaks out in craziness or defiance, we might look closely at it, before running for cover and before attempting to restore a familiar order. For some reason, in the poetics of experience, when we encounter apparent meaninglessness, meaning is revived. If we are going to be curious about the soul, we need to explore its deviations, its perverse tendency to contradict expectations (hooks, 1995).

## Case Illustration

The following is one more example of a therapist inducing a novel experience by being simultaneously in charge, provocative, firm, self-deprecating and impotent, and assertive, with beneficial effect. Notice there is a difference between this therapeutic interaction in which the therapist's behavior raises anxiety slightly and the relationship defined by business guidelines that would help someone to understand something by using reason.

The G's were a family of five: mother, father, two daughters, and a son, Bob, 17. Bob was upsetting everyone because he was interested in witchcraft. He dressed in a dark, Gothic manner and painted his fingernails black. His parents were stiff and tight, embarrassed by their son, and assumed everyone thought of him as an idiot. With the help of the school and their pastor, they came to view Bob's role-playing as a mental disorder. Halfway into a very tense first interview the parents could only talk about Bob and elaborate on what they feared and disliked in him, it became apparent to me, the biometaphorical psychiatrist, that Bob did not have a thought disorder: he was being an annoying adolescent. I said, "You know, I think Bob is a creative kid, but what worries me is that he has turned into such an isolate." And turning to Bob, "Had you thought of trying to cultivate some of your pals into a coven, so that you have some disciples? You know you can't be a successful witch without disciples." The mother, a very humorless sixth-grade teacher, lips pursed in permanent disgust, went after this 60-year-old psychiatrist as though he were eleven, "That's ridiculous. We didn't come here for more silliness." She paused. Then challenging the therapist, "Why are we here anyway?" Smiling, and without pause, the therapist answered, "I'll tell you something. I have been ridiculous for a long time, and I'm good at it. I suppose you're here to learn a different way to be ridiculous." The content of this clumsy message had abrasive and rude elements, but simultaneously and nonverbally, it was nondefensive, playful and inviting. But most important, it was oddly self-deprecating, a social non sequitur. Continuing, the psychiatrist asked the mother how she arranged to upset her parents when she was in high school. Within the next ten minutes, her jaw loosened, and, smiling broadly, the mother laughed at some of her own exploits as a high school senior, while her husband and son looked on amazed. In her heart of hearts, she liked her son's way of being idiosyncratic. She feared he would grow up to be scared like his father. The dominant mother/teacher role had stepped aside, and in her amused, nonanxious remembering, we had access to her personhood (Keith, Connell, G.M. & Connell, L.C., 2001).

The psychotherapeutic method I am describing is not about making progress toward specific goals. It is about a process. We work with families in a way that helps them to change their living process by creating a context in which they experiment with the unwritten rule system they live by, the rule system that dominates their relationships. The therapist joins the family and then changes in ways that disrupt the rule system. What we do is very similar to play therapy in which a special space exists for having a special experience. That special space is my office. The specifics of the outcome are not all that important.

How do we know we are successful? We are successful when the family takes back responsibility for their own living. The outcome in this idiosyncratic model is also idiosyncratic, and the outcome does not belong to the therapist, it belongs to the family. The ending often surprises me. I seldom use medication, so the result has little to do with medication, but lots to do with some symbolic change. The symbolic change can cause a profound shifting for which there are no words; it is often stimulated by acceptance of the fact that family members are not the center of the absurd universe, but "just another schmuck." Or they become frustrated with my bemused unwillingness to stimulate hope.

Questions about medications come up inevitably and often. Many patients arrive already treated by their family doctor or pediatrician. The brain, the genes, and the synapses, as explanations for psychopathology, all come up as ways to deal with the unknown that haunts. My response is that I believe that changes in the human relationships are what are most important and most enduring.

Occasionally patients include in their agenda a wish to stop taking medications. If they want to get off them, I ask them to take the matter up with the physician who put them on the medication. If that doctor does not want to take them off, I suggest they find out from him what he thinks will happen if they stop the medication, get instructions from him on how to stop the medication, and then remove themselves from medication with full responsibility for the outcome.

Stopping medications does not always end happily. One reason is that many of these medications that affect synapses do so by altering cellular structure within the central nervous system. Thus, when the medications are ended, unpleasant feelings arise. This does not prove the medications are needed; it suggests the nervous system requires time to accommodate to the absence of the chemical agents. Pharmacological agents create a physiological need for themselves.

Another, very important reason that ending medications may cause trouble is that the medication has an impact on the symbol system of the family. The medication, apart from its chemical effects, becomes a household deity. It becomes the foundation of well-being. If the medication disappears, anxiety or apprehension appears. "If there is a medication, then we will be fine. If no medication, who knows what will happen?" Its absence raises the expectation that the patient will be symptomatic, and the processes that led to the symptoms in the first place are likely to recur.

### Case Illustration

I saw a physician and his family because his 12-year-old daughter had a habitual cough. The presenting problem was resolved within a few visits, but the parents continued in marital therapy. The physician father was boyish, positive, and earnest in a way that put pressure on his wife; a grown-up was needed, and he wasn't a candidate. Although they lived a hundred miles away, I saw them eight times in four months, and they ended sessions because life was much improved. Eight months later they returned for more therapy. When they returned, I learned the wife's internist had started her on Zoloft eight weeks prior to the interview. The husband said, "She is so much better on Zoloft. I would be worried if she decided not to take it." "I only took it for two weeks," his wife said, flatly, contradicting his enthusiasm for medication.

## SUMMARY

In my way of working with families, the family replaces the medication as the agent for repair and change. Through a combination of social, economic, and cultural factors, psychotropic medications have become a dominant way of dealing with the problems of mental health. Psychotropic medications suppress symptoms and alter the consciousness of the patient, the family members, and practitioners. In addition, the overt goodwill and optimism of biomedicine can produce iatrogenic illness by removing initiative from the hands of patients and their families. It also interferes with the way we balance the complexities of freedom and responsibility, with the result that inside our culture at the beginning of the twenty-first century, a *dependency* develops on medical science to provide new truths, for which too many wait hopefully and probably in vain.

This essay is written not to stimulate defiance in practitioners or in patients, but as a way to nudge the biomedical way of thinking a little and to contaminate conventional thinking about psychopathology. It is important to pay attention to how the social fabric influences behavior, but this information comes not from the simple history of cause and effect, but from the symbolic history of the family. My desire is to give therapists and patients an alternative way of thinking about personal problems and pain, a countercultural way that can remove symptoms, enrich living, and deepen relationships.

## REFERENCES

Bateson, G., & Bateson, M. C. (1987). *Angel's fear*. New York: Macmillan.

Brown, N. O. (1966). *Love's body*. Berkeley: University of California Press.

Castaneda, C. (1987). *The power of silence*. New York: Simon & Schuster.

Eco, U. (1995). *Six walks in the fictional woods*. Cambridge, MA: Harvard University Press.

hooks, b. (1995). *Art on my mind: Visual politics*. New York: New Press.

Keith, D.V. (2000). I look for I: The self of the therapist—part ii. In Michele Baldwin (Ed.), *The use of self in family therapy* (2d. Ed.). New York: Haworth Press.

Keith, D. V., & Kaye, D. L. (2001). Consultation with the extended family: Primary process in clinical practice. *Child and Adolescent Psychiatry Clinics of North America*, 10(3) 563–576.

Keith, D. V., Connell, G. M., & Connell, L. C. (2001). *Defiance in the family: Finding hope in therapy*. Philadelphia: Brunner-Routledge.

Kleinman, A. (1988). *The illness narratives*. New York: Basic Books.

Marron, J. T. (1997). Personal communication.

Chapter 2

# When More Is Less: A Common Difficulty in Collaborative Treatment of Human Distress

Phoebe S. Prosky, MSW

*The table was a large one, but the three were all crowded together at one corner of it. "No room! No room!" they cried out when they saw Alice coming. "There's plenty of room!" said Alice indignantly, and she sat down in a large arm-chair at one end of the table.*

Lewis Caroll, *Alice's Adventures in Wonderland*

## INTRODUCTION

Our current understanding of the multidimensionality of psychological events reveals that we have choices as to how to describe them. Each choice brings with it its own hypothesis about the etiology of the event and determines the appropriate interventions for addressing it. For example, an event may be described as a state of depression (mind), a change in body chemistry (body), a detachment from important others (context). Each of these descriptions implies its own etiology and its own therapeutic response.

Furthermore, the view from any of these perspectives is formed with reference to the particular viewer's previous experience and knowledge. And in addition it is formed with relation to its place in the world and its time in history. If we look, for example, at a trance experience, we can describe it from any of the preceding three vantage points—mind, body, or context. And then each of us viewing it would describe it drawing on his or her own stored base of experience. And the view would be further colored according to its place and time, seen as inspired, or out-of-it, or accessing supernatural powers. We can see then that explanations of psychological events are determined by what aspect of the event is viewed, and by whom, where, and when. For this reason any explanation can capture only a facet of an event and is at all times a description of the interface of event and observer, place and time (even when the observer is the self). Any view that claims to have *the* definitive description of the event fails to acknowledge the event's multidimensionality and in so doing falsifies its description. The discovery of this multidimensionality, often referred to as complementarity, is relatively new in the Western scientific paradigm. It flows from Einstein's relativity theory and the ensuing developments in general systems theory (Schilp, 1957, ch. 7). The idea of complementarity is that discoveries through time are not a unidirectional progression from ignorance to truth, as is often thought, but more like slices of a pie, revolving in a circle, all the slices participating in the description of a universe too grand and complex to be captured by any one explanation.

One of the current trends in psychotherapy, in response to the idea of multidimensionality, is collaborative health care, in which professionals of different backgrounds work together in a team with people in distress (McDaniel & Campbell, 1997). This is clearly an important and valuable development and advances the application of systemic thought. However, at the same time, a second trend in mental health—biological psychiatry— has been so universally embraced that its etiological base, related to brain chemistry, has eclipsed the various etiologies underlying the other professional approaches:

> The last three decades have seen the steadily rising dominance of medication in the treatment of the array of human experiences we call psychopathology, mental illness, psychiatric disorders. (Keith, p. 1).

Thus, at the same time that we are espousing teamwork among professionals with differing points of view in response to our multidimensional understanding, we have withdrawn wholesale the etiological supports for viewpoints alternative to the biological:

> "Chemical imbalance" is a persuasive metaphor freely used in Modern Psychiatry to support the use of psychotropic medications. This formula-

tion of human problems is derived from the epistemology of medical bioscience. Family therapy/ecosystemic thinking represents an alternative epistemological system with a different view of the human condition which leads to different clinical interactions. (Keith, n.d., p. 1)

The acceptance of the bioscientific etiology as core, combined with the collaboration of a multidisciplinary treatment team, has often created an "as if" situation in which collaborative treatment *looks* multidimensional but is in fact governed by the etiology of a single perspective—the biological. Stripped of their etiological bases, alternative interventions can manifest only as pale shadows of their inherent potentials. In short, at the same time that we have advocated for the multidimensionality of collaborative health care, we have robbed the field of psychotherapy of the riches of its etiological multidimensionality.

In truly collaborative mental health work, the working hypotheses of all the approaches involved have to be understood and accepted by all the professionals and made available to the clients as having descriptive value in approaching the problems at hand. To practice in this way would require more comprehensive interdisciplinary education of professionals so that they grasp the place of the working hypotheses of each discipline in approaching a situation of human distress. Such an education would help all the professionals involved toward a more total appreciation of life in all its complexity. And it would make them more meaningful resources to their clients in their efforts to help them toward a more complete view of their situation.

## Case Illustration

The following case illustrates the problem in those collaborations based on the etiology of only one of the points of view of the professionals involved: A multidisciplinary team is assembled to work with a situation, but a biological etiology is declared as the base of the work. The other points of view are utilized only for intervention—not for their viewpoints—and under these circumstances can deliver only a fraction of their potentials. The approach *appears* to be multidimensional, but in fact it falls far short of the mark.

In the discussion of the case, the focus will be on the role of the family therapist on the team and the *contextual* view. A similar discussion could be had around the approaches of other team members. In this instance we will see how the family systems view of the situation was stripped of its working hypothesis, namely, that the symptom bearer's symptoms express the stress and distress inherent in the context, thereby rendering the systemic view impotent. The story is told in the author's own voice.

The family was referred to me by a local mental health clinic with the request that I be the family therapist on a team of clinicians, including a psychiatrist, a case manager, and a respite worker.

I was to meet with the family in my office and participate in team meetings at the clinic.

The family was composed of George and his second wife, Lillian, Janine, age 10 (George's daughter by his late wife Carol, who died of cancer shortly after childbirth), Michael, age 3, and Rebecca, age 2 (both the children of George and Lillian). After Carol's death George was left to cope alone with his infant daughter. He worked in a hospital in a supportive capacity and recounted what a struggle he had trying to care for Janine and make a living. He emphasized that, in the press of things, he paid close attention to her physical needs but could not also attend to her emotional needs. Fortunately, his parents lived nearby, and Carol's parents, though living at a distance, were very much involved—too involved, George would say—and spent a lot of money on Janine and whatever time they could. George married Lillian when Janine was 5, and Lillian moved into the house with George and Janine. Subsequently, George and Lillian had two children together.

When I met the family, they had just been through a thirteen-week intensive home-based intervention, precipitated by Janine's third psychiatric hospitalization (which was succeeded by her fourth). She was described by her family as an uncontrollable monster when she became angry, escalating in her behavior to such an extent that George had, on more than one occasion, called the police. They further feared her destructive behavior around the two younger children.

Our treatment team was headed by the psychiatrist who administered medication. At the point that the family therapist was included, the situation under treatment had already been defined as having a biological etiology: the psychiatrist had diagnosed Janine as having attachment disorder and ADHD and described her as having a brain chemistry in need of adjustment by the proper medication. Several medications had already been tried, most of which worked initially and then lost effectiveness. Each time a medication became ineffective in curbing Janine's outbursts, the psychiatrist hospitalized her. At ten years of age, Janine had already experienced several psychiatric hospitalizations.

It had been accepted by all those already involved when I arrived on the team that because of this brain abnormality, Janine would probably have to remain on medication for the foreseeable future. The other professionals involved were expected to provide their treatment based on this assumption.

However, in fact, the respite worker viewed the situation very differently in spite of her acquiescence. Janine and she had spent large amounts of time together, including going camping and other activities for whole weekends at a time. The respite worker reported no unmanageable behavior, and she and Janine had formed a strong bond, a statement with which everyone agreed (despite the diagnosis of attachment disorder). However, as the respite worker's position on the team was both subordinate to the psychiatrist's and ancillary, the respite worker's view did not intersect with the view held by the psychiatrist in any way that could meaningfully provide for the family an alternative hypothesis of etiology and response. Her idea of a different etiology was only *implied* in her report, since she was not equipped to develop her experiences with Janine into a conceptual paradigm for comparison with the biological view of the psychiatrist. So Janine's behavior with the respite worker was viewed as a kind of strange anomaly and was set aside, as though it were a jigsaw piece belonging to a different puzzle (which in fact it was). The family had accepted the counsel of the psychiatrist, and the biomedical etiological view prevailed.

As family therapist my opening session was with George and Lillian as parents of Janine to learn their view of the problem. I was impressed with the strikingly clinical way George described Janine, speaking in terms of "incidences" and "episodes." His frame of reference was more clinical than any therapist would have used in talking with a colleague about a client. There were no terms of endearment, no indication of emotion, except for references to anger, which seemed to be expressed by the parents through withdrawal of attention. Stepmother Lillian echoed all of George's descriptions and expectations.

The second session was held with the whole nuclear family present in order to understand more about their ways of interacting with one another. During this session Janine gravitated to the piano in my office. Three individual sessions with Janine followed this family session. These were scheduled in order to accommodate the clinic's treatment expectations. But also the parents were resistive to participating regularly in family therapy, because they had received a biological definition of the problem from the psychiatrist and could not understand why they were to participate in to the treatment of Janine's brain disorder. During these three individual sessions, Janine and I sat at the piano. She loved playing and learned fast, gobbling up everything I could teach her. We went halfway through a beginning piano book in these three meetings. In one session Janine played spontaneously as loudly as she could, banging the whole keyboard with her fingers, up and down the octaves. Periodically, she would stop and look over her shoulder. I asked her why, and she said her father didn't like loud noises. The work in these sessions on her life experiences took place between the bar lines. When her father would bring her and pick her up, I shared with him what I had learned about Janine from the session and made suggestions about parenting her.

At the second of these sessions, when he brought Janine, George told me that the new medication she was on was working well, and there had been no outbursts on Janine's part. He said it looked like they had finally found the answer in this medication. I told him, with emphasis, in front of Janine, that there were many things at play in Janine's progress: Janine was doing her part in our sessions, and he and Lillian and been working on parenting issues. I said that in my view all of these were contributing to the progress he experienced. When he came back to pick up Janine, he said he guessed it *was* a combination of everything that was working. They made a third appointment for Janine. That, however, was to be the last for the time being. George thought that I was just teaching Janine to play the piano and that a piano teacher could do that. Things were going well, and he thought they should discontinue her sessions.

A few weeks later I received a call from the clinic, which had in the meantime been overseeing Janine's medication. Janine had been hospitalized again. Neither the family nor the clinic had called me about this most recent crisis. The psychiatrist had made this decision without any input from the treatment team.

When Janine came out of the hospital, the clinic called a case management meeting with the psychiatrist, respite worker, case manager, family therapist, and parents. Everyone except the psychiatrist was there at the appointed hour but could not begin to meet because the psychiatrist was in charge of the meeting. When he came some fifteen minutes later, he reviewed the problem, emphasizing that Janine suffered from attachment disorder and ADHD. He made comments outlining the limitations and appropriate expectations of "ADHD kids." He checked in with George on how Janine's latest, posthospitalization medication, Ritalin, was working. The parents revealed that they were distraught with this latest hospitalization and at their wits' end as to how to deal with the situation. Nothing had worked for long.

I turned to the parents and commented that their decision to describe the problem solely as an illness in Janine did not seem to be working. I proposed that if they wanted to try describing it as a family problem for a while, they would have a fresh avenue for finding a solution. They agreed and asked what that would mean. I described my idea: that they would work as a whole family, looking at everybody and everybody's part in the family. I told them not to agree too fast, as it would demand a lot of them. They thought a bit and agreed again. As I recall, the psychiatrist did not comment on my suggestion. The case manager however was quite excited about the freshness of this idea and later called to tell me so.

I began again to meet them as a family. In a couple of weeks' time, I suggested a home visit to the family for dinner, to which they were very receptive. When I arrived, Janine greeted me with enthusiasm. She took me to see her room, which was located in the dark cellar, in the farthest corner from the stairs. She commented that I should watch out for the jumping spiders on the cellar floor which she said frightened her. Her room itself was well lighted and appointed and constituted a sort of oasis in the darkness of the basement. Then we went to the beautiful wooded area behind her home where she had constructed a kind of fort of twigs around the base of a tree. She invited me in. She said she had hidden there one night when her father had called the police. She said she loved being in the woods. We spent a long time exploring there. When we returned to the house, we sat down to dinner. While Janine was telling a story, first Lillian, then George got up and left the table, and I suddenly realized that Janine and I were sitting by ourselves while she completed her story. After dinner I learned that at bedtime Janine was given a kiss and hug and sent off alone downstairs to her room. Her siblings and parents slept in rooms two stories above hers. Janine's isolation in the midst of her family was underscored by these situations, giving the diagnosis of Attachment Disorder a contextual dimension.

That evening I made the following suggestions to the family. (a) Spend more time with Janine at bedtime, in her room, perhaps reading to or with her. (b) Let go of expectations from past interactions. George saw Janine as a potential time bomb and was poised at every moment for a recurrence of her outbursts. When things would go better, he would wonder when the next explosion would come. (c) Get piano lessons and perhaps rent a piano for Janine. (d) Reorganize the house so that Janine's room would not be in the basement, separate from the rest of the family.

In response to these recommendations George bought Janine an electronic keyboard and placed it in her room in the basement. This was a pale enactment of my suggestion. A keyboard does not have the percussive potential of a piano for banging on; furthermore, a piano is usually located in the house in such a way that everyone is a part of the experience while it is being played, not tucked away in a bedroom. As for the sleeping arrangements, George would not consider a change. He said this would be impossible because of the configuration of the house (which he himself had designed) and the ages of the two younger children.

Janine's posthospitalization course went well, and the usual time for a relapse passed. Everyone was getting along better. A second case management meeting was called to check on progress. George expressed his satisfaction with what was happening with Janine. The psychiatrist asked to what he attributed the change. "Ritalin" was his speedy reply.

The difficulty with this conclusion from a family systems viewpoint was that the systemic hypothesis of etiology (i.e., that the client's symptoms are a signal of distress in the larger context) had not been acknowledged. The medication addressed the symptomatology, but not what it signaled from a contextual viewpoint, and so masked the signs of distress from that quarter, signs that had acted as a kind of map of that territory. According to the systemic hypothesis, the distress related to the context would now seek new avenues of symbolic expression, which might take the form of increased symptomatology in Janine or symptomatology in another family member or relationship. The problems only *appeared* to have been solved for the time being; a whole sector of the situation had not been considered.

At this point the therapeutic work was to be suspended for the summer. Janine was going off to *four* consecutive sleepaway camp experiences in as many different camps, the family's way of occupying her while school was out, and yet another sign of her contextual alienation. I called for a session with the father alone. I told him that I was going to discontinue my work with them, but that if at any time in the future the medication did not suffice, I would be happy to work with them again. He was quite agreeable to leaving it at that. I also let the clinic know I was terminating my work with the family. They accepted this. Had I agreed to continue working in this situation, any success related to a family systems view would have been attributed to the medication and seen as affirming the conclusions of the biological view (and the family) that Janine's problem was basically a brain disorder. I was not willing to contribute to this definition because of its long-range disempowering implications for Janine and the unknown long-term effects of medication on children (Fisher & Greenberg, 1996, p. 365). I therefore withdrew my treatment. If the medication held, then the problem was solved in the eyes of the family, and the situation would continue to be defined in that way—an outcome I was powerless to impact. If, however, the medication did not prove to be the answer, family therapy would not also have failed by association. If the family sought a different view, family work would still be available as a different direction with the opportunity to redefine the situation in a way that did not place the whole burden of the problem on Janine's small shoulders.

## SUMMARY

This clinical vignette provides us with an example of the problems often involved in collaborative treatment. The family had accepted a single viewpoint with regard to a multidimensional event. This one view provided a path for symptom management but was by itself insufficient for resolution and growth. The treatment effort *appeared* to be multidimensional because it involved different kinds of professionals and different treatment modalities. But it was in fact completely determined by a single etiological hypothesis.

In this case my efforts as a family therapist to work within the clinic system in a collaborative team approach only contributed to the problem. In a treatment program whose whole course was being attributed to a brain disorder treatable by medication, any success was attributable to the effects of the medication; any success that followed from my efforts worked perversely to maintain the idea that the problem was medical and the solution pharmaceutical. And in that program, no one but Janine had to change. Furthermore, the collaborative intervention helped create the false impression that every possible approach to a solution was being tried. If the daughter was hospitalized again, family therapy would be very likely added to the list of failed treatment attempts—even though family therapy had never really begun.

## REFERENCES

Fisher, S., & Greenberg, R. (1996). *From placebo to panacea*. New York: Wiley, 365.

Keith, D. (n.d.). Epistemology and Experience in the Clinic: Family Therapy for Chemical Imbalance in Children: Four Cases. Unpublished paper.

McDaniel, S. H., & Campbell, T. L. (1997). Editorial: Training Health Professionals to Collaborate. *Families, Systems and Health*, 15(4), 353–359.

Schilp, P. (1957). *Albert Einstein, philosopher scientist*. New York: Tudor Press.

# Foreword to Chapter 3

In the first two essays we have set forth our theme and our concerns. Now we would like you to join us for a helicopter ride over the whole territory in which our theme plays itself out so that we can view its extent. The Auerswald essay that follows will be our vehicle. Please climb aboard.

"Dick" Auerswald was a friend and inspiration to both of us. He died, too soon, in 1998, his work too little recognized. His death came swiftly. It left a large hole in the fabric of systemic thinking in family therapy. In the years before his death, he developed and self-published a wonderful collection of his papers, which he left us as a patch for the fabric of our field. Entitled *Ecovision, Volume I, Essays: 1964–1993*, it preserves for us the legacy of his wonderful invigorating thinking. The essay that follows is from this collection. It does not talk about the issue of pharmacology specifically, but it pays attention to the epistemology that underlies what we are talking about in *this* collection. The premises on which family therapy is based are different from the premises that underlie psychiatric thinking. This is an epistemological problem, a problem based on different ways of thinking about human experience. This Auerswald essay is one of the best sources for clearly understanding this fundamental difference in thinking patterns.

The essay is well written, but mental energy is required to integrate what it says. You may want to read it several times. In the first part, Auerswald talks about epistemology and paradigms and models. It lays the groundwork for the second part, in which he develops the mechological paradigm and the ecosystemic holodigm. The mechologic paradigm works well for designing and building machines but when applied to human experience is value-neutral and leads to events like the holocaust, which are constructed on logic. The ecosystemic holodigm is the kind of thinking that energized the early family therapy movement and is better suited to thinking about human relatedness. The third part of the paper delineates an operational paradigm, which Auerswald describes as "modes of thought."

In our book, we hope we have moved the discussion about the dialectics of family therapy and psychopharmacology into what Dick called Mode Four, at least some of the time. Mode Four, a free associative level, he defines as ". . . shared creative thought carried out together by a community of individuals. (Example: a synergistic conversation carried on by a group which creates a new possibility. Ego ownership is abandoned and the participants experience full 'we-ness.')."

Later, in the clinical section of the book, another Auerswald essay, "Thinking about Thinking in Family Therapy," acts as a review of some of the same material and then applies it clinically.

# Chapter 3

# Family Healing and Planetary Healing: Three Paradigms in Search of a Culture*

Edgar H. Auerswald, MD

*"Oh, Kitty, how nice it would be if we could only get through into Looking-glass House! I'm sure it's got, oh! such beautiful things in it! Let's pretend there's a way of getting through into it, somehow, Kitty. Let's pretend the glass has got all soft like gauze, so that we can get through. Why, it's turning into a sort of mist now, I declare! It'll be easy enough to get through——"*
      Lewis Caroll, *Alice's Adventures in Wonderland*

Seminal thinkers in our century in increasing numbers have pointed out that escape from the current self-destructive trajectory of human evolution will require a "paradigm shift" from the mechanistic and reductionistic paradigm of dominant Western thought to an ecological paradigm which directs thought and reality definition in such a way as to prevent impending ecological disaster and to promote and support the evolution of a world-wide community of differences. As family therapy has been exploring the nature of paradigm shift since such a shift resulted in its emergence as a domain of

*Family Healing and Planetary Healing: Three Paradigms in Search of a Culture. Published in the proceedings of the international congress, "Toward an Ecology of the Mind: Then Healing Dimensions in Family and Society," Budapest, Hungary, July, 1989.

thought, it would seem that family therapists may be able to make a meaningful contribution to the search for such a transformation of thought/reality. This paper is a report on a project designed to explore the nature of the Western paradigm and to develop a nonmechanistic nonreductionistic paradigm to be "shifted to" by exploring the epistemological transformation which has been taking place in twentieth-century science. The possibility of a contribution from family therapy is critiqued in this context.

If our species survives its current self-destructive tendencies, it seems likely that the twentieth century will be known by future generations as a century of transformation. As an evolutionary outcome of the technological explosion created by Western science, most humans now share a vantage point which provides a view of what is going on throughout our planet. I think you will agree that the panorama thus exposed to all of us is disquieting. This global scene stimulates visions of a world-wide harmonious connected community, while simultaneously exposing how disconnected we have become, and how unwilling or unable most of us are to accept certain of the differences among us.

Also exposed is a set of conditions which tells us that we are an endangered species. It has become apparent that among our species is a large segment which is behaving in a manner which could turn our green earth into a planet which cannot support complex life forms like ourselves. We see that the technology which provided us with this view has also evolved the means of our total destruction. We now know that it will be necessary to evolve a global community which embraces differences while maintaining harmony and a global culture which pays meticulous attention to the avoidance of behaviors which generate ecological disasters.

That task, it turns out, is easier said than done. The creation of harmony and assured ecological viability cannot be attained if each of us asserts and stands with certainty on what he knows. It is, in fact, precisely such assertions which create continuing conflict and disconnection and which generate ecological disaster. It is becoming increasingly clear that it will be necessary for us to examine how we know what we think we know. The word for the study of how we know what we think we know is epistemology, so another way of saying this is that it is necessary for us to engage in epistemological explorations (see note 1, p. 55).

Given the above conditions, then, it is not surprising that in our field of psychotherapy there has been a movement toward the application of our skills in the relational domain in systems larger than that of the individual person; the first such system thus embraced has been that which is most visible and powerful in our day-to-day lives, the family. Here, as in all of science, there is renewed interest in epistemological issues.

It is also not surprising that natural scientists who study the lives of species have also become sensitive to the relational domain, to how species interact with each other and with their natural environment and that they too have become concerned with healing, with the creation of harmonious communities of differences. Here, too, the epistemological questions have surfaced.

The new science of ecology and what we call family therapy emerged side by side in the mid-years of the twentieth century, and they share the same roots. Both are engaged in the study of what prevents the creation of harmonious communities of differences, and in the development of methods for healing and preventing conditions that create debilitation and death. Both focus on the domain of relations, the domain in which individuals and species interact, interpenetrate, connect and disconnect, and thrive and decline. There is correspondence to be found in the work of family therapists and ecologists. Ecologists are becoming healers while family therapists become ecologists. Members of both endeavors are becoming epistemologists.

This concern for how to create harmonious communities of differences and how to prevent ecological disaster is happily no longer confined to circumscribed professional groups. Humans throughout the planet are developing an ecological consciousness. There is now a general concern with how we can create a world-wide harmonious eco-community of differences.

So it would seem we family therapists who have been concerned with the alleviation of distress and the prevention of death and debilitation in individuals and families may have some unique and important experience to report as a contribution to the necessary task of alleviating distress and preventing the debilitation and death of our species.

Such a contribution can be both epistemological and operational, but its precise nature is not immediately clear. As family therapists, we know that understanding and clarity require the location of an issue in context. So, to seek an answer to the question of what we can contribute, let's look at the global context.

I will begin by quoting the words of two of the preeminent thinkers of this century. First, the words of Albert Einstein: "Everything has changed but the way we think." "We shall require a substantially new manner of thinking if mankind is to survive."

Then the words of Gregory Bateson: "The point is that the ways of nineteenth century thinking are becoming rapidly bankrupt—here I want to call attention to a condition of our time—that as the conventional ways of thinking about mind and life collapse, new ways of thinking about these matters are becoming available, not only to ivory tower philosophers but also to practitioners and to the 'man in the street.'"

Both of these men were referring to a transformation in *how* we think, not *what* we think—to how we know what we think we know, and how we assign the status of reality to what we know.

When Einstein spoke of survival, he was speaking of escape from what he perceived as the high probability that humans who possessed nuclear weapons would inevitably use them. Bateson shared this concern, of course, but his concerns also included a number of other ecological disasters which he saw evolving long before most of us, and, much more than Einstein, he was an epistemologist, which is to say that he was more aware of the detailed differences between those various ways of thinking that determine how each of us comes to know what he thinks he knows. He tells us that the "new manner of thinking" so devoutly desired by Einstein is already available to us. He is, perhaps more than any other, eminently qualified to make this statement, since he devoted his life to the development of ideas that contribute to the new manner of thinking which he called ecological.

Thomas Kuhn described the process of transformation in the thinking of scientists from one reality construct to another as a paradigm shift, and many authors now apply this term to transformations outside of science as well. In this language, what Einstein and Bateson both considered a necessity for continued viability of our endangered species is a widespread paradigm shift. If the survival imperative voiced by these men is taken seriously, as we now know it must be, it would seem that if action to accomplish such a shift can be designed and undertaken, it will be necessary to clarify the paradigms to be shifted from and to.

An effort to accomplish such clarification has been going on at the Center for Applied Epistemology (see note 2, p. 55). What follows is a report on the outcome of that work so far. Before proceeding, however, let me clearly define how the word *paradigm* has been applied in this work, and also introduce and define another term, which allows for more clarity when comparisons are made between local paradigm shifts and the global shift to which Einstein and Bateson refer.

The definition of the word *paradigm*, at least in English dictionaries, is: "a model of how things should be." This definition, as you can see, contains an imperative embodied in the word *should*. Immanent in all paradigms, of course, is a set of premises. The dictionary definition of the word *premise* is: a statement on which reasoning is based." There is no imperative in this definition, but there is another word which can also denote a statement upon which reasoning is based which does carry an imperative. That word is *precept*, the dictionary definition of which is: "a command, a *rule* of conduct." If the conduct referred to is cognitive, then it would seem that a paradigm is formed when a set of premises constructed in thought that are related in such a way as to project a model become precepts or rules. Thus a paradigm can be defined as: "a set of precepts, or rules, which imperatively direct thinking or reasoning in a manner that supports and maintains a particular model of how things should be."

In practice, then, a paradigm can be described either with a set of ideas expressed as defined premises, by premises expressed as precepts, or by a set of precepts expressed as rules which represent the essence of those premises or precepts.

The word *paradigm* and the definition I arrived at are deficient in one respect. The distinction of a paradigm of paradigms which projects a model of a complete reality—that is, one which is capable of projecting a model of "all of it," so to speak—from a paradigm which models a specific domain of reality—"some of it," so to speak—is not made. To correct this deficiency, and thus to avoid the confusion it can create, I have suggested elsewhere that a paradigm of paradigms—that is, a paradigm which is capable of modeling "all of it"—be designated a *holodigm*, and that the word *paradigm* be restricted to denoting those which are capable only of modeling "some of it." I will be using these two terms and their adjectival derivatives, *paradigmatic* and *holodigmatic*, in this way as I move along.

This distinction, once made, turns out to be more interesting than it appears at first glance. It exposes the probability that a paradigm, to be viable and ultimately useful, cannot long stand alone. It must project a domain of reality which is congruent with a total reality projected by a holodigm. Also exposed is the possibility that a paradigm may be used as if it were a holodigm when it is not. These observations turned out to be important in the work I will describe, for reasons I will later explain.

The first paradigm I wish to present is composed of a rule set. It has been referred to variously as the Western paradigm, the Occidental paradigm, the Cartesian-Newtonian paradigm, the mechanistic paradigm, etc.

The set was arrived at by observing the premises expressed in the science and predominant philosophy of the years following the work of Immanuel Kant until the end of the nineteenth century, when syllogistic logic had been well developed, and logical positivism and Newtonian science reigned supreme in Occidental thinking. Since these premises, which are those of the Age of Reason, continue to predominate and to be expressed in the general exercise of reason in the Occidental world today, it was possible to check out the set empirically by direct observation.

It is the paradigm of mechanistic, reductionistic, atomistic, centripetal reasoning which has projected the reality model accepted by humans in the Occidental world for at least the past three centuries. The logic of this thought/reality system is the syllogistic logic based on the mathematics of the nineteenth century and before. The premises represented by these rules are those of Cartesian-Newtonian science. The core premise which holds the rest of the premises together is expressed by the *Rule of Single Fixed Reality* and the *Rule of Mechanistic Form* which holds that the universe is constructed as a gigantic machine. It is for this reason that I have designated this set as "The Rules of Mechologic." It is as follows:

## THE ABSOLUTE RULES OF MECHOLOGIC*

1. Rule of Single Fixed Reality
2. Rule of Mechanical Form
3. Rule of Separate and Infinite Time and Space
4. Rule of Three-dimensional Space
5. Rule of Linear Time
6. Rule of Objectivity
7. Rule of Conservation of Substance
8. Rule of Name as Thing
9. Rule of Hierarchy
10. Rule of Substantive Abstraction
11. Rule of Dissipative Energy
12. Rule of Understanding by Analysis
13. Rule of Linear Causal Process
14. Rule of Idea as Thing
15. Rule of Pejorative Dualism
16. Rule of Certainty

This paradigm, which directs the thought which spawned the industrial revolution and the opposing ideologies which evolved therein, became the predominant thought system used by all Occidental humans, and it remains dominant to this day. Occidental societies were constructed on the basis of political-economic systems (ideologies) which are representations of the reality model projected by this paradigm.

That reality model is the one familiar to all of us. It is that in which objects and "objective" ideas exist substantively in an infinite and separate time and space. Space is three-dimensional, and time ticks off at a steady rate as measured by clocks. Objects and ideas are generally arranged in hierarchical order according to form, activity, or some value set. Substance and energy can be neither created nor destroyed.

In this reality model, there is one reality and one truth. There is one universe, and the task of science is to discover the true laws which govern it. Paradox forms the boundary of reasonable thought, and thus such laws must be devoid of paradox.

The rules of the paradigm are therefore easily recognizable and self-explanatory to Occidental humans. In recent decades, as a result of the adoption of the  ideologies of this reality in other parts of the world, they

---

*For definitions of each rule, see Appendix pp. 57–58.

have been put to widespread use, and thus have become recognizable throughout our planet.

I wish to emphasize four points regarding this paradigm. The first is that *it is pejoratively exclusive.* It is held together operationally by three of its rules—the Rule of Pejorative Dualism, the Rule of Hierarchy, and the Rule of Certainty. These are the rules of the paradigm which allow decisions to be made.

The Rule of Pejorative Dualism could also be expressed as the either/or rule. It requires that alternative ideas be mapped on the polarities of antonymic pairs that express values—pairs such as good/bad, useful/useless, sinful/righteous, right/wrong, and so on. Out of a range of possible choices, it allows for the discarding of all save one. That one is then declared good or right or true, and the others bad or wrong or false. In the search for truth, *THE* single Truth, the Rule of Certainty can be evoked. The remaining rules are used in the development of concepts that are subjected to such judgment. The outcome is that all ideas which do not fit into the reality model of the paradigm are simply discarded as irrational and wrong or untrue.

The viability of this system of thought is sustained by the use of these rules to cope with paradoxes which form the boundary of reason. A paradox can simply be mapped as a pejorative antonymic pair, one pole of the paradox declared right and the other wrong, and the pole declared wrong discarded. The result of this operation, however, is that thought directed by this paradigm continually turns centripetally inward on itself. It becomes pejoratively exclusionary and unreceptive to creative change.

The rules of the paradigm really are rules. They accept no deviation from their commands. The reality system thus becomes self-constitutive and self-perpetuating.

The second point I wish to emphasize is that this paradigm *contains no built-in morality.* It is completely amoral. Using the Rule of Pejorative Dualism and the Rule of Certainty, a mechological thinker can rationalize any idea—even Auschwitz, for example. Morality in the societies and cultures formed by this paradigm depends on metaphysical paradigms of nonempirical origin, so that a morality can be (and was) constructed which reinforces the idea of Auschwitz.

The third point I wish to emphasize is that this paradigm *is not a holodigm.* As Bateson pointed out over and over again, it has no capacity to deal adequately with the domains of human relationality and creativity. Logical thinking in the Age of Reason deals with people as objects that bounce off each other or that articulate like parts of a machine. The system only allows for thought about how an objective entity acts *on*—that is, *effects*—another objective entity. It cannot handle how events *connect* in the relational domain—that is, how living entities or ideas interpenetrate or merge or interact and relate with one another. Thus, the domain of mechological reason has no place for human passions, fantasies, dreams, feelings, couplings, conflicts, play, or creativity, not even for the nuances of human development.

This observation, of course, is not surprising to us Occidental thinkers. We have always considered these domains to be unreasonable. Sigmund Freud located them outside of the reasonable ego in the unbridled id, and solved the problem of their reasonable legitimacy by inventing the mechanism of sublimation.

The fourth point I wish to emphasize is that the paradigm when put to use in thinking about these unreasonable domains not only excludes them but also, by its method of understanding and its use of pejorative exclusion, *actively creates disconnection* in these domains. The rules of the paradigm as thought system require that in a search for understanding of any entity or phenomenon, objective or abstract, one must disconnect the elements of the entity by breaking it down into its parts. This, in itself, is not necessarily problematic, but as the system contains no rules which allow it to handle the relational domain, it contains no rules which allow for the relational reconnection of the parts. All it can encompass is thinking about how the disconnected parts act on one another in a linear view of cause and effect, and in such thinking the parts remain fundamentally disconnected.

In "hard" science, where reality status required mathematical cohesion, until the end of the nineteenth century, it seemed possible that this deficiency could be overcome. It was assumed that mathematical formulae which seemed *generic* to physical reality could be stated as immutable laws which reconnected the parts. In this century that assumption has turned out to be highly questionable, if not entirely illusory. It has been suggested by responsible "hard" scientists that what Newtonian physics spawned in the Age of Reason is a magnificent empirical art form which was pragmatically very useful, but which, in the end, could not qualify for the status of either reality or absolute truth.

In the "soft" sciences of the Age of Reason the assumption that the parts could be reconnected by the discovery of immutable laws has also been central, but no such immutable laws have emerged. Here, the assumption is even more questionable.

There is still no provision in the mechological paradigm for reconnection of the parts defined in reductionistic analysis.

This paradigm, nevertheless, has created some highly attractive outcomes. It projects the reality in which technological advances have created the machines which shape our modern world, with all its benefits. These machines have expanded our senses, our knowledge base, and our mobility in a manner which has allowed some of us to live longer and to overcome want, and even to create a seemingly endless frontier as we move out into our galaxy. Unfortunately, among those machines are also those which comprise devastating weaponry, including nuclear weapons, those which seem to rob us of our humanity, and those which are polluting our earth, thus creating a growing variety of present and impending ecological disasters—in short, those which threaten life on earth.

It is the paradigm that, based on these threatening outcomes, has been declared bankrupt, damned, and repudiated by nearly all of the important philosophers of the latter three-fourths of the twentieth century. Especially, it has been attacked as a paradigm which creates a kind of species solipsism and hubris which disconnects us from the rest of nature and blinds us to the long-term outcomes of our actions.

It is, therefore, presumably the paradigm to be moved from in the paradigm shift we seek.

It is, however, the paradigm which drives the thought and projects the reality in which those who inhabit the dominant power centers of our planet live. It won't go away. It can't go away. It can't simply be moved from. It spawned the system which currently supports the world's economy. It is the paradigm of production, and those who use it can claim rightly that it has spawned most of that which most of us have called progress, in the sense that it has markedly raised the standard of living for a substantial minority of the world's population, enough so that, to many, it has seemed possible that its benefits could be extended to all people of the world. Even if the political ideologies which grew in this paradigm are reconciled, it still won't go away.

So, it would seem, if we are to make the necessary paradigm shift, we will have to move to a holodigm which can include this paradigm of production, and which can direct us in its usage. We will need to continue its use to make machines, but we must do so in a manner in which ecological disasters will be avoided. This holodigm, then, must be one which can project a reality in which a whole new economic paradigm can be developed, an eco-economics (or more appropriately an economics that takes the *eco-* in the word seriously), if you will, in which the machines we make and the way we use them ultimately and permanently support life.

The second paradigm I wish to present is presented as one to be moved to. It is also stated as a set of rules of thought. Before presenting it, I must state how it was developed and why the means used were chosen.

This paradigm was developed by collecting the premises which have been expressed by scientists during the twentieth-century epistemological transformation of scientific thinking that began with the emergence of relativity and quantum physics around the turn of the century, and moved into a new phase in midcentury with the emergence of nonlinear mathematics and the study of chaos. That transformation, as you know, resulted in an explosion of scientific endeavor, the emergence of several new sciences, and the development of a number of new technologies.

The paradigm immanent in this transformation did not throw out the use of the mechological paradigm. It retained it and now uses it in two ways. First, while the laws of Newtonian science, which both contributed to and emerged from mechological thinking, were stripped of their mantle of absolute truth, the reality model it projected was not pejoratively discarded, and it continues to be used as a useful tool. Second, scientists had continued to think mechologically in order to construct the machines they used in their experiments. Whatever the paradigm was that had emerged in the twentieth-century transformation, it was, it seemed, inclusive and not exclusive.

Also, given that anyone can invent a new paradigm, in a search for a paradigm to be moved to, it appeared necessary that the method for development would have to maintain a strong commitment to empirical process (see note 3, p. 56). One way to maintain this commitment seemed to be to study a paradigm developed by those who were most committed to empiricism—that is, by "hard" scientists.

This choice of where to look for the missing paradigm turned out to be a fortunate one. As the work of developing it was begun, it was anticipated that the task would be very difficult. It was assumed that it would be necessary to look at the thinking of those scientists who participated in the transformation and to extract their premises from the nature of their work. It seemed unclear whether it would be possible to maintain even a semblance of soft empiricism. It turned out, however, that the scientists who were involved in the transformation were directly developing new premises, and that they stated these premises, often with great clarity, when they published their work.

For example, Einstein's theory of relativity stated new premises (new, in the domain of contemporary science, that is) regarding the nature of time, space, and motion and matter and energy. Heisenberg's principle of uncertainty stated a new premise with regard to the nature of truth. Bohr's principle of complementarity stated a new premise with regard to the connectedness of seemingly opposed dualisms which leads to a new premise on the nature of paradox. Bateson's redefinition of the nature of mind was stated as a new premise, as were many other of the concepts he developed. The work of Maturana and Varela on the autopoietic nature of life processes was stated as a new premise. Prigogine's work on the nature of transformation was stated as a new premise. Bohm's description of the implicate and explicate universe stated a new premise. In presenting his equations which formed the foundation of chaos theory, Edward Lorenz stated a new premise which was elaborated by Mandelbrot in his work on fractal geometry—etc., etc., on and on.

The task of developing this paradigm turned out to be much easier than had been expected. It did not require much interpretation, although it did require some synthesis. Mostly, however, the work turned out to consist of compilation, the elimination of duplication, and, most difficult, the choice of words. The paradigm which emerged from this work is as follows:

## THE GUIDING PRINCIPLES OF ECOLOGIC*

1. Principle of Multiple Evolving Realities
2. Principle of Space–time
3. Principle of Universal Cognition
4. Principle of Event as Information
5. Principle of Attractors
6. Principle of Pattern as Related Events
7. Principle of Pattern Emergence
8. Principle of Monistic Connectedness
9. Principle of Event-shape as Ecosystem
10. Principle of Understanding by Contextualization
11. Principle of Paradox as Punctuation
12. Principle of Conservation of Ideas
13. Principle of Name as Shorthand Representation
14. Principle of Heuristic Truth
15. Principle of Continuous Creation
16. Principle of Human Participation

Now I must state some *qualifying* observations which emerged during this work.

First, the rule set I have presented to you is not one which has been subjected to widespread consensual validation. Since a theory can be defined as a yet-to-be-validated paradigm, it is, in a sense, a theory of a paradigm.

Second, early in the work of compiling these rules it became apparent they are not rules of the same order as those which make up the mechological paradigm. Their content does not carry the continuous imperative of a fixed rule. The paradigm as a whole turns out to be one of emergence and growth which itself will continue to grow and evolve, and so, of course, will the rules which express it. Ten years from now, if I present this paradigm, it will have changed. It is for this reason that I have identified these rules as guiding principles.

In one sense they could still be considered rules, however, because they do express an imperative directed at the *method* of thinking while not restricting the content.

*For definitions of principles, see Appendix, pp. 58–60. See also note 4.

In order to test whether this list of principles collectively deserves the status of a paradigm—that is, whether it works—the list must be approached as if it does express a paradigm. My own experience in the use of this paradigm as thought/reality system leads me to believe that it does work and that, with modifications, it will survive. This, of course, remains to be seen.

Ultimately, of course, the final test which will determine whether the rules hang together as a system for use in thought and reality construction is whether they can spawn a new formal, though evolving, system of logic. The work of developing such a system has only just begun, although the Laws of Form of G. Spencer Brown and the nonlinear mathematics of complexity theory seem so far to be a promising basis for the development of such a logic.

Some additional *nonqualifying* observations which emerged from this work are also of interest.

These rules, of course, are much less self-explanatory to us "reasonable" humans than those of the mechological paradigm. Generally, they do not seem familiar to Occidental thinkers. The core premise of this paradigm, expressed by the *Rule of Multiple Evolving Realities,* is that while we do not know whether there is a reality "out there" that humans can ultimately perceive or whether human themselves construct their reality entirely, we can stand with impunity on the premise that, at the very least, humans contribute to the construction of that which they accept as reality through a process of dynamic editing directed by paradigms which are imbedded in a common holodigm.

Of interest, too, is an observation which emerged during the work of compiling these principles. None of them is really new. As they were extracted from the work of twentieth-century scientists, it is possible to attach names to them (e.g., the source of rule no. 2 is obviously Einstein, the source of rules nos. 3, 8, and 9 is Bateson, the source of rule no. 6 could be Heisenberg or Gödel, the source of rule no. 4 could be Bohr, the source of rule no. 10 could be Bateson or Prigogine, etc.), but all of the ideas expressed in the premises stated by these scientists can be found in texts written by philosophers over the course of millennia. The core premise behind rule no. 1, for example, was expressed tangentially by Plato in his allegory of the cave. What is new is the confluence of these ideas into a connected paradigm in our twentieth century.

Also, it must be noted that unlike the mechological paradigm, which projects a concrete reality for which our language has been tailor-made, there is not yet a language sufficient to the description of the nonconcrete reality projected by this ecological paradigm. What I can do is describe it using visual metaphor.

The rules of this paradigm create a way of thinking that allows one to "see" a domain in which events which comprise information connect to form emerging, receding, transforming patterns that are describable, not in terms of fixed qualities or quantities, but rather as interacting, interlocking, and interpenetrating scenarios. In the act of such "seeing," the observer becomes a participant in the scenarios which are "seen." The observer thus has influence in the scenarios "seen" to an extent which seems roughly inversely proportional to the complexity of the view.

I would like to emphasize the following four points with regard to this paradigm:

First of all, although it may be too early to tell, *this paradigm appears to be a holodigm*. Whereas the mechological paradigm is pejoratively exclusive, this ecological paradigm is inclusive. Once again I must use visual metaphor. On the terrain of the reality projection of the ecological paradigm sits the mechological reality of the Age of Reason, and the mechological paradigm as thought system is available for use as needed. This ecological paradigm, however, *does* encompass the domain of relationality and creativity. It gives form to the domain which in mechological reality appears as unformed and chaotic.

The second point is that in contradistinction to the mechological paradigm, this paradigm *actively supports* the domains of relationality and creativity. It exposes disconnectedness and allows for the observer as participator to create connections.

The third point is that while objectivity is confined to the mechological paradigm, the use of which is included in this paradigm, *at least* "soft" *empiricism can be maintained in the domain of creativity,* and it appears possible that "hard" empiricism may be possible based on the nonlinear mathematics which is emerging from chaos theory. Bateson's emphasis on "rigor and imagination" comes to mind. Both, it appears, are possible in thinking directed by this paradigm.

The fourth point I wish to emphasize is that, on first glance at least, this *ecological paradigm appears to include at least the rudiments of a built-in morality*. Its active support of relational connectedness and creation would seem to imply support and veneration for that which is alive, for life itself. It should be possible to build an ethic based on this morality. As this ecological paradigm, as holodigm, includes the mechological paradigm, this morality could correct the lack of morality in the paradigm of the Age of Reason. The ability to rationalize any idea through mechological thinking would be controlled. The morality of ecological thinking as the context for mechological thinking, for example, would prevent the rationalization of an Auschwitz.

Now I would like to introduce a third paradigm. This paradigm is one of a very different order. While the paradigms above are epistemological, this one is operational. It is stated not as rules, but rather as definitions, and was developed for purely pragmatic purposes. In order to contrast the two paradigms I have already presented, it became necessary to learn to think as purely as possible using first the rules of one paradigm and then those of the other. Those who engaged in an effort to learn this within my horizon have been humans who had learned to think and reason within the mechological thought/reality system. Thus, when an effort was made to think together in the new paradigm, it often degenerated into an exercise in which much time was spent pointing out how one or another of those thus engaged had fallen back into the reductionistic, dualistic, atomistic, centripetal thinking of familiar mechologic. A gimmick was needed which could get past this state of affairs. Accordingly, I invented a paradigm which is roughly rooted in the structure of Bateson's levels of learning paradigm, but which instead is expressed as modes of thought. As you will see, it turned out to be useful in ways beyond the purpose for which it was it was intended. The paradigm is as follows:

## MODES OF THOUGHT

*Mode Zero* is defined as that thought which is automatic and out of consciousness which results from biological inheritance, repression or repetitive learning. (Examples: biological message systems, memories too painful to remember, the unconscious thought in which one engages when driving an automobile over a thoroughly familiar road while thinking consciously about other issues.)

*Mode One,* primarily used for learning, is thought which allows one to adapt to a fixed environment. (Example: the thought required to drive on the same highway before it has become thoroughly familiar.)

*Mode Two* is thought which allows one to adapt to changing or multiple environments. (Example: the thought we engage in to adapt to the complexities of everyday living.)

These three modes (zero, one, and two) are purely adaptive, and the usual progression from one to another is centripetal from Mode Two to Mode One to Mode Zero. Centrifugal progression to Mode Three requires a qualitative jump.

*Mode Three* is creative thought carried out individually that remains ego-bound. (Example: the fantasy that the driver engages in which leads him to an idea of a better route to take, or the artist creating a work of art, or the psychotic creating his private reality. The sense of ego ownership of these creations is maintained.)

*Mode Four* is shared creative thought carried out together by a community of individuals. (Example: a synergistic conversation carried on by a group which creates a new possibility. Ego ownership is abandoned and the participants experience full "we-ness.")

*Mode Five* is experienced as beyond "we-ness" It is pure being, oneness with "all of it," with eternity.

Modes Three and Four are not concerned with adaptation, but are entirely creative, and the usual progression from one to the other is centrifugal from Mode Three to Mode Four. Occasionally there is progression from Mode Four to Mode Five, an experience that Western theologians would call the experience of God, that philosophers would call pure Being, that Eastern theologian/philosophers would call enlightenment, and that could be considered beyond creativity as an experience rooted in Creation (capital C).

The idea of how to use this paradigm was to develop ways to induce a group into Mode Four and then to think ecologically together. In the effort to implement this idea, some very interesting observations emerged.

What became apparent was that the mechological paradigm as thought system is perfectly suited to thinking in Mode Two and Mode One, and remains as the basis of Mode Zero thought, whereas ecological thinking was nonproductive in these modes. Conversely, ecological thinking was perfectly suited to thinking in Modes Three and Four, whereas mechological thinking was nonproductive in these modes.

Not only that but when mechological thinking became separated from the context of ecological thinking and took over the group, the creative capacity—that is, the Mode Four group itself—disintegrated, and either-or conflicts arose. Mechological thinking in the adaptive modes, it appears, is anathema to the creative modes.

Another important observation was that there is cross-fertilization between the two domains of the adaptive and the creative. Experiences generated in the implementation of adaptive action were useful in the creative domain when stated as ideas in the form of questions, and, of course, ideas generated in the creative domain were useful in the adaptive domain. In fact, the nature of this cross-fertilization allowed for the maintenance of soft empiricism in the process thus generated. Creative thinking in Mode Four, though stimulating and pleasurable, turned out at times to be a wild and impractical exercise without such soft empiricism. A Mode Four group, it seems, must begin its creative work with an idea in the form of a question, an attractor idea, so to speak.

The conclusion that can be drawn from these observations is that mechological thinking in the adaptive modes is necessary for construction of the tools, the machines, the technology of adaptation, and for planning the linear sequences of action necessary for putting those tools into adaptive action, whereas ecological thinking is necessary for use in the relational and creative domains, and as the context for choosing how to use mechological thinking in a manner which can support, not destroy, life.

Finally, I must present another set of observations that emerged, serendipitously, in this work which was carried out primarily by people trained in the behavioral sciences. Thinking ecologically within and about this paradigm, it becomes clear that mechological thinking in Modes Two, One, and Zero projects a reality which is the domain of neuroses which are disorders of adaptive function based by definition on internalized conflict created by either-or thinking.

It also appears that Mode Three thinking is the domain of psychosis, which, as H. S. Sullivan and others have pointed out, can develop when engaged in by a person who, for any of a number of possible reasons (only one set of which is biological), is so communicationally disconnected from all others that consensual validation of the ideas and images s/he creates does not occur, who assigns reality status to her/his creations, and who, by so doing, sets in motion a cybernetic process which reinforces and enhances his/her disconnection. The oft-stated observation that artists seem more at risk for madness than nonartists supports this view.

Mode Four grouping, it also appears, forms the basis for that form of connectedness that we call community—that domain of relational connectedness where in various configurations people think, create, play, generate and support families and tribes, resolve conflict, and relate in spontaneous ways.

Finally, Mode Four also appears to be the domain in which ontological freedom can be attained, by which I mean it is a domain in which participating humans are free to define themselves and their being by choice according to an infinity of shared possibilities. This observation deserves a book in itself.

The question, of course, remains: how useful are these paradigms and the observations which emerged during their development to the needed task of developing a means of creating a widespread transformation of thought and reality which can allow our species to escape from the ecological dangers which surround us? That question cannot, of course, be fully answered yet. Nor can I argue my conviction that they are very useful adequately in a short paper. I will be doing that elsewhere. I will, however, assert with conviction that the mechological paradigm which sources these dangers is totally insufficient as a basis for evolving solutions. And I can also share some brief versions of some of the scenarios from the use of the ecological paradigm in group four interaction.

For example, imagine that the arms treaty negotiators learn how to form a Mode Four group and to think ecologically. If they did, given the nature and morality of such thinking, it is difficult to see how they could do anything but construct a plan to get rid of all nuclear weapons.

Or imagine that ecological thinking was predominant in Germany in the 1930s. How, under such circumstances, could Adolph Hitler have come into power?

Or imagine that the delegates to the United Nations all learn how to form a Mode Four group and to think ecologically. Suppose, then, that each of them also forms a Mode Four group of the leaders in various domains in the country they represent and teach these groups to think ecologically. Suppose, then, that this network of Mode Four groups accepts the task of designing a reality in which a harmonious planetary community of differences exists, and in which the threats of ecological disaster now apparent on our planet including that of nuclear war, do not exist. Central to such a plan would be a new model of world economics—an eco-economics.

Then, once that task has been accomplished, suppose the United Nations group reverted to mechological thinking and designed a sequence of action with the goal of operationalizing that reality, and obtained commitment from the leaders of the national and transnational political and economic power structures of our planet to abide by this plan and carry out the sequence.

While it is unlikely that the third of these fantasies will become reality, the first of them could. Furthermore, the media these days are full of information which suggests that ecological consciousness is growing rapidly in our species. If enough people learn to think ecologically, the same outcome of a harmonious planetary community of difference could conceivably be reached via a planet-wide transformation. Let's hope so. Einstein was probably right.

At the very least, ecological thinking projects a reality which comprises a route of escape from the immobilizing restrictive redundancy of mechological thinking. Too, we humans, in this reality, are not biological machines with a built-in killer instinct or an immutable capacity for blind aggression in the service of survival, which must be controlled by reason, and which frequently gets out of hand. We are what we have known ourselves to be all along. That is, we are beings who sometimes hate, but, more often, who love. As social beings, we are relationally dependent. We seek connectedness with other humans, without which we fail to thrive. But we also seek the experience beyond time, the experience of eternity. We are capable of conscious participation in the creative evolution of ourselves and our surroundings. We are not passive recipients and observers of our destiny, nor are we stuck with a dualistic relational connection with nature in which we are either victims or controllers. We can, though perhaps within limits, create our own destiny. Now, let's get back to the original question. What can the experience accumulated in family therapy contribute to the needed global transformation?

In mechological reality the answer is preordained. There the global issues about which I have written are disconnected from the issues dealt with in that part of reality made up by families and family therapy. There it is obvious that family therapists, as such, cannot affect the socioeconomic and political state of the world, the states which create ecological disasters. There what we do when we move into families as healers has very minor relevance to the threat to our species. All we could hope to do in this reality is to call the families' attention to this threat, and we will be loath to do that since it will interrupt our use of the technical intrafamilial interventions we use and raise an anxiety-provoking issue seemingly far out of context.

In mechological reality, the answer to the question is: not much, if anything.

In ecological reality, however, such is not at all the case. The applicability and usefulness of the ecological thought/reality system in what seem to be lesser domains, especially those which directly involve people in the total context of their lives, is a test of whether or not the ecological paradigm deserves the status of a holodigm. Such a test is highly relevant to the viability of the ideas which generated it.

Many of the ideas central to family therapy are clearly relevant. For example, the notion of reframing arose very early in the family therapy movement. Isn't ecological reframing precisely what is needed to accomplish a global transformation. We family therapists have developed many methods for reframing. Might not those methods (sculpting or narrative construction, for example, in which we construct an empirical art form which, when described, gives us a way to talk about relational connections) prove useful in larger domains?

In the dialogue among family therapists, we have learned a lot about cybernetic causality. Isn't what we have learned relevant to an understanding of the evolution of ecological disasters?

We have also learned much about how to utilize the ideas of one of those I quoted at the beginning of this paper—Gregory Bateson—in pragmatic ways. Isn't that experience relevant to the larger field? I can share one example from personal experience which supports this.

When I introduced the Modes of Thought paradigm into the conversation which is our Center, I modeled it roughly on a simplified version of Bateson's Levels of Learning paradigm. Only after I had introduced it did I realize that it was a framing paradigm for what I, and, I think, many ecosystemic family therapists do in family therapy.

Don't we join with the families who consult us and attempt to form a Mode Four group in order to think creatively together? Then, don't we convert the distress reported by the family into a question or questions to be answered by the explorations within that group? Once we have determined those questions, don't we seek out an ecological scenario which contains the reported distress in our search for answers? Don't we sometimes invite others who can help in this task to join the group? Then, once we are satisfied that the we have understood enough of the scenario, don't we use known techniques or invent ways to intervene in order to change the scenario in a manner which will eliminate the debilitating distress? Don't we, in this process, teach the family to think ecologically, at least in relation to the scenario we have discovered? Don't we induce them to abandon the linear and reductionist explanations for their distress with which they have been stuck? Don't we hope that this experience of Mode Four ecological thinking will persist for them and give them a means of preventing the development of further distress as they live on? Sometimes, if the family and situation permit, don't we engage in teaching these lessons beyond that which is necessary to alleviate a symptom or change behaviors? I think that is what we do when we seek a healing transformation in ecosystemic family therapy. Some of us have used our experience of this kind while working with families in efforts to produce transformations in larger social systems. This experience, too, is valuable.

I say that all of this experience is valuable. In ecological reality, the answer to the question of what the experience accumulated in family therapy can contribute to the imperative of global transformation is: much!

To make that contribution, however, we will have to sharpen our definitions. We will have to pay attention to some distinctions that are not generally made. To begin, we will need to distinguish paradigm and holodigm, mechological thinking and ecological thinking, mechological reality and ecological reality, and, if we do, other needed distinctions will undoubtedly emerge as we evolve.

One such additional needed distinction has already emerged. The catchwords in our field are now *system* and *systemic*. We will need to distinguish mechosystems and ecosystems, and *mechosystemic therapy* and *ecosystemic therapy*. What I have been arguing in this essay is that the difference is profound.

## NOTES

1. I must point out here that, to the extent that each of us is defined by what we think we know, the study of how we are (or be) and the study of how we know merge. The philosophical distinction of epistemology and ontology has turned out to be illusory in this century. The pathway of epistemological exploration pursued by science and the pathway of ontological exploration pursued by philosophy end up as one. Both domains of exploration require freedom from constraints. In this paper I am following the epistemological pathway pursued by science, not only because science is the domain in which I have lived, but also because at the location in which the paths merge, it appears to me that the constraints to ontological freedom are largely epistemological.

2. The Center for Applied Epistemology is not an organization. It is a conversation among a group of people who are interested in the epistemology of ecology in which I participate. The promotion and maintenance of this conversation is a project of the Aion Foundation, Inc. of San Francisco.

3. *Empiricism* is a word which calls up a can of worms. There are many who would argue that the concept of empiricism is inexorably bound by its origins to reductionistic science, and that its use in this work creates an irreducible paradox. I use it herein (in the absence of a better word) only to describe a process in which ideas are generated in a manner based on shared observations and widespread acceptance.

4. I cannot in this short paper explain the origin and definition of the rules of this paradigm sufficiently to make it easy for the reader to grasp them. Since your only recourse is to peruse them and think about them, I can facilitate that task somewhat by telling you that rules 8, 9, 10, 11, and 12 all express premises that delineate the dynamics of rule no. 7, the Rule of Continuous Creation.

## REFERENCES

This paper was presented at the "bridge" conference held in Budapest in July 1989, entitled: "Towards an Ecology of Mind: The Healing Dimension in Family and Society." Because most of the ideas I have presented were drawn from a wide range of literature, from my own life experience, and from a multitude of conversations with others, I cannot always clearly identify their sources. The following, therefore, is an incomplete bibliography. What I have tried to do is construct a reading list for those who are interested in pursuing the relevance of the assertions I have made. It is the kind of list that makes one want to apologize. There are so many other publications which could appear in addition to or instead of those chosen, and it is likely that on another day I might make a different list. Also, sections in some of these books are difficult for most of us family therapists. Stay with the text, and never mind the equations.

The list is not in alphabetical order. Instead, I have ordered it in a sequence which I think, if followed, might facilitate the task. Adherence to this sequence is, however, not all that important.

Bateson, G. (1979). *Mind and nature: A necessary unity.* New York: E. P. Dutton.
Bateson, G., and Bateson, M. C., (1987). *Angels fear.* New York: Macmillan.
Kuhn. T. S.. (1970). *The structure of scientific revolutions* (2nd Ed.). Chicago, University of Chicago Press.
Zukov, G. (1979). *The dancing Wu Li masters.* New York, Morrow.
Planck, M. (1936). *The philosophy of physics.* New York: Norton.
Einstein, A., & Infeld, L. (1961). *The evolution of physics.* New York: Simon & Schuster.
Bohr. N. (1958). *Atomic theory and human knowledge.* New York: Wiley.
Heisenberg, W. (1974). *Across the frontiers.* New York: Harper and Row.
Bohm, D. (1981). *Wholeness and the implicate order.* Boston: Routledge and Kegan Paul.
Prigogine, I., and Stengers, I. (1984). *Order out of chaos.* New York: Bantam.

Hawking, S. W. (1988). *A brief history of time.* New York: Bantam.
Gleick, J. (1987). *Chaos: Making a new science.* New York: Viking Penguin.
Briggs, J., & Peat, F. D. (1989). *Turbulent mirror.* New York: Harper and Row.
Bateson, G. (1972). *Steps to an ecology of mind.* New York: Ballantine Books.
Maturana, H. R., & Varela. F. J. (1987). *The tree of knowledge,* Boston: Shambhala.
Watzlawick, P., Ed. (1984). *The invented reality.* New York: W. W. Norton.
Skinner, Q. (1985). *The return of grand theory in the human sciences.* Cambridge: Cambridge University Press.
Spencer-Brown, G. (1972). *Laws of form.* New York: E. P. Dutton.

## APPENDIX

## The Rules of Mechologic

1. **Rule of Single Fixed Reality**
   Definition: There is one reality. There can be more than one version, but, ultimately, only one is true.
2. **Rule of Mechanical Form**
   Definition: The universe is a machine made up of parts which articulate to make the whole.
3. **Rule of Separate and Infinite Time and Space**
   Definition: Time and space are separate. Time is time, and space is space. Process is what happens in space as it moves through time.
4. **Rule of Three-Dimensional Space**
   Definition: Space is an unbounded empty container with three dimensions—height, width, and depth—and that which is contained therein has these dimensions.
5. **Rule of Linear Time**
   Definition: Time moves inexorably on a line that stretches from past to present to future as measured by clocks.
6. **Rule of Objectivity**
   Definition: Space is filled with substantive objects (things) moving in time. Each object has three dimensions modified by various characteristics which distinguish it from others. To "be objective" is to pay meticulous attention to each object and its characteristic.
7. **Rule of Conservation of Substance**
   Definition: Things can be broken down into smallest parts which are immutable (can neither be created nor destroyed).
8. **Rule of Name as Thing**
   Definition: The name of the thing is the thing named.

9. **Rule of Hierarchy**
   Definition: The natural arrangement of things in space is hierarchical as determined by some dualistic value set, most frequently powerful/powerless or good/bad or a variation thereof.

10. **Rule of Substantive Abstraction**
    Definition: Mass and energy is energy. Together they comprise the machine. Mass is the measure of substance and energy is the measure of power. Mass can neither can be created nor destroyed (i.e., creation took place a long time ago and provided us with a fixed amount).

11. **Rule of Dissipative Energy**
    Definition: Energy/power/work "run down" (dissipate).

12. **Rule of Understanding by Analysis**
    Definition: Understanding is acquired by breaking a thing down into it component parts and seeing how they articulate (seeing how the machine works).

13. **Rule of Linear Causal Process**
    Definition: Parts articulate as they move through time, and cause precedes effect on the time line (e.g., A causes B causes C causes D). There can be combinatory causes (e.g., A and B can combine to cause C). Progression of causes and effects from past to present is called history.

14. **Rule of Idea as Thing**
    Definition: Ideas are abstract things with dimensions and characteristics which occupy space and obey the rule of linear causal process.

15. **Rule of Pejorative Dualism**
    Definition: The universe is dualistic and to maintain order (through the making of decisions) all things must be mapped on pejorative dualism as represented in language by antonyms and labels. The most often used pejorative dualisms are true/false, good/bad, necessary/unnecessary, righteous/evil.

16. **Rule of Certainty**
    Definition: Truth is absolute and immutable.

## Ecological Paradigm (Holodigm?)

1. **Principle of Multiple Evolving Realities**
   Definition: There can be more than one holodigmatic or paradigmatic reality.

2. **Principle of Spacetime**
   Definition: There is one four-dimensional space–time continuum.

3. **Principle of Universal Cognition**
   Definition: Mind is that ubiquitous activity of the universe that makes possible the creation of order out of chaos.

4. **Principle of Event as Information**
   Definition: Information is a difference which makes a difference, and an event is a happening that makes a difference.

5. **Principle of Attractors**
   Definition: Events are connected by an organizing event or set of events that express an idea. In human cognition, an attractor is an idea expressed as a question.

6. **Principle of Pattern as Related Events**
   Definition: As events cluster in the *domain of relations,* they form discernable patterns.

7. **Principle of Pattern Emergence**
   Definition: As patterns of connected events form in the implicate domain, they emerge and become discernible in explicate domain.

8. **Principle of Monistic Connectedness**
   Definition: All patterns discernible in the explicate domain of the universe are connected in the implicate domain.

9. **Principle of Eventshape as Ecosystem**
   Definition: As patterns are event–shapes established in the relational domain, and as ecology is the study of the relational connections of living organisms with each other and with their physical environment, such a discernible pattern is referred to as an ecosystem.

10. **Principle of Understanding by Contextualization**
    Definition: Understanding of a given event is acquired by examination of the genesis, growth, stability, and transformation or disintegration of its membership in a pattern and the nature and function of the connections formed.

11. **Principle of Paradox as Punctuation**
    Definition: In thinking, when a paradox is encountered, it is a signal to expand the field of thought.

12. **Principle of Conservation of Ideas**
    Definition: Ideas are patterns of information, and those which do not appear to fit into larger patterns are not to be discarded, but, instead, are to be set aside in a manner which maintains their accessibility for subsequent thinking.

13. **Principal of Name as Shorthand Representation**
    Definition: A name is not that which is named. It is, instead, a symbolic representation constructed for purpose of facilitating communication.

14. **Principle of Heuristic Truth**
    Definition: Truth is impermanent; it exists only within the pattern which generated it, and it "runs out" when the pattern is transformed or disintegrates.
15. **Principle of Continuous Creation**
    Definition: The universe is constitutive of itself; that is, it continually creates itself creating itself.
16. **Principle of Human Participation**
    Definition: Humans are active participants in universal cognition and thus in continuous creation.

Part 2

# Theoretical Dimensions: Dilemmas and Contradictions in the Approaches of Family Systems Therapy and Psychopharmacological Practice

# Introduction to Part 2

Auerswald points out in his essay that at this time our ecological awareness requires that we shift from rule 5 of the Mechologic Paradigm, the Rule of Linear Causal Process, to rules 7, 8, 9, and 10 of the Ecological Paradigm, Principle of Pattern Emergence, Principle of Monistic Connectedness, Principle of Event-Shape as Ecosystem, and Principle of Understanding by Connectedness. Family systems work made this shift half a century ago.

Today's biopsych model, however, has reverted back to the Mechologic Paradigm and the idea of simple linear cause and effect as it advocates that all mental events are simply the result of shifts in brain chemistry. Clinical contexts, regardless of discipline (psychiatry, psychology, or social work), are dominated by psychiatric thinking and language. The linear language that goes with psychiatric practice, medicalized psychiatric diagnosis, is so implicitly part of the values and the semantics that support American society that it is almost impossible to comment on it. How can you raise a question about those beautiful colored slides providing data combined with a lecture by a well-dressed man from a major medical center who speaks so rapidly and with such assurance? Where do you start the discussion? Yet start it we must, for this retrograde slide into the mechologic lexicon of linear causality in biological psychiatry sends us backward in time and threatens to extinguish the discoveries in family systems theory over the last fifty years, discoveries which correspond to the ecological insight so critical to our survival today.

The following essays begin a finely nuanced discussion by examining the issue of Family Therapy as an Alternature to Medication, from similar but varied perspectives. All of the writers in this section are physicians, most are both psychiatrists and family therapists. In the latter cases, their work as psychiatrists is deeply affected by their experience as family therapists. In this section papers by Freeman, Pakman, Schaefer, Ducommun-Nagy, and Mei present cultural critiques and guidance about the relation of family therapy to the use of psychotropic medications. The issues we are dealing with in this book are elusive. They are best understood by looking from multiple perspectives. The authors in this section provide multiple, but connected, viewpoints related to thinking about family therapy. These are papers that transcend dichotomizing; they stay in the dialectic, better, in the holodigm. Each shares an honest wondering about dilemmas that arise out of family therapy practice in a culture that is persuaded that psychopharmacological agents are good.

The world goes wrong when it depends upon theory to cover its effects, when it depends upon the "system" to care for people. Beliefs and identities are a crucial component in this area of concern. The forces affecting mental health care all seem to represent goodwill and a desire to improve our world, but in their combined effort they repress freedom and creativity and have such persuasive power over all. The forces are the pharmaceutical companies in concert with managed care corporations, but their methods are catalyzed by the bureaucratic globalization of mental health care practices. Pharmaceutical companies and managed care companies collude to pressure physicians to use these agents inappropriately. Thus the term *biological psychiatry* is used as a mechanism of persuasion. Commonly in practice, the biological mechanisms of the psychotropes are oversimplified and misapplied.

In the opening essay in this section, Freeman notes the conflicts, the arguments, the disagreements within family therapy. He helps to develop a discussion, which leads to an ecosystemic view of *personal responsibility* and this level of responsibility is crucial to clinical practice. Freeman is dealing with the question: What does *this practitioner* do with *this family* in *this situation*? In medical practice the customer is not always right. The reflective practitioner takes a position, not as a way to achieve dominance, but, first, as a way to take care of himself and his integrity and, second, as a way to give the family something to push against in the interest of increasing the health of the members.

Pakman's is a multihued and richly textured essay that attends to three significant forces in the mental health field and the impact of their combination. He deepens his discussion by starting with an etymological framework, which leads him to consider *mythos*. "Myths bring a different tradition, a basic constituent of human culture, expressing by their mere presence, with no claims at proof, important aspects of people's identities." This is the multifaceted, finely patterned point that makes the paper so valuable. Pakman's critique is developed from, and firmly rooted in, a refined and poetic systemic perspective. It not only arouses creativity, but provides a discussion for establishing a perspective and implementing practices, which might correct the disturbances in the current system.

Schaefer begins with a history of science perspective to comment on the current situation. History shows that the explanatory capacities of science and the belief systems derived from science are limited, but that scientific methods have no way to acknowledge these limits. His is an effort to integrate biology into the system thinking view and ultimately into clinical practice. He describes and explores an interface between biogenetics and psychotherapy, that is, how psychotherapy has a biological effect. He pays attention to the impact of *DSM* on the language for describing psychiatric troubles. His case examples come from children growing up in families with few resources who thus receive their health care from public systems. Dr. Schaefer is a thoughtful, gracefully reflective child psychiatrist in the public sector.

Dr. Ducommun-Nagy's contribution gives yet another useful perspective. She is a psychiatrist who was trained in Europe and has practiced in the United States and in Switzerland. She is well known for her work in contextual family therapy. In her essay she comments on the role of medications in different practice settings and different countries. There are curious differences, which suggest that psychotropes are as much an interpersonal message as they are a physiological agent. These observations help us to be skeptical of the unambiguous statements that are used to promote these agents. The case examples demonstrate events in her experience with patients, where there is surprising behavior not explainable by medication treatment or intentional psychotherapy. The examples remind us of the enigmatic nature of mental health problems.

Zhao Mei's article asks us to rethink entirely the nature of illness. She discusses principles of the Chinese system of medicine, which vary greatly from Western concepts, and gives us some brief vignettes to illustrate this point of view.

## Chapter 4

# Psychobiological Family Therapy: Toward an Ecological Psychiatry

Larry S. Freeman, MD

*"Then you'd better not fight to-day," said Alice, thinking it a good opportunity to make peace.*
*"We must have a bit of a fight, but I don't care about going on long," said Tweedledum. "What's the time now?"*
*Tweedledee looked at his watch and said, "Half-past four."*
*"Let's fight till six, and then have dinner," said Tweedledum.*
*"Very well," the other said, rather sadly: "and she can watch us—only you'd better not come very close,"he added: "I generally hit everything I can see—when I get really excited."*
Lewis Carroll, Alice's Adventures in Wonderland

The world of mental health practices is fraught with debate, conflict, and confusion. Nowhere is this more evident than in the contrasting practice patterns and theoretical underpinnings of family therapists and psychopharmacologists. The unfortunate result has been a "failure to communicate" or, worse, a communication that one or the other approach is "wrong." These beliefs in the incorrectness of others' work, and the rightness of one's own and like-minded clinicians', stem from conflicts of values, world views, politics, economics, and personal biases (Fancher, 1995). This state of affairs is likely to continue as long as these fundamental practices are seen to be in conflict, or even merely different yet compatible. Unless they are reconciled, this tension will continue. An alternative, a theory and clinical practice that takes a both/and approach, offers the promise that this can change. The many resources and approaches to helping troubled persons could then be integrated, complementary, and synergistic (Havens, 1973).

Recent issues of the *Journal of Marriage and Family Therapy* and *Family Systems and Health* are excellent examples of this state of affairs. The *JAMFT* discussion centers on the issues of medication in assisting teenagers battling depression. The lead article (Sparks, 2002a,b) clearly takes a strong position of advocacy for alternatives to medication from a postmodern, narrative, feminist perspective. The author clearly and successfully challenges many medical practices, as well as the theory and evidence that support them. In addition to advocating for the right of her 16-year-old client Amy to choose her treatment, she protests—with some validity—the marginalization of psychotherapists. Her incisive critique of the "science" of drug trials and stress upon the importance of patient empowerment in the therapeutic alliance are critically important. While vigorously distinguishing herself from medical providers, she claims that she empowers her clients, respects their choices, and does not privilege one approach over another. Unfortunately, to strengthen her argument, she creates a stereotype, "white-coated male physicians" who construct "a passive tentative single patient" and "subdue and pathologize women's complaints" by prescribing medication. The end result is that one is left feeling one must take a side in the debate over ways to assist the troubled.

The responses to her paper are similarly distorted by the political pressures reflected in and reinforced by the seemingly irreconcilable positions. Denton stresses the need of "evidence-based practices both for the good of people who are suffering and the field of family therapy." He argues "family therapy has an *ethical* [italics added] obligation to move towards a standard of evidence-based practice." Overall, the tone of his article is patronizing and grounded in a truth which cannot be questioned. "Sparks does not add anything to the literature on the treatment of adolescent depression" (Denton et al., 2002).

Although empirical validation of proposed treatments can be a step forward, it must be weighed against other considerations, recognized as a hoped for, rather than an achieved, objective, and valid in some but not all worldviews. The political, theoretical, and economic contexts of such studies must be recognized as influences on the design of the studies, the questions asked, the data collected, the information revealed, and the interpretations made. The risk of "scientifically validated evidence of experts defining acceptable practices" (Zubialde & Aspy, 2001), and the hope that "standardization will bring quality and efficiency," carry considerable risks of privileging some difficulties, approaches, and outcomes over others. The values, politics, and economics embodied in these choices, that construct the "reality" of any given "scientifically valid study" (Goldberg & David, 1991), are likely to remain obscure (De-Grandpre, 1999; Valenstein, 1998).

The response of a family and community-centered child psychiatrist captures the dilemma. Combrinck-Graham "confesses" to prescribing medications and responds to the clearly political thrust of the lead article by implying that the "moral high ground" is what is at stake (Combrinck-Graham, 2002). Rather than defining it as "working without medication," she stakes a claim to it by indicating she addresses both medication issues and "all the other factors which contribute" to people's symptoms. Proposing a both/and rather than either/or approach to medication and psychotherapy, her position on the legitimate questions regarding if and when to prescribe remain clouded by moral and political concerns.

At the heart of this debate is a political and ethical snarl, what Hawaiians term *hihia*. As long as arguments for and against the many approaches to helping troubled people are couched in these terms, the fields of psychiatry, family therapy, and mental health in general will be ensnared in unnecessary and harmful controversy. We will not improve our ability to understand (Chessick, 1992) and assist our patients as deeply, broadly, and efficiently as we would if we could move beyond these cultural and political differences. Until we do, we will not be collaborators so much as friends and foes, less able to further our field and possibly inflicting suffering, if not actual harm, upon those whom we claim to serve (Pukui et al., 1972, p. 71).

## THE POLITICS OF UNCERTAINTY

> Though essential, the difficulty in using reflection successfully stems from its central mission of calling attention to our deficiencies.
>
> (Zubialde and Aspy)

Controversies of this sort arise in human discourses when the discussion is point/counterpoint, thesis/antithesis, and there is insufficient synthesis of differing views. The root of the debate lies in insufficient knowledge, misunderstanding, or lack of sufficient will and cultural support to find a way of reconciling seemingly disparate views. For this to occur, some common ground must be found. In order to do this, it is helpful to identify the core difficulty that is embedded in and hidden by the debate. In this instance, I submit that *confusion over the issue of personal responsibility* underlies the intense affect and selective emphases of the various "sides of the debate." This confusion has effects upon clinicians, patients, caregivers, and the culture in general. The result is a pervasive and recurring process of "mystification" ( Laing & Esterson, 1964), "confusion about the causes of certain events," with the result that the distinction between praxis and process becomes blurred. "Praxis expresses the intentions of a person or group of persons; process refers to events which have no author." (Esterson, 1970). Mystification arises when one's acts are seen "as if they are the result of process rather than one's intentions," as well as when individuals are held responsible—that is, "blamed"—for events over which they have little say. A dramatic example is that of a psychotic young man whose father stated that his son's difficulties stemmed from having the largest feet in the family (Whitaker, personal communication, 1975).

Mystification tends to arise when there is uncertainty about the origins and meanings of certain events, or when attributions regarding the players in those events, oneself or others, are vague and "not authored." Legitimate motives, grievances, and aspirations are subverted by a *mystifying explanation* of their worlds. Personal agency and choice are undermined. Confusion over the responsibilities of a given person or group of persons for how things occur is the result, creating a tinderbox for the spark of difference to flame into conflict. The intense affect regarding the meaning and resolution of emotional suffering, shared in its many forms by all concerned, can be seen to be rooted in the anxiety created by this impasse.

This confusion over the issue of personal responsibility in a complex world has many sources. It is manifested in legal, religious, economic, political, and philosophical domains in cultures throughout the world. In mental health care, different disciplines, and schools within disciplines, subscribe to "ideologies" about the origins and meanings of any number of "symptoms." Each ideological faction pursues a discourse that inhibits reasoned and comprehensive assessment of both what is known, and what is not. Each model fails to acknowledge that it emphasizes some part of the whole over others, with the result that it is as if some models do not even exist.

Process manifests itself in a variety of ways in the mental health world: the psychopharmacologist who does not attend to the effects of marital strengths and challenges on-target symptoms of medication treatment; a developmentally oriented individual therapist whose approach prolongs therapy (so-called therapy interminable) of a marital difficulty by seeing one partner to the exclusion of the spouse; the family therapist who attends only to "observable interactions" and considers the inner experiences of people a "black box"(Watzlawick et al., 1967) and overlooks developmental and neurophysiological vulnerabilities in individuals.

The intellectual gymnastics that each of these approaches must utilize are primarily "a reality edit" (Bateson, 1972, 1979) which amounts to a decision to "see" in a certain way (White, 1986). This results in the emphasis on some aspects of the ecology of suffering and the deemphasis if not denial of others.

As a result there is an undeclared struggle regarding "which edit is best," that is, most valid, most effective, most ethical. The fact that this struggle is itself harmful is not addressed. Instead since nobody wishes to lose an argument over who is right and who is wrong, each simply becomes more strident and self-assured, more committed to a given "edit," and less willing to reveal the uncertainties that inevitably arise when a preferred method of treatment is insufficiently effective. *It is this failure of individual clinicians and the models they embrace to reveal uncertainty that induces mystification.*

Mystification is a state that can potentially arise in patients, families, social systems, and clinicians. For "consumers," it tends to occur in regard to explanations of causation that then dictate treatment and ascribe specific meanings to their experiences. For clinicians, it occurs because of role confusion or their own unawareness of edits they are making, as well as edits that are "prescribed" to them and which they are expected to accept without question and frequently without seeing that this has occurred. The problem is not in the edit itself, but rather in the rigidity of thinking that arises when a person becomes too attached to a given edit, and most especially by a failure to acknowledge that the edit is being made and is one's choice rather than the "truth." As a result of this, all parties share the experience of being constrained, by their own models or those of others, from exploring relevant factors and providing the most comprehensive understanding of the genesis, maintenance, and resolution of human difficulties.

## THE MEANING OF SUFFERING

It sounds like your son is ADD or ADHD. I know, because I am one.
(Conversation overheard at a YMCA swimming pool)

Life is not easy. "The purpose of life is to be happy" (Dalai Lama, 1995). Would that this were so simple. Compassion, acceptance, tenderness, and freedom are always in demand. The literature of our profession, and its effects in the larger society, is subject to cultural and political pressures that subvert these truths. These pressures amount to pressures to "edit" the entire story of the ecology of suffering. The creation of edits is the first step toward defining a point of view that argues that suffering is symptomatic of the pathological effects of selected "causative" factors, while negating others. Treatment is then dictated by the theory of causation to which any given practitioner subscribes, or that he accepts without comment as presented to him by the referring party or the patient requesting assistance.

The experience of suffering organizes and focuses the attention. Feeling anxious, angry, confused, sad—these daily experiences are cast as symptoms of disorders. The interpretation adopted reflects the accepted reality of a given edit. The model to which a person subscribes determines what symptoms mean and how they might be ameliorated. Practitioners and patients thus become caught in a web of meanings that reflect a particular viewpoint. Patients "become" their symptoms, and ultimately their disorders. Practitioners allocate subjective experiences of suffering to their preferred models; experiences become symptoms that affirm the truth of a given perspective. For example, anxiety is a universal human experience, a signal to the organism that there is an uncertainty ahead. This is quickly transformed into evidence of neurophysiological derangement, (or) negative cognitions, (or) oppressive social structures, (or) family conflict. Each and all of these formulations have in common the transformation of suffering into pathology, and the the practitioner risks becoming wedded to only one point of view.

The "clinical gaze" (Foucault, 1965) too often has had deeply troubling effects on patients and healers alike. Fundamentally, this consists of the objectification of others and sometimes the self, as well as the loss of self-reflection. As a result, clinicians run the risk of overlooking their basic assumptions, the effects of their values and beliefs upon how they "observe." Patients are encouraged or tempted to transform personal experience into evidence of disorder or disease. Because self-regulation is a hallmark of health (Friedman, 1995), and for sentient beings this requires self-reflection, this undermining of the ability to constructively question one's own and others' basic premises is damaging to both clinical care and the "personal knowledge" (Polanyi, 1974) of patients, their families, and clinicians. The well-being of patients and providers suffers.

In order for a given clinical practice to proceed smoothly, those in need and those who are providing their care have to join together and share a common vision. Faced with uncertainty about the meaning of symptoms, participants in the clinical encounter are prey to the process that is identified by Chomsky as the "manufacture of consent" (Achbar & Wintonick, 1994). Chomsky argues that *necessary illusions* are created which become organizing precepts in people's perceptions and understandings about themselves and the worlds they inhabit. These premises are held internally, largely out of awareness, as well as reinforced by "prevailing wisdoms" analogous to dominant discourses described by Foucault (Foucault, 1980). Necessary illusions become extremely influential when they amount to "emotionally potent oversimplifications," which set the tone of discussion. Akin to the "strange attractors" in chaos theory (Gleick, 1987), these embedded assumptions function as catalysts that hasten the conversation toward arguing over differences. Once begun, this pattern promotes ideological narrowing, so that a circular and reinforcing process is established in which some topics are selected over others, concerns are distributed in particular ways, and issues are framed and information filtered with the purpose of promoting a particular agenda.

In the fields of health and mental health care, there are effects on both the content of the debate and the process of inquiry. On the two extremes, psychopharmacologists suggest more and more drugs and drug combinations, while social theorists emphasize the construction of reality to the point that sometimes it seems as if very little is as it is, but simply as it is seen. Each side has become wedded to one point of view so that openness to the other is discouraged. We are less "scientific" and more political as a result of these unbridged differences. Furthermore, the debate over which thought system to embrace is itself an emotionally potent oversimplification that turns uncertainty into a struggle over who is correct. Thoughtful critique is usurped by a political process. One is encouraged, even required, to pick a side (Haley, 1988). This occurs between professionals, between professionals and people requesting assistance, and within families themselves.

The concrete and specific effects of these forces in the clinical moment are quite clear. For those people who have adopted physiological explanations for subjective symptoms of distress, as well as unacceptable or unwanted behaviors, new symptoms invite more drug treatment. If a given drug or drug combination is insufficiently effective, the questions asked presume that the solution lies in pharmacological intervention. Conversely, those who see medicines as a crutch or an indication of sickness, or, worse, badness, stoutly resist the true benefits medicines might provide them.

The physiology of experience thus becomes over- or undervalued. To this is added a political or moral vector—"doctors are experts"; "clients' choices much be honored." Both parties to the clinical encounter risk being disempowered by these edicts. The patient who is reluctant to take medicines is characterized as resistant or lacking in insight. The doctor who declines to prescribe medication that is requested by a patient or referring party is seen to be uncooperative or as not validating that person's perceptions. Too often, referrals for evaluation really amount to prescriptions for clinicians' behavior.

The complementary roles of healer and patient are distorted by these factors. The mere possibility of turbulence in the healing process is damaging to that effort, and when it truly occurs, it adds to the suffering of all involved (Frank, 1973).

## AN ALTERNATIVE

A scientist is known, not by his technical processes, but by his intellect; the essence of the scientific method of thought is that it proceeds in an orderly manner toward the establishment of a truth.

(Peabody, 1930)

The fields of medicine and family therapy each have their own ethical and epistemological premises. Applying medical ethics to systemic thinking creates common ground for both. Issues at the interface create opportunities for research and reflection.

Family therapy was part of a revolution in human consciousness. Beginning with Freud's unconscious, followed by the discovery of cybernetics and communication theory, the psychology and behavior of the person became a conversation about the individual in context (White, 1986) and the internal schemata—the "assumptive world" (Frank, 1973)—that are constructed by a person's development and experience.

In spite of this, the thought system of "causation," and a political and moral tradition of labeling individuals, remained the social matrix of the field. Family therapy became reductionist in its efforts to *explain* schizophrenia, delinquency, anxiety, and other difficulties. The ecological view was undermined in a search for credibility in the marketplace of ideas. It became an article of faith that social experience—in the family, the community, or the culture at large—caused or created or induced these disorders. Many studies that were (merely) interested in the relationships of things remain some of the best of our literature, yet neglected because they did not succumb to these pressures (Auerswald, 1968, 1985a, 1987b; Boszormenyi-Nagy, 1972; Ferreira, 1963; Ford, 1983; Giacomo & Weissmark, 1987; Kantor & Neal, 1985; Napier, 1978; Searles, 1965; Stierlin, 1977; Vogel & Bell, 1960; Whitaker,1976; Wynne, 1971).

System concepts stress the hierarchy of systems and subsystems in the living world (Engel, 1980). A truly systemic view would not negate molecular and cellular variance any more, or less, than attachment issues or social norms (Kitwood, 1993; Norman & Malla, 1993; Post, 1992; Scheflen, 1981; Siever & Davis, 1991). All would be relevant. The issue would no longer be what information is desired or admissible. Instead, the search would be for a description of the relationships among systems and subsystems. The advantage of this conceptualization is that the questions for the practitioner using such an approach provoke further study and learning. If an individual has symptoms potentially amenable to drug treatment, that assessment can be made so that there is no uncertainty on the part of the clinician about whether this is a realistic option in planning an overall treatment plan (Swedo et al., 1998). Such an assessment, however, is done in such a way and at such a time as to consciously strive to create a therapeutic process whose outcome reflects the premises and values of the practitioner's approach to the work.

## THE UNIVERSE OF EXPERIENCE

> Science is the pursuit of knowledge of the physical universe through systematic observation. Whatever we say in science is a limited and approximate description of reality.
>
> (Fritjof Capra, 1991)

An alternative to competing edits and the politicization of care is the ability to select differing perspectives according to the requirements and circumstances of a given case, while maintaining a core of clinical integrity that allows for different postures but a persistent ethical foundation. This is encouraged by the enumeration of a paradigm which is "both/and" rather than "either/or" in describing the ecology of suffering, and which harmonizes with the variance of the structures and processes (Varela, 1989) of human individuals and human systems.[1]

The human animal is above all a social creature. Kramer (2000) provides a remarkably elegant and clear, yet open and curious starting point to describing a theory of the person in her social ecology. Kramer's view is that the structure of the brain will have been shaped by the evolutionary pressures that also influence humans to develop vastly more complex social structures than other animals do. The brain is part of the social order, part of the interactional system, rather than separate from it. Human brains are designed for information gathering and retrieval, abstract reasoning, and complex social behaviors. The human being is a "meaning making creature" (Frank, 1973; Frankl, 1946; Stern, 1985). The biology of experience is social, psychological, and physiological (Brothers, 1989). Kramer questions the claims of "biological psychiatry," recasting it as physiological psychiatry and suggesting that the premise that it is more "scientific" because it is "biological" is not valid due to its limited—edited—version of what constitutes a "biological" psychiatry. Since the brain is part of the social order, it is influenced by experience while also shaping experience. Clinical care must account for the circularity of interactional processes involving both the brain and the environment and recognize that at times physiological processes in the brain—and other systems in the human body—may hinder social competence.

Of the many beauties in this view, the deconstruction of two dichotomies that have plagued mental health looms largest. No longer is the mind/body split tenable, the individual/social split is also rendered meaningless. Most remarkably, therefore, so is the body/group split.

Now all levels of existence are regarded as interconnected. That interconnection is not in the cause-and-effect way that leads to speculation about causation and reductionist thinking. Rather, instead of one thing "making another happen," various events and attributes are correlated with one another in a variety of ways. It becomes possible to ask questions about the role of social and political events in supporting family strengths and weaknesses and at the same time to correlate these speculations with physiological measures (as yet to be determined) of "mental illnesses."

A difficulty arises with this approach. Since it is necessary for one to attend in a certain way, and consequently not in other ways, there needs to be some basis for the way the attention of the clinician is employed. The data of observation need to be organized in some fashion (Taylor, 1979).

The advantages of general systems theory in addressing this challenge lie in its flexibility, comprehensiveness, and neutrality. General systems theory is useful in understanding such disparate phenomena as the role of a principal in a high school and the letdown reflex in a lactating mother. It is comprehensive because it does not accept edits without acknowledgment; it welcomes new information, for example, allowing for the fact that another baby's cry in some instances can induce a mother's lactating response. The neutrality of general systems theory rests in its not having a political agenda; it is "clinical" in this purified sense and not contaminated with values, agendas, and resentments. Thus, it can be helpful in discriminating the different roles and functions of a private high school principal from those of one who is in a public school.

General systems theory has had mixed reviews because it has been misapplied as well as swept up in the political debates that have raged in the field of family therapy. Misapplied because of (a) the selective emphases of various family therapy models, each of which adopts some systems concepts and neglects others, and the difficulties of these models in reconciling themselves to one another, and (b) the urge to fund a reductionistic explanatory justification of various phenomena in order to gain validity in "scientific" circles. Decisions to concentrate observation in one or two levels of systemic organization were then, and remain, methodologically useful but must be acknowledged. When they are not, knowledge claims exceed genuine understanding and validity. For example, relationship stress with one's parents became an explanation for a variety of ills; the mind was seen as a "black box" (Watzlawick et al., 1967).

Properly applied, general systems theory invites continuing questioning, openness to new information, and fascination and even awe for the complexity of life itself. It is a cornerstone in the foundation of an ethical and respectful practice of healing. It requires attention to all levels of the *psychosocial biosphere*. It allows emphasis on one part of the whole, or one relationship of many, but discourages blindness to the context of that decision and focus, and that that decision has been made. It brings forth patterns that hitherto have been invisible.

The benefits of general systems theory rest more with its paradigmatic effects than with any particular strategic technique. "Thinking systems" means being curious about the structure of a given level in a system (e.g., the effects of hospital architecture on patient anxiety), the processes at a given level in a system (e.g., the effects of a mother's grief on a child's self-esteem), and, uniquely, interlevel processes (e.g., the effect of a mother's grief on a childs adrenal functioning; the impact of harsh self-criticism by a manager of a health service upon patient satisfaction). The questions invited seek descriptive rather than explanatory answers, yet those questions can also be asked.[2]

General systems theory and medicine now can be seen to intersect at the point of ethics. The primary edict of medical care, "First do no harm," is always subject to constraints: "unless you must." Medical ethics urge awareness of potential, at times predictably likely, adverse effects of any chosen treatment. In psychiatry this poses a challenge to practitioners and patients to appreciate and seek to account for the many seen and unseen motivations and responses that arise in any given (clinical) encounter (Riker, 1997). Medical ethics require resources to respond effectively to (a) emergencies and (b) unwanted results arising from a given clinical decision and action. General systems theory suggests those effects may be quite diverse and widespread; ethology reminds us that these effects will be communicated from one person to another, and at many levels of experience.

Medical ethics also call for the physician to provide the best care that he or she can to a given patient. The quality of care is measured according to its effects on the person's overall well-being, along with the treatment of a given condition. This is where general systems theory encourages a medical ethic that is broader, and more comprehensive, than the norm that isolates the responsibilities of the clinician to his or her actions with regard to a given problem or to an individual patient. Instead, a systemic medical ethic is one that asks the question "What is the best care for not only this condition, or this individual, but for the ecology in which he or she resides?" It also asks about the unforeseen and unintended adverse consequences not only for the condition, other conditions, or the individual, but for the person's social network (Whitaker & Miller, 1969).

Ethically grounded, ethological, general systems theory provides a template to describe what is observed, its potential relationship(s) to other observations, what is not being noted but may be important, what changes would tend to foster individual and group competencies, and the impact of health systems organization as well as cultural norms on the type, quality, and nature of services offered (Freeman and Clarkson, 2001).

## PSYCHOBIOLOGICAL FAMILY THERAPY

Treat the disease, heal the illness.

(Freeman, 1993)

A healing practice must have a described version of health or wellness, of what it is trying to achieve. This will reflect a recognition of the physiological requirements for optimal adaptation (i.e., certain givens such as needing iron in one's diet); and a model of ideal functioning (being) that is sought or maintained. Psychobiological family therapy seeks to integrate (a) ethological views of human anatomy, physiology, and relationships with (b) general systems theory, in order to have a clinical model that (c) promotes ethically based practices (d) meant to support individual and community growth.

The meta theory of psychobiological family therapy, and the clinical decisions that ensue therefrom, can be captured in the following tenets:

> Symptoms are indications of disharmony, dysfunction, or growth.
>
> Symptoms reflect dissonance at various levels in the system or between different levels of the system. They are "emergent properties" of a "web of susceptibility"(Kleinman, 1988) that is intrinsic to systemic functioning.
>
> Assessment of the political meanings of symptoms is necessary to minimize the potentially limiting effects of "reality edits" that run counter to comprehensive clinical care.
>
> Living systems must grow to be alive, otherwise they shall stagnate (Greenspan, 1997).
>
> All people share similar genes and similar vulnerabilities.
>
> Some people have considerably higher vulnerabilities of a given type than others.
>
> Vulnerabilities (can) become "pathologies" as a result of the interaction of the person with her or his environment; this can also *not* occur when vulnerabilities are dealt with in a different way (Chess & Thomas, 1999; Kleinman, 1997).
>
> This means that difficulties may become catalysts for a second-order change in the system's organization and functioning. They can precipitate growth and adaptation, or further dysfunction (Reiss, 1981).
>
> Because of this, strength-based approaches to care are the starting point in developing a relationship to the patient, the problem and the symptoms.
>
> In addition, symptoms both have and create meaning: it is the clinician's task to be a catalyst for second-order change and to be a guide in the search for growth-inducing meanings.
>
> Responsible acts are measured according to their effects upon oneself and upon others. One bears responsibilities (a) for oneself, (b) to others, (c) for others, (d) to oneself.
>
> Ethical care addresses these responsibilities for the person owning the problem, the people who are intimately related to her, and the caregivers who seek to assist (Vogel, 1994).
>
> The individual with a vulnerability and the people around him share different types of responsibility in minimizing the expression and influence of these vulnerabilities. Much of a person's growth as a creative and spirited person is rooted in dealing with these responsibilities.

## SIGNS, SYMPTOMS, AND SUFFERING

"Let me give you my analysis," the interrogator told Arkady. "Soviet psychiatry is on the threshold of a major breakthrough, a major statement on the entire basis of mental illness. In a just society, there are no valid reasons to break the law except mental illness. Those who do, suffer from a psychological disturbance we term pathoheterodoxy. Like other criminals, you have unreal expectations, you overestimate your personal powers, you feel isolated from society, you swing from sadness to excitement, you mistrust the people who most want to help you, you think you are the exception to every rule.

"We now have proof that the nervous system of a criminal is different from that of a normal person. After a few days in an isolated cell, all develop catatonia. I myself have placed a needle 2 cm deep into the skin of such a pathoheterodox personality and observed the total absence of pain."

"Where did you place the needle?" Arkady asked.

(Smith, 1981, pp. 198–99)

Every symptom cluster has a political element to it. The politics of symptoms are expressed in debates over (a) what constitutes a symptom; (b) who "has" the symptom; (c) what difficulties are expressed by the symptom; (d) whether treatment is directed at symptoms or the underlying difficulty it is perceived to represent; (e) what resources will be brought to bear to deal with the symptom or the underlying difficulty; (f) who will be allowed or expected to fulfill the various functions necessary to carry out a treatment plan; (g) the quality of the relationships among providers and patients; (h) the meaning attached to changes that occur over time as treatment proceeds; and (i) when therapy and treatment are completed.

In each of these domains, the debate has theoretical, economic, and political elements. Theories of "reality" and "science" are in potential conflict. What symptoms mean and how to address them are under continual review. Who should provide resources and why must be negotiated. Relationships of power must be assessed. Access to information is variable from case to case and at different times in a given case. Control of access to information establishes political power and frames the discourse of suffering, the approaches to managing it, and decision making regarding what resources will be deployed.

The cultural context of a given healing practice has varying impacts upon the intimate clinical encounter. As a result, there is a "political force field," a matrix of meanings, agendas, and relationships, that has continuing effects upon how services are provided and for what ends. An extreme example of this was the policy implemented in Afghanistan prohibiting women from seeing male physicians. Similarly, in parts of New Zealand, issues that are important in constructing the therapeutic alliance are handled by developing monolithic policies. Many there have advocated "gender appropriate therapy," which decrees that females should only see female clinicians, and males only see males, and "culturally sensitive therapy," in which people are only to see others of the same ethnic background. In the United States school counselors commonly assign to primary care physicians the role of providing predetermined medications for students whose behavior is considered problematic. In all these instances these forces undermine the integrity of the clinical process. The fundamental purpose of a healing action is to offer assistance and relief, do no harm, and seek optimal outcomes. The political and cultural pressures on clinicians and patients, and their relationship, must be accounted for by clinicians in order to minimize their destructive effects. Psychobiological family therapy seeks to address these issues throughout the process of assessment and treatment.

## THE PROBLEM OF RESPONSIBILITY

The strategies and priorities of the psychobiological family therapist are organized around questions of personal responsibility, both for the identified patient and those in her or his care network, natural and professional. There are four types of responsibility, which are under consideration at any time.

### Responsibility for One's Self

All persons grow into increasing degrees of personal responsibility. The young child's first experience with this is the development of a capacity for concern for others (Winnicott, 1965). This originates in the child's identification with a responsible caregiver, which fosters the child's awareness of a self whose needs and behavior create demands upon another. As the child matures, and throughout adulthood, responsibility for self grows through (a) increasing mastery of tasks (tying shoes, doing homework, following diet and exercise recommendations), and (b) deeper self-awareness and recogition of the effects of one's actions, feelings, and values upon others.

### Responsibility for Others

The parent-child relationship is prototypical of accepting responsibility for others. Countless acts by parents in caring for their offspring express acceptance of, and at times appreciation for, the personal growth that is catalyzed by this responsibility. Growth in this responsibility domain occurs through both accepting increasing responsibility for others (e.g., taking on additional duties with aging parents or a chronically ill child) and acknowledging the limits of one's responsibility to another (e.g., a parent of a teenager coming to accept he cannot constructively manage his own anxiety regarding his child's choices by trying to control the child's activities, friends, and interests; also, a spouse accepting that it is her husband's, not her own, responsibility to be sensible in dealing with his health issues).

## Responsibility to Others

This is enacted at the interface of responsibility for oneself and responsibility for others. This is a matter of accountability, of accepting that one is answerable to others for the choices one makes. The spouse who is not making wise choices regarding his own health is not only failing to be responsible for himself, he is also shirking his responsibilities to his wife and children. Similarly, the spouse who remains overly involved with directing and controlling her mate's behaviors with respect to a health issue is not being accountable for her own limitations. She is behaving as if she has more "control" than is valid. This, in turn, fails to acknowledge to her partner that she cannot do for him what he must do for himself. Responsibility to others is expressed through openness and accountability for the effects of one's acts upon them; it is self-reflection brought on by feedback from others. It is at issue in all our relationships (Ignatieff, 1984), not only our intimate ones.

## Responsibility to Oneself

This refers to the existential yearning to be more fully oneself (Taylor, 1991). It involves an acceptance of one's talents, desires, and limitations as a starting point to creative living. Openness to feedback from within that is usually dormant results in "personal knowledge" (Polanyi, 1974) about what motivates, invigorates, and excites one. It values creativity and growth as ends in themselves. The small musings and whisperings that occur throughout life are not suppressed or ignored so completely that they fail to provide a platform for questioning one's life as it continues. This can occur in quite limited and finite ways, as when a person tries to master a sport or musical instrument, and in the more profound ways that occur when these musings lead to major changes in the course of one's life. Examples of the latter could include a career woman's decision to postpone returning to work after having had children because she discovers more value and meaning in child rearing than she had anticipated; similarly, a woman who has had children and values the voice that urges her to return to school for education in a new career.

The domains of responsibility interpenetrate one another, one becoming a catalyst for growth in another. All relationships potentially traverse these realms, so that, for example, issues of responsibility for the self of one person are affected by issues of responsibility to the self of the other, and responsibility for others deepens responsibility for the self.

## RESPONSIBILITY IN THE MODERN AGE

The many discourses that comprise the sum of what is known and proposed about the sources and resolution of human emotional suffering suggest their own ethical premises regarding issues of responsibility. The two forces cited earlier that underlie so much of the conflict and confusion in the field— mystification due to the confusion of praxis and process, and reality edits— distort the concept of responsibility that applies to individual patients, their families, and the clinicians and social systems who serve them.

Psychobiological family therapy brings the notion of responsibility as the foundation for ethical practices and creative health into the foreground of clinical care. The four domains of responsibility present opportunities for the clinician to intervene, with her underlying premises of health, illness, and suffering guiding the timing and thrust of any given choice (Kaiser, 1965).

As a result, strategies employed are understood as efforts to promote responsibility in any of the domains. Accurate assessment of praxis and process, and curiosity about the entire ecology of a clinical problem (Hillman, 1964) rather than selected reality edits, provide the foundation for a clinical posture that is growth-oriented, in-spirited, and systemic and that accepts the many types of vulnerability to which people and groups of people are subject while drawing upon their strengths and aspirations.

## A STORY

If you don't know where you're going, any road will get you there.

By the age of 12, DJ had developed a relational style that confused those around him and kept them guessing and off-balance. He was behaving oddly at school as well as at home. He appeared depressed, and had long carried a diagnosis of attention-deficit disorder, one made by his pediatrician when he was 5 or 6. His parents had divorced two years earlier; his father had been treated for cancer, apparently effectively, during the same period, and had then been overseas for a year; and his father was now remarried to a woman who saw herself as "good with kids," having raised three adult children of her own. Since the divorce of DJ's parents, the conflict between them had continued unabated.

DJ's mom, Martha, asked her ex-husband, Rob, to approve home schooling for DJ in the sixth grade. Rob declined, indicating that because DJ had been homeschooled in the fourth grade and had had to repeat it in public school, he could not support this decision. Martha was concerned that DJ's "sensitive nature" prohibited his having a successful experience in the tougher public school environment. She was concerned about a history of "schizophrenia" in her family, that it might "affect" DJ. Martha also had strong religious beliefs that contributed to discomfort with the values in public schools, and created conflict with her ex-husband and his new wife. She clearly wanted to protect her son from both the harshness of peer relations and cultural influences.

During the divorce she had agreed to DJ's being prescribed an antidepressant "after praying about it," feeling he needed medication to "mend his broken heart." Treatment with stimulants at 5 and 6 had been helpful to his work at school before the family difficulties intensified. Since then the results were more difficult to assess. DJ and his family had lived in several locales, and he had been in individual counseling several times both before and after his parents' divorce.

DJ was on a summer visit with his father and stepmother when Martha inquired about the home-schooling plan. One week after Rob refused, she sent him an E-mail telling him to "take responsibility for DJ." His wife, Donna, agreed, and they had decided to discontinue both the antidepressant and stimulants which DJ had been on. Some time after this, as he continued to have difficulty and appeared depressed, his pediatrician had prescribed a new antidepressant. His odd behavior, immaturity, and low academic performance were gradually resolving over the fall. Meanwhile, his mother had relocated to the area where Rob and Donna lived and visits had again occurred, in the aftermath of which DJ had been even more "eccentric."

Unexpectedly, late in the fall, Martha went to DJ's school and "removed him" prior to a scheduled weekend visitation. Rob only found out that this had occurred because DJ called to tell him what his mother was planning and that he was fetching some clothes. Rob phoned Martha and told her not to take their son; she did so anyway. This triggered the reinvolvement of the courts, and the father's request to see me.

DJ indicated to me he disliked trying to talk about his feelings the way his counselor wanted him to and did not wish to continue to see her. He stated that she didn't understand him, "I'm a boy." He made ironic comments about his parents' conflict while indicating strong loyalty to both. He had in the past indicated thoughts about suicide and feeling stupid; he talked to himself at school, banged his head on the table, and mimicked sexual acts. He refrained from cultivating friendships "because you lose them anyway." Despite the complex and conflictual emotional field in which he had found himself, on the first day I met DJ, I was able to see an inquisitive, playful, creative, and unpredictable boy. He had good eye contact, tracked the conversation well, and listened carefully while making it clear he would remain "hidden" behind his flamboyant mannerisms.

My approach to this from the beginning was meant to clarify how the tumult in DJ's family was affecting him, reduce the damaging effects of that upon him, and determine to what extent DJ's difficulties reflected personal vulnerabilities (ADD), as opposed to the relationships and history in which he found himself. I surmised that his personal identity had been grossly contaminated by his parents' values conflicts about religion, school, medication, and how they "saw" him, by the loyalty conflict that warring parents induce in a child, and by the evident attributions from his mother that he was a "special" child who could not make it in the larger world, a view that his father did not support.

In order to accomplish this, I chose (a) to see DJ alone, join with his immature and outlandish and magical expressions, and establish a posture in our own relationship that indicated "I sense that you are competent but hurting, and cannot tell me how until you know me better and feel that we have a relationship that will endure"; and (b) to meet with the parents to establish that I was "on neither side" regarding medications or placement of DJ and that I expected them to deal with the issues between them for DJ's benefit; and (c) to meet with school personnel to reduce the possible reinforcements to a deviant identity that could arise in DJ's interactions with peers and adults in the school setting. I wanted them to see DJ as deeply confused by his life story, but not "sick." I also demurred on the issue af resuming stimulants, indicating that his improvements at school were encouraging, and that his parents' disagreement over the wisdom of such treatment was a relative contraindication to doing so. This would remain under consideration. Only after some of this had occurred would I review the issue of medicines. This was because to change medicines now would add further uncertainty to "knowing DJ" and also because it would risk being seen as taking a side in the parental struggle over how DJ should be viewed. Was he a vulnerable soul, as Martha believed, or a boy whose mother had encouraged him to be deviant and had discounted his strengths, as Rob believed. In essence, I agreed with both attributions.

Initially, matters intensified. DJ remained indirect, metaphorical, and puzzling in his verbalizations and mannerisms. He refused to respond in a confirming manner to anything I said or asked as long as it was not also "crazy" like he was. At school he became more bizarre; his mother pushed harder to have him removed or placed "on medication." The principal gravely told me that her many years of experience indicated that DJ was schizophrenic. He raged, had tantrums, banged his head, and made sexually explicit comments to peers and staff, but never hurt anyone. When problems arose, he would indicate a desire to return to his mom but did not do so at any other time.

Ultimately, DJ was able to make it clear that his unpredictable future led him to hate himself and refrain from building a life at school, with peers, and with me. Gradually, though, he was able to rely more on his father and stepmom. He liked coming to see me even as he indicated how topsy-turvy his world was and continued to "hide" behind confusing communications. We had a secret bond, an understanding that DJ was "acting crazy" (Searles, 1965) when he chose to remain mysterious.

A turning point came when he indicated he wanted to come less often. He had had too much counseling already in his life and nothing had ever changed. He clearly felt that he just went to counseling, without any prospect of its truly helping him, and that it was something to be endured. I explained to him that he had not asked me to help him change or resolve anything, and that my intent was to see him as long as necessary so that when I did stop stop seeing him it would be because counseling was no longer needed. Unlike prior counseling, I wanted this to make a difference, so he could go on without any counseling at all. He returned the next week and indicated that he wanted to learn how to "express my feelings."

Over the ensuing months, DJ became more transparent and direct with me and others. He finally indicated he wanted to remain with his father; he prevaricated when his mother came to a session to discuss placement, but finally told her that he wished to remain with his father. He reported that school was hard, and his dad, mom, and stepmom agreed to a blind trial of stimulants, to which he responded with improved academic performance and greater enjoyment at school. Peer relations normalized.

The custody battle heated up. I had referred the parents to another therapist for counseling and there had been little progress in resolving their differences. I made the referral because it was important for me to be an advocate for DJ's health and well-being. I positioned myself to be a catalyst for more effective organization of the family, and to stress the responsibility of both parents to prioritize his needs above the ongoing marital conflict. Evidently Martha changed her mind several times about their counseling and where DJ should be. Despite this, DJ indicated he now "could express his feelings so I don't need to come anymore." He wanted to play with boys in his neighborhood instead.

When his mother abrogated an agreement negotiated by her and Rob's attorneys to present to the court, DJ "revisited bizarreness," but this time his dad and he were able to sort it out and he regained his hard-earned maturity and self-respect. He wanted to continue with the scheduled termination of therapy. Our last day together, he was a delightful 13-year-old boy with a supportive stepmother whom he teased but respected and appreciated. He wanted to continue with his medicine for ADD because schoolwork went so much better. He could thank me for my help. He knew he could return, but for now we were done.

This case highlights several principles of systemic practice based upon fostering an ethic of personal responsibility.

The therapist is responsible for seeking collaborative and respectful relationships with parents while at the same time preserving clinical integrity and avoiding being coopted by one or another political vector in a child's world. This creates the greatest likelihood of an optimal outcome.

The therapist must see the individual and the system and the effect of each on the other.

The therapist must be aware of and acknowledge what is not known while retaining clinical decisiveness based upon a clear understanding of how the process of therapy must proceed in order to be most beneficial. This was reflected in the decision to see DJ individually for the most part, since his personal identity was so wrapped up in the family conflict and in a defensive "eccentricity."

Attention to the internal dynamics of the clinician who seeks a "nonedited universe" reveals the political forces discouraging that approach. Ethical care is rooted in the clinician's own struggle with ethical dilemmas (Riker, 1997). In this case, a desire to be neutral between two warring parents, both about "what" DJ was and how to deal with it/him, gave way to advocacy for the child as it became clear the parental war would continue.

A personal and strength-based orientation empowers patients who wish to grow and resolve matters but may alienate those who wish to "act out" their personal issues irresponsibly. DJ's mother failed to be responsible to DJ. Her initial "pathologizing" concerns created a somewhat adversarial set that she did not change when they were addressed as she wanted (e.g., wanting medication before it was prescribed, then devaluing DJ's considerable growth in competency without it, then not being satisfied when her original wish—Ritalin—was met). She failed to see the impact her "stance in the world" had upon her son, who was both angry at her and worried about her.

Tracking the issues of responsibility throughout the family helps the clinician to assess and prioritize goals and strategies. DJ came to see that he could not be responsible for himself—his behavior, his feelings—as long as he took so much responsibility for his mom. He owed it *to* himself to be a kid instead of her caregiver. As he took less responsibility for mom, he was encouraged to be more responsible to his dad, stepmom, school, and, ultimately, himself.

The assessment of the individual neurophysiological and psychobiological vulnerabilities are best done when there is a minimum of interference by the family and social context. When these conditions are not met, medication prescriptions and changes are postponed, thereby becoming an inducement to deal with the "noise in the system" that confounds accurate assessment of symptoms. An accurate "medical diagnosis" is difficult, and at times impossible, if there is too much interference by the ecology of the child who is carrying those symptoms.

The overall therapy process is growth oriented. Here the child grew in self-responsibility and expression; the marital-divorce impasse evolved so that DJ was out of the middle; the mother's stigmatizing attributions of DJ's craziness and specialness, and the father's reactivity to them, gave way to an identity perceived by himself and his father and stepmother as a bright and sensitive boy whose competence was enhanced by stimulants for schoolwork needs and not for behavior problems.

The aim of therapy is authenticity and self-regulation. For DJ, therapy changed from something he would go to "forever" because he "needed it" to a resource to help him to be more authentic and able to care for himself, a resource that he would outgrow.

A systemic therapist is faced with an ethical difficulty when a decision to focus on an individual or on the medication is made while a broader therapeutic alliance with a larger system has not yet been established. As a result, the therapist is ethically bound to account for the possible unwanted consequences of such a decision, so that the result is one of continued growth of the individual rather than affirmation that he is, or has, the problem. Not uncommonly the clinician must reluctantly accept that, at least for a while, an optimal "ecological" outcome is not possible.

## THE THERMODYNAMICS OF CONSCIOUSNESS

The therapist, like "the philosopher, is a perpetual beginner."

(Merleau-Ponty, 1968)

From an evolutionary perspective "We humans have in our several cultures, then, all the things which worked in the past and were selected for by the needs of a former present. One can say that the same principles at work in natural selection in the biotic world also apply to ideas. It is particularly important today to explore what kind of an animal our many cultures have made us into."

(Mason, 1990)

The thought system herein termed psychobiological family therapy suggests a cascade of questions that result from the "conversation" among many clinical models. These questions, arising at the creative edge in therapy and in theory, constitute the effort to find further synergies among treatment models. Taken together, they create and constitute an "ecology of curiosity."

The clinical moment is fraught with overtones of the unspoken and unacknowledged. In the practice of psychobiological family therapy, the clinician attends to several of the levels of systemic structure (individual, marital, cellular) at once, listening for themes and isomorphs within, and especially across, levels in the patient's expression and experience of his predicament. This expression is verbal and behavioral, conscious and unconsciousness, intended and unintended.

The therapist's experience is one of weighing different values and perspectives. Medical ethics and systemic inclusiveness form the basis of analysis, with the therapist's role the promotion of the growth of all concerned. The therapist's goals are process oriented, defined in general as facilitating a therapeutic experience through the evolution of personal responsibilities. The goals for the patient—that is, the sought-for conditions that define health—are both individual and group based. The welfare of the individual and her body are rooted in the health of the system.

Psychobiological family therapy is not "eclectic" in the sense that an underlying value system and concept of the role of the therapist remain clear and constant. Guidelines for determining the timing of interventions assist and support the therapist in maintaining an ethical core, or compass, and a destination, or beacon. Much like sailing, the therapist does not try to dominate the currents and obstacles in her path; she employs a "causal agnosticism" (Hoffman, 2002) that encourages her to use the ebb and flow of feeling, thought, and action to determine her next move.

Medications are but one of many strategies that may be employed to complete the "search for a structure" (Freeman, 1990) that growth-oriented therapy needs, a structure in which trust, safety, and a therapeutic contract for change can thrive.

## NOTES

1. The contributions of ontological biology have fascinated family therapists. The notion of "structural coupling" has enormous heuristic value in planning a therapeutic stance which fosters an increasing intimacy and the possibility of change in the therapeutic encounter. Yet there has been debate about the concept of "structure" as it is applied to individuals and families (Chubb, 1990). A distinction is made that suggests families have no structure, only process, while individuals do have structure, that is, "thingness." While any concept imported from one discipline to another can be misused, it does create new possibilities for seeing that can be quite powerful. In this instance, I submit that both individual organisms and the social networks they create are processes (Merleau-Ponty, 1968), whose recursive stable patterns constitute what is meant by "structure."

2. This is a reference to the debate in family therapy about domestic violence and systems theory (Dell, 1989; Goldner et al., 1990; James & McIntyre, 1983; Mackinnon & Miller, 1987; Paterson & Trathen, 1994). Systems theory encouraged observation of the victim's behavior as a possible factor influencing that of the abuser. This was (mis)taken to mean that the victim was to blame, a concept itself not compatible with systems theory. In any case, systems theory does not preclude the issue of choice: The abuser, provoked, does not "have to" be violent. Systems theory both holds the abuser responsible and organizes data into a meaningful perspective that wonders what all the influences are upon violent acts. Causes and effects—broken bones, psychological trauma after a rape—are reconcilable with systems theory just as Newtonian mechanics are compatible with Einstein's theory of relativity. In each instance a heuristically valid "edit" is the basis of compelling observation.

## REFERENCES

Achbar, M., & Wintonick, P. (1994). *Manufacturing consent: Noam Chomsky and the media*. Canadian film.

Auerswald, E. H. (1968). Interdisciplinary versus ecological approach. *Family Process*, pp. 202–215.

Auerswald, E. H. (1985). "Thinking about thinking in family therapy." *Family Process*, 1–12.

Auerswald, E. H. (1987). Response to "The problem of gender in family therapy." *Family Process*, 29–31.

Auerswald, E. H. (1987). Epistemological confusion in family therapy and research. *Family Process*, 317–330.

Bateson, G. (1972). *Steps to an ecology of mind*. New York: Ballantine Books.

Bateson, G. (1979). *Mind and nature, a necessary unity*. New York: Bantam Books.

Boszormenyi-Nagy, I. (1972). Loyalty implications of the transference model in psychotherapy. *Archives of General Psychiatry*, 374–380.

Brothers, L. (1989). A biological perspective on empathy. *American Journal of Psychiatry*, 10–19.

Capra, F., & Steindl-Rast, D. (1991). *Belonging to the universe*. San Francisco: HarperCollins.

Chess, S., & Thomas, A. (1999). *Goodness of fit: clinical applications from infancy through adult life*. London: Brunner/Mazel.

Chessick, R. (1992). *What constitutes the patient in psychotherapy*. London: Jason Aronson.

Chubb, H. (1990). Looking at systems as process. *Family Process*, 169–175.

Combrinck-Graham, L. (2002). "Commentary: Confessions of a prescription writer." *Journal of Marital and Family Therapy*, 47–50.

Dalai Lama. (1995). Foreword to Epstein, M., *Thoughts without a thinker*. New York: Basic Books.

DeGrandpre, R. (1999). *Ritalin nation*. New York: W. W. Norton.

Dell, P. (1989). Violence and the systemic view: The problem of power. *Family Process*, 1–14.

Denton, W., Walsh, S.R., and Daniel, S. S. (2002). Evidence-based practice in family therapy: Adolescent depression as an example." *Journal of Marital and Family Therapy*, 39–46.

Engel, G. (1980). The clinical application of the biopsychosocial model. *American Journal of Psychiatry*, 535–544.

Esterson, A. (1970). *The leaves of spring*. London: Penguin Books.

Fancher, R. (1995). *Cultures of healing*. New York: W. H. Freeman.

Ferreira, A. (1963) "Family myth and homeostasis." *Archives of General Psychiatry*, 457–463.

Ford, F. (1983). Rules: The invisible family." *Family Process*, 135–146.

Foucault, M. (1965). *Madness and civilization*. New York: Vintage Books.

Foucault, M. (1980). *Power/Knowledge: Selected interviews and other writings*, ed. C. Gordon. New York: Pantheon Books.

Frank, J. (1973). *Persuasion and healing*. Baltimore: Johns Hopkins University Press.

Frankl, V. (1946). *The Doctor and the Soul*. New York: Barton.

Freedman, D. (1992). The search: Body, mind, and human purpose." *American Journal of Psychiatry*, 858–866.

Freeman, L. S. (1993). Thinking about thinking in psychiatry. Presented at the Australia and New Zealand Royal College of Psychiatry Annual Meeting, Auckland, New Zealand.

Freeman, L. S. (1990). The search for structure in family therapy. Presented at the Annual Conference of the American Association for Marital and Family Therapy, Washington, DC.

Freeman, L. S., & Clarkson, H. O. (2001). The effects of health care organization on clinical care. Presentation at the annual conference of the American Academy of Child and Adolescent Psychiatry in partnership with the Royal Australia and New Zealand College of Psychiatry, Honolulu, HI.

Friedman, E. (1995). "Biology and family therapy." Presentation at the First Annual Conference of the Collaborative Family Health Care Coalition, Washington, DC.

Gabbard, G.O. (1992). Psychodynamic psychiatry in the "Decade of the Brain." *American Journal of Psychiatry*, pp. 991–998.

Giacomo, D., & Weissmark, M. (1987). Toward a generative theory of the therapeutic field. *Family Process*, 437–459.

Gleick, J. (1987). *Chaos: Making a new science*. New York: Viking.

Goldberg, C. D. S., & David, A. S. (1991). Family therapy and the glamour of science. *Journal of Family Therapy*, 17–30.

Goldner, V., Penn, P., Sheinberg, M., & Walker, G. (1990). Love and violence: Gender paradoxes in volatile relationships. *Family Process*, 343–364.

Greenspan, S. (1997). *Growth of the mind*. New York: Addison-Wesley.

Haley, J. (1988). Schizophrenics deserve family therapy, not dangerous drugs and management. *Family Therapy Forum*, March–April, 3.

Havens, L., (1973). *Approaches to the mind*. New York: Little, Brown.

Hillman, J. (1964) *Suicide and the soul*. Dallas: Springs Publication.

Hoffman, L. (2002). *Family therapy, an intimate history*. New York: W. W. Norton.

Ignatieff, M. (1984) *The needs of strangers*. New York: Viking.

Kaiser, H. (1965), *Effective psychotherapy*. New York: The Free Press.

Kantor, D., & Neal, J. H. (1985). "Integrative shifts for the theory and practice of family systems therapy. *Family Process*, 13–30.

Kitwood, T. (1993). Person and process in dementia. *International Journal of Geriatric Psychiatry*, 541–545.

Kleinman, A. (1988). *Rethinking psychiatry.* New York: Free Press.

Kramer, D. A. (2001). The biology of family therapy. *Child and Adolescent Psychiatric Clinics of North America,* 625–639.

Laing, R. D., & Esterson, A. (1971). *Sanity, madness, and the family.* New York: Basic Books.

MacKinnon L. K., & Miller, D., "The new epistemology and the Milan approach: feminist and sociopolitical considerations," *Journal of the Association of Marriage & Family Therapists*, 152, 139–156.

Mason, D. T. (1990). *Blue baroque*, A play presented at Fairhaven College, Western Washington University, Bellingham, WA.

Merleau-Ponty, M. (1968). *The physical and the invisible.* (A. Lingis, Trans.). Evanston: Northwestern University Press.

Napier, A. Y. (with Whitaker, C. (1978). *The family crucible.* New York: Harper & Row.

Norman, R. M. G., & Malla, A. K. (1993). Stressful life events and schizophrenia I: A review of the research. *British Journal of Psychiatry,* 161–166.

Patterson, R., & Trathen, S. (1994). Feminist in(ter)ventions in family therapy. *Australia and New Zealand Journal of Family Therapy*, 91–98.

Peabody, F. W. (1930). *Doctor and patient.* New York: Macmillan.

Polanyi, M. (1974). *Personal knowledge.* Chicago: University of Chicago Press.

Post, R. M. (1992). "Transduction of psychosocial stress into the neurobiology of recurrent affective disorder. *American Journal of Psychiatry*, 999–1010.

Pukui, M. K., Haertig, E. W., and Lee, C. A. (1972). *Nana I ke kumu (Look to the Source, Vol. I).* Honolulu: Queen Liliuokalani Childrens Center.

Riker, J. H. (1997) *Ethics and the discovery of the unconscious.* Albay, NY: State University of New York Press.

Scheflen, (1981) *Levels of schizophrenia.* New York: Brunner/Mazel.

Searles, H. (1965). *Collected papers on schizophrenia and other subjects.* New York: International Universities Press.

Siever, L. J., & Davis, K. L. (1991). A psychobiological perspective on the personality disorders. *American Journal of Psychiatry*, 1647–1656.

Smith, M. C. (1981). *Gorky Park.* New York: Ballantine Books.

Sparks, J. A. (2002). Taking a stand: An adolescent girl's resistance to medication. *Journal of Marital and Family Therapy*, 27–38.

Sparks, J. A. (2002b). "Taking a stand: Challenging medical discourse." *Journal of Marital and Family Therapy,* 51–59.

Stern, D. (1985). *The interpersonal world of the infant.* New York: Basic Books.

Stierlin, H. (1977). Counter transference in family therapy with adolescents. *Psychoanalysis and Family Therapy.* New York: Basic Books.

Swedo, S. E., Leonard, H. L., Garvey, M. G., Mittleman, B., Allen, A. J., Perlmutter, S., et al. (1998, February). Pediatric autoimmune neuropsychiatric disorders associated with streptococcal infections: clinical description of the first 50 cases. *American Journal of Psychiatry*, 264.

Taylor, C. (1991). *The ethics of authenticity.* Cambridge, MA: Harvard University Press.

Taylor, W. (1979). Using systems theory to organize confusion. *Family Process,* 479–488.

Valenstein, E. S. (1998). *Blaming the brain*. New York: Free Press.

Varela, F.J., "Reflections on the circulation of concepts between a biology of cognition and systemic family therapy." *Family Process,* 28, 1, 15–24.

Vogel, E. F., & Bell, N. W. (1960). The emotionally disturbed child as the family scapegoat. In Bell, N. W., & Vogel, E. F. (Eds.), *The family*. Glencoe, IL: Free Press.

Vogel, L. (1994). *The fragile "we": Ethical implications of Heidegger's Being in Time*. Evanston, IL.: Northwestern University Press.

Watzlawick, P., Beavin, J. H., and Jackson, D. D. (1967). *Pragmatics of human communication*. New York: Norton.

Whitaker, C. A. (1976). The hindrance of theory in clinical work. In Guerin, P. J., *Family therapy, theory, and practice*. New York: Gardner Press.

Whitaker, C.A. (1975). Personal communication.

Whitaker, C. A., & Miller, M. H. (1969). A re-evaluation of psychiatric help when divorce impends. *American Journal of Psychiatry,* 611–688.

White, M. (1986). Negative explanation, restraint, and double description: A template for family therapy. *Family Process*, 169–184.

Winnicott, D. W. (1965). *The maturational processes and the facilitating environment*. New York: International University Press.

Wynne, L. C. (1971). The injection and concealment of meaning in the family relationships and psychotherapy of schizophrenics. *Psychotherapy of Schizophrenia*, Proceedings of the IV International Symposium Excerpta Medica, Amsterdam.

Wynne, L. C. (1984). The epigenesis of relational systems. *Family Process*, 297–318.

Zubialde, J. P., & Aspy, C. B. (2001). It is time to make a general systems paradigm reality in family and community medicine. *Families, Systems, and Health, 2002*, 345–359.

# Chapter 5

# A Systemic Frame for Mental Health Practices

Marcelo Pakman, MD

*For some minutes Alice stood without speaking, looking out in all directions over the country—and a most curious country it was. There were a number of tiny little brooks running straight across it from side to side, and the ground between was divided up into squares by a number of little green hedges that reached from brook to brook.*
Lewis Carroll, *Alice's Adventures in Wonderland*

Three significant forces have reshaped the mental health field in the last decade. I will name them in order from those more specific to the mental health domain to those that are more general and contextual:

1. The first one has been the fascinating, prodigious development of *psycho-neuro-pharmacology*. The "decade of the brain" was signaled by significant resources, unequaled in almost any other area of research, poured into the development of new pharmaceutical agents. Fifteen years ago we had only a small percentage of the pharmacological agents currently available to treat mental conditions and influence human behavior. Most of them were what are now called "dirty drugs," because they caused significant side effects and were poorly targeted to specific pharmacological actions. Since then the understanding of the chemistry, the physiology, the

micro anatomy and the development of neuronal processes has expanded together with its clinically oriented outcome.

2. The second significant force shaping the mental health field as part of the health field at large has been the "*managed care movement*," which flourished in the context of a need to respond to a health crisis signaled not only by an endless, uncontrolled rise of medical costs, but also by the spread of neo-liberal economic policies, uncontested since the end of the cold war. The concept of "managing" areas of social practice (until the mid 1980s framed mostly as needed social services), imposing restrictions based mostly on financial considerations, became acceptable. With it we witnessed the growing emphasis on "cost containment" and the need to "optimize resources," as well as the increasing attention to developing "evidence based" treatments, "quality assurance," and the promotion of research on "treatment outcomes," all of them congruent with the new financially based approach. This "managed care" force significantly changed the whole practice of mental health and gave the final farewell to the old psychiatric hospitals—a farewell that had begun in the 1960s, fueled by a progressive community mental health stance, and was finalized in the 1990s for more market-related reasons.

3. The third force impacting the mental health field and the health field as a part of many other social systems and domains has been the process of "*globalization*" (Pakman, 2000). Fantastic technological developments in communication and new rules for international financial transactions fed the planetary homogenization of practice, ideas, concepts, esthetics, policies, and educational materials, at least as far as the digital divide allowed.

But what are the implications of being globalized? The mental health domain, for instance, was deeply formatted by these homogenized practices embodying the process of globalization. It was increasingly informed with the concepts that managed care made mandatory for the health care "industry," and pharmacology, invigorated by its research developments and by the significant financial resources of the manufacturing laboratories, was promoted to a dominant place in practice, congruent also, as we will see, with the managed care principles. This process was also facilitated by a social climate conducive to adopting material, clearly visible causes as exclusive explanations for events (paradoxically at the very moment of the defeat of "materialism" by the liberal capital forces). It was further facilitated by a crisis in social sciences in academia, which, while profiting from the technological advances of the globalization process, neglected to see its impact on the everyday world in which applied sciences merged with economic and financial realities. While academicians were fascinated with the academic debate on postmodern trends, and concerned with going beyond "modernism," globalization processes were transforming whole fields of practice, unaffected, to a great extent, by the postmodern academic turn that was absorbing the best energies of social scientists.

The shaping of the mental health field by these forces did not happen without a cost. The main unwanted consequence has probably been a twofold development of the mental health field, with a continuous and on-going tension between a *central* and a *peripheral* trend of development, which evolved in a rather uneven way.

The dominant center stage has been progressively occupied by approaches that, although named bio-psycho-social, are characterized by the primacy of two elements promoted by the shaping forces of the field we identified before:

- *Pharmacology*, considered to be better researched, more efficacious and, in a vaguely defined way, more "scientific," and promoted by the already mentioned psycho-neuro-pharmacological developments.
- *Procedures* that progressively replaced theories in the actual practice of psychotherapy, at least at the level of community mental health in which most people receive mental health services, and were instrumental in implementing new ways of structuring organizations. These procedures, being necessary for services to be adequately processed and paid by the insurance companies, thus guaranteeing the revenue on which the survival of those institutions depends, became the main embodiment of the managed care movement in everyday practices. These procedural trends would deeply transform by psychotherapeutic practice and organizational structure.

This homogenization tended, unfortunately, to push many interesting practices to the margins of the field, discouraging those professionals with expertise and enthusiasm who remained invested in their development.

Let us explore now in more detail the two main components of the center stage, pharmacology, and procedure-driven psychotherapy and organization, before focusing on the consequences for the mental health field of their promotion to center stage. We will leave for the end the practices that have been demoted or marginalized.

## A SYSTEMIC VIEW OF PHARMACOLOGY

An etymological inquiry may add interesting insights for a systemic view. The etymological roots of the term *pharmacology* are found in the Greek terms *pharmakon,* "remedy," and *logos,* "reason." Thus, pharmacology would be the reasoned discipline of remedies. The earliest records of medicinal plants and minerals come from Chinese, Hindu, and Mediterranean civilizations. In 2735 B.C. the Chinese emperor Shen Nung described the fever-reducing capabilities of a substance. The Greek physician Galen described many remedies in the second century B.C., medicinal agents are already mentioned in *De materia medica,* from the first century B.C. The first Western treatise was written by Dioscorides in the first century A.D. The medieval apothecaries both prepared and prescribed drugs, but the Arabian influence in Europe during the eighth century A.D. brought about the separation of the duties of pharmacists and physicians, reinforced by a law enacted in Bruges in 1683 forbidding physicians to prepare medications for their patients. In 1546 the first pharmacopeia appeared in Nuremberg; others followed soon in Basel, Augsburg, and London. In 1617 the Society of Apothecaries was founded in London, inaugurating pharmacy as a profession. In the early nineteenth century some apothecaries specialized in the preparation of medical compounds, thus developing pharmacology as a specialty, while the establishment of the Pharmaceutical Society of Great Britain, in London, in 1841, was the foundation of scientific pharmacological education and training. Around that same time, French and German chemists isolated many active substances from their plant sources, and in the later nineteenth century, the German Schmeiderberg introduced pharmacology into academia. Pharmacological research expanded after 1930 and boomed after World War II in the United States of America and Europe (Encyclopedia Britannica, 2002), fueled by a significant economic development, knowledge acquired during war times, and an interest in the human rights aspects of medical care.

These are aspects of the history of pharmacology from the point of view of the rational tradition of *logos,* which means not only "reason," but also "word," thus the rational word, whose value can be argued and demonstrated through reasoning (Encyclopedia Britannica, 2002). But I would like to develop a stereoscopic view, adding the mythical word to the rational one, as a way to add depth for a systemic inquiry (Bateson, 1979). From the Greek term *mythos,* which means not only "fiction" or "story," but also "word," myths bring a different tradition, a basic constituent of human culture expressing by its mere presence, with no claims at proof, important aspects of people's identities (Encyclopedia Britannica, 2002).

Let us now go, in this next section, to the mythical word as related to our subject. I will present the mythical account interspersed with some viable interpretations.

In the Greek mythical tradition Asklepios (Latin: Aesculapius), the god of medicine, spent time in the forests gathering the herbs he used as remedies (Seton-Williams, 1993). He carried prepared samples in an ivory medical cabinet (Graves, 1997). A son of Apollo, the god of healing, truth, and prophecy, Asklepios learned the art of healing from the centaur Chiron, the first physician and the first one to understand the use of herbs

(Kerenyi, 1951). Chiron was immortal, but while trying to heal another centaur, he was scratched by an arrow tainted by the poisoned blood of the Gorgon Medusa, and, overcome by unceasing agony, surrendered his immortality voluntarily (Grant & Hazel, 1973). It was also blood from the Gorgon Medusa that Athene gave to Asklepios to carry always with him in two phials: with the blood taken from her left side Asklepios could raise the dead; with the blood from her right side, he could destroy instantly and instigate wars.

When Asklepios used his powers to resuscitate several heroes, Hades, the god of the kingdom and of shadows, complained to Zeus that Asklepios was interfering in his kingdom stealing souls from his domain. Zeus, responding to the complaint from Hades, killed Asklepios with his lightning, together with the man he was trying to resuscitate at that moment (Graves, 1997). However, Zeus accused Asklepios of being bribed with gold, without admitting he was responding to Hades' complaint. It is reasonable to imagine that people were probably more prone to justify killing a physician for accepting a bribe than for trying to resuscitate a client, thus Zeus used the more popular argument.

Apollo, father of Asklepios, avenged his death by killing several Cyclopes (Kerenyi, 1951), who made Zeus's thunderbolts, the weapons he used to kill Asklepios. In response Zeus resuscitated Asklepios, and Apollo put him in the sky as a constellation, under the form of a serpent-holder (Grant and Hazel, 1973). In this way Zeus, a great politician, managed to placate Apollo, whom he wanted to keep on his side, giving him his son Asklepios back. Apollo, himself a good negotiator as well, understood that Asklepios had to be deprived of his healing powers, thus was "promoted" to the skies, where he has ever since held an important symbolic role.

The staff of Asklepios with a snake coiled around it became the symbol of medicine (Encyclopedia Britannica, 2002). The ability to control the poisonous snake by transforming its poison into remedies, congruent with the myth of the blood of Medusa, seems to be part of this symbolic representation. In Epidaurus, the cult place of Asklepios, people slept in the temple, hoping to be cured while dreaming (Kerenyi, 1951). Consciousness was to be excluded from the curative process for it to occur. From Epidaurus, his cult was introduced to Rome in 293 B.C., together with the cult of Hygieia, to whom Asklepios chose to delegate the duty of compounding remedies. She was the goddess of health, her animal was also the snake, and she was gradually identified in Rome as Salus, the deity of safety and welfare, appearing as Salus Publica, "public health" (Encyclopedia Britannica, 2002).

It is pertinent to remember here, in light of this overview of the mythical tradition, that Jacques Derrida (1982), in his study of Plato, brought attention to the term *pharmakon*. He points out that *pharmakon* means both "remedy" and "poison." This is congruent with the image of the snake through which Asklepios' aspiration to power over life and death is represented. The term *pharmakon* is closely related to *pharmakeus*, "magician" or "sorcerer," and to *pharmakos*, "scapegoat." So *pharmakon* was not only what Asklepios used as a remedy to resuscitate, but also what he used as a poison to kill. The fact that both remedy and poison were the same substance (Medusa's blood) further stresses the double-sided quality of *pharmakon*. In using *pharmakon* as a remedy and poison, Asklepios became a *pharmakeus*, a magician. Magicians operate without the intervention of consciousness, as the rituals of Epidaurus showed. As such they would purify from evil, either eliminating with their remedies the *pharmakos*, the scapegoat inside the individual, to save the individual, or eliminating with their poison the individual as *pharmakos*, a scapegoat, to save the community.

But there are two other interesting aspects to consider here:

1. The magician himself could be eliminated as a *pharmakos*, a scapegoat, if he abused his powers, as happened to Asklepios himself when Zeus decided to kill him. More reflexive, Chiron resigned himself of his immortality when confronted with his negative side, eternal suffering. Apollo himself, first vengeful and resentful against Zeus, ended up serving him again when Zeus gave Asklepios back to him, although he understood that Asklepios' excessive use of healing powers had to be stopped, and put him as a symbol on the sky. Ultimately, Chiron, Zeus, Apollo, all admitted that *hubris*, the "out of measure" condition of humankind, needed to be limited.

2. The *pharmakeus*, the magician, does not have to operate exclusively through a remedy or poison understood as a drug, because "the most effective of all medicines," *ariston pharmakon*, is, according to Plato, *epistemen*, "knowledge." It was because he provided "knowledge" as *pharmakon*, "poison, " thus becoming a *pharmakeus*, a magician, who seduced his disciples, that Socrates, for instance, was condemned to die by *pharmakon*, "poison," thus becoming a *pharmakos*, a "scapegoat." When knowledge is an expression of *hubris*, it can also become a poison more than a remedy. Knowledge becomes a poison, more than a remedy, when limits are not established by a reflective process and the teacher uses his knowledge without the intervention of the consciousness of the learner, and thus without conscience, becoming a seductive magician. This is why the Greek term used for this type of knowledge, which could become poisonous in the hands of a seductive

magician, *epistemen*, is different conceptually from the Latin term *conscire*, "knowing together," with the participation of consciousness (Humphrey, 1992).

Drugs as well as knowledge, pharmacology as well as psychotherapy, can suffer from the same illness: they can be used based on a logic of scapegoating, of elimination of the evil, without a limiting reflection, without consciousness, ultimately without conscience, becoming poisons more than remedies, and leading to doomed relationships between the patients and the healing professionals.

So, we have been alerted about many risks during our mythical journey: the omnipotence of those who handle remedies operating unilaterally; an underlying scapegoating logic of simplistically eliminating evil without a more seasoned consideration of multiple factors and specific circumstances, leading to the risk of iatrogenia (remedies becoming poisons); the lack of reflection in healing practices leading to the need to set limits because they disrupt ecological forces; and last but not least, that all those factors can also be a risk when what mediates the medical-patient relationship is knowledge (that is to say, an informational process, as in psychotherapy and organizational ideology) and not drugs.

In more contemporary terms, we would say that operating unilaterally is simplistic, that trying to optimize only one variable operating without an ecological multifactorial view is asystemic, that acting without consideration for specific circumstances is disembodied, and that applying our knowledge/power (Foucault, 1980) in a technocratic way without self-observation is irreflexive. We will see how all these risks are actually present in the version of psychopharmacology, psychotherapy, and organizational structuring promoted to center stage in the last decade and how they have helped to legitimize simplistic, asystemic, disembodied, and irreflexive practices (Pakman, 1999).

## PHARMACOLOGY AS PROTAGONIST

What type of pharmacology and biology has been promoted to center stage? Although complex at the level of research, the version of psychopharmacology reaching the practicing clinician tends to be rather simplistic.

At the level of the interface between the manufacturer and those prescribing medications (psychiatrists, other physicians, and clinical nurse specialists) simplistic decision trees are promoted, to replace decision-making processes that are more seasoned and complex. Representatives from the manufacturing laboratories, frequent visitors to medical offices, are now trained to put pressure on the customers on which they depend, those prescribing psychotropics. With the passion of the converted, those less reflexive, try forcefully to highlight the benefits of their products and to influence the decision-making process of the professionals. Among their usual interacting techniques, they frequently ask directly: "How do you decide what type of medication to use in your X type of patients (X being depressed, psychotic, manic, etc.)?" These questions are not aimed at knowing how professionals think. They are opening gambits to pressure professionals into deciding to follow certain patterns. In fact, decision making among professionals is complex and follows a tacit "knowledge-in-action" process (Schön, 1983) that, as a general rule, professionals themselves have a hard time explaining. As we know, the epistemological training of psychiatrists, physicians in general, and clinical nurse specialists goes from poor to nonexistent. The inability of practitioners to articulate their expertise makes them more accepting of the charge that their practices are not rigorous, opening them to easy colonization by the simplistic decision trees that manufacturers increasingly try to impose on professionals, disguising them as scientific ways of doing things that would replace their apparently sloppy, nonrigorous practices.

Although giving gifts to professionals is very limited in the United States of America compared to Europe (where professionals regularly receive expensive travel packages, tickets for artistic or sporting events, etc.), giving materials for patients and objects with advertising labels for medical offices are still part of the setting of current American psychiatry. Representatives also have access to the prescribing profile of every single physician in a given region, being thus able to target specific doctors less permeable to advertising strategies. Under the label of education, professionals are asked to accept invitations to dinner, during which some revered "expert" (in general well intentioned) is going to educate the "second class" professionals, frequently people with enormous practical expertise, who sometimes even have theoretical expertise in areas submerged in the pharmacological tsunami swamping the mental health field.

With increasing frequency, some professionals, far from the actual research arena and without a seasoned knowledge to critically appraise research findings, establish with the prestigious pharmaceutical industry a relationship based on belief and mediated by the new priests representing the industry. Psychiatric practice ends up being colonized, and skillful and experienced professionals end up replacing their own criteria, seasoned and complex, with consultations from these rapidly trained laboratory representatives who bring the word of the "experts."

Thus, psychiatrists have suffered a significant demotion in the last decades: under the pressure of other expanding (and less expensive) mental health professions, they have barricaded themselves behind their prescribing privilege in order to maintain their hierarchical positions in the field. Psychiatrists barely succeeded in maintaining their incomes, which did not increase at the rate of most other medical specialties. Meanwhile, in order to dedicate themselves to the exclusive territory of psychopharmacology, psychiatrists abandoned the world of psychotherapy to the point of having only a very basic knowledge of it and no expertise in its practice. Not having a deep expertise in basic pharmacological research either, they have become the front door clerks of the industry, still brandishing the prescription pads as a symbol of a dwindling power. Their marginal status in mental health organizations does not escape the awareness of recently graduated physicians who increasingly choose other specialties.

In current psychiatric practice, the word of the experts is highly determined by market needs and strategies. If we pay close attention, we can see this in the fluctuating lines of argumentation used by the pharmaceutical industry. When the serotonin selective reuptake inhibitors (SSRIs) came to the market, increasing selectivity to target specific neurotransmitters was shown as preferable in order to avoid side effects. Those medications targeting multiple receptors were then called "dirty." But a pharmaceutical company produced a new drug and, instead of being shy about targeting multiple neurotransmitters, promoted that quality as an advantage, a dual mechanism of action, and named it as a new class of antidepressants, the serotonin norepinephrine reuptake inhibitors (SNRIs). Those companies advertising SSRIs that, according to their reduced selectivity, were "dirtier" than others, immediately forgot selectivity and started presenting their product as having advantages based on a dual mechanism of action. In another example, a widely circulated story tells that the very name of the SSRI was coined rapidly and conveniently, replacing what until then was "uptake," by "reuptake," and adding another "S," standing for "selective," when it became evident that a category of antidepressants called SUI (serotonin uptake inhibitor) was too suggestive of suicide to be attractive when marketed to depressed people. If the story is not true, it is nonetheless congruent with the modus operandi of an industry. Myths, again, reveal important aspects of human interactions.

The rapid and easy, user-friendly decision trees promoted by trainers with less professional education than those they want to influence overlook significant components of the complex patient-physician relationship that is essential to medical professional advice. Physicians do not treat floating, isolated brains in controlled research settings, nor isolated synapses. However, a rather disembodied view of mental health is being promoted. Serotonin and dopamine being the same in every neighborhood, we do not need to pay too much attention to contextual issues if we think in terms of neurotransmitters. Psychopharmacological interventions, based only on basic neurochemical knowledge, are still social practices, open to the variables of all social processes. If research funding were oriented not only to the pharmacological aspect of drugs but included sociology, social psychology, and communication, studies could focus on the role of other forces in pharmaceutical utilization. Most psychiatrists know of many patients who decide their allegiance to medication based on the commercial and sometimes generic names of the products; patients who, regardless of the claimed targeting properties of certain psychopharmacological agents, believe they have improved areas that there is no pharmacological justification to improve; patients who agree to stay on a medication because they feel "more relaxed," something they expect that a medication for "nerves" should do, but deny any improvement in areas and symptoms actually targeted by a given medication; patients who accept and prefer to stay on a medication because it is part of the sick role they need to maintain for other reasons; patients who claim improvements after taking sporadically medications that work pharmacologically only when taken regularly; etcetera. If a more complex view of pharmacology were to be promoted, we would probably be able to know more about such situations, as well as the industry's marketing strategies and its decisions to go for official approval of a medication for certain conditions and not others, thus creating a specificity that is preordained, once more, for marketing reasons.

Direct advertising has lately also become part of the picture. With the argument of "empowering" the consumer, the pharmaceutical industry again promotes simplistic direct connections between particular types of symptoms and specific medications. Although nothing illegal happens, and lies are not told, the whole range of expertise and the complex assessment needed for adequate professional advice tends to be bypassed. As a result, patients request specific agents for treatment and join professionals in endlessly repeating the "chemical imbalance" credo, until nobody seems to remember the poor explanatory power it holds. After all, love, or any other emotional state, could also be defined as a chemical imbalance if we were to eliminate all the interactive, interpersonal, social aspects of its construction.

Pharmacology, and biology in general, are of course not necessarily rooted in simplistic thinking, but in the way they have been channeled in the domain of practice, now transformed into a market, we almost never hear about concepts like "calibration" of the nervous system, the importance of timing in neurotransmitting, the nonsynaptic neurotransmitting processes, and the nuances of neurodevelopment, all of which would give a much more complex view of the relationships between brain functioning, human connections, culture, and language (which, by the way, is also a chemical brain process, as is everything else we experience). Thus, at a conceptual level (and as we will later see, at a pragmatic level as well), asystemic practices are promoted in which pharmacology stands tall and alone, as a unilateral dimension, abstracted from the situated life of the person, the family, and the social network. Pharmacological knowledge, spread powerfully with the resources of the industry, and legitimized at every possible level by a scientific label, becomes the basis for a technocratic clinical application. Practitioners with no training in critical inquiry end up using user-friendly knowledge prepacked for the "busy professional" by an industry dictating the lyrics of an irreflexive practice.

## PROCEDURAL PRACTICES

When young professionals from different theoretical persuasions are welcomed to the field, they have so many procedures to follow for their practices to be reimbursed, that being socialized very rapidly into following them is a *condition sine qua non* for them to be able to practice. Procedures include everything from intake forms and clinical documentation guidelines to organization of required multidisciplinary teams, from billing requirements to the organization of professional time, from the required use of certain diagnostic categories to the prescribed guidelines for liability risk reduction, from credentialing committees to treatment protocols, from organizational structures to institutional policies, from training to supervision, from administrative policies regulating interactions among mental health workers and between them and their clients to compliance with state and federal regulations of agencies increasingly dedicated to prevent and detect fraudulent practices.

These procedures have become the most constant feature across mental health institutions, in which homogeneous forms and documents, as well as cloned committees, set the pace for globalized practices. Although most mental health administrators were trained in one of the mental health professions, they have become specialists, increasingly distant from clinical practice. They are the ones who usually interface with policy makers and funding providers and convey to clinicians the structures that regulate the implementation of procedures. Although some institutions are more sensitive to the concerns of the real providers of direct care and try to get the input of those providers to inform administrative decisions, a growing dissatisfaction pervades the ranks of mental health professionals, who tend to complain that they are at the bottom of the hierarchy of mental health structures, at least when decisions are made that will guide the practice of their professions. Professional associations try at times to voice the concerns of their constituencies, but they frequently lack financial resources, an essential factor in becoming a forceful lobby. Other times, the ethos of professional associations is totally congruent with the forces formatting the field, and thus they lack the critical ability necessary to maintain a balance. A polarized atmosphere, in which criticism is equated with a lack of collaboration, has also become part of a field navigating the stormy seas of a world disrupted now by terrorism, and the antiterrorist campaign in response to it that risks weakening civil liberties. The concepts promoted by managed care are embodied in institutional procedures. Although the procedures are justified in principle by legitimate requirements, following them leads to conflicting realities. "Cost containment" and the need to "optimize resources," necessary measures due to the financial crisis of the mental health system, led to an increasing number of clinicians working on a fee-for-service basis. Committed to meeting certain levels of productivity, measured in patient-hours per week, all clinicians have to frequently overbook clients, given that clinics working with multiproblem patients tend to have high no-show rates. If we add phone contacts related to patient care, and necessary documentation for which those clinicians are responsible, the time for quality peer interaction drops to a minimum. Something similar happens with psychiatrists and clinical nurse specialists, who are frequently pressured to see patients for 15 minutes with the rationale that all they are asked to do is "to review their medications"; a 30-minute visit remains a luxury affordable in those institutions better governed by common sense. During those 15 minutes clinicians are supposed, at a minimum, to maintain a relationship with their patients, evaluate their clinical status, discuss the specifics of treatment options and side effects, include other people from the social network or the health care system of the patient, write prescriptions or contact pharmacies, and write or dictate documentation. Time and productivity pressures combine in this way with other restrictions of the procedures-driven practice to further constrain the potential of the field and channel professional activity in ways that end up being necessarily simplistic.

An important consequence of these pressures (unacknowledged in cost-effectiveness equations) is that there is no time for actual clinical discussion and coordination of care of patients shared by professionals in the same clinic, and even less with professionals in other institutions, unless professionals use their own unpaid time for that. This adds to the fact that both at the biological and at the more hierarchically relegated psychosocial level, skills and ways of thinking have been adopted, both in practice and in education in mental health, that promote isolated practices lacking integration among the disciplines of the mental health field (psychiatry, nursing, psychology, education, social work, chemical dependency, etc.). So the dashes among the publicly proclaimed bio-psycho-social approach have been rather symbolic in practice. They have not been accompanied by practices that honor those supposedly integrated approaches. The term *systemic* has also suffered a demotion by generalization; it may be used to designate, for instance, any encounter between people working for different systems, and not a complex and transdisciplinary way of thinking and operating.

These isolated practices have further amplified the tendencies dominant in academia, where "disciplinary" knowledge (Pakman, 2000), compartmentalized among professions, still structures the syllabi of most graduate and postgraduate training. Professional training for a transdisciplinary practice is still an oddity, and no special credentials to work in family therapy, systemic interventions, and network approaches are required, while individually based approaches better suited to marketing in the current context gain recognition.

Lack of connection and conflict also typifies the relationship of the mental health field with the health field at large, as well as with other systems with which the field shares many of its "customers," namely the legal system, the school system, the welfare and disability system, the human rights system, and the always contested, erratically defined and politically heated chemical dependency system. Thus, the current context promotes asystemic thinking, which mirrors the fragmented sources of funding that makes it so difficult to develop programs focused on areas of care (children, adolescent, families, domestic violence, etc.) in a coordinated multidisciplinary form.

The multidisciplinary teams, the mainstay of "quality assurance," do not compensate for the lack of contact among professionals. Their members are sometimes people with the necessary professional credentials but dedicated mostly to administration, and even when that is not the case, they cannot replace what contact among those actually caring clinically for a given patient would yield. Given the volume of cases they have to process, they end up having a rather perfunctory supervisory function which mostly assures the quality of the paperwork, which becomes the virtual reality of a disembodied mental health care. This colludes with psychotherapeutic work based on rather abstract and supposedly universal entities like "self-esteem, " "personality," "diagnostic categories," in which professionals with training almost exclusively centered in the individual and individual psychological categories, become blind to the ecological and situated social texts of mental phenomena.

The reasonable motto that only "evidence based treatment," supported by research on "treatment outcomes," deserves recognition and funding, obscures the vicious cycle in which research for pharmacology is strongly funded, whereas research on ecological and systemic approaches is virtually nonexistent. This belief system designates the same kind of practices as valuable, as a self-fulfilling prophecy that pushes to the margin any innovative approach, disincentivating creativity. Lack of professional, financial, or academic recognition punishes those who fall beyond the scope of practices occupying center stage.

Under the pressure of minority groups, some professional organizations, and the most democratic elements in the legal and the political system, "diversity committees" and "human right committees" are now a common feature of mental health organizations. They are a welcome addition to the field, because they help to legitimize those dimensions as an essential part of democratic systems of care. Unfortunately, their impact has been greatly reduced by the fact that adding diversity does not automatically change the qualities of the systems within which they operate. Specifically, training in "cultural competence" and "cultural sensitivity" is like a prosthetic additions to the modus operandi of institutions along the lines I have been describing, which remain largely unchanged. In practice, "cultural competence" training becomes, in a paradoxical way, instructions for dealing with specific groups of people, as if the problems of nonminority patients were assumed to be nonproblematic for practitioners. "Cultural sensitivity" training becomes a way to "tolerate" those who are different, with all the actual ambiguity attached to this advertised "tolerance." More reflexive ways of integrating diversity concerns into current practices are difficult (Pakman, 1998). "Human rights" committees are frequently a means for "customers" to complain about care received, sometimes because they have no other way to express their dissatisfaction with the health care system. The broader issue of access to care as a human right is not a concern of these committees, and the exponents of a human rights perspective are usually not invited to the table at which policies and funding are discussed and decided.

Mental health professionals may believe, when they start their practices, that procedures are only "paperwork" and that requirements that they attend institutional meetings  are only organizational matters no institution can do without and marginal to their professional activities, but their professional minds are sooner or later formatted by them. Frustration and dissatisfaction frequently follow. In this way the whole interaction between professionals and patients (now renamed consumers in the fashionable market language, the use of these terms is endorsed because it empowers patients) is structured. Increasingly those procedures end up replacing theories of practice in mental health, and even more, becoming major contributors to the theories-in-use (Argyris & Schön, 1974; Schön, 1983) of tacit knowledge that professionals follow in the actual practice of their profession.

Although colonization by procedure-driven practices is more obvious in community mental health institutions, no practitioner is totally free of their pressures, because third-party payers have similar requirements for private practitioners, and because some of the procedures have become part of a legitimized state-of-the-art practice: today the risk of being sued for malpractice always looms, and nobody would dare to deviate from the norm. Procedures are the instrument of efficient forms of distributed power (Foucault, 1978, 1982) in which each of us ends up controlling him- or herself without Big Brother having to do it. They are also formidable ways of smuggling ideologies into institutions, in the disguise of obviously helpful ways of organizing professional practices.

One further consequence of this state of affairs is that, given that the organization of the services is conducive to both a technical application of

practical knowledge and organizational fragmentation, sealed then to critical inquiry, the irreflexive nature of all these practices is perpetuated. The
disjointed, isolated, asystemic way of operating and the technical-rational
(Schön, 1983) quality of the procedures make it difficult for the professionals to see the progressive narrowing of choices. Professionals and poor
and minority patients end up mirroring each other in this regard.

## THE INVISIBLE MARGINS

We have seen how pharmacology and procedure-driven practices collude
to result in organizational practices that tend to be simplistic, asystemic,
disembodied, and irreflexive. In spite of this complicated situation, we
have less prominent, less visible, and less recognized developments at the
margins of the mental health field, where many practitioners and professionals keep actually engaging, against all odds, in creative thinking and
practice.

The complexity of the problematic situations they have to deal with in
their daily practice and the lack of legitimization of their problems and of
satisfactory ways of addressing them have impelled many professionals to
act to promote integration with medical care and collaboration with multiple social systems, family and network approaches; they are thus reframing in action their professional practice. These practices have the potential
to further develop skills and ways of thinking that are complex, embodied,
systemic, and reflexive, and in need of recognition and visibility.

So the problem is not one of a polarity between a biological approach
and a psychosocial one. Actually this polarity is in itself reinforced by a
field radicalized by nonintegrated, poorly collaborative, and simplistic
views. The problem is that these views pervade the whole field, including
both the biological and the psychosocial approaches; they occupy center
stage and relegate to the margins practices that are still needed in those
areas in which mental health seeks more internal integration as well as
better interdisciplinary, not exclusively individually centered, multisys-
temic practices.

Biological and psychotherapeutic approaches cannot be properly integrated within the fragmented structure of current systems of care. They
could be integrated within the frame of a major change encompassing both
types of approaches, united under a common umbrella of reflexivity, open
to a systemic view of health, respectful of levels of complexity and atten-
tive to the situated, embodied circumstances of peoples lives. That reflexivity would be implemented by professionals able to look at their own
practices to deconstruct their impact on people's lives. If we apply the
same qualities of systemic, complex, embodied, and reflexive thinking to
the problem at hand, we have to understand that no change of this magnitude would be possible without the participation of managed care and

other funding sources, academia and research institutions, mental health administrators and policy makers, who would also have to deconstruct their own practices and honestly evaluate how they contribute to maintaining an undesirable state of affairs.

Within such a context of a concerted effort for a transformation of mental health care, professionals would have room for their "expertise at the fingertips" (Hoffman, 2002) to be recognized and validated. They would not be approached by academicians to get data from them while their knowledge is seen as hierarchically inferior. They would not be exposed to the double bind of asking them to be congruent with abstract theories without recognizing the actual situations in which they work, which lead to the developments of theories-in-use built from the procedural sources within which they operate, as well as from many other non-professional sources of knowledge-in-action (Schön, 1983). They would not be asked to blindly follow procedures and comply with regulations. Professionals would then welcome the introduction of reflective settings for them to make their theories-in-use explicit and open to critique, as long as their efforts were accompanied by a similar exercise from the other actors in the mental health system.

We need to make a "reflective turn" in the mental health field, starting from our actual practice (Schön, 1991) in which professionals display a knowing-in-action which makes them effective in spite of many obstacles—that same knowing-in-action which today renders them ineffective because of the many restrictions from multiple sources never opened to critical inquiry.

If this reflective turn is to occur, professional training and practice, rather than being limited to a technical and abstract knowledge which increasingly condemns professionals to frustration and exposure to the impossibility of applying their abstract theories within the current mental health system, will encompass both a "poetics" and a "micro-politics" (Pakman, 1999, 2000).

A poetics is made of the task-specific abilities and skills professionals develop over time to operate in the framing of problematic situations as problems, and either the solving of these problems or their transformation into dilemmas. Although it also includes a technology, a poetic tradition deviates from the most prevalent practice in psychotherapy in that it does not try to find the meaning of people's behaviors by reading them through a ready-made grid or code. It grants meaning to every human behavior, looking into the context of its emergence to understand how competent actors develop viable ways of behaving in the actual settings of their lives. It does not lock professionals in the role of privileged holders of universal hidden codes to decipher behavior, codes whose meaning escapes their agents. Instead, meaning is understood to be inherent in behavior to begin with. The onus is on the professionals to find the context in which competent behavior becomes understandable and open to evaluation by social agents. A poetically based tradition operates through reflexive methodologies, looking into the complex nature of people's lives at the crossroads of multiple social systems.

A micro-politics is made of the abilities and skills professionals develop over time so as to make the social/institutional/political situations in which they find themselves operating better suited to allowing their poetics to be effective. Professionals trained in operating micro-politically as a legitimate and central aspect of their task would not feel weakened in their professional identities when they try to reconfigure the actual ecology of their practice in interaction with actors from other relevant social systems.

Poetics and micro-politics operate conjointly as deconstructive endeavors for a critical social practice, one that sees the systems that organize mental health care as constitutive of the mental processes and identities of the social actors involved. Reflexive methodologies, like reflecting teams (Andersen, 1987, 1991), work on professional "prejudices" (Cecchin, 2001), "appreciative inquiry" (Srivastva & Cooperrider, 1998; Cooperrider, Sorensen et al., 2000) and "qualitative reflexive research" (Steier, 1991), are instances of the type of structures conducive to introducing the types of skills that make this social practice viable. In a similar spirit, I have consistently implemented, during the last years, "design studio" methodologies (Schön & Rein, 1994) in the mental health field, both in supervision and organizational consulting (Pakman, 2000, 2002). In the "design studio," mental health professionals learn to critically evaluate how the institutional structures they are a part of construct the identities of themselves and their "customers," how the fate of interventions is multiply determined and open to continuous reshaping by many actors in the actual situation in which they are operating (Schön & Rein, 1994), how to make procedures and their underlying ideology visible, and how to micro-politically negotiate frames to increase the chances of their technical knowledge being more effective. Systemic thinking then becomes a way to consistently find the reflexive distance from which to critically evaluate the assumptions of particular ways of framing human problems without the constraints of any single discipline or scientific or lay knowledge.

With this double focus, poetical and micro-political, in mind, professionals who presently feel at a disadvantage among the actors in the mental health structure might feel encouraged to participate with other actors developing programs sensitive to the public health dimension, aware that simple things work well and that minor concerted efforts generate cascades of events in positive directions, open to the complexities of lives at the crossroads of multiple social systems, and eager to constantly re-examine their everyday expertise gained in the trenches of their actual practice. I do not see any good reason for such a practice and philosophy of hope to be given up to its dusk.

## REFERENCES

Andersen, T. (1987). The reflecting team. In *Family Process, 26,* 415–428.

Andersen, T. (Ed.). 1991). *The reflecting team.* New York: Norton.

Argyris, C., & Schön, D. (1974). *Theory in practice: Increasing professional effectiveness.* San Francisco: Jossey-Bass.

Bateson, G. (1979). *Mind and nature: A necessary unity.* New York: Dutton.

Cecchin, G. (2001). Personal communication.

Cooperrider, D. L., Sorensen, P. F., Whitney, D., Yaeger, T. F. (Eds.). (2000). *Appreciative inquiry: Rethinking human organization toward a positive theory of change.* Champaign, IL: Stipes Publishing.

Derrida, J. (1982). *Dissemination.* Chicago: University of Chicago Press.

Encyclopedia Britannica (2002). s.vv. Asclepius. Hygieia, Logos, Myth, Pharmaceutical, Pharmaceutical industry, Pharmacology, Salus. http://www.britannica.com.

Foucault, M. (1978). *Discipline and punish: The birth of the prison.* New York: Random House.

Foucault, M. (1980). *Power/knowledge: Selected interviews and other writings, 1972–1977.* Edited by Colin Gordon. New York: Pantheon.

Foucault, M. (1982). Space, knowledge and power. In Rabinow, P. (Ed.), *The Foucault reader.* New York: Pantheon.

Grant, M., & Hazel, J. (1973). *Who's who in classical mythology.* New York: Oxford University Press.

Graves, R. (1997). *The Greek myths.* London: Penguin Books.

Hoffman, L. (2002). *Family therapy: An intimate history.* New York: Norton.

Humphrey, N. (1992). *A history of the mind.* New York: HarperCollins.

Kerenyi, C. (1951). *The gods of the Greeks.* New York: Thames & Hudson.

Pakman, M. (1998). Education and therapy in cultural borderlands: A aall for critical social practices in human services. In *Journal of Systemic Therapies, 17*(1), 18–30.

Pakman, M. (1999). Designing constructive therapies in community mental health: Poetics and micropolitics in and beyond the consulting room. In *Journal of Marital and Family Therapy, 25*(1), 83–98.

Pakman, M. (2000). Disciplinary knowledge, postmodernism, and globalization: A call for Donald Schön's "Reflective Turn" for the mental health professions. In *Cybernetics and Human Knowing*, Vol. 7 (2–3), 105–126.

Pakman, M. (2002). Unpublished manuscript.

Schön, D. (1983). *The reflective practitioner.* New York: Basic Books.

Schön, D. (1991). Introduction. *The reflective turn: Case studies in and on educational practice.* New York: Teachers College, Columbia University.

Schön, D., & Rein, M. (1994). *Frame reflection: Towards the revolution of intractable political controversies.* New York: Basic Books.

Seton-Williams, M. V. (1993). *Greek legends and stories.* New York: Barnes & Noble.

Srivastva, S., & Cooperrider, D. L., (Eds.) (1998). *Organizational wisdom and executive courage.* San Francisco: New Lexington Press.

Steier, F. (Ed.). (1991). *Research and reflexivity.* London: Sage.

Chapter 6

# Can Giving Heal? Contextual Therapy and Biological Psychiatry

Catherine Ducommun-Nagy, MD

*Alice looked around her in great surprise. "Why, I do believe we've been under this tree the whole time! Everything's just as it was!"*

*"Of course it is," said the Queen: "what would you have it?"*

*"Well, in our country," said Alice, still panting a little, "you'd generally get to somewhere else—if you ran very fast for a long time, as we've been doing."*

*"A slow sort of country!" said the Queen. "Now, here you see, it takes all the running you can do, to keep in the same place. If you want to get somewhere else, you must run at least twice as fast as that!"*

Lewis Carroll, *Alice's Adventures in Wonderland*

## INTRODUCTION

Since psychopharmacological interventions have become the dominant way of treating mental illnesses, why would anyone refuse to concede victory to the camp of biological psychiatry? If mental illnesses were simple brain diseases that medicine will soon cure, it would be wonderful. It would be one of the greatest achievements of modern medicine to provide a true causal treatment for illnesses that affect the lives of millions of people around the world. Yet, is this a realistic view of the future?

As someone who has practiced both family therapy and psychiatry for more than twenty-five years, I know that we are far from finding a true cure for mental disorders, and I do believe that family therapy and specifically contextual therapy (which I will expand on later in the essay) can offer to patients something that medications will never provide: a chance for healing through relating, or more specifically, giving.

I do not pretend to be an expert in psychopharmacology: I have never participated in any neurobiological or psychopharmacological research. On the other hand, in my practice of psychiatry, both with children and with adults on two continents, I have gathered a vast experience in the practical use of psychotropic medications and a sense of what can be realistically expected from psychopharmacological treatments.

As a contextual therapist for many years, I have also developed a good sense of what patients can gain from relational therapy. Furthermore, a formal training in the history of sciences and more specifically in the history of psychotherapy (Ducommun, 1984) has given me a keen eye for detecting inconsistencies in theories and in the presentation of scientific findings.

I would like the reader to go with me on a journey that will take us from the first days of my training as a young psychiatrist in Switzerland to the present in Philadelphia.

Along with me, the reader will discover that, when it comes to mental health sciences, one day's truth may well end up being another day's aberration, the science of one country a fiction in another. There is a saying "From the sublime to the ridiculous, there is only one step." We may never reach the sublime—a true scientific knowledge about the etiology of mental disorders—but we need to avoid the ridiculous—a false pretense about what we can offer to our patients.

We need to gain a realistic understanding of what pharmacotherapy can offer before we can have a useful discussion about the place of family therapy in today's treatment of mental illnesses. We also need to examine some of the limitations of classical family therapy.

In brief, we need to remain open to any hypotheses for the etiology of mental illnesses, and we need to develop a broad understanding of all the determinants that can affect our patients' behaviors and their relationships with others. Contextual therapy, with its multidimensional view of relational reality, can help us move in that direction.

## BIOLOGY AND PSYCHIATRY

By now, biological hypotheses dominate the field when it comes to the exploration of the origin of mental illnesses. But even the most sophisticated models have fallen short of producing irrefutable etiological explanations for any of the mental disorder listed in the *Diagnostic and Statistical Man-*

*ual of Mental Disorders* produced by the American Psychiatric Association, currently in its fourth revision.

The validity of the *DSM* and its usefulness have been challenged not only by outsiders like family therapists but also at times by psychiatrists. Several years ago the American Psychiatric Association put the question of the use of *DSM* to a vote. Members were asked to choose between a continued use of the *DSM* system and the International Classification of Diseases established by the World Health Organization. Although they chose in favor of the *DSM* system, members have recently challenged some of its features. The column " Talk Back" in the "Opinion" section of the October 2001 issue of *Clinical Psychiatry* reflects the position of several psychiatrists who responded to the suggestion that the *DSM* system needed a complete overhaul. Several listed serious limits to the present version, one being that "psychiatry faces complex diagnostic problems because there is a paucity of biological markers to categorize psychiatric diseases." One of the recurrent arguments is that the way in which diseases are grouped is not based on an understanding of the biological processes that lead to mental illnesses.

Could we eventually group disorders by types of "chemical imbalances" rather than by observed symptoms? One can already answer that, in all likelihood, most of the symptoms that we can observe are under the control of more than one neurotransmitter and involve more than a single neuronal pathway.

The complexity of brain functions is such that there are theoretical reasons for believing that we will never be able to track all the neuronal pathways and all the neurotransmitters involved in even a single symptom or a specific behavior. For instance, until recently we have assumed that schizophrenia was simply the result of an increase of dopamine in the central nervous systems; therefore, most medications used to treat it have been dopamine antagonists, the typical antipsychotics. We are now confronted with the possibility that "schizophrenia may also be explained as the result of abnormalities in the interactions between all the monoaminergic systems and, in particular between the dopaminergic and the serotoninergic systems rather than in the abnormalities of any one simple system" (Akpaffiong, Lecca, Jackson, & Ruiz, 2001). These hypotheses lead us far away from the simplistic view that mental illnesses are the result of a chemical imbalance that can be easily corrected by administering the right medication.

There is one exception to our lack of clear etiological knowledge. A few years ago Rett disorder, which is listed under developmental disorders, received a definitive explanation: the presence of a single defective gene. Interestingly, among all disorders listed in the DSM, it is only one that requires the presence of a physical criterion, a deceleration of the head growth during infancy (American Psychiatry Association, 1994).

We know that Down's syndrome, which entails both mental symptoms, including mental retardation, and physical findings, does not appear in the *DSM* classification and is considered to be a medical condition. Therefore, under the current multiaxial assessment system, Down's syndrome, as a medical condition, is listed under axis III.

Rett disorder and Down's syndrome are very similar disorders. They are both genetic disorders entailing combined physical and mental symptoms, even if the first is caused by a single defective gene and the second by the duplication of one chromosome. It would be hard to deny that children with Down's syndrome do not present with developmental delays in many areas. Mental retardation is a symptom common to both.

Why, then, should Rett disorder belong to the axis of major mental illnesses and the other to the axis of physical conditions? Was Down's syndrome simply forgotten and should it be added to the list of mental disorders in the next version of *DSM*? Or should Rett disorder be removed from it for being in fact a medical condition?

While all these questions may indeed undermine the validity of the *DSM* classification system, the following point must be underscored: If all mental illnesses were truly brain disorders, they would be in fact organic disorders. Therefore, they would need to be listed under axis III of the current system, and axis I would become empty. The *DSM* system would become obsolete. In effect, *DSM* would be extinguished by its own criteria, not because of a vote by members of the American Psychiatric Association, or because of criticism of its limitations by outsiders and even by insiders.

Fortunately for *DSM,* it will not be forced to extinguish itself soon. We are years away from fully understanding the scope of the biological elements that are involved in these disorders. We need to remember only that since no one has the key to their precise etiology, we cannot say that we can treat them "scientifically."

## TWO CONTINENTS, MANY WAYS OF PRACTICING

Having practiced psychiatry and family therapy on both sides of the Atlantic, I have come to the realization that the field of psychiatry is at a very different place from any other field in medicine. I was trained in Switzerland in the late 1970s, first as an adult and later as a child and adolescent psychiatrist. I moved to the United States in 1987. Since then I have maintained contact with Europe and observed the evolution of psychiatry and family therapy on both continents; my account should illustrate how the treatment guidelines and the approaches to the treatment of mental illnesses are different in different cultures. In medicine and surgery the situation is vastly different; it is difficult to find any differences between the treatments offered in Europe and in the United States. This contrast should serve as evidence of the fact that psychiatric illnesses, unlike medical ones, cannot be treated on the basis of a clear understanding of their etiology.

### Switzerland, the Late 1970s: Adult Psychiatry

My training in adult psychiatry took place in a unique institution: the Secteur Psychiatrique Ouest of the Canton (state) of Vaud mental health system. This organization was to provide psychiatric services for the entire population of a quarter of the state including adult, child and geriatric services. The adult services comprised three teams working on the site of a mental hospital and three satellite offices in small towns. The hospital was unusual for two reasons: It was originally built as an exclusive private hospital and was later purchased by the state and was still staffed by a personnel trained to cater to the wealthy of the world; most of the senior staff lived on grounds, and some of the doctors were expected to live on the grounds, too. Doctors could not simply forget about their patients while they were off duty. They shared the same dining room and the same gardens. Patients knew whether a given staff member was at home or not just by checking the parking lot.

I had to learn two things from this experience: Seeing patients suffering from the most severe forms of mental illnesses day after day and sharing to a great extent their daily routine forced us to find a way to address them as fellow humans rather than as a special breed of people that we were treating but would have never associated with in our daily life. We also had to learn about boundaries: How were we to maintain personal privacy and patient-therapist boundaries in an environment where our lives were to a great extent visible to our patients?

While the décor evoked an affluent past, the patients themselves were referred to the various units of the hospital not because they could afford such a place for their treatment but simply because they lived in the communities served by the organization. Furthermore, they were assigned to specific units not by age or diagnosis but by postal codes.

Each of the three teams was assigned to serve a determined geographical area, whose patients were referred to the corresponding satellite clinic for outpatient therapy or hospital unit if they needed hospitalization. In such a setting, it was difficult to ignore the social environment of the patients or the patients' families: Each of us knew several families in which more than one member needed treatment, which made us aware of some of the dynamics described by the pioneers of family therapy.

Since the first family therapy training program in the area opened only at the very end of the 1970s, we were trying to see families without much to rely on. We were applying what we could find in the few books available to us on the subject at the time. Later we started to benefit from the input of visiting leaders of family therapy, first on the occasion of some of the early family therapy conferences that took place in Europe, later when leaders of the family therapy movement were invited to visit newly opened training programs. In 1980 I was introduced to Ivan Boszormenyi-Nagy, MD, during one of his early visits to Switzerland. He interviewed the family of one of my individual patients. This encounter confirmed my interest in family therapy. This was my first step toward a commitment to contextual therapy, first by trade and later by marriage.

Otherwise, many forms of therapies were offered to the patients beside biological therapies. Patients were offered intensive psychodynamic psychotherapy if we believed that they could benefit from it. Patients also received a vast array of treatments ranging from group therapy to occupational and music therapy.

Social rehabilitation was one of the major focuses of the team's intervention. Besides full-time hospitalization, patients with chronic illnesses were offered many possible options within the hospital program. They could leave for the day to work or could go home for the night without having to be assigned to a different team. Weekend hospitalizations were used to prevent relapses in drug-addicted patients who would go on drug binges during weekends, or to protect dependant patients who became more suicidal when unoccupied. Patients were sometimes placed in sheltered group homes, and sometimes in adult foster care placement.

Patients who needed constant hospitalization because they could not adjust socially to any of the other programs were occasionally taken out of the hospital for a brief vacation. They would leave with some dedicated staff members and stay for a few days in a vacation home. Some were sent to spend a few days in small hotels that had a contract with the hospital. Homelessness of the chronically ill patients was virtually unknown, and most of them were employed, if not in some regular job, at least in a sheltered workshop.

In general, biological treatments were the main fare for our sickest patients. One needs to remember that one of Switzerland's main industries is the pharmaceutical industry and that Switzerland has developed many of the medications available on the world market. Only with the globalization of industries in the recent years did Switzerland lose some of its central role in that area. Many compounds authorized in Switzerland never hit the market in the United States or did so at a much later time.

One of my assignments was to monitor the treatments ordered by several attending psychiatrists. Many of the doctors were trained outside of Switzerland and used medications that they were familiar with rather than the ones commonly used in Switzerland. This forced me to learn about so many compounds that, by the end of my training, I had gathered personal knowledge about most of the drugs produced not only in Switzerland but in all of Europe, many more than were being used in the United States at the time.

We had the belief that medications were more efficacious if administered directly into the bloodstream. Acutely ill patients spent most of the day lying in bed with an IV drip of antidepressants or neuroleptics. After two or three weeks, we started to give them medication by mouth.

Chronically ill patients were often offered a depot form of neuroleptics. If they had been discharged from the hospital, a visiting nurse who was part of the team would go to their home to administer the medication at scheduled intervals.

All of us were trained in the prescription and use of shock therapy. Electroshocks were recommended for the same indications for which they are used today. We still occasionally used a form of insulin shock, the "humid shock," in which the patient received a dose of insulin that did not induce coma, but fainting. We believed that this would help patients in regressing to a situation of physical discomfort similar to the situation of a baby and that it would allow for "remothering" by a nurse who would stay at their side like a mother would with a sick baby. We believed that if the symptoms leading to the hospitalization could have been the result of unmet dependency needs, patients would be cured after such an intensive administration of care.

Only rarely did we need to use any kind of containment, but in crisis situations patients were placed in a seclusion room and a chemical restraint was administered, usually a cocktail of two neuroleptics and a benzodiazepine.

Interestingly, while our patients were generally treated with great respect by staff, the standards for the protection of their civil rights were rather low. Patients were not given much of a chance to refuse treatment. Commitment laws protected patients by requiring the signature of two physicians to commit a patient to a mental hospital; however, these two physicians could not belong to the same institution. This offered some guarantee of objectivity. On the other hand, once the patient was admitted, the length of stay was at the discretion of the treating psychiatrist. Patients who were committed were visited by a mental heath delegate on a regular basis, but if they started to complain about their hospitalization, the only answer they would get from the delegate was: "Why would you like to leave such a beautiful place, and all the doctors are so nice!"

## Switzerland, the Early 1980s: Child Psychiatry

In the French-speaking part of Switzerland, child psychiatry was a bastion of classical psychoanalysis. All the symptoms of mental illness observed in children were believed to have a psychogenic origin. This included autism. The only exception was mental retardation. Based on this assumption, it was logical that psychopharmacological interventions were not considered useful.

Characteristically, children were treated by intensive analytical psychotherapy, analytically inspired play therapy and by an array of adjunctive therapies like speech, movement, music, and occupational therapy.

Even people who were less drastic in their beliefs and could endorse a biological basis for at least some of the conditions observed were very hesitant about using psychotropic medications. They were concerned about the risk of affecting the development of the brain in an adverse way and were generally extremely hesitant to prescribe any medications—even stimulants—to youths under the age of 16 years.

In any event, medications were reserved for extreme situations. I used them at such rare intervals that I remember one occasion on which it took me an entire day to locate a prescription pad at an agency, and when I did, I discovered that the address printed on the pad was the location of the agency a decade earlier.

After a stay of several months in Philadelphia to train in contextual therapy, I returned to Switzerland to become the director of a 25-bed residential treatment program for children suffering mostly with autism and psychosis. Shortly after my arrival I inquired about medication administration, since no child seemed to receive any. The answer was "You can prescribe anything you want, but you need to remember that you are the only one who is authorized to administer medications, since there are no nurses here." I was living 10 miles away and the only alternative was to bring the child to the nearby pediatric hospital for each dosage of the medication. Was I willing to return to the program every night and on weekends to distribute medications? Not quite. I can therefore attest that it is possible to run an entire inpatient program for severely disturbed children using hardly any medication, not even for crisis management.

The institutionalization of these children, sometimes for years, was justified by the belief that these children had developed symptoms because of a noxious psychological influence by their parents. These children needed a corrective psychological experience gained from intensive individual therapy and contact with a highly trained staff.

Family therapy was not seen as useful: Why reexpose children to the pathogenic influence of their parents? Parents were kept at bay, and direct contacts between parents and therapists were not encouraged. Social workers spent a lot of time calling mothers to give them news about their child so that they would not be tempted to try to reach the child directly outside of strictly scheduled interactions. They were less inclined to involve fathers in the process. They were very strict in their supervision of the direct interactions between the parents and the child, and visits were scheduled only as deemed appropriate by the therapist. Very rarely, one of the social workers would ask me for help and use my skills as a family therapist.

During the same period, I was providing clinical services and supervision to a team serving a population of mentally retarded, often multiply-handicapped children and adolescents. There was no question about the origin of their symptoms. They were organic in nature. Many children had a known diagnosis of Down's syndrome, several had a congenital disease, and some were born very prematurely and presented with neurological disorders and blindness. I do not remember any child receiving psychotropic medications but cannot exclude the possibility that some did.

What I remember mostly was the devotion of staff and parents, mitigated by their occasional bouts of discouragement, at which time they started to blame one another for the child's lack of progress. I started to use contextual therapy and its main strategy—multidirected partiality—to decrease people's reliance on blame and to help parents and staff to understand each other better for the benefit of the child.

### USA, the Late 1980s: Adult Psychiatry

After years of practice in Switzerland, I moved to the States. That forced me to make a lot of adjustments in my practice of psychiatry. I was rather disoriented in my understanding of care delivery systems and I was surprised by the society's lack of responsibility for its weaker members. It took me a long time to fully apprehend the impact on therapy of the commercialization of mental health care delivery—a for-profit venture in which a service was heavily marketed to those who could afford it, with little consideration for those who could not. I soon noticed that patients were often kept in treatment for as long as insurance coverage lasted and quickly discharged around the time it was exhausted. A lot of providers did not seem to worry that their clients were losing their chance to receive outpatient therapy because they had reached the limit of their coverage while they were hospitalized. As long as they could charge their services to the insurance company before others would, they were satisfied. To that extent, when managed care arrived on the scene, it appeared to me initially to be a reasonable means of protecting these patients. This positive impression lasted only until I realized that it was not the patients' interest that managed care companies were protecting but the financial interests of the companies and their stockholders.

The lack of coordination of care was very disturbing to me. There was very little chance for coordination between inpatient care and outpatient services since each institution was functioning independently. In addition, in the few instances in which policies were put in place to secure some kind of coordination, the information was getting lost because of the steady turnover of therapists at each place.

I was impressed by one element of American psychiatry: the importance given to the participation of patients in their treatment. The extent of the patient's rights was dazzling. Patients were truly informed about their treatment and about their options, including their right to refuse treatment altogether. It was mindboggling to me that teenagers could have a right to decide on their mental heath care, as is the case in Pennsylvania, where therapists need to obtain the consent of their patients as soon as they reach the age of 14 years.

I was also very impressed by the knowledge of patients who were able to shop for the therapy they wanted. The fact that patients could openly blame their therapist for the lack of progress in their treatment was surprising to me. I was used to patients who did not dare to challenge their therapists. Furthermore, we had been taught to interpret such an attitude as a resistance to treatment, not as a valid complaint about the therapist' s possible lack of skills. This was a huge eye-opener.

On the other hand, the freedom of patients to challenge their therapists had a troubling consequence. American therapists could be sued by their patients for all sort of reasons and had to practice defensively. I was very much disturbed by this discovery. It was already bad enough that patients were often mistrustful and needed to be reassured, but what if the therapists had to mistrust their patients because of the risk of unfair accusations?

As far as therapeutic modalities were concerned, I did not experience a drastic change of practice when I moved from Switzerland to the United States. There were no surprises in the biological treatments offered to the adult population in this country. I already knew that the choice of approved medications was more limited and the recommended dosages higher. It was not unusual to find medications prescribed at ten times the dosage that would have been used in Switzerland. For instance, I was trained to prescribe Haldol (haloperidol) at the dosage of 2–8 mg per day, sometimes even less. I suddenly saw patients who were taking 20–60 mg of the same medication. How could we explain that Swiss patients could display a good improvement with so much less medications than their American counterparts? Maybe it was the cheese.

Family therapy was, of course, much more readily available here than in Europe, and I used to joke that there were more family therapists on my street than in all of Switzerland.

While psychoanalysis had been a very powerful movement in American psychiatry, its influence was clearly on the decline by the time I came to Philadelphia. This was the most visible in the treatment plans set for individual patients: "Measurable goals" was the leitmotiv. Behaviors needed to change no matter what their origin. If things did not work out as well as we expected, it was not because the symptoms were the results of deep-seated unconscious internal conflicts but because our reward system needed improvement. It was as if a drawer opened at the end of the nineteenth century by Freud, which contained all the discoveries of the psychoanalysts, was suddenly closed. We were back to the era of moral treatments: Like the proponents of rational therapy, we were expecting our patients to act as if all their behaviors were under the sole control of their reason. The frequent use of hypnosis rather than analytical therapy was another trend toward preanalytical treatments.

## USA, the 1980s: Child Psychiatry

The move away from psychodynamic interpretation toward behavioral treatments was most marked in child psychiatry, but the use of psychotropic medications for children was still modest. While stimulants were prescribed frequently, other psychotropic medications were used cautiously.

Although it was true that child psychiatrists were much more likely to prescribe psychotropic medications to children than their European counterparts, the prescribing guidelines had remained rather strict. Physicians would hesitate a long time before prescribing a medication not clearly endorsed for patients of that age, which limited pharmacological interventions to the very few that were approved for the use in children by the Food and Drug Administration.

## USA, 2002: Adult Psychiatry

The treatment of adults has not changed drastically in the last decade. As has been the case in child psychiatry, behavioral interventions have become more frequent and interpretation of behaviors based on a psychoanalytical model more rare. Short hospital stays and the use of psychotropic medications are the norm. The reimbursement of mental health services has been separated from the reimbursement of medical services. The access to care is strictly limited by managed care companies, sometimes to the point of ridiculing any therapeutic intervention, as was the case when companies started to ask to review the progress of some patients every 12 hours. What is missing the most is a true commitment by society to helping its sickest members.

## USA, 2002: Child Psychiatry

As far as child psychiatry goes, an interesting development has taken place: Children treated within the child welfare system may in fact receive better treatment than children treated in the private sector, since private insurance companies are much more likely to use drastic cost-containment strategies than are state-funded agencies, including state-funded managed care companies supervising the use of public funds for the treatment of the

mentally ill. In addition, charitable institutions are often comfortably en-
dowed and much more willing to absorb the cost of nonreimbursed treatments than are the for-profit organizations in which children of affluent
families are more likely to receive treatment.

A drastic change occurred in the last few years. Psychiatrists who in
the past would have refused to consider the use of a medication not specifically approved for a given age group are now willing to prescribe dozens
of drugs that are not approved by the Food and Drug Administration for
that age group.

This is based on the belief that if enough people do the same thing,
their prescribing habits will fall under the famous "standard of practice,"
which will counterbalance the lack of FDA endorsement. I am still very
disturbed by the contrast between this attitude and the continued conser-
vatism of my European colleagues. A "monkey see, monkey do" attitude
could become the justification for some questionable treatments. It is
frightening to realize that if too many people, encouraged by pharmaceutical companies, move toward a noncritical use of these medications, the few
cautious practitioners remaining could fall under the criticism of "not ad-
hering to standard practice." Fortunately, another requirement, the practice
of "prudent care," may help them to resist the current prescribing trends. I
do believe that some practice patterns are clearly not prudent, including
the trend to polypharmacy.

The movement of the recent years is not only leading to an increased
reliance on psychotropic medications for treatment of children, including
an absurd increase of the prescriptions written for stimulants, but there is
also a return to the use of old neuroleptics to address behavioral disturbances, despite recommendations that newer ones be used.

Children who have been neglected, abused, or exposed to violent cir-
cumstance are more likely to become enraged. Most of these children are
not psychotic, but they cannot trust! Early on, they have been hurt by the
people who were supposed to care for them. Staff become an easy target for
displaced anger. When young patients encounter the despair of untrained
and overworked staff, their rage can escalate to the point that these children
become a real danger to others. This is when they are likely to receive a seda-
tive cocktail of medications, which usually includes at least an old antipsychotic like Thorazine (chlorpromazine), sometime a second antipsychotic,
and a minor tranquilizer like Benadryl. Most of the time these potent medications are administered by injection. Surely no one believes that rage is the
result of a brain disorder that Thorazine could fix, yet most of the time staff
is helpless and often cannot find a better way of dealing with the situation.
Often the painful and intrusive nature of the procedure and the unpleasant
side effects of the medication reinforce the mistrust and the anger of the
youths, and their perception of a hostile and frightening world is confirmed.

As the situation develops, these clients are more and more likely to actually hurt staff and even to be arrested for assault. Once they are adjudicated delinquents, these youngsters need to leave the mental health facility for a specialized institution: In situations in Philadelphia with which I am familiar, these young patients are sent to specialized institutions in Texas, where they are expected to attend very strict behavioral programs. The staff has hope that the youths who leave will benefit from their new programs but often talk about them as if they already know that some will eventually hit death row after committing a heinous crime.

The state of affairs in child and adolescent psychiatry is sad. There is an urgent need for more commitment by society to reach these children before they get too discouraged to respond to our interventions.

## THE CURRENT STATE OF AFFAIRS
## IN PSYCHOPHARMACOLOGY

In this section I would like to share with the reader some of my impressions about the treatment options offered to today's psychiatrist. Nonmedical clinicians run the risk of misjudging the effectiveness of medication in both directions: exaggerated expectations or unwarranted skepticism. American psychiatrists may be misinformed about some facts well known to their European counterparts; they often believe that some drugs are new that in fact have been used for years in Europe. To that extent a short review based on my clinical experience and historical perspective may be of use to both groups of readers.

That all companies try to peddle their own products and convince people that theirs are the best is not disturbing to me at all. Business is business. What is more disturbing is the loss of independence of the academic institutions that are supposed to provide us with objective information. We need to form our opinions based on our own observations and using our own capacity to look at data with a critical eye. I want also to remind the reader that I do not aim at the discussion of all the possible drugs available on the American market, but at the discussion of some examples of well-known drugs in each group.

Given the fact that most readers may be unfamiliar with the chemical or generic name of these medications I will discuss medications using their brand names along with their generic names.

### Antipsychotics

While progress has been made in the treatment of schizophrenia, we are far from having reached the point at which we could offer a cure for this condition, despite the 50 years or so that have passed since the very first neu-

roleptic, Largactil (chlorpromazine), came into use. Conventional neuroleptics like Largactil and its derivatives have been effective in decreasing
aggression and hallucinations as well as delusions, but they have been disappointing in the treatment of the "negative" symptoms of schizophrenia,
apathy and social withdrawal.

In recent years psychiatrists have increasingly prescribed atypical
antipsychotics, which are allegedly more effective in treating negative
symptoms and less likely to cause tardive dyskinesia, an irreversible
damage to the nervous system resulting in characteristic abnormal movements. Only one point has been forgotten: atypical neuroleptics were
known already in the 1960s. Under the name Leponex, Clozaril (clozap-
ine) was already used in Europe at least twenty years before it became
known in America. At first it was prescribed to patients according to the
simple prescribing preferences of their psychiatrist, not to the severity of
the patient's condition. At the end of the 1970s, Leponex was removed
from the market in connection with a number of deaths caused by agranulocytosis, a condition in which the body stops producing white blood cells
and stops fighting infections. Most patients did not experience any set-
backs from a change to a conventional medication, but some patients who
had been greatly helped by this medication never regained their prior level
of functioning once they had to switch back. This discovery led to insight
into the uniqueness of this medication.

What American psychiatrists seem to ignore is the tremendous effort of
the Swiss pharmaceutical industry to replace Leponex by a comparable but
safer product. Several atypical antipsychotics were used already in the seventies, for instance, Entumin (not known in the United States), but none
proved as successful as Leponex in reducing the negative symptoms of
schizophrenia.

Since no medication could match it, Leponex, under the new name
of Clozaril, was reintroduced on the market in the early 1980s with a lot
of restrictions and stringent monitoring requirement to prevent fatalities.
Since then, there have been several new attempts to produce similar
but less dangerous drugs. Several of them are now among the most prescribed psychiatric drugs, for instance the frequently used Risperdal
(risperidone).

The pattern remains the same: a great hope followed by disappoint-
ment. These newer medications are less likely to induce tardive dyskinesia.
Nonetheless, they lack the neuroleptic effect sometimes useful for severely
agitated and extremely aggressive patients and they don't quite match
Clozaril for effectiveness in treating negative symptoms.

Besides that, though these medications are much less dangerous than
Clozaril, they can have substantial side effects of their own, including, for
some, the risk of weight gain and an increased risk of diabetes. In conclu-

sion, despite over 40 years of trials on two continents, the ideal drug for the treatment of schizophrenia has yet to be found.

Furthermore, it is now clear that some of the debilitating factors of this illness may not lie in the presence of hallucinations or social withdrawal, but in the presence of cognitive disorders. Kraepelin coined the term *dementia precox* to describe schizophrenia and was criticized for it (Zylboorg, 1941). He may come back into fashion. Recently, researchers have started to use anticholinesterase inhibitors to treat schizophrenia, which is the type of medications used to treat Alzheimer's dementia.

### Antidepressants

The picture is somewhat better when it come to the treatment of depression. We do have medications that are both safe and effective. The early medications, the tricyclic antidepressants, which were developed mostly in the 1960s, were effective. Still, they had significant side effects and were potentially dangerous. Taken in overdose, these medications lead to cardiac arrhythmia and death. How could any psychiatrist feel comfortable prescribing a medication that suicidal patients can use to kill themselves? For that reason, depressed patients needing medication were often hospitalized until the depression had improved to the point that the risk of suicide was no longer a concern.

The discovery of the newer antidepressants, mostly the so-called selective serotonin reuptake inhibitors, SSRI-antidepressants, has represented true progress. These medications are generally safe, even in the hands of suicidal patients, and their use has decreased the pressure to hospitalize them. For most, they have only minimal side effects, and they are generally rather effective. Since patients tolerate these medications better, they are more willing to be treated before they get so sick that they have no choice.

This has led to the interesting observation that patients did not improve simply in the area of depression but that they described a change in their general behaviors. These medications do not only improve depression; they make people less irritable, possibly less aggressive. In short, they appear to affect some of the patients' characteristic behaviors and change the way they react to world, which has led to the belief that they could in fact treat not just the depression but the personality itself (Kramer, 1993).

The story of the treatment of bipolar disorders is to a great extent a success story, too. Lithium can be very helpful in stopping and preventing manic episodes and in decreasing the risk of suicide, but, unfortunately, lithium can reach toxic levels very easily. "Will lithium prevent a death or cause one?" is the question that comes to the mind of any physician who treats suicidal patients. Furthermore, the long-term use of lithium can lead to serious kidney problems.

While treating this disorder entails risks, not treating it is much worse. We should remember that before the use of lithium, the course of the disease was such that people got worse with age and a great number of them died either of suicide or of dangerous behaviors and even exhaustion during manic episodes. Even with state-of-the-art treatment, the risk of death from the disease is still one of the highest of any mental illness, alongside schizophrenia.

Other mood stabilizers are less dangerous than lithium but may be less potent. They come from the class of anticonvulsants and are more and more frequently prescribed. The most common are Depakote (valprolic acid) and Tegretol (carbamazepine). While they are less likely to lead to fatalities if misused, these two medications also have serious potential side effects, including a risk of hepatic failure for Depakote and agranulocytosis for Tegretol. In addition, like lithium, these medications require monitoring of blood levels.

### Treatment of Children

The use of psychotropic medications for children has changed rapidly. More and more children are treated with the same medications given to adults while the data about the long-term safety of these medications on the developing brain are still lacking. One of the most common pharmacological interventions in that age group is the use of stimulants.

These medications can be quite successful for the treatment of decreased attention, increased impulsivity, and poor concentration. On the other hand, these medications are largely overused and prescribed too soon, without an attempt to understand all underlying factors that could lead to disruptive behaviors. They can lead to side effects like lack of appetite and insomnia, and their prescription needs to be closely monitored to avoid abuse, not so much by young patients as by unscrupulous caregivers.

There is no recognized pharmacological intervention for the treatment of conduct disorder, but aggressive and antisocial youths are very likely to receive medication anyway. More and more often, neuroleptics are prescribed for agitated and aggressive youths, which is in contradiction with guidelines that recommend the use of this kind of medication only for people suffering from psychosis.

### Treatment of the Elderly

The elderly population now has the benefit of new pharmacological intervention, the use of anticholinesterase inhibitors, which seem to slow down symptoms of dementia.

## GIVING, A HIDDEN THERAPEUTIC RESOURCE

### Mr. G.

Mr. G. was diagnosed with schizophrenia in his twenties and lived in a state hospital for a good part of his life, not doing too much in a unit for chronic patients who were receiving custodial care. Even though his treatment history could not be retrieved, it seems that he had received rather adequate treatment with standard typical antipsychotics over the years.

When he reached his fifties, a big change occurred in his life: He was transferred to a much smaller hospital where he was admitted as a " new patient." He was described as a man who had many residual symptoms of schizophrenia, and who had no social skills, but who was not actively hallucinating. While staff believed that he was still delusional, he was rather careful not to discuss his thoughts with others, which showed that he was capable of a certain sense of reality.

While he was expected to attend individual and group therapy, no one had ever succeeded in engaging him in either. While the unit had a therapist trained in family therapy, he was not offered family therapy because he had no known family. No one would come to visit him, and, to the knowledge of staff, no one was calling him on the phone. He hated individual therapy almost as much as the young residents who were assigned to his case: They did not know what to discuss with him, and he was unable to tolerate spending any time with someone without feeling threatened. During groups, he was generally pacing outside of the circle of patients, not paying attention to anything.

He was very disabled and no one expected that he could ever leave the hospital to live on his own, but with a lot of effort, staff finally managed to persuade him to attend a sheltered workshop. His job was very simple: ordering crayons in boxes according to colors. He liked the opportunity to leave the hospital for a few hours every day and to have a pretext for missing therapy sessions.

On and off he had to miss work because he had an episode of more active psychosis. On such occasions he became more paranoid and could not tolerate his boss anymore. At times these episodes were treated with an increased dose of, or a change in, medication, at times not. No one could identify triggers to those periods and no one could explain why he would suddenly recover and return to his prior level of functioning. In any event, some elements never changed: his social withdrawal, poor hygiene, and weird way of dressing. Nurses were fighting with him daily to get him to shave and to wear his underwear inside his trousers rather than over his shirt and stretched to his shoulders. Every one in the hospital knew him for this weird habit.

One day, to everyone's surprise, he had shaved and was wearing a nice suit and no underwear was visible. A fancy tie graced his shirt. He was immediately asked about the change: "What is happening Mr. G.?" He replied, "What? I am going to visit my brother!" Indeed, we discovered that he had a brother. He had finally approached his social worker with just enough information to be granted permission to leave the hospital for the day and visit him.

### Mrs. R.

Mrs. R. was a patient in the same hospital as Mr. G. She was also admitted for schizophrenia, and also treated with classical antipsychotics. She presented very differently. A neat person always dressed in elegant outfits, she was otherwise very actively psychotic. She was hearing voices, kept up long dialogues with invisible partners, and was unable to function socially.

She refused to attend the sheltered workshop, refused to attend any treatments, whether individual or group therapy. She had no family and no visitors, but she liked to watch people. Instead of attending the program's activities, she would spend hours in the lobby of the hospital where she was often seen making circles with the smoke of her cigar. Everyone knew her and usually greeted her with a "hello, Mrs. R.," but she would not respond.

One morning, one of the physicians arrived at work in a very distressed mood following some bad news. The inattentive receptionist greeted the doctor with a cheerful "Hi, Doc." Mrs. R., who was sitting in the lobby talking to her imaginary partners, suddenly got up and placed herself behind the doctor, who was waiting for the elevator. She whispered: "Doctor, you should go home! Don't work if you feel that bad!" As soon as she finished her sentence, she went back to her seat.

### Anna

Anna, a teenager who had lost her parents early, had been raised by an older sister but had great difficulties in accepting that her sister could marry. From the time of the sister's marriage, things went downhill, and soon Anna had to be placed in foster care. She continued to be very demanding and eventually was asked to leave. She was placed with a third family and soon needed hospitalization for severe mood swings and for suicidal ideation. She started also to present with problems with food intake. Her weight fluctuated dramatically; at times she was almost emaciated, and at times she experienced rapid weight increase. Occasionally, she would self-mutilate.

Given the severity of her symptoms, she was admitted to a residential treatment program in which she received intensive individual therapy, and therapy with her sister and with her foster mother. She was also following a strict behavioral program. In addition, she had been placed on a variety of medications to stabilize her mood. Eventually one medication started to appear somewhat better for her than the others and she started to make some improvement.

Nonetheless she remained enormously demanding of staff attention. It was rare that a full week would go by without an incident that would require a crisis intervention. Her staff had great concerns about letting her leave the campus but eventually agreed that she could attend some activities organized by the program's chaplain. Residents were invited to participate under supervision in some charitable activities such as working in a kitchen for homeless people, visiting elderly people in a nursing home, or taking toys to homeless children.

Residents who wanted to participate in these activities had to demonstrate stability and earn the required behavioral point for the week, which required that they not act out. Anna managed to attend one of these activities almost by chance, having for once maintained an appropriate behavior for one week, but soon this became one of her greatest motivators: She wanted to do well so that she could go out and help others. As she improved, she could make new plans for her life and eventually was ready to leave the program. At the time of leaving, she was asked to describe what had helped her the most. Without any hesitation, she replied: "The chaplain and learning that I could not spent the rest of my life feeling miserable because I could not receive all that I wanted: I needed to start giving."

## What Can We Learn?

Three patients on two continents share a similar reality: they have spent long periods in hospitals, received many treatments, and taken many medications. Each of them was cut off from an ordinary life. To many, they would appear to be hopeless cases, and in many ways they were. After all, despite years of treatment, two of these patients were still extremely disturbed and unable to function outside of an institution. The other was not able to function without a lot of support and did not believe that she could eventually return to a normal life.

They were severely ill patients suffering from a range of conditions—schizophrenia, mood disorders, and personality disorders. One thing is sure: medication may have helped them not to get worse, but it did not cure any of them.

On the other hand how can one say that a man who cares to dress up for a brother is just a hopeless schizophrenic? How can one say of a woman who is more sensitive to the suffering of another human being than the staff around her that she has no capacity for reality testing? Is the young woman of our story a "demanding borderline" or a generous contributor to society?

We need to realize that our patients, even the sickest ones, can contribute in a meaningful manner to relationships and have a need to give as much as they need to receive. If we can learn that, we can mobilize therapeutic resources that neither psychopharmacologists nor classical family therapists are familiar with: the resource of receiving through giving.

## FROM PSYCHIATRY TO CONTEXTUAL THERAPY

### The Beginnings of Psychiatry

People interested in the history of psychiatry might find the excellent book *A History of Medical Psychology* by G. Zilboorg (1941) useful. The first psychiatrists were men who were influenced by the ideas of their time. For instance, a sense of social responsibility inspired by the Quaker movement played a definite role in the development of early American psychiatry. The first private psychiatric hospital in the United States, Friends Hospital in Philadelphia, was founded by the Quakers in the early 1800s. An early French psychiatrist, Philippe Pinel, was inspired by a sense of justice and protection of human rights when he asked for the permission to release the mentally ill from their chains during the French revolution. The goal of these early psychiatrists was more to better the fate of the mentally ill than to cure them. They were fighting for them against ignorance, ostracism, and at times actual cruelty. They were simply advocating for their humane treatment. If any attempt was made to influence the course of the disease, it was usually limited to the use of drastic physical means, like a spinning chair. The idea was that if patients could spin long enough to become unconscious, their brains could be shaken back into shape.

During the nineteenth century custodial care of patients with psychosis was the norm. Most of the nineteenth century psychiatry was characterized by a tremendous effort at describing psychosis in great detail. But even at the onset of the twentieth century, psychiatrists had difficulty in envisioning that psychotic patients could be cured, and custodial care was still the norm.

### The Beginnings of Psychotherapy

The earliest forms of psychotherapy relied either on hypnosis and suggestion or, conversely, on rationalization. Rational treatments, called also moral treatment or medical moralization, relied on the idea that patients could be helped to abandon symptomatic behaviors by reasoning with them. While these approaches led to the development of cognitive therapies, they did not produce any significant results in the treatment of psychotic patients. The hope that delusional patients could be helped to abandon their distorted views by rationalizing with them was short-lived.

During the same period, Freud had become interested in trying to understand the origin of unusual neurological deficits that could not be correlated with any objective organic lesions. It was his genius to discover that they had their origin in the psychology of the patient and could be reversed by psychological methods.

Based on his successes, Freud moved on to the exploration of the psychological origin of psychiatric rather than neurological symptoms. He turned his exploration to the psychological origin of phobias, compulsions, and hallucinations. As blindness or the paralysis of an arm did not originate in the damage to a nerve but in the psychology of the patient, phobias or compulsions or psychotic symptoms did not originate in the dysfunction of a brain. These symptoms were the result of a compromise between contradictory forces in the psyche of the person. From then on psychoanalysis developed into the vast field that we know today. Freud's very genius in discovering the nonorganic nature of symptoms has been at the root of one of the biggest challenges met by today's psychoanalysis. If an entire theory is based on the idea that observed symptoms do not have an organic base, how can this theory accommodate psychopharmacological interventions based on the opposite assumption, the organic base of the same symptoms?

Furthermore, it is possible that the psychoanalytical movement may have in fact contributed to a certain delay in exploring biological avenues to help patients with psychosis and other severe mental disorders. By the 1950s it was difficult to find a chairman of psychiatry who was not an analyst. Looking for brain disorders as an explanation for psychiatric symptoms would have forced them to move away from the discovery so central to the analytical movement—the psychogenic origin of psychiatric symptoms.

## The Early Days of Family Therapy

A look at the background of the pioneers of family therapy in the 1950s reveals that most of them were psychiatrists by training. For that reason they should have been well equipped to compare the results of family therapy with the results of psychopharmacological interventions, but in fact they were not in a position to do so, and for a good reason. The use of psychotropic medications and the array of medication available was so limited that there was no reason to try to compare the two kind of treatments.

The majority of the founders of the family therapy movement, if they were not fully trained analysts, had been exposed to the theories developed by Freud. While each of these pioneers may have had a different rationale for doing so, they all ended up breaking one of the fundamental rules of psychoanalysis. Instead of maintaining the absolute confidentiality of analysis, they were interested in seeing patients with their relatives. By doing so they took the risk of entering an area that was completely uncharted, and they could not turn back to analysis for help.

Soon family therapists needed new tools and turned to general systems theory when they realized that behaviors, besides being psychogenically determined as described by analysis, were also determined by supra-individual forces. They started to describe health and pathology in systemic terms and to develop interventions accordingly. Soon a very rich literature developed to describe these new phenomenon and to design treatment strategies (Wynn, 1982).

Some started to believe that so-called mental illnesses were in fact manifestations of these supra-individual determinants and that the main issue in therapy was to fight the forces of homeostasis. They discovered that any change in one individual was counterbalanced by a pressure to return to the previous state of functioning. Early family therapists went further to discover that symptomatic behaviors could actually meet the need of family members for unchanged relationships. Symptoms were understood as a compromise between centrifugal forces, like the striving for autonomy, and centripetal forces, like the striving for togetherness and undifferentiation. Family members needed to be helped to accept changes and face losses. This was a common point of understanding among the early family therapists; from then on, each of them developed a particular style of achieving this goal. In any event, patients were seen as people who needed to be liberated much more than healed. For a good review of the field, the reader is referred to *The Handbook of Family Therapy* edited by A. Gurman and D. Kniskern (1991), which remains to date one of the most extensive sources of information about the family therapy movement and the various schools of family therapy that have developed over time.

### Family Therapy and Pharmacotherapy

It is easy to see why most family therapists have trouble to this day in addressing the issue of pharmacotherapy for the treatment of mental illnesses: They share with the analysts the belief that mental illnesses are not actual brain diseases. While the analysts saw symptoms as the result of unresolved internal conflicts, the family therapists saw them as the result of contradictory forces: the thrust toward autonomy on the one hand and the pull of homeostatic forces on the other. For different reasons neither group has been well prepared to integrate biological causalities into their respective models of therapy.

I have by now demonstrated that we need to be able to recognize the actual limits of psychopharmacological interventions. We need also to recognize the arrogance of those family therapists who have tried to explain everything by circular causality. The field of family therapy has paid a big price for it, not just in a loss of credibility in the eyes of the scientific community, but in the resentment of many parents because they feel blamed unfairly for the mental illnesses of their offspring (Ducommun-Nagy, 1999).

## CONTEXTUAL THERAPY

### From Biochemistry to a Theory of Relationships

Unique among the pioneers of family therapy, Ivan Boszormenyi-Nagy, founder of contextual therapy, can claim actual training in biochemistry, which he obtained at the University of Budapest in the late 1940s. This was part of his effort as a young psychiatrist to find the etiology of schizophrenia. Eventually he spent six years doing biochemical research on the correlations between mental illnesses and intracellular metabolism (Boszormenyi-Nagy, 1958/1987). He later returned to clinical research and became one of the founders of family therapy and the originator of contextual therapy. His interest in the biological determinants of mental illnesses is reflected in an approach to family therapy that leaves a place for biological hypotheses in the etiology of mental illnesses, hence for the possibility that medications can be useful to treat them.

Contextual therapists may not be trained as psychopharmacologists if their professional background lies outside of the field of psychiatry, but their model of therapy leaves a place for psychopharmacological interventions. Contextual therapists can afford to recommend the use of psychotropic medication during the course of family therapy without having to fear inconsistency. Instead, the recommendation of a combined intervention can be the reflection of clinical maturity. Contextual therapists can accept that there are multiple determinants that can account for any observed symptom or any observed behavior and more than one therapeutic resource to rely on.

### A Multidimensional View of Relationships

Not all clinicians are ready to recognize and work with a synthesis of the biological determinants discussed by the neurobiologists and the psychopharmacologists, the psychological determinants described by the psychoanalysts and the cognitive therapists as well as the supra-individual, systemic determinants described by the classical family therapists. Even fewer clinicians recognize the role played by another factor that seems to be at the source of our very humanness: our capacity for fair giving and our expectation of a fair return. This aspect of relationships is at the core of the so-called dimension of relational ethics described by Ivan Boszor-menyi-Nagy in his main books (Boszormenyi-Nagy & Spark, 1973/1984, Boszormenyi-Nagy & Krasner, 1986; Boszormenyi-Nagy, 1987).

Unlike feedback mechanisms that affect each of the individuals involved in the interaction in a similar ways, the balance of giving and receiving, the level of obligation or entitlement that one person has accrued vis-à-vis the other, is unique to that relationship. As givers, we expect fair returns, and as receivers we know that we have incurred obligations that we need to meet if we want to secure the long-term viability of our relationships.

### Giving and Receiving

The main clinical conviction of contextual therapy stems from the observation that even the sickest of our patients, as described in the few examples earlier on, have not lost a capacity to care about others and try to give to others, even if they can do so only in a limited fashion due to their illness.

Helping patients to find an avenue for fair giving may lead to at least as much clinical improvement as helping them in claiming their due. While most therapists understand that deprivations can lead to faulty emotional development and pathology, it appears to contextual therapists that patients who are blocked from giving to others may suffer even more.

Patients with conduct disorders and antisocial personality disorders have been considered incapable of caring or giving. We should not infer from our perception that since they are incapable of caring, they do not suffer from being blocked in their capacity to give. We tend to describe these patients as people who behave as "entitled." They are out to take what does not belong to them and punish innocent people for not meeting their immediate needs.

This we can see easily, but what we fail to see is that often they are hurt givers. Most of the time, these patients have in fact turned against society after having experienced a rejection in their attempt to give to others in the earlier part of their lives. As they start to turn their resentment toward others, or turn toward others to claim compensation for past hurts, they incur a new round of rejections, which feeds into their conviction that the world is an unfair place and that they can only get what they can grab.

In being blocked from giving to others, they are hurt as much as the patients with psychosis or depression. By offering our consideration to them as hurt givers, we introduce the possibility that they might want to reengage in the constructive process of giving, which will eventually lead to some benefits for them and the people around them.

Our most disturbed patients, like people with schizophrenia or severe mood disorders, may be blocked in giving because of their thought disturbances, their lack of social skill, apathy or depression, but they should nonetheless be addressed as people who can benefit from giving.

## Self-Delineation and Self-Validation

In each of the case examples cited, one of the main issues at stake was the continuation of the self, and the included fear of the dissolution of this continuity, either because of the loosening of thought processes, as with the first two patients, or because of self-destructive urges, as with the third young woman. In having an opportunity to give to others, they were able to regain a self-definition and a self-worth, temporarily for the first two patients and more permanently for the third one.

We need to remember that for many patients who are socially isolated by their disease and also mistrustful of others to the point of being unable to relate with anyone, voices—even harsh ones—can be less distressing than the silence resulting from a successful treatment with antipsychotics. On a few occasions I have seen patients who had been suffering from severe auditory hallucinations become abruptly suicidal when an antipsychotic turned out to be effective in quelling the voices.

In those cases, patients were able to describe the experience not as an improvement but as of an abrupt loss of meaning, a threat of annihilation. Being able to give can be the only hope of emotional and even physical survival, the only path toward relevance. This holds true for clients with severe depression as well.

## Autonomy and Dependence

As contextual therapists we learn that we depend on others not just to meet our material and emotional needs, but for our very existence as separate selves. For contextual therapists the notion of autonomy is a paradox: "I need you to define me as separate from you. If this is true, you are in fact part of me because without you I could not exist as me." This notion is at the core of Boszormenyi-Nagy's dialectic view of relationships (Boszormenyi-Nagy, 1958/1987). Not only do we need others to meet our emotional needs, but our very existence as selves depends on the existence of others. In giving, I recognize the other as different from me, that is, I can delineate myself, and at the same time, I earn a merit, that is, my self-worth increases. Our dependence on others for our very existence as selves constitutes a separate aspect of relationships not fully accounted for by any of the other dimensions of relating, defined by Boszormenyi-Nagy for the first time in 2000 as the "ontic" dimension of relationships (Ducommun-Nagy, 2002).

## CONCLUSIONS

In the discussion of the place of family therapy in today's world, we have been able to see that neither classical family therapy nor psychopharmacology has been able to give a complete answer for the etiology of major mental illnesses. Nonetheless, both have contributed to improving our understanding of these conditions.

On the whole, we are like a team of engineers trying to build a bridge over a big valley. We know where the road should start—the genes—and where it should go—the behaviors, but we do not know yet if we will ever manage to finish the bridge. For now, the best we can do is to build as many pillars as we can—our knowledge of subjects as diverse as neurobiology, endocrinology, pharmacology, cognitive development, psychoanalysis, systems theories, anthropology, and relational ethics, to name a few. Our hope is that one day we will have been able to build enough pillars and that each will be high enough to carry that road. In the meantime, we need to do our best to help our patients lead as fulfilling lives as possible, no matter whether we can actually cure their illnesses.

If it is true that giving can protect any of us, including our most vulnerable patients, from the dread of meaninglessness and annihilation, then giving is possibly one of the most potent medicines that we can offer. Psychotropic medications like antidepressants and antipsychotics can help our patients to regain an optimistic view of reality, a better reality testing, but their self-worth as human beings will continue to depend on their capacity to risk giving and on the capacity of the people around them to accept receiving.

Our job as therapists is to improve our understanding of all the elements that can lead to blocked giving and to improve our clinical skills so that not only our patients but anyone in their families can learn the same truth: Giving is an act under our control, receiving is only a hope. We may be entitled to compensation for past injustices, but we may never receive it, whereas we know that we can gain a strong inner reward from our capacity to give generously.

\* \* \*

I want to express my gratitude to my husband Ivan Boszormenyi-Nagy for his encouragements and comments about the manuscripts. I also want to thank Gunter David, MFT, for his editorial suggestions.

## REFERENCES

Akpaffoing, M. J., Lecca, P., Jackson, D. M., & Ruiz, P. (2001). The role of dopaminergic and serotoninergic systems in the treatment of schizophrenia. *Psychline*, (3) 4.

American Psychiatric Association. (1994). *Diagnostic and statistical manual of mental disorders* (4th ed.). Washington DC: American Psychiatric Association.

Boszormenyi-Nagy, I. (1985). A theory of relationships: Experience and transactions. In Boszormenyi-Nagy, I., & Framo J. (Eds.). *Intensive family psychotherapy.* New York: Brunner/Mazel (original work published 1965).

Boszormenyi-Nagy, I. (1987). *Foundations of contextual therapy.* New York: Brunner/Mazel (original work published 1958).

Boszormenyi-Nagy, I., & Krasner B. (1986). *Between give and take: Clinical guide to contextual therapy.* New York: Brunner/Mazel.

Boszormenyi-Nagy, I., & Spark, G. (1984). *Invisible loyalties.* New York: Brunner/Mazel (original work published 1973).

Ducommun, C. (1984). Paul Dubois 1948–1918, Sa place dans l'histoire de la psychotherapie, Gesnerus 41, *Zeitschrift de Schweizerichen Gesellshaft für Geschichte de Medizin und Naturwissenschaften* [Paul Dubois, 1848–1918, his place in the history of psychotherapy].

Ducommun-Nagy, C. (1999). Contextual therapy. In Lawson, D. & Prevatt, F. (eds.), *Case book in family therapy,* Belmont, CA: Brooks/Cole and Wadsworth.

Ducommun-Nagy, C. (2002). Contextual therapy. In Kaslow, F. *Comprehensive handbook of psychotherapy* (Vol. 3). New York: Wiley.

Gurman, A. S., Kniskern, D. P. (1991). *Handbook of family therapy* (Vol. 2). New York: Bruner/Mazel.

Kramer, P. (1993). *Listening to Prozac: A psychiatrist explores antidepressants, drugs, and the remaking of the self.* New York: Viking/Penguin.

Wynne, L. (with Gurman, A., Nagy, I., and Ravich, R.) (1982). The family and marital therapies. In Lewis, J.M. and Usdin, G (eds.) *Treatment planning in psychiatry.* Washington D.C.: American Psychiatric Association.

Zilboorg, G. (1941). *A history of medical psychology.* New York: Norton. Reprint 1967.

Chapter 7

# Medicating the Ghost in the Machine

Paul Schaefer, MD

*"Well, it's no use your talking about waking him," said Tweedledum, "when you're only one of the things in his dream. You know very well you're not real."*

*"I am real!" said Alice, and began to cry.*

*"You won't make yourself a bit realler by crying," Tweedledee remarked: "there's nothing to cry about."*

*"If I wasn't real," Alice said—half-laughing through her tears, it all seemed so ridiculous—"I shouldn't be able to cry."*

*"I hope you don't suppose those are real tears?" Tweedledum interrupted in a tone of great contempt.*

Lewis Carroll, *Alice's Adventures in Wonderland*

## INTRODUCTION

Since the first observation of microscopic life in the mid-1600s, there has been a tension in the development of biology between two streams of thought sometimes called vitalism and reductionism.

Vitalism maintained that life itself could never be reduced to chemistry and physics.[1] It maintained that there was a "vital essence" that explained manifestations of life for which the sciences couldn't account. Reductionism insisted that the processes of biology were all dependent on physical phenomena that eventually could be learned and studied through the sciences. Neither one of them could explain life in its fullness. Or explain why a living thing dies at a particular moment.

Why was the microscope important?

The first notable instance of how lenses affect what we see was just after they were significantly improved by Dutch opticians in the 1600s, with the development of technology that allowed precision shaping and polishing of glass sufficiently pure to curve light with a resultant visible image.

The Italian Galileo was the first to get into trouble. In 1609 he used the telescope invented by Dutch opticians the year before to observe the night sky. He was the first to observe the moons of Jupiter. Although that seems of little note today, when we have sent space probes beyond the reach of Jupiter, in the 1600s it was big news. He was the first to note that Copernicus was not just right in theory, but in fact. The earth was not the center of the universe. And Jupiter, which was one of the planets that supposedly was orbiting the earth, had satellite moons of its own. These moons were orbiting not Earth, but Jupiter itself.[2]

The next notable use of the highly polished lens was by a Dutchman by the name of Leeuwenhoek (Britannica 2002). He used lenses differently in order to be able to see the minuscule. He was the first to describe microscopic organisms, such as bacteria and protozoa. He worked to dispel the notion of the spontaneous generation of life, which was the prevalent belief about how certain life-forms arose, such as weevils in wheat granaries.[3]

Science grows by building on the work of others. It is a combination of great records of observation, combined with attempts to link the observations in a meaningful schema. Post-Renaissance science has insisted on linking the observations primarily in mathematical schemata. Observation is improved by improving the instruments with which we observe. Both the microscope and the telescope have greatly expanded our realm of observation.

The phrase "the ghost in the machine" was coined by the British philosopher Gilbert Ryle in 1949,[4] as a criticism of the Cartesian split between the mind and the body. He may have been influenced in his phraseology by German romantic novelist E. T. A. Hoffmann, who in 1817 wrote "The Sandman," a story about a man's uncanny love-attraction to what was then called an automaton, meaning an animated machine.[5]

Since then the phrase has acquired multiple meanings. It can describe one's feeling on first seeing an animated machine and not knowing what makes it do the wonderful things it does. The explanation is that there seems to be a ghost in the machine, because the workings are not known. Tribal peoples who have never seen a television might use this metaphor, if they were told that the television was just a machine.

The explanatory principle of the "ghost in the machine" also describes the tension between vitalism and reductionism: we don't know enough of the workings of the biology of humans to explain the wonderful things they do, so they must be caused by a ghost in the machine. Some call it the soul.

Ghost and machine refer to different levels of abstraction. Each offers different explanatory advantages. Neither is adequate to describe the fullness of human life. But both are important. The ghost notion is important because it describes a higher level of abstraction than current science can reach. The machine notion is important because some of our current science can explain certain qualities of life purely from physical principles.

In the world of medicine, particularly in psychiatry, therapeutic interventions are sometimes based on the ghost metaphor, sometimes on the machine metaphor. Both can be effective, if integrated with the biggest metaphor, which is the one where symbol meets reality between living human beings.

Since Hoffmann wrote his story of the animated machine, our notion of science has expanded to include multiple levels of dimension, or system levels of the sciences.

Physics is the lowest level, meaning it has primary importance. Physics deals with fundamental forces and elementary particles. It also works in a statistical way with large populations of particles, and it applies to the motion a body of any size. Chemistry deals with things bigger than elementary particles: atoms and molecules and single charged particles and their interactions. Biology deals with much, much larger than elementary-particle-sized things: meaningfully organized chemical aggregates and the complex interactions that occur between and among them in living things. Social science deals with the interactions of aggregates of one particularly powerful biological organism: homo sapiens.

At each level, complexity increases.

The more complex sciences (including family therapy theory) take longer to establish their validity and to make their important discoveries. This is because they are built on the findings of sciences at lower levels of complexity, which also take a long time to develop. It was not until the end of the nineteenth century that Michelson and Morley demonstrated that the speed of light is the same for all observers, independent of their own velocity. And that realization was based on experimental observation that previously was not possible, because technology had not yet advanced enough to allow such precise measurement, before 1897, when Michelson and Morley established the fact that allowed Einstein to develop the equations of special relativity in 1905.[6]

The lower levels of complexity, those that have equations to map their existence, describe the machine. The higher levels of complexity, those that have only metaphor to map their existence, describe the ghost. The social sciences, and family therapy in particular, exist mostly in the realm of the ghost.

The constructivist family therapy literature that cites how "lenses" affect what we see draws on this history of science. It does this even as new instruments for expanding human perception continue to be developed. In the last decade of the twentieth century instruments were developed that are beginning to enable us to visualize the brain thinking.

With new noninvasive brain-imaging techniques, we have begun to be able to watch the brain think and correlate it to things we would call mind, or ghost. Brain scans have shown the changes that occur in certain kinds of therapy, and how these brain changes are similar to those caused by medication.[7] Others have shown how the brains of patients change as they hallucinate.[8] Still other scans have shown how subjects' brains change when they free-associate.[9]

We are now at the beginning of a period of discovery of the interface between the ghost and the machine. But that is not the end of the story. There is a twist in the plot.

## CURRENT SITUATION

A 13-year-old African-American girl is discharged back to her family after her second stay in a psychiatric hospital. This time she has stayed six weeks. She was placed on five different psychotropic medications sequentially over that time. She was discharged on only three of them. Changes were made too quickly, long before the chemical actions of any of the medications on her brain had adequate time to show the fullness of their effects.

Her discharge diagnoses were attention deficit disorder and psychotic depression.

Considering those two diagnoses alone, a humorously inclined reader might guess that she would have said to her psychiatrist: "Doc, I need a stimulant, because I can't pay enough attention to my hallucinations!"

A 12-year-old African-American boy is discharged after five days in the psychiatric unit on several psychotropics, one of which is an antipsychotic, and his diagnosis is psychosis not otherwise specified.

In each case the length of the child's stay in the hospital was determined by an ongoing "dialogue" with the insurance company. The first case was far longer than the norm. The second was about average for the situation. They illustrate how the insurance industry has developed a shared economic interest with the pharmaceutical companies: both make more profits when more people are on more medications, up to a certain limit.

For the pharmaceutical companies, the shared benefit is from increased sales. For the insurance companies, it is serendipity. They benefit from the fact that the medications have few enough side effects that they can be used in larger populations than was possible with the earlier psychotropics—and from the fact that these new medications have powerful behavioral effects.

Unfortunately, neither the ghost nor the machine is being respected in this way of dealing with patients. The medications are not being used appropriately even if the machine is the only way of viewing patients, and the social context is being abjectly neglected, so there is little realm for the ghost.

Ironically, these developments in the insurance and pharmaceutical industries were preceded and to some extent catalyzed by a development in organized psychiatry: the decision by the APA in 1980 to adopt a purely phenomenological diagnostic manual (*DSM-III*) that would supposedly be "atheoretical," and thus would help advance research by specifying categories more exactly, and it would help clinical practice, because it could be used across disciplines by practitioners of various theoretical models.

*DSM-III* united pharmaceutical and insurance companies far more than it united clinicians.

The reason *DSM-III* did not unite clinicians is because its language was less rich than each of the theoretical languages in which the clinicians had been trained and had experience. Those theoretical languages are all hyperdimensional, meaning there are more than three dimensions, and their number is constantly capable of expansion. But the dimensions they measured were not the same as those that the *DSM-III* measures.

Because the *DSM* system is only phenomenological, it represents neither the ghost nor the machine. It is based on an inadequate attempt to codify the ghost. It takes very little notice of the social context, relegating all social things to the fourth axis. It has no way of talking about the unconsious fantasies ghosts have of one another. Nor does it describe the fantastic dances social systems do with one another. And we all know that ghosts *do* dance.

The chief usefulness of the *DSM-IV* clinically is for psychiatrists who prescribe psychotropic medications. For those clinicians, the *DSM* system is essential. The medications have all been studied based exclusively on *DSM* system categorization. So those are the situations in which the medications must be applied. Even so-called off-label applications of the medications are based on the *DSM*.

The use of the *DSM* rigorously in a situation of adequate trust that allows people to tell their hyperdimensional stories to the doctor provides for the safest possible use of psychotropic medications, as long as this use is informed by the fact that the family is hyperdimensional and that the *DSM* is only intersecting some of the many dimensions in which they live.

Psychotropic medications can be quite valuable. Bipolar disease, major depression, and schizophrenia are three conditions for which the new medications have increased the level of functioning and thereby the quality of life. The appropriate use of medications for people who have been appropriately diagnosed with these conditions has enabled deeper relational capacity in family members.

The greatest misuse of the *DSM* is in its misapplication. And unfortunately, with the pressure of insurance reimbursement schedules, the *DSM* is widely misapplied. When a combination of forces causes a twelve-year-old boy to bounce in and out of the hospital, suddenly on two new psychotropic medications, with an essentially inadequate history to justify the diagnosis, we must ask what has been lost through this coalition of forces.

The integrity of one person is lost. The integrity of the person's connections to family and friends is lost. If someone is misdiagnosed because of the combination of financially motivated pressure from the insurance providers and the availability of medications that cause few side effects but nevertheless cause powerful psychic effects—if someone is misdiagnosed like that, the world is much poorer.

The way the entire family loses is this. It is inevitable that families face things they have never faced before. Some of them are of such magnitude that the family does all it can to survive. This causes different systems to go into operation in different families. If the so-called symptomatic person is silenced with a psychotropic medication, then the family never gets to take the leap to the next level of adaption to this variety of conflicting emotional needs. The family tends to attempt to satisfy as many of the needs of the individual members as it can. A psychotropic medication misused can cause the family to fail to meet this goal, and the family is stunted, though the identified patient may be less miserable.

Because I am a child psychiatrist, I have seen far more of this loss with children than with adults. I have seen many cases of parents with developmentally delayed children, where the parents have limitations of their own, mentally and emotionally. In those cases, the parents seldom meet a therapist sophisticated enough to understand both the developmental level of the child and the parent and to translate the interventions to both. Instead, the child gets "diagnosed" with a mental disorder, and once medication is prescribed and the parent sees some kind of improvement, this seems to the parent proof that their child has a disorder. I see it as a failure of development on both parts. I see it also as an impoverishment of the world.

## HISTORICAL OVERVIEW

The understanding of the brain has barely begun. The last century has seen an explosion of knowledge in the fields of biology and medicine. Advances in medicine and surgery have greatly improved the health of everyone who has access to the medical system. Enormous progress has been made in understanding the physiology of the heart, lungs, kidneys, and liver. At the same time, very recent changes in the funding of medical services have decreased the quality of care in every specialty. Nurses have been laid off, and some of their duties have been given to ancillary staff who do not have the clinical training to understand them. Physicians have less time with patients. They are forced to submit to endless, veiled disconfirmation by pseudo-colleagues (doc-to-doc), in the form of telephone interviews with physician insurance reviewers (personal communication with David Keith, MD).

Progress in psychiatry has been much slower than that in other medical specialties. This is because the brain's functions are far, far more complex than those of the other organs. The next closest in the complexity of the chemical changes that characterize its functioning is the liver. Someday science may well discover chemical changes in the brain that are meaningfully linked to changes in the liver.

Since the development in the past ten to fifteen years of new brain-scanning methods (PET, regional blood flow), we have gained the ability to watch the brain think. And we are beginning to amass data from other areas of biological research that suggest an early model of how the brain's chemistry is affected by experience. For the first time, we are beginning to understand the chemical changes that are caused by psychotherapy.

Additionally, psychiatry itself has made enormous progress in the past hundred years. Freud's groundbreaking *Interpretation of Dreams* was published in 1900.[10] In it Freud developed the first highly articulated metaphorical language of the ghost. He strongly maintained that even seemingly nonsensical behavior or language could be intelligible if seen through the appropriate lens, which was his growing theory of unconscious life intersecting with consciousness. His was the first widely applied theory of psychotherapy.

During the past century enormous progress has also been made in the realm of the machine metaphor of human life. There have been significant breakthroughs in our understanding of the biology of major depression, bipolar disorder, and schizophrenia, with very clear and incontrovertible genetic connections established for each disorder. For these three debilitating illnesses, significant progress in psychopharmacology has produced drug treatments that significantly improve the quality of life for people who are appropriately diagnosed with any of there illnesses.

Group psychotherapy developed in the past seventy years, as did family therapy in the past fifty years or so. Both of these developments have also led to great improvements in the level of functioning for people who have access to them.

Many of the founders of family therapy were analysts or had been in analytic training. It is clear that they learned significant things from their analytic training that they then applied in their family therapy work, while devising new language to describe the complexities of what they were experiencing.

The account family therapy pioneer Murray Bowen[11] gives of his experience at the NIMH is fascinating combined with his account of his repeated failure to graduate from the analytic institute. In his collected papers he describes the studies of couples therapy being done at that time in which both husband and wife were being treated separately with psychoanalysis. When couples were then treated psychotherapeutically in the same room at the same time (family therapy), it was discovered that symptom relief occurred much more quickly than with the two separate psychoanalyses.

Prior to the family therapy revolution, psychiatric treatments were either somatic (e.g., drugs, electroconvulsive therapy, needle showers, insulin shock) or psychoanalytic. And psychoanalysis did provide significant relief from psychic pain. It also facilitated people's growth; it had a humanism inherent in it that was the best counterbalance to those awful somatic treatments.

When DSM-II was published in 1968, the psychiatric world was dominated by the psychoanalytic perspective; the terminology of that manual reflected this perspective. DSM-II was very short and was considered of little importance in terms of therapeutic psychoanalytic practice.

When *DSM-III* was published in 1980, it was a radical break with the past because it deliberately eschewed psychoanalytic and any other theoretical language in the interest of providing a detailed descriptive phenomenology. It was done specifically enough to allow the collection of a wealth of clinical data through research. It has done that. It was also designed to be modified over time after the research data came back that indicated a need to change the diagnostic categories. This is why we had *DSM-IIIR* and then *DSM-IV*. Each evolved into the other, based on research data gathered from studies using the previous version.

But none of the DSMs include contextual data in the formulation of the primary diagnosis. The contextual data are included in other axes. The phenomenology is based on only one person. There is a vast unexplored territory, which is the phenomenology of relationships. Psychiatric symptoms (e.g., depressed affect, anxiety, hyperactivity, sleep disturbance, etc.) must always be explored in the context of contexts. That is to say, not just in the context of the individual's narrative of experience, but also in the context of surrounding relationships.

Yet I must also say that the *DSM-IV* does have some sophistication. For instance, attention deficit hyperactivity disorder is often misdiagnosed because clinicians do not read the criteria in *DSM-IV* carefully enough. It is described as a symptom complex of distractibility, impulsivity, and hyperactivity occurring in more than one context that causes distress in a person's functioning. However, there are exclusionary criteria that are often overlooked. The first says that the increase in these symptoms should be greater than expected taking the child's mental age into account. A 3-year-old cannot pay attention as long as a 6-year-old, nor can an 8-year-old mentally retarded child whose mental age is 5. The second exclusionary criterion that is usually overlooked is that this symptom complex of hyperactivity, distractibility, and impulsivity cannot be attributed to any other mental disorder. The most common mental disorders that could cause this symptom complex would be anxiety disorders and depression.

The *DSM* is essential to the physician who prescribes psychotropic medications. The medications were developed and tested using the *DSM,* so those are the only situations in which you know what they will do. If you are going to prescribe these medications, you absolutely have to use the *DSM.* And you have to use it rigorously.

Let me be plain: the best use of the *DSM* for the clinician is in prescribing psychotropic medication. Let me be more plain about this: the *DSM* has no ability to encode the richness of family experience that it is necessary for a family therapist to understand in order to know how to intervene therapeutically. *DSM* gives diagnostic advice primarily with regard to the therapeutic use of medications. It is simplistic because it refers only to individuals. When you prescribe a medication, it is essential to pay the most attention to the individual level. However, if you prescribe psychotropic medication without paying attention to the levels above the individual, such as relational context in the family, you will certainly make more therapeutic mistakes than if you take into account the systems above the individual.

## A SCIENTIFIC MODEL FOR THE INTEGRATION OF REAL BIOLOGY WITH REAL THERAPY

A new model is needed. Family therapy and medication are inappropriately apposed as opposites. Could ghost be an alternative to machine, in the imagining of metaphors to describe humans and their meaningful interactions? What is needed is beyond the ghost and the machine: a model that allows the integration of what is known biologically about human behavior with what is known in the realm of psychotherapy and family therapy in particular.

In the language of family therapy, what must be done is to retain the knowledge that has been gained by understanding families as systems, and then to gain greater knowledge about subsystems, such as the brain. In particular, family theory must investigate further the interfaces between subsystems. The truths that brain scientists have been uncovering are important for family theorists and therapists because the progress of medical science has also been informed by systems theory.

The model I suggest to replace the ghost and the machine is based on one presented by the nobel laureate Eric Kandel in two articles in the *American Journal of Psychiatry* in 1998 and in 1999.[12,13] His model is so fine, and so rooted in real, current science that I could hardly improve on it.

However, Kandel considers mostly the biological correlates to key concepts in psychoanalysis, and he does not really consider the ways that social structures affect brain chemistry, except to say that they certainly do, but are probably better investigated on a higher level of abstraction than brain chemistry.

Which is precisely what theories of family therapy are.

Kandel's model is built on five principles. Each principle is firmly based in the findings of contemporary science.

1. All mental processes, even the most complex psychological processes, derive from operations of the brain. . . .
2. Genes and their protein products are important determinants of the pattern of interconnections between neurons in the brain and the details of their functioning. Genes and specifically combinations of genes exert significant control over behavior. . . .
3. Altered genes do not, by themselves, explain the variance of a given major mental illness. Social or developmental factors also are very important contributions. . . . Behavior and social factors exert actions on the brain by feeding back upon it to modify the expression of genes and thus the function of nerve cells. Learning . . . produces alterations in gene expression. All of nurture is ultimately expressed as nature.
4. Alterations in gene expression induced by learning give rise to changes in patterns of neuronal connections.
5. As psychotherapy . . . is effective and produces long-term changes in behavior, it does so through learning, by producing changes in gene expression that alter the strength of synaptic connections and structural changes that alter the anatomical pattern of interconnections between nerve cells of the brain.

Kandel states that the "details of the relationship between the brain and mental processes—precisely how the brain gives rise to various mental processes—is understood poorly, and only in outline." However, the most significant points in this model are that learning changes the expression of genes and that these changes in gene expression then change how neurons are interconnected. And that all social experiences, including psychotherapy, cause changes in the brain.

He indicates as well that though social behavior also derives from operations of the brain, the biological level is often not the best level of analysis of group behavior. He does not consider in that article the interface in clinical practice between pharmacotherapy and psychotherapy.

Yet that is precisely the level family therapists must know more about if they work with families in which one or more members are on psychotropic medications. Furthermore newly developed insights from brain science do provide chemical explanations for some key therapeutic truths. Pressures from the insurance industry make it more difficult to apply what we know therapeutically. But it is now clear that they do not allow for the therapeutic application of what we already know biologically.

For instance, Winnicott's notion of the holding environment[14] is one that is routinely interefered with by insurance companies that limit the number of sessions approved for a given diagnosis. And the holding environment does not just apply to psychoanalysis. It is part of the beginning stage of any kind of psychotherapy, and involves the establisment of trust.

Biologically, the holding environment can be seen as that which allows brain changes to consolidate. Therapeutic change takes place through learning, which changes the expression of genes, which change patterns of neuronal connections. Because they are biological processes, they take time to occur, and they occur slowly sometimes, and after enough of them accumulate, they achieve a jump in growth. The holding environment provides the safety to expose the brain to different path possibilities and the time necessary for them to grow into long-term brain structure.

When it is interfered with by the denial of service, ground that had been gained therapeutically frequently reverses. The biological changes are not given the time and the protection necessary to consolidate into long-term memory.

Another example of biological backing for what is known therapeutically occurs in working with different subsystems of a family, including other generations. Family members are linked biologically. Even though memories of a given event differ in family members' retelling, that memory substrate is biological. Many of the biological links are unconscious, too. The research that Minuchin[15] did on a family with a diabetic member is an example of this. While videotaping a family session, at given intervals, blood was drawn from each member. Blood levels of free fatty acids (a stress indicator, among other things) were shown to be linked in time, even in the nondiabetic members, and their levels were related to the emotional content of the videotape.

Changing family patterns requires building new memories of relating differently, which is a biological process. If the changes occur in only one subsystem and there are higher-level systems that have not changed, the therapeutic effect will recede after therapy ends.

Here additional information about how psychotropic medications work and how they affect family dynamics must be included, because this is another area where insurance companies do not use the most advanced level of biological understanding in various ways when they limit service.

The length of time that is required for psychotropic medications to exert their full effect is determined by a number of factors. The half-life of the medication determines how long it takes to reach equilibrium blood levels. Some medications have active metabolites whose half-lives also effect the time to equilibrium. Time to equilibrium is important for assessing whether a medication has been at an adequate level to have a therapeutic effect.

Many psychotropic medications work primarily by causing secondary changes in brain chemistry. All of the antidepressants work this way, as does the anxiolytic Buspar. What this means is that the antidepressants cause one change in the brain (e.g., inhibition of serotonin reuptake), which then causes a number of other changes which take time to occur before they become therapeutically evident. In the case of the antidepressants, what is thought to be the clinically significant chemical change is down-regulation of postsynaptic receptors, whether serotonin, norepinephrine, or dopamine.[16]

Once the secondary changes occur, an individual's symptoms start to change. This is the point at which insurance companies often start suggesting that treatment is no longer necessary. The secondary changes that are caused by antidepressants can take up to six months fully to manifest themselves.

## CASE DESCRIPTION TO ILLUSTRATE THE MODEL

When I first met Miriam Hayes, she was $13^{1}/_{2}$. She and her family had been referred to our agency for "wraparound" services, which might include such things as in-home family therapy or the appointment of a mental health worker to attend school with the child to keep her out of trouble. I met them for the psychiatric evaluation that would reauthorize the services the treatment team felt were appropriate. The evaluation involved a group interview with the mother and daughter, as well as the team, which consisted of two master's-level clinicians, a mental health worker, myself, and a case manager.

Miriam had recently been discharged from a six-week-long stay in the inpatient unit of a local psychiatric hospital. She had been admitted there because of depression, running away, and so-called out-of-control behavior. She was discharged with a diagnosis of psychotic depression and attention deficit disorder. She had been given trials of five different psychotropic medications and ultimately was discharged on three of them.

When I met her, I was wary because of this extended stay in the hospital. In the present era of managed care, children who stay in the hospital that long have very unusual stories. I did not want to miss vital details of Miriam's story.

Sometimes, of course, children stay in the hospital longer because of the intersection of forces that include psychopharmacology and the insurance industry. In these cases, the child ends up staying longer in the hospital because seriously symptomatic behavior is still occurring and because the psychiatrist is adjusting doses of medications or changing them. The managed-care reviewers do not grant extra hospital days in order to observe the behavioral results of the secondary-messenger changes the psychotropic medications have initiated. But they do grant days to stop one medication because it is ineffective and start another. And, of course, any medication that depends on secondary changes and dosage adjustment can take several months to assess with regard to its effectiveness. Any insurance reviewer who grants extra hospital days for a child to change medications when sufficient time has not been allowed to observe the effects of the first medication is practicing bad medicine.

Miriam's mother (Ms. Hayes) was angry with her the day I first met them. She was telling me that Miriam was still as oppositional and disrespectful as when she went into the hospital. Miriam wanted to wear her sneakers to school the day before. Ms. Hayes would not allow her to do this because they were wet from the rain. As a result, Miriam walked barefoot to school. Eventually, Ms. Hayes found her and brought another pair of shoes to her.

At this juncture, given the hospital's discharge diagnosis (psychotic depression), I was not sure whether this was simple adolescent assertion of autonomy or whether it represented some level of psychotic disorganization. Because psychotic disorganization can be very dangerous, it is important to detect it. So I asked Ms. Hayes to help me understand some things. I asked her to begin with some history that would help bring me up to the present time.

She went back fairly early. Miriam had been born two months prematurely, and her biological mother was suspected of having been abusing drugs and alcohol during pregnancy. At two months of age, she was placed with a family friend after having suffered a broken right femur (which suggested abuse or neglect). At the age of $2\frac{1}{2}$, she was placed with Ms. Hayes after being diagnosed with failure to thrive. She was adopted by Ms. Hayes at age 5.

Miriam had certainly been neglected as an infant, and possibly abused as well. It is clear that trauma and neglect have a serious deleterious effect on brain development after birth,[17] so it is quite possible that Miriam was experiencing post-traumatic symptoms of stress-induced brain changes at a time in her life when her brain was still developing significantly through early childhood.

By the age of 6 she was manifesting problematic behavior that grew to the point that Ms. Hayes had her evaluated at the neurology clinic of a university hospital. She was diagnosed with ADHD and treated with Ritalin first and then Cylert when she developed side effects to the Ritalin. Ms. Hayes eventually discontinued this, too, because she felt it was not helpful.

Ms. Hayes then jumped forward six years to relate the happenings of the previous year that had had a significant impact on Miriam. The family had recently moved from a "drug-infested" neighborhood to upstate, in order to be with Ms. Hayes's sister, who was having knee surgery. They stayed there three months. At the end of this time, there was a terrible assault by a male teenager on some of the children in the family. One of the daughters was raped, and three of them were physically attacked. All of them were threatened and intimidated, although Miriam was not present for this. She knew of it in detail from talking with her sisters.

Additionally, after that initial assault, the entire family was apparently persecuted on this block. The details of the persecution were not exactly clear due to limited time in the interview but involved severe intimidation, to the point that the family moved away from upstate in May.

The subsequent fall, Miriam had three different teachers because each of her previous teachers had left the school or quit. Ms. Hayes told me there was great chaos in that classroom. She also told me she feared Miriam might have been assaulted or raped while she was in that classroom, because at that time Miriam became much more aggressive and at times frightened of men.

By November Miriam was hospitalized at the children's psychiatric unit of a university hospital. She stayed there for twenty days and was discharged back to home. Several months later, she was also admitted to the partial hospitalization program at a large private psychiatric hospital for eleven days due to depression with suicidal ideation and oppositional behavior.

At the end of March she was admitted to the inpatient unit of another private psychiatric hospital because she had run away from home and shown other kinds of oppositional and defiant behaviors. She remained there until the middle of May and received medication trials of Wellbutrin, Effexor, Desyrel, and Risperdal.

She was initially started on a trial of Wellbutrin, which was eventually increased up to the level of 150 mg BID but was discontinued after it was felt that she had not responded to it. She was then given a trial of Effexor, which was increased to a dosage of 75 mg three times a day. She began to show a decrease in depressive symptoms, but she had persistent nausea and vomiting, which led to discontinuing the medication. The Desyrel had initially only been used as needed for insomnia and was apparently gradually increased to 75 mg by the time of discharge. She was discharged on Risperdal 1 mg BID, Desyrel 75 mg at bedtime, and Tenex 1 mg BID. That was when I first met Miriam, as they began the outpatient wraparound treatment under my supervision.

In discussing this initial history, I have to make several points simultaneously, because they are all immediately apparent. The first is that this child was neglected at an early age, and possibly abused, meaning she may have lasting neurological effects that influence her anxiety level, her tolerance for chaos, and the variability of her mood.

The second is that this child appeared with a very serious diagnostic label: psychotic depression. It is serious because it can be unpredictably dangerous to self or others. Great care must be taken in disagreeing with another psychiatrist's diagnosis of psychosis.

The third is that some of the stories of the family's history were terribly unfinished and lacked vital information. For instance, the story of the persecution after the assault on the family while they were upstate was unfinished. So also was the story of what led the family to uproot so easily in order to stay with Ms. Hayes's sister. The stories that led to her various psychiatric admissions were also unfinished.

The fourth is that though it is always difficult to second-guess another psychiatrist's work from reading a chart, it was clear that Miriam was exposed to bad medication management. For instance, the Effexor was increased too rapidly, which worsened the nausea that can accompany it as a side effect. I could guess that it was increased rapidly because of the pressure to adjust a medication as quickly as possible for insurance reasons. And the diagnosis of ADHD was not questioned, despite the fact that that diagnosis cannot be made if another mental disorder could cause the same symptoms. Post-traumatic anxiety is clearly one condition that can cause the symptoms of ADHD, and one that it seemed quite likely that Miriam suffered from. Both the Wellbutrin and the Tenex had been chosen because they are indicated for ADHD, but neither is recommended for post-traumatic anxiety.

Over time, because we were able to assign a mobile therapist to go into the home each week and a mental health worker to go to school with Miriam, we were able to accumulate much more information. I began working with Miriam and her mother on a plan to discontinue as much of the medication as could be done safely. I saw Miriam weekly for a time, as the medications were being discontinued, to watch for possible reemergence of psychotic symptoms. Within several weeks, Miriam had developed enough trust to reveal that she had fabricated the story about having hallucinations. She told me that she had only said that to get the psychiatrist to stop bothering her.

We also learned that all of Miriam's siblings had been adopted, and several had special needs. Her younger brother was mentally retarded. Her 11-year-old sister had recently been in a motor vehicle accident and may have suffered brain injury in the accident. In the single meeting that the family brought her to, she was unable to stay in her seat. She was talking almost constantly, and teasing Miriam, sometimes pulling at her hair. We eventually learned that the home was full of this level of activity, and there was not a lot of space in the home. The children were generally in one room all at the same time. Ms. Harris would tolerate a high level of chaos chronically until she could no longer stand it and then would shout at the children.

Miriam's school behavior was not problematic at all. She had no trouble focusing, controlling impulses, or paying attention. She got along well with peers for the most part. As the medications were slowly discontinued, her attentiveness actually improved, because she was no longer sedated. Ms. Harris stopped the Tenex and the Risperdal impulsively after she saw that Miriam was doing well with lower doses of them and did not tell me this until our next appointment several weeks later.

By the next appointment, Ms. Hayes was already beginning to regret taking her daughter off the medications. She began to wonder whether her daughter's recent oppositionality was related to stopping them. As I explored the background of the recent oppositionality, I realized it had nothing to do with stopping the medication. As I reflected this back to the mother, she resisted somewhat and tried to make plain to me how awful her daughter's behavior could be at times. She then insisted to me, "When she was in that hospital, she called the doctor a bitch! The doctor called me up at home and told me how surprised she was!"

Miriam disputed this, as if she remembered it either not at all, or differently. The mother insisted, and Miriam grew more withdrawn. While the mother was talking, I found myself smiling. In the pause that was created by the daughter's withdrawal, I spoke up and said with some seriousness, "I was smiling while you were talking, because I was hoping your daughter called her 'Dr. Bitch.' "

At this, the whole room burst into laughter, the daughter and the mother together, along with the other staff. And it was such a long laugh that people were surprised to be enjoying it so much. The laugh had opened the mother's and the daughter's ears at the same time. My joke linked the mother's insistence on respect with the daughter's need to return disrespect that she felt. And it also reminded the mother of the ways she has felt disrespected by doctors.

After that laugh, it was much easier to talk to them. I told Ms. Hayes I saw no need for medicine now, but I wanted them to be in touch with me if things changed. Her body is the same at school as at home, and her body needs no medicine at school, so it is clear she could control herself at home, if the right things are done, one of which is more intense family work.

Over the months of working with Mirian and her mother, it became clear to me that both the diagnosis of ADHD and that of psychosis were based on inadequate history and had been wrongly applied. It also became clear that this family was one that had so many stories to tell that the psychiatrists they had previously seen seldom had sufficient time to listen to them.

The prevalent myth of the chemical imbalance that causes disturbances that can be diagnosed using *DSM-IV,* combined with the selection of powerful psychotropics with fewer side effects and pressures from health insurers to make a diagnosis quickly and start medications, led in this situation to a serious misdiagnosis.

In this situation, most of the things that were related to Miriam's behavior were in the realm of what would be called a ghost in the machine. She certainly was neglected at an early age. She was probably abused at that age as well. But her story is one of many in which there is an inadequate history. If she was abused as well as neglected, she may have had brain changes from that, brain changes we are only beginning to understand. In the face of serious symptoms, what was available of Miriam's history, guided by *DSM-IV* criteria, was sufficient to start the treatment. It was clearly insufficient for understanding the meaning of her life experience.

## CONCLUSION

Working psychopharmacologically with one member of a family does not change the family dynamics. It just offers an opportunity to change them. If the therapist does not intervene after the changed psychopharmacology, then the system reverts to the best possible replication of the old system after the intrusion of another element (the symptomatic behavior, followed by the medication).

Therapy can change the brain's set-point for the tolerance of chaos. If therapy does not create a holding environment that exposes the family to new learning over the time period required to change the biological substrates in a long-term way (which includes secondary messenger changes, and transcription of new protein products and the time required to replace the population of previous connections with the population of neurons making the new connections)—if the holding environment cannot be held that long, the family's brain set-point for chaos remains the same, and soon after therapy ends, the family will reproduce a new version of the same chaos.

Having effective medications to treat depression or obsessive-compulsive disorder (OCD) does not mean that family therapists are put out of work. Their job actually gets harder, because they need to know something about how these medications work on the brain. And they need to know about where they stand with regard to the notion of brain and behavior. And they have, as family therapists, to pay much more attention to the changes possible—after medication therapy has begun—in family structure and in intrapsychic shifts that allow other windows in some members to open. They need to pay more attention to three-generational balances of caring, because the medications can cause action on each of these levels in a clinically significant way.

It is in this spirit that I have developed two sets of guidelines. The first set is for nonmedical therapists. The second set is a summary of some of the guidelines I use for myself, which may be useful to readers who are psychiatrists.

## GUIDELINES FOR NONMEDICAL THERAPISTS

Always question the diagnosis. Learn to use the *DSM-IV* yourself. It is relatively easy to learn to use it, and there are casebooks that teach it.

Learning the *DSM-IV* enables the therapist to ask informed questions. It also gives the therapist some guidelines about what to expect of medication management and assessment. Choice of medications is based on the *DSM-IV* diagnosis and evidence from clinical studies that use it.

Especially always question a diagnosis that comes from a hospitalization. Psychiatrists do not have enough time during a hospitalization to get to know patients by themselves or in the context of their families. Patients do not have enough time to build sufficient trust in the treating doctor to reveal essential pieces of history. As a result, the diagnosis is often wrong.

Additionally, inpatient psychiatrists know that they can get an extra day or two from the insurance companies if they can argue that they need time to adjust the medication or to add a new one. This practice is especially problematic when you consider that medications are being adjusted that affect a person's soul based on a very shallow knowledge of the patient by the doctor.

If one of your patients has been psychiatrically hospitalized, get another psychiatric evaluation as soon as you can after the hospitalization is over. Get the evaluation by a psychiatrist whose judgment and skill you know and trust, if you can.

Learn the names and classes of common psychotropic medications. There are four basic classes: anxiolytics, antidepressants, mood stabilizers, and antipsychotics. If you learn just the most common medications from each class, you will be able to interface with the medical establishment and the insurance reviewers with greater ability to challenge the denial of service.

## GUIDELINES FOR PSYCHIATRISTS

Argue with managed-care reviewers about the need to allow time for secondary messenger changes to occur after adjustment of medications. This is pharmacologically and clinically sound. A medicine cannot be judged ineffective if it has not been given enough time to allow the secondary changes to occur. They must occur anew after each dose increase.

Memorize the half-lives of all the medications you use, and use those to argue pharmacologically. After starting a new medicine at a single dose, it takes four to five half-lives of the medication to reach an equilibrium level in the serum. Discharging a patient before the new medication has reached an equilibrium level is not really medically sound when the patient has been admitted for a life-threatening condition. Imagine the insurance reviewer discharging a patient with a life-threatening arrhythmia before he or she was stabilized on antiarrhythmics. Then argue from that perspective.

Learn the *DSM-IV* well enough from memory to argue specific points with reviewers. For instance, when attention deficit hyperactivity disorder is one of the diagnoses that is under consideration, insist on the necessary time to exclude any other mental disorder as potentially causative of the same symptoms, such as anxiety or depression. No child should ever be started on medication for ADHD after a single forty-five-minute interview with a psychiatrist.

Use the other axes to argue for more treatment as well, especially the fourth (psychosocial problems) and the fifth (level of functioning).

Never accept the written history that is given you as reason not to explore the same history yourself. Assume the aspect of a literary critic while reading the histories of others: view them as different perspectives on interactions of which you were not part.

Listen to the ghost and learn from it. Learn to discriminate between the ghost and the medicine, and medicate only the machine.

Never medicate the ghost.

## NOTES

1. "Nature, philosophy of." *Brittanica 2002*. Copyright © 1994–2002 Britannica.com Inc. September 22, 2002.
2. Ferris, T. (1988). *Coming of age in the milky way.* New York: William Morrow and Company.
3. "Leeuwenhoek, Antoine van." *Britannica 2002*. Copyright © 1994–2002 Britannica.com Inc. September 17.
4. Ryle, G. (1949). *The concept of mind.* London and New York: Hutchinson's University Library.

5. Hoffmann, E. T. A. (1969). *Der sandmann, das öde haus: nachtstücke.* Stuttgart: Reclam.
6. Ferris, T. (1988) *Coming of age in the milky way.* New York: William Morrow and Company.
7. Eisenberg, L. (1995). The social construction of the human brain. *American Journal of Psychiatry,* 152: 1563 b-1575 b.
8. Cleghorn, J. M., Franco, S., Szechtman, B., Kaplan, R. D., Szechtman, H., Brown, G. M., Nahmias, C., and Garnett, E. S. (1992). Toward a brain map of auditory hallucinations. *American Journal of Psychiatry,* 149: 1062–1069.
9. Andreasen, N. C., O'Leary, D. S., Cizadlo, T., Arndt, S., Rezai, K., Watkins, G. L., Ponto, L. L., and Hichwa, R. D. (1995). Remembering the past: two facets of episodic memory explored with positron emission tomography. *American Journal of Psychiatry,* 152: 1576–1585.
10. Freud, S. *Die traumdeutung.* (1900). Leipzig and Vienna: Franz Deuticke.
11. Bowen, M. *Family therapy in clinical practice.* Northvale, NJ: Jason Aronson, 1985.
12. Kandel, E. R. (1998). A new intellectual framework for psychiatry. *American Journal of Psychiatry,* 155, 457–469.
13. Kandel, E. R. (1999). Biology and the future of psychoanalysis: a new intellectual framework for psychiatry revisited. *American Journal of Psychiatry,* 156, 505–524.
14. Winnicott, D. W. *Playing and reality.* New York: Basic Books, 1971.
15. Minuchin, S. (1974). *Families & family therapy.* Cambridge, MA: Harvard University Press.
16. Stahl, S. M. (1996). *Essential psychopharmacology.* New York: Cambridge University Press.
17. Teicher, M. H. (2002). Scars that won't heal: the neurobiology of child abuse. *Scientific American,* 286, 3, 68–75.

Chapter 8

# Rethinking Illness

Zhao Mei, MD

*"You are old, father William," the young man said,*
*"And your hair has become very white;*
*And yet you incessantly stand on your head—*
*Do you think, at your age, it is right?"*
Lewis Carroll, *Alice's Adventures in Wonderland*

Society is plagued by disease: indeed, disease is a part of the human condition. Despite advancements in medical technology and understanding, the abundance of medications and the proliferation of doctors, nobody is safe from its clutches. Disease is constantly around us and in us in one form or another.

Western medicine has an important role to play in health management, but we need to realize that this is not an exclusive role. Despite the amazing and rapid advancement in medical science in the past years, there are still many diseases whose causes are unknown and invisible. Good health is the result of finding and maintaining a physical, mental, social, and emotional balance so that the body can tap into its inherent healing power.

As a doctor, surgeon, and gynecologist in China for over twenty-five years, I was initially trained in Western medicine and have seen patients in large hospitals and small clinics and treated them for everything from colds to cancer. I have run expensive and highly technical diagnostic tests, prescribed medications, and performed operations. My patients looked to me to treat their disease and thus restore them to good health.

From the start of my medical career I have blended traditional Chinese medicine practices with my Western medical approach. But upon coming to the United States in 1991, I have practiced Chinese medicine exclusively, trading invasive procedures and chemical medications for herbal treatments, acupressure, and Qigong practices of therapeutic movement and meditation. I have shifted my focus from treating disease to restoring the body's power to attain and maintain good health.

In the course of making this transition from Western to Eastern integrated treatment philosophies, I also have had to rethink the way I look at illness and, consequently, the way I view good health.

As defined by the World Health Organization, health is a state of complete physical, mental, and social well-being and not merely the absence of disease or infirmity. To take this definition one step further, we need to look at health as a relative balance of our internal and external social and natural environments. Therefore, health and illness is not only a biomedical model, but also a bio-psycho-social model; medicine is not only a natural science, but also a social science; the treatment of disease is not only a medical task, but also a job for the whole of society.

To achieve optimum health, we must find a way to regulate our internal functions—such as the nervous, circulatory and hormonal systems—as well as our conscious and unconscious thought and emotion. Also, though we often have little control over our external environments, we can learn to control our reactions to and feelings about the world around us.

Let us look at the wide range of elements the Chinese system of medicine views as contributing to illness. We begin with the environment. In our highly industrialized and technologically advanced country, people live in polluted environments with their daily lives driven by increased stress and competition. This stress is rooted in financial burdens and obligations, but also, and perhaps more important in social components, such as ecological imbalance, violence, pornography, broken families, and economic crisis.

Under constant pressure from societal and family needs, people are generally spending more time at stressful jobs and less time relaxing at home with their families. With this increased exposure to higher pressure, the damage to one's physical and psychological body and well-being becomes more apparent and severe. People tend to become more nervous, depressed, anxious, angry, sorrowful, and fearful—all negative feelings that can lead to the development of illness.

Stress and pressure can take charge of one's body and manifest more commonly as chronic illnesses, such as heart disease. Based on one analysis done in one Chinese medical journal, (Yang Sheng 2001) 10% of illness is caused by microorganisms, 10% by genetic factors, 30% by environmental factors, and the remaining 50%, directly or indirectly, by lifestyle and stress. For that reason, unlike treatment for a bacterial infection, in which we can tackle the problem by using antibiotics, these chronic illnesses require a comprehensive approach. We cannot simply rely on doctors prescribing medications and performing surgeries.

Moving from the environment, we come to the internal climate of the individual. In Chinese medicine, mental activity is thought of as related to particular organs. Anger is seen as related to liver function, sadness to the lungs, thinking to the spleen and stomach, excitement and happiness to the heart, fear to the kidneys. As these expressions and emotions become fixed, our related internal organs and functions become more distressed and chronic illness develops.

A Chinese anecdote tells about a sculptor who spent his time carving intricate statues of ghouls and demons. After many years of this work, the sculptor's face was fixed with deep lines and a permanent scowl. The sculptor went to a *qigong* master and asked that his face be healed and his expression softened. "First," the master told him, "you must do something for me." The master instructed him to carve six statues of Guan Yin, a graceful female Buddhist figure symbolizing kindness, mercy, and beauty. After six months, the sculptor presented the completed statues to the master. "I see that you already have sent good *qi* to heal me," the grateful sculptor said, his now smooth face beaming. "No," the master said with a quiet smile. "Through your work, you have healed yourself."

The constant career, social, and economic pressures of today's active society affect our internal health much as demons and ghouls affected the sculptor's face. In order to combat these pressures and take charge of our own healing, we need to develop a more peaceful, natural, and resilient spirit.

For instance, a rubber band hangs down flat in its natural form. But if you wind it, the rubber becomes stretched and twisted and will remain in this unnatural form under force, a state that is called distortion. But release the pressure, and the piece of rubber will try to return to its original shape, its natural state. The more elastic a thing is, the better its ability to bounce back. Our body is much like the piece of rubber. In its natural state it is meant to be a relaxed and supple form allowing the nurturing and healing power of *qi* to flow into us and through us.

Sometimes we become ill and remain so because of the benefits that may come to us as a result. For example, a child who is uncomfortable in school has a stomach ache and finds that he will get to stay home from school because of it. He is likely to link stomach aches with staying home and in an unconscious way may actually develop stomach aches to avoid school. Over time such activity may actually create stomach illness. The psychological has worked its way into the physical.

Our health can even be affected by people and things at great distance from us. Negative feelings toward a relative we refuse to have contact with can do damage. The unfinished business of those who have gone on before us can play itself out on an unconscious stage in our psyche with a resulting health problem. And even larger historical trends can have a direct bearing on how we find ourselves physically.

Additionally, the media sometimes confuse or misinform the public about health-related issues by giving false or incomplete information. Thus, while we are generally more informed about disease and health these days, our information often is negative, misleading, or contradictory. Therefore, we must gain a true understanding of the nature of disease if we are to take the first step toward attaining good health. For example, we have seen that the subject of vitamin supplement usage has had a cyclical ride from moderate use to megadosing back to moderate again. An adequate diet should provide energy and essential amino and fatty acids, vitamins, and minerals. Functioning as coenzymes and hormones, vitamin supplements are very important in vital metabolic pathways. Overdosing with vitamins, however, can be very dangerous because it disrupts the body's natural balance.

We often think of hospitals as places for the treatment of illnesses and regaining health, but even here adverse events can happen. Many times a misdiagnosis, an accidental drug overdose, or complications from drug side effects can subsequently lead to the development of more illness and even death in some cases. Also, the signals doctors send their patients when diagnosing and treating disease are often negative and unsympathetic. A man recently came to me suffering from a chronic hepatitis and resulting liver cirrhosis. When diagnosed five years prior to our meeting, doctors told this patient that he would soon need a liver transplant. Subsequent discussions with doctors invariably focused on viral counts, liver damage, and limitations resulting from this damage. Though doctors were following accepted protocol, the patients was left with an abundance of fear and little hope, conditions that affected his spirit and aggravated his condition. The missing pieces of the conventional treatment puzzle are emotional and social support for the patient.

In traditional Chinese medicine, the digestive and reproductive systems are the foundational systems of the human body: people need to live and to continue to reproduce. All the other systems revolve around these two. As we know, a healthy digestive system is essential to maintaining life, for it converts food into materials that build and fuel our body's cells. It is also a complicated organ system which takes food in, digests and breaks it down, absorbs the nutrients into the blood stream, and gets rid of the indigestible portion. Not surprising in a modern society such as ours in which food is abundant, many diseases of the digestive system are primarily related to "indigestion." Indigestion arises when we eat something that doesn't agree with our stomach, whether it is too cold, too hot, too spicy, too oily, or too salty. Indigestion can also occur if we ingest toxic materials, such as some food additives.

To summarize, food is transformed to nutrients only after proper digestion, whereas indigestion of food can create diseases. Most of us understand this basic physiological formula, but what we overlook is a second, and more important, cause—the psychological component of these digestive difficulties. Our inability to digest the stresses and responsibilities of life psychologically is a greater stress to our digestive system than the biological and physiological factors.

Here is an example of how stress can induce and promote disease. There was a Chinese student, a bright and healthy young man, who came to the United States on scholarship to study in a local community college. After three years, he had achieved the highest scores in many of his classes and was often praised for his dedication to his academic work. One cold winter morning while he was out shoveling snow, he suddenly started vomiting blood and was later found unconscious. Subsequently, he was sent to the local hospital. There he was diagnosed with a ruptured gastric ulcer after a procedure called an upper endoscopy. Later he told doctors that since coming to the United States, he had had to work extremely hard in order to overcome the language and cultural barriers and to adjust to college life. On top of this, he had had to work different part-time jobs to pay for his education. Eventually, despite his young age, the pressure and stress from the combination of these factors had resulted in a bleeding gastric ulcer that nearly ended his life.

Another important organ system, the reproductive organs, allows us to produce offspring and to continue the human race. As with illnesses in the digestive system, problems in the reproductive system, especially gynecologic problems, are often directly related to disruptive family environments and unhealthy family relationships. Aside from genetic, infectious, and trauma-induced disorders, many gynecologic conditions, mostly uterine diseases, can be induced by intense emotional responses to infidelity and maternal misdeeds and misgivings. Prolonged repressed anger and feelings of betrayal associated with incidents of infidelity are common emotional triggers for many gynecologic problems. The anguish a mother feels for her children can lead to physical and emotional problems. Events such as these can be concealed quite easily from one's conscious mind; any guilt and restlessness eventually become rooted in one's unconscious and may affect the physical reproductive system.

In China there is a big lake, called Wash Hard Lake, which has water so pure and clear that you can see the bottom. People walk to the lake from far away in order to wash their hearts—to wash out sadness, jealousy, crazy thinking, grief, worry, a fixation with pornography. After they have washed there, they feel cleansed and understand what they need to do. They experience a great feeling of relief.

In the Chinese system of health, disease is seen as coming from the heart. It is said that when the heart is calm and in its natural state, we have both safety and health. But when the heart is not calm, we create illness. All of the things I have mentioned above can cause turbulence of the heart. Even strong desire disturbs the calm of the heart.

Now, this heart is not the physical heart. It is more akin to consciousness. Through unconsciousness disease is born. Our various unconscious beliefs affect our facial expressions. When we look at people's faces and trace the fixed qualities, we can see aspects of anger, fear, and other emotions etched there. The psychological is holographic with the physical. In Chinese medicine the psychological controls the physical, so if we can direct our consciousness toward health, we can have a good measure of control of our health.

Some people have developed an identity around their illness. When this is the case, it is difficult to utilize their minds in the service of healing, since their identity depends on their being sick. They may therefore come to be unable to wholeheartedly wish for health. This will seriously impair their ability to heal.

Thinking about health is always a very complex matter. There may always be genetic, infectious, and trauma-induced precipitants on the purely biological plane. But after taking these into account, Chinese medicine first addresses the psyche. Take cancer. In the Western approach the doctor shocks the patient's psyche by giving him or her the diagnosis of cancer, and then a prediction of how long the patient is likely to live. Immediately, a course of medication or surgery is begun, and it shocks the body. In a Chinese approach, when the diagnosis is given, the patient would be instructed to wait a bit to allow the shock to the psyche to dissipate. He or she would be instructed to contemplate his or her situation and consider what stressors might be present in his or her life. This approach addresses the patient first on the level of psychic events.

According to Chinese medicine the invisible heart has the capacity to heal, and we can all access it. If we accept the notion that we create illness through our lifestyles, then we have the ability to cure our illness by tapping our inherent healing capacities. If we resign ourselves only to the healing powers of medicine, then we lose the idea that we have within ourselves the power to heal. And in the treating of the invisible heart medicine will not help. So while searching for ways in which we have contributed to our own illness may be uncomfortable, we may benefit greatly from it by tapping into our own ability to heal.

A 16-year-old boy who came to see me had suffered from severe depression to the point that he was not able to continue his sophomore year in high school. He had seen a psychiatrist, who prescribed antidepressant medications and had at this point changed them four times without improvement. Furthermore, the boy was suffering from side effects of the medications, including nausea and insomnia. He had decided to stop taking the medications and came to consult me. I taught him *qigong,* which he began practicing faithfully. He also joined a martial arts school. Gradually he began to feel better and regained the energy and concentration to resume his school work with a home tutor who was very caring and helpful. He has now caught up with his junior year course work and plans to return to school for his senior year this fall.

This inner ability to heal has to do with *qi,* according to traditional Chinese medicine. It is believed that *qi* is a basic substance of which the world is comprised. Everything in the universe results from the movements and changes of *qi.* It is invisible and intangible, but its polymerization can transfer to other forms that are visible and tangible. The body is seen as having two forms—the visible physical form and the invisible universal *qi* form, which includes a vital force, healing power, energy source, mind, spirit, wisdom, intelligence, emotions, etc.

The principle of traditional Chinese healing philosophy is that the body can supplement and support the internal healing *qi* by making connections with the universal *qi.*

*Qigong* is a method or skill of training the *qi* through breathing and relaxation exercises, visualization, meditation, and other natural methods. It has been used in the prevention and successful treatment of acute and chronic diseases such as diabetes, cancer, and heart disease. It also provides assistance to AIDS and MS patients. *Qigong* has achieved the status of science with a new and vigorous body of scholarship investigating and certifying its benefits. It has gained the attention of the worldwide medical community.

To gain a full understanding of *qigong,* we have to retrain our thinking and reevaluate our conceptions. The practice of *qigong* seeks to guide a person to a new realm, a different pathway of thinking. It requires self-discipline and a determined commitment to consistent practice of its essential elements. The practitioner must associate his or her mind, postures, and breathing and act on the whole body. On the one hand, *qi* actively self-regulates the functional activities of the body and it maintains a dynamic equilibrium. On the other hand, it enables the body to produce an "energy-storing" reaction, which reduces energy consumption and increases energy accumulation, producing the effects of regulating yin and yang. The practice of *qigong* takes its practitioner to that special, powerful state of mind in which physical changes occur concurrently through practice. By actively introverting conscious activity to remold, perfect, and improve his or her life, the practitioner can bring it back into a precise balance that will yield optimum health.

## REFERENCE

Long, Zhixian. (2001). "Developing natural healing methods beneficial to mankind," *Chinese Yang Sheng Baojian,* April, 7–8.

# Part 3

# Political Issues: The Mechanisms Behind the Accelerating Growth of Psychopharmacological Practices

# Introduction to Part 3

It is not the judicious prescribing of medication in a particular instance that is at issue in this section. Psychotropic medication is a resource to be drawn upon in certain instances for certain people. What is at issue is the domination by economic and political forces of a field that traditionally has been, and by nature must continue to be, shaped in response to the needs of the people seeking its services.

The care of people's emotional needs in this country has traditionally been the charge of religious and social service organizations, the majority of which have been nonprofit or government-sponsored organizations. The people drawn to work with people's emotional difficulties have traditionally seen their work as something of a calling—a kind of central principle in their lives, orienting them toward bettering the lives of others. Because of the values in the larger culture, those people have always understood that their financial remuneration for this work would be modest.* This has been acceptable to these people because their bottom line is not the dollar, as in business, but rather the opportunity to perform acts for the betterment of others. In fact, it is this spirit of involvement with others—the therapeutic relationship—that is the only element of psychotherapy that quantitative research findings repeatedly correlate with successful outcomes.

What we are taking issue with, then, is the blurring of the boundary between healing and commerce. The managed-care industry, as an arm of the insurance business, has purely commercial roots. While maintaining its commercial status and its responsibility to its stockholders, it has now laid claim to territory traditionally reserved for the healing arts: decisions about who will receive care and what kind of care that will be. The production of pharmaceutical substances, on the other hand, is part of the healing tradition. Marcello Pakman, in his chapter, tells us that until the seven-

---

*Even though psychiatrists usually receive more than moderate remuneration, their economic status among physicians is the lowest.

teenth century physicians made their own remedies, and only thereafter did the profession of pharmacist come into being. Yet it has now become big business, and its primary allegiance, as with managed care, must be to its stockholders.

Should the managed-care industry increasingly dictate the practice of healing? Should the pharmaceutical industry increasingly employ commercial marketing tactics? The medicalization of the health insurance industry and the commercialization of pharmaceutical production raise many questions. Can the merchant-customer relationship provide the healing quality necessary to helping people transform their emotional lives? What is the relationship between commerce and politics?

In order to attempt to answer such questions, we need political and economic information about both the managed-care and pharmaceutical industries and insight into how the relationship between them affects the lives of those who seek care. The two chapters that follow give an account of some of the economic and political effects of the blurring of the boundaries between healing and commerce.

"The Myth of the Magic Pill," by Duncan, Miller, and Sparks, questions the basis of the widely held "chemical imbalance" theory as the cause of emotional distress and the claims that medications are more effective than talk therapy. It investigates how these popular myths originated. It further critiques the research that supports the claims of the effectiveness of medications. It then describes, using glimpses from case material, a therapeutic stance with a different basis and a wider range of treatment possibilities.

"Pig Pharma: Psychiatric Agenda Setting by Drug Companies," by Beder, Gosden, and Mosher, addresses the political issues attendant on the blurring of the boundary between healing and commerce. It sees the commercial interests of the pharmaceutical industry as having so great an impact that they undermine representative democracy itself in the ways mental health services are provided and mental health laws implemented. It describes the rerouting of public policies by strong special-interest lobbies to expand sales instead of benefiting the public good. It investigates grassroots coalitions that are actually fronts to influence the policy agenda for mental health. It looks at the ways that policies tailored for commercial interests are not beneficial for those seeking mental health.

Chapter 9

# The Myth of the Magic Pill

Barry Duncan, PsyD, Scott Miller, PhD,
and Jacqueline Sparks, MS

*"One side will make you grow taller, and the other side will make you grow shorter."*
*"One side of what? The other side of what?" thought Alice to herself.*
*"Of the mushroom," said the Caterpillar, just as if she had asked it aloud; and in another moment it was out of sight.*
Lewis Carroll, *Alice's Adventures in Wonderland*

Shelley fights back the tears as she utters in a voice barely audible to her family physician, "Things have just gotten to be too much. At first I didn't want to get up for work, and now I don't want to get up at all." Shelley feels hopeless, desperate, and fragile. In times gone by, she rallied during the tough times and met obstacles head on. But this time is different: no last-minute heroics or rising to the occasion, no platitudes or pep talks that have always worked for her in the past. The doctor looks at the ten-item questionnaire Shelley completed in the waiting room; it accurately reflects her poor appetite and loss of pleasure in sex or anything else for that matter. Her physician explains that such "neurovegetative symptoms" are a sign of "clinical depression," a *medical* illness resulting from a chemical imbalance in the brain. She also tells Shelley that though the problem is serious, there is no need to despair because the illness is now treatable. The doctor gives Shelley a brochure that says treating depression is just like using insulin for diabetes. By taking an antidepressant, Shelley will increase a critical chemical that is in short supply in the brain. As the examination nears completion, the physician suggests that Shelley seek out the support of a "talk therapist" inasmuch as combining medication with psychotherapy can sometimes enhance the chances of recovery. She nods her agreement. Prescription in hand and samples in her purse, Shelley leaves the office feeling comforted: her problem has a name, a cause, and a known cure.

The practice of attributing emotional suffering to chemical imbalances in the brain is now commonplace and embraced by the public and mental health professionals alike. So popular is it, in fact, that since the antidepressant Prozac—the first SSRI, or selective serotonin reuptake inhibitor—was introduced in 1988, over 300 million prescriptions have been written for the drug and its two chemical cousins, Paxil and Zoloft. Pharmacological treatment is not only popular for adults but also the fastest-growing form of intervention for children. In 1996, 600,000 prescriptions for Prozac alone were written for kids under the age of 18 and 203,000 for children between the ages of 6 and 12. Three thousand perscriptions were written for infants under the age of 1!

So ubiquitous have these drugs become that almost everyone has either taken, or knows someone who is taking, medication and reporting feeling better as a result. Sure, the pharmaceutical companies can be criticized for excessive promotion and marketing. Learning that Eli Lilly long ago created a peppermint flavored version of Prozac even though it is not approved for use with children and even requires a warning label ("safety and effectiveness in pediatric patients has not been established") is enough to make most people temporarily uncomfortable. By now, though, most Americans have come to expect occasional excesses from businesses competing for market share in the capitalistic society in which we live. And while most mental health professionals would acknowledge that the explanation given to clients is a gross oversimplification of actual brain functioning, few reject the biochemical model altogether. Fewer still question the effectiveness of the drugs, and virtually no one challenges the idea that combining medication with therapy is the best of all treatment options. At least it includes what talk therapists have to offer. The problem with these common beliefs and practices emerges, however, when they are examined in the light of scientific research. Empirically, there is *little support* for the idea that

- emotional suffering is caused by a biochemical imbalance in the brain;
- drug treatment is superior to psychotherapy (even for "severe" depression); or
- outcomes are better when therapy is combined with drugs.

Let's start with the mantra of American psychiatry: the biochemical imbalance. What our culture calls "depression" is a complex condition of mind, body, life, and heart. Yet in the past ten years we have been subjected to a simplistic version of a medieval morality play extensively (and expensively) promoted by pharmaceutical companies and rarely examined critically. Replayed endlessly in magazine ads, radio announcements, and television shows, endorsed by federal agencies and mental health organizations, this drama always shows some poor soul possessed by a "Chemical Imbalance Demon" being exorcised by a high priest with a prescription pad. Never mind the fact that standard medical textbooks say there is no such thing as a simple "biochemical imbalance" which accounts for emotional problems. Indeed, as neuroscientist Elliot Valenstein points out in his excellent book *Blaming the Brain* (1998), the arguments supporting biochemical imbalances are unconvincing and the research is rudimentary at best. Valenstein suggests that psychotropic drugs create, not cure, biochemical problems because of the brain's plasticity and rapid adaptation to pharmaceuticals. And yet the message continues to be broadcast to the American public: emotional suffering is a medical disease and one should run, not walk, to the nearest Church of Pharmacology for a cure. "Biochemical imbalance" is as much a part of American vernacular as "Did somebody say McDonalds?"

Consider, for example, the following excerpt from a *60 Minutes* documentary that aired in 1993 at the beginning of the SSRI's meteoric rise to power:

> *Host:* For 10 years, D has been suffering from depression, a serious illness. Sometimes she spends weeks on an unmade bed in a filthy apartment. She told us that she didn't care about anything, and she often thought of suicide.
>
> *D:* I've sometimes been afraid to take the subway home because I might throw myself in.
>
> *Host:* Most doctors believe chronic depression like D's is caused by a chemical imbalance in the brain. To correct it, the doctor prescribed Prozac.
>
> *Host:* . . . and two weeks later, we paid her another visit. I can't get over it. You're smiling.
>
> *D:* Yeah.
>
> *Host:* How do you feel?
>
> *D:* Great. I feel great. I feel like—like a different person. Somebody else. Somebody—something left my body and another person came in.
>
> *Host:* She no longer spends her days in a filthy apartment. So *two weeks* after you started on this drug, whammo.
>
> *D:* Right.
>
> *Host:* You stopped being depressed . . .
>
> *D:* I stopped being depressed . . .

*Host:* . . . got out of bed . . .

*D:* Mmm, hmm.

*Host:* . . . fixed your apartment, fixed yourself . . .

*D:* Fixed my life.

*Host:* . . . and you're losing weight.

*D:* Yeah. Mmm, hmm. Yep. I'm happy about it. I think it's great.

In this narrative, depression is not a bundle of miseries shaped by many forces, weak and strong: a sedentary, lonely, dishonest, impoverished, or selfish life; perhaps the loss of love, health, beauty, or community; feelings of powerlessness arising from unsatisfying work, oppressive socioeconomic factors, addicted children, or a difficult relationship; frustrated ambitions; difficulties in knowing, speaking, and meeting one's needs or in getting along with one's family or other people. No, D on *60 Minutes* is suffering from a purely biological illness, a "chemical imbalance." Its resolution does not require her to get meaningful support from others, to establish a collaborative relationship with a good psychotherapist, to change her attitudes and actions, or to make any personal effort. There is only one solution needed, and only one offered: the passive consumption of a pill.

For decades, pharmaceutical companies and their handmaidens have spent billions of dollars promoting this simplistic message, and it has only intensified since the introduction of the "miracle SSRIs." Trumpeting these drugs' supposedly vast advantage over earlier antidepressants and therapy, drug company representatives rent booths at psychiatrists' conventions; buy advertising in medical journals; hand out manufacturers samples to MD's; talk to journalists; and fund the seemingly incontrovertible drug research that provides the intellectual undergirding for this miracle play. More recently, the pharmaceutical industry has bypassed these traditional "middle men of mental health" and marketed their wares directly to the general public. Antidepressants are now as normal and pervasive as aspirin—like Visa, it's everywhere you want to be. Zoloft's logo smiles from plastic prepaid phone cards, coffee mugs, luggage tags, and complimentary pens and pencils. A commercial during the World Series asserts the powers of Paxil to cure social anxiety. A colorful tissue box in a physician's office proclaims: "Sue's playing with her kids again" on one side and "Walter's fishing again" on the other. The reason for the turnaround? "Just like normal—thanks to Prozac!"

Then there's the National Depression Screening Day (NDSD). All across the country, hospitals, mental health clinics, physician's offices, and even libraries, grocery stores, and shopping malls are helping people suffering with depression, many of whom apparently do not even know they are suffering from it. Sponsored by the American Psychiatric Association and the National Institute of Mental Health (NIMH) and supported by mental health organizations and patient groups, this project has grown to include over 3,000 sites. In 1998 it screened a record 90,000 people. Over the radio and on television the message is the same: depression, the silent killer, is a treatable, physical disease, like high blood pressure. "Help" is just a phone call away.

At the screening sites the message continues: mild forms of depression can be helped with counseling; moderate or severe forms of the disease require medication. Never mind that no depressed person we know of would ever describe his or her own suffering as "mild." It's like "I'm mildly pregnant." But, of course, that is precisely the point. Why? Because in spite of being jointly *sponsored* by the American Psychiatric Association and the NIMH, NDSD is actually almost completely *funded* by drug companies. In fact, six of the seven major funders are pharmaceutical companies. Kathleen Day reported in her 1995 article "Depression Awareness—or a Prozac Pitch?" in the *Washington Post*, that Eli Lilly alone provides 50% of the funding! The same article reported student and parent complaints that the project, extended into schools, seemed little more than a plug for Prozac. Say no to drugs, but say yes to Prozac. Perhaps Prozac needs a cool image for maximum impact—perhaps something like Joe Camel.

Primary-care physicians, who write most prescriptions for antidepressants, are prime targets for this national marketing extravaganza disguised as a public awareness project. For example, after a recent Depression Day, the managed mental health care firm, Pacificare, reported that the typical physician in its plan, with the help of the quick and dirty questionnaire administered to Shelley, now identifies two to four depressed patients a day and prescribes medication. The message is well crafted, and it works. If Prozac, Paxil, and Zoloft were books, they would be runaway bestsellers: $7 billion was spent on them last year.

Finally, consider the recent White House Conference on Mental Health. Leading luminaries in the field of medicine gathered together to discuss "cutting edge" discoveries in the treatment of emotional problems. As columnist Arianna Huffington later pointed out in a June 1999 article (Arianna Online), however, the whole affair was "mainly a cheerleading session for drug manufacturers," with the plenary sessions looking like "infomercials." Arianna's take on the conference message was that, contrary to the first lady's suggestion, it doesn't take a village to raise a child, just a pill. Arianna's conclusion notwithstanding, this "historic" conference provided commentary on the pervasiveness of the bad-chemicals-on-the-brain theory of human suffering and the belief in the myth of the magic pill.

Their widespread popularity suggests that antidepressants, especially SSRIs, are not merely one good therapeutic tool among many, but miracle drugs, manna from the gods, universal panaceas. They have no serious side effects, so the conventional wisdom goes. They supposedly work for everybody, and far faster and more effectively than therapy for serious depression, making them the obvious treatment of first resort. They help a profoundly depressed sufferer get out of bed and walk and have "proved"—so the popular wisdom goes—that the causes of depression and other forms of human suffering lie not in our stars or our relationships but in our cells.

The message behind the miracle play is demoralizing and disempowering to both clients and therapists—to say nothing of its being utterly unrealistic. Yet professional associations representing therapists seem to have believed the drug companies' publicity and accepted their second-class status, assuming the primacy of pharmaceuticals is based not on great marketing, but good science. They have become acolytes, worshiping before the altar on which the magic pill is displayed. For example, having apparently resigned themselves to a "if you can't beat psychiatry, then join them" philosophy, the American Psychological Association is fighting for prescription privileges for psychologists. At the same time, the American Association for Marriage and Family Therapy (AAMFT) is funding their campaign for wider recognition as a legitimate provider organization by seeking grants from various pharmaceutical companies. A few years back, AAMFT joined Glaxo-SmithKline (a drug company) to produce a brochure called "Intimacy and Depression: The Silent Epidemic." Drugs are spotlighted as the treatment of choice for depression. Curiously, family therapy is never mentioned, and therapy of any kind becomes a poor second cousin to medication—"antidepressants are usually effective, [but] psychotherapy can also be useful," the brochure condescendingly points out. It also laments the many sexual side effects of antidepressants, but suggests that other choices exist *without* sexual side effects. Luckily, Glaxo-SmithKline makes Wellbutrin, an antidepressant whose major marketing distinction is its lack of sexual side effects. Wellbutrin is not mentioned in the brochure, allowing AAMFT to maintain its posture of never endorsing products, but a veiled and ghostly endorsement nonetheless hovers around the entire production, whatever the high-minded denials. Family therapists and other nonmedical therapists can either accept a second-class status, or face daunting odds in protesting the erosion of valued traditions in their professional organizations.

While most people first became aware of our concerns about medication when we protested the AAMFT and Glaxo-SmithKline relationship, we actually began questioning the veracity of the magic pill many years ago. While a graduate student, Barry worked in a residential treatment center for troubled adolescents. When the psychiatrist was on vacation, 16-year-old Ann was admitted and assigned to Barry. Ann was like many of the kids, abused in all imaginable ways, drop-kicked from one foster home to another, attempted suicide on a number of occasions, and been in numerous hospitals and runaway shelters. In spite of all that, Ann was a pure delight—creative, funny, and hopeful for a better future. Therapy went great, Barry and Ann hit it off famously, and Ann settled in and attended high school for the first time in several months.

Three weeks later the psychiatrist returned. Though Ann was adamantly opposed to medication—she said she had been down that path already—the doctor ordered an antidepressant and lithium. Barry protested, citing evidence of Ann's improvement, but to no avail—he was only a mental health grunt and a student to boot. Ann soon ran away and went on a three-day binge of alcohol and drugs. A carload of older men who picked her up while hitchhiking ended the ride with a gang rape. Adding insult to injury, Ann was forcefully injected with an antipsychotic when the police brought her back to the center. When Ann described this experience to Barry, she saw the horror on his face and reassured him that she had suffered far worse indignities than being forcefully tranquilized. It was little solace for either, though.

When Ann persisted in her ardent protests of the drugs, Barry encouraged her to talk to the center director. Rather than listening, however, the director defended the psychiatrist. The director later admonished Barry for putting ideas into Ann's head and told him to "drop it." Instead, Barry spent days researching the literature. What he found surprised him. In contrast to what most clients were told, little was known about how psychotropic drugs actually worked. There were drugs like cocaine, for example, which blocked the reuptake of the brain chemicals believed critical to depression in exactly the same way as antidepressants but did not have any "therapeutic effect." Furthermore, while increases in these "critical" neurotransmitters resulting from antidepressants were actually present within hours of the first dose, they did not result in any therapeutic benefit for four to six weeks! Moreover, there was no empirical support for prescribing these drugs to children—let alone multiple drugs.

Finally, Barry was shocked to find that the effectiveness of the drugs was suspect. He found a 1974 review of 91 studies that reported that tricyclic antidepressants had no better effect than a sugar pill in nearly one-third of the published reports. Though largely overlooked, this finding is particularly noteworthy because participants who showed rapid improvement to the fake pill (called "placebo responders") were eliminated from these studies! Furthermore, as research with negative results is less likely to be published, one can safely assume that the extent of the placebo response rate was considerably underestimated in this review. Simply put, Barry had unexpectedly discovered that the emperor had no clothes. What did Barry get when he confronted the psychiatrist with these facts? He got fired. Ann survived as usual, resisting when she could, and unfortunately viewed this experience as just another cog in her wheel of abuse from her "helpers." Barry left demoralized but determined never to be in the dark again, complicit by virtue of ignorance.

Despite the endless PR and advertising, the campaign to medicalize problems in living cannot succeed without therapists' cooperation. Drug companies need talk therapists to promote their message. Increasing their market share requires that everyone come to believe that chemicals are both the cause of and the cure for emotional difficulties. As Barry discovered, raising a voice of concern is risky. As the old saying goes, there's not much difference between holding up your head and sticking your neck out. However, continuing to acquiesce to the biological perspective and prostituting ourselves for whatever is left over after the "real doctors" have finished eating will only insure our permanent placement at the "kiddies'" table. This doesn't mean simply closing our mouths and refusing to take the medicine we're being told is good for us. Rather, it means looking at what the research literature really says and then using that information to help clients navigate the many choices available to them. In particular, in order to stay the rising tide of biological fundamentalism, clinicians need to be aware of several serious shortcomings in the research.

To begin with, SSRIs do not work for everybody, not even for those who are desperate to believe in them. Just consult the *Physician's Desk Reference*. It reports that adverse reactions cause 15–16% of people to discontinue treatment and that little is known about their effectiveness or consequences beyond 12 weeks of use. A 1999 report issued by the Agency for Health Care Policy and Research (AHCRP) found that in spite of being marketed as having "fewer side effects," those actually taking the new and improved drugs didn't think so. In fact, they were just as likely to drop out of research studies because of side effects as those who took the older tricyclic drugs. Patients on SSRIs are more likely to complain of diarrhea, nausea, insomnia, agitation, headache, and sexual problems. The tricyclic antidepressants are more likely to cause dry mouth, constipation, dizziness, blurred vision, tremors, and adverse cardiovascular effects. Pick your poison.

Unfortunately, dropping out of a research study is among the least problematic side effects of these pharmaceuticals. Adverse drug reactions are in fact the third leading cause of death in the United States! In a 1995 study published in the prestigious *Archives of Internal Medicine*, pharmacists Lyle Bootman and Jeffrey Johnson investigated 3.1 million hospital admissions and estimated that 200,000 people die per year from drug complications. This figure is equivalent to a 757 jet packed full of passengers crashing every eight hours every day of the year! The same study set the cost of such "reactions" at $77 billion annually.

The adverse effect getting the most coverage lately, especially since the 1999 Columbine shootings and the death of Phil Hartman in 1998, is the increased chance of violence. According to psychiatrist outcast Peter Breggin, in his 1999 book *Your Drug May Be Your Problem,* "there is substantial evidence that . . . SSRIs can cause or exacerbate depression, suicide, paranoia and violence." Psychologist Ann Blake Tracy investigated 32 murder/suicides in her book *Prozac: Panacea or Pandora*? She found that 24 of these 32 cases were taking SSRIs. Is this just the raving of lunatics? Yes according to spokespersons like Frederick Goodwin, former director of the NIMH, who boldly asserts that the question of psychotropic drug safety and effectiveness "has long been settled by a mass of scientific evidence and by the testimonies of hundreds of thousands of patients, their families, and caregivers." When this "mass of scientific evidence" is considered, however, the supposed superiority of biological intervention is exposed as a house of cards built on a foundation of sand.

First, consider the report of the AHCPR, which reviewed more than 300 randomized trials of the SSRIs for depression. The report concluded that the SSRIs were no more effective in treating depression than the older and much less costly tricyclic antidepressants. Moreover, in contrast to the 75–80% success rates frequently touted in promotional literature by drug companies, the AHCRP reported a much more modest 50% response rate to the drugs. In other words, only half of those given an antidepressant actually experienced some benefit. While at first glance this figure may still seem impressive, the researchers found that 32% of people in the studies they reviewed responded just as well to an inert, inactive placebo! This means that the newer antidepressants only outperformed sugar pills by 18%—a finding hardly worth writing home about. Responding to similar data published by AHCPR in 1993, psychiatrist Walter Brown ironically stated, "That's not an astonishing effect," and provocatively proposed that placebo should be the first line of treatment with depression.

Recall the stunning changes in D in the *60 Minutes* broadcast. Her changes occurred in just two weeks although prevailing guidelines for Prozac are four to six weeks. Which did she respond to? The active drug or placebo factors? Blinded by expensive marketing, Americans have been led to believe that the virtually universal effectiveness of antidepressants is a matter of scientific record, conclusively demonstrated in strict, controlled, double-blind, placebo studies—the gold standard in medical research. But, in fact, the exaggerated claims from mediocre results are not based on empirical proof but on relatively flimsy data and flawed experimental designs.

In their provocative tour de force, *From Placebo to Panacea*, Professors Roger Greenberg and the late Seymour Fisher demonstrated that the validity of controlled studies, in which a placebo is compared to the "real" drug, depends upon the participants and the raters who measure the effects not knowing who is getting the real drug and who is getting the placebo. They pointed out, however, that the use of inert sugar pills as the placebo in the vast majority of drug studies actually makes it possible for everyone involved to tell who is taking the real drug. Simply put, those taking the active medication will be more likely to experience the standard side effects—dry mouth, weight loss or gain, dizziness, headache, constipation, nausea, insomnia, and so on—clear signals that they are taking a powerful drug—while those taking the sugar pill will not. As a result, the "double-blind" study is immediately "unblinded"—a fact that seriously compromises any conclusions that can be drawn.

Paradoxically, side effects *by themselves* are likely to account for the effect seen in antidepressant studies. Roger Greenberg and his associates examined 13 studies (*all* of those available at the time) on Prozac and reviewed their findings in a 1994 issue of the *Journal of Nervous and Mental Disease*. They found that side effects were themselves positively correlated with improvement: the greater the experience of side effects, the better the outcome was judged to be by both patient and clinician. A meta-analytic review of drug treatments for obsessive compulsive disorder similarly found judgments of therapeutic benefit rose as the experience of side effects increased. These studies suggest that a sudden nudge to clients' physical perceptions seemed to jump-start their own capacity for emotional regeneration.

Psychologists and respected scientists Irving Kirsch and Guy Sapirstein (1998) make a persuasive case that antidepressants may have no effect on depression other than that produced by the perception of side effects and the power of placebo. Their meta-analytic review of 19 studies involving 2,318 patients showed that 75% of the beneficial effect of antidepressants can be ascribed to the placebo effect. The remaining 25% of the positive effect of antidepressant is attributable to the side effects. This review demonstrates that antidepressants are equivalent to credible, but non-antidepressant drugs; in other words, when an *active* placebo is used (one that mimics the side effects of the real drug), the advantage for the antidepressant disappears—there is no difference in discernible effect between the placebo and the drug being tested. Several other recent meta-analytic studies from independent research groups have validated the finding that placebo accounts for most of the antidepressant effect.

Finally, drug studies often look better than they are because they rate improvement by looking to clinicians' perceptions, not clients'. They usually rely on clinician-rated measures of depression (the Hamilton Depression Rating Scale or the Global Assessment Scale, for example) rather than client-rated measures (like the Beck Depression Inventory or the Lambert and Burlingame Outcome Questionnaire). But clinicians and clients differ substantially in their reading of how much improvement in emotional well-being the drugs bring about. In 1986 outcome researcher Michael Lambert and colleagues discovered in their meta-analysis of antidepressant studies that clients reported significantly less improvement on drugs than did their therapists. Six years later, in 1992, Greenberg and colleagues published another more extensive meta-analysis of 22 antidepressant studies involving 2,230 patients—and compared the effects of a placebo with both "old" (Elavil, for example) and "new" (Prozac) antidepressants. They found that both old and new antidepressants showed an advantage (about 18%) over the placebo on *clinician-rated* measures, but none on *client-rated* measures.

In short, when clients rate their *own* responses, they usually experience no improvement on antidepressants beyond what can be attributed to hope and expectation. If clients don't feel "better" after taking medications, how meaningful is any "improvement" their therapists think they see? As a final example of the exaggeration of meager findings, consider a study recently showcased as "the one" that finally demonstrates the benefit of Prozac with children (Emslie, et al., 1997). Set aside the problem of the inert placebo and compromise of the double blind. This study showed *no differences* between the Prozac and placebo groups on all measures, both clinician and client rated (totaling five), *except one*. One clinician-rated measure of improvement showed superior performance of the Prozac over the placebo condition at the end of the study. The conclusion published in a major journal: "Fluoxetine was superior to placebo in the acute phase treatment of major depressive disorder in child and adolescent outpatients with severe, persistent depression."

*You be your own judge.*

Antidepressants are heavily marketed as more effective than therapy for severe depression, and as the pharmaceutical bubble continues to swell, managed-care plans have inexorably pruned therapy to a bare minimum in favor of medications. But research has for years demonstrated that drugs are no more effective than therapy—and there is growing evidence that they may even be *less* effective. As just one example of such research, consider the largest and most methodologically sound study conducted to date comparing psychotherapy with drug treatment: The Treatment of Depression Collaborative Research Project, or TDCRP, led by psychologist Irene Elkin (Elkin, et al., 1989). This 1989 NIMH project, which involved psychiatrists and psychologists in several cities, randomly assigned 250 participants to four groups: Aaron Beck's cognitive therapy, Gerald Klerman and Myrna Weissman's interpersonal therapy, antidepressant treatment, and finally placebo. Overall, the four treatments—including the placebo—worked with about the same effectiveness!

Since the study was first published, there is now research evidence that changes brought about by therapy are more likely to persist over time. In 1992 researcher Tracie Shea and colleagues published an 18-month follow-up study of clients in the original 1989 NIMH multisite project. The psychotherapies outperformed the medications and placebo on almost every outcome measure. More therapy clients than drug clients recovered without a subsequent major depressive relapse, while those receiving the antidepressants sought treatment more often during the follow-up period, showed a higher probability of relapse, and experienced fewer weeks of minimal or no symptoms than either the two therapy groups or the placebo group.

Over the decades generations of therapists have come to suspect it isn't so much *what* they do—what theory, what model, what technique, or even what medication—that helps people, but who *they* are and who their *clients* are, as well as the idiosyncratic personal *fit* between themselves and the people who come to see them. Now there is a growing body of solid evidence for this widespread intuitive wisdom. A study conducted by Sidney Blatt and colleagues based on the same massive data pool comprising the 1989 NIMH project, reinforced evidence that has been emerging in other studies for years: the difference in outcome was related more to differences among clients and therapists than to treatment methods. Blatt found, however, that some therapists were more effective than others. Who were they? The researchers learned that the clinicians most successful in treating depression were more likely to use psychotherapy alone—they rarely used medications at all. "More effective therapists have a psychological rather than a biological orientation in their treatment approach," Blatt concluded.

But wouldn't the best of all possible worlds be one in which medications were *combined* with therapy, for a kind of double-whammy treatment effect? This idea that in treating depression both together must be better than either alone has become the newest orthodoxy among many professional groups. In fact, this sensible-sounding "compromise" actually promotes the use of medications by implicitly suggesting that virtually anybody who enters therapy for any reason could usefully take them, and many practices funded by managed care now routinely require all therapy clients to undergo medical evaluations as a prerequisite to treatment. And yet there is little evidence in favor of the two-is-better-than-one approach. In 1998 Larry Beutler, researcher and senior editor of *The Journal of Consulting and Clinical Psychology*, challenged anyone to find current scientific literature supporting this now-conventional belief. No one can. Consider a meta-analytic study by Yale psychiatrist Bruce Wexler. He concluded his review of seven well-controlled studies of 513 patients with this simple comparison: of clients with major depression, 29/100 would recover if given drugs alone, 47/100 would recover if given therapy alone, and 47/100 would recover if given combined treatment. On the other hand, drop-out or poor response can be expected in 52 drug patients, 30 therapy patients, and 34 combined patients. Further, a 1995 *Consumer Reports* study (Seligman, 1995) concurs that medication plus psychotherapy contributed no more benefits that psychotherapy alone. These findings suggest that therapy alone should usually be the initial plan as it would not expose clients to the unnecessary costs and side effects of combined treatments.

Reality check: The preponderance of scientific evidence shows that therapy is as effective or more effective than medications in the treatment of depression, even if severe, especially when client-rated measures and long-term follow-up are considered. In all of the healing arts, there is no single explanation or simple, infallible remedy for any of the problems that beset humankind. And yet the growing focus on biological determinism in mental health with the accompanying pharmaceutical hard-sell suggests not only that there are always solely biological explanations, but perfect, fail-safe biological solutions as well—simple pills that mark *fini* to everything from mild depression and nervous tension to panic attacks and bipolar disorder to full-blown psychosis and schizophrenia. How did this medically anomalous, weirdly simplistic point of view come about? If the science behind the alleged superiority of psychotropic drugs is so lacking, how did medications come to hold almost unchallenged sway over both public and professional opinion?

In the days of the Watergate investigation, the chief informant known as "Deep Throat" advised investigative reporters to "follow the money" to discover the source of illegal behaviors, which eventually led them to the President of the United States. Something like the same advice might help explain why psychotropic medications have permeated every aspect of our culture. Follow the money, and you will begin to understand the logic behind the growth of the pharmaceutical behemoth. A recent piece of investigative journalism in the *Wall Street Journal* (Tanouye, 1998), for example, reported that 96 % of the research studies of any drug funded by its manufacturer turn out favorable results, while only 37 % of the studies *not* funded by the manufacturer find in favor of the new drug. Like a flower opening itself to the sun, the research results tend to lean toward the money source. Similarly, a study published in October 1999 in *The Journal of the American Medical Association* (*JAMA*) by Mark Friedberg concluded that drug company sponsorship is associated with a reduced likelihood that unfavorable results will be reported. In a scientific version of the piper calling the tune, the drug company that is paying for the research tends to get the kind of research its leaders want.

Given this bias, it is even more distressing to consider how many pro-drug articles are published that *fail* to disclose ties to drug companies. The American Medical Association provides ethical prohibitions against physicians accepting payments, funding, reimbursements, or inducements of any kind without disclosing their relationships to drug companies. But it happens anyway, all too often. An investigation by Terence Monmaney of the *Los Angeles Times* (1999) found that the renowned *New England Journal of Medicine* published articles by researchers with drug company ties who did not identify potential conflicts of interest. In an analysis of 36 articles since 1997, eight articles were found with undisclosed financial links to drug companies that marketed treatments evaluated in the articles. Another recent example is provided by an article in *JAMA* that reported the sorry state of affairs of American sexuality, saying that as many as 43% suffer from sexual dysfunction. *JAMA* belatedly disclosed that the authors of the study were paid consultants to Pfizer, makers of Viagra, and may have had a conflict of interest in pronouncing the nation's libido in such a dysfunctional condition.

Although the AMA takes conflicts of interest seriously, it cannot apparently keep up with all the violations. With so much drug company funding, it is impossible to police. In addition, there is a major loophole in the guidelines. While disclosure is mandated in medical journals, it is not required in any publications that go directly to the general public. It is almost as if the AMA were saying that it is important for doctors but not the general public to know about potential breaches in objectivity. A physician can write an article in a magazine with widespread circulation or author a book that sells millions and never have to breathe a word about her affiliations. Add to this disclosure deficit the many TV appearances made that implicitly support drug company interests.

Just as bad money drives out good, heavy marketing seems to blunt or even nullify the effects of good but negative research when it does occur. *Consumer Reports* (Gurin, 1992) estimated in a 1992 issue that the $65 billion drug industry spends $5 billion a year on promotion and publicity for its products—the "educational" and "public service" efforts and multimedia advertising blitz already discussed, for example. Psychotherapy cannot begin to compete with the billion-dollar drug industry when it comes to promoting the value of therapy even though the data are clear: psychotherapy is, hands down, as good as, or better than, medications when head-to-head comparisons are made.

Psychiatrist gadflies Peter Breggin and Loren Mosher have documented the powerful influence of drug company money on continuing education and psychiatric journals. Mosher, in a 1999 *Psychology Today* article, estimates that drug companies spend an average of $10,000 per physician, per year, on "education." Fully 30% of the budget of the American Psychiatric Association is underwritten by drug advertising, and pharmaceutical companies substantially support psychiatric conferences through displays and unrestricted grants. How does all this money impact the psychiatric profession? As Abraham Lincoln once said, "Moral principle is a looser bond than pecuniary interest."

Mosher calls the relationship between drug companies and psychiatry an "unholy alliance" that "is dangerous because researchers and psychiatrists . . . remain biased in favor of drug cures, downplay side effects and seldom try other types of intervention." It is understandable that biological psychiatry is now embraced almost exclusively in medical schools and residency training programs. "Biochemical imbalance" is the battle cry of the profession. In interviews with the media, psychiatrists often resemble the brainwashed soldiers in the *Manchurian Candidate* (starring Frank Sinatra), robotically espousing the ubiquitous biochemical imbalance as the cause of a plethora of problems.

And therapists of all stripes are joining them as drug companies extend their influence—and the potential conflicts of interest—to other mental health professions. For example, with the help of an unrestricted grant from GlaxoSmithKline, the 1998 conference of AAMFT highlighted the Intimacy and Depression campaign at its opening session—a session generally reserved for one of the real movers of the family therapy field. Instead, without disclosing GlaxoSmithKline involvement, the session, using *Party of Five* clips and an *Oprah* style format, presented an hour and a half commercial for Wellbutrin without, of course, ever mentioning the drug specifically. The tragedy of the sexual side effects of antidepressants was repeated 11 times, and 6 times the point was pummeled into the audience of 2,000 therapists that treating depression need not include depriving clients of a sex life. Therapists were encouraged to inquire about side effects and inform clients that alternatives exist to help them.

Two of the presenters were affiliated with GlaxoSmithKline. The psychiatrist who drove home the point about sexual side effects of antidepressants was on Glaxo's advisory board, speaker's bureau, and had had her research funded by them. She, with the psychologist on the panel, wrote GlaxoSmithKline's own brochure about the Intimacy and Depression Campaign (IDC). By depriving the audience of the consideration of any possible conflicts of interest, AAMFT violated the standards of the Accreditation Council for Continuing Medical Education (ACCME) in two ways. AAMFT did not acknowledge Glaxo's support in the conference brochure (Standard 5c) and did not disclose the faculty relationships with Glaxo (Standard 7b).

With all this largesse and publicity raining benevolently down, is it any wonder that people and therapists tend to become hypnotically fixated on the brouhaha about a "revolution" in psychopharmaceuticals and overlook the boring fine print of the drug studies with their more negative implications? Most important, the fact that drugs do not live up to their miracle status does not discredit those that have been helped. Medication has its place—if only it would stay there! To give the devil his due, we believe that antidepressants can be very helpful at times—especially for those who believe in them. Because they've gotten good press, they can positively harness the placebo effect, reinforcing Sir William Osler's dictum that "One should treat as many patients as possible with a new drug while it still has the power to heal." They sometimes do help free people from paralyzing self-doubt, obsessions, and bulimic cravings—people who have conscientiously tried therapy with no results. Because they're widely touted as simple and effective, they encourage people who might otherwise be too ashamed and reluctant, to talk to another human being about their unhappiness and pain. Because they offer concrete, immediate action, they hearten people with the thought that at least someone is doing *something* to help them. Finally, some people find it easier to begin contemplating their distress when they can attribute it to their biochemistry rather than to circumstances in their personal lives. So drugs should not be banished from the sanctuary of psychotherapy; rather, therapists and consumers should get a grip, stop kowtowing to their supposedly superior powers, and think of them as one valid choice among many—and certainly not as the treatment of first resort.

But where does this sobering evidence about psychiatric drugs leave us when we are face-to-face with smothering despair? Consider Alina. At the first session, her therapist listened with growing concern as Alina talked about her fourth attempt to live apart from her abusive husband—the sense of having failed, failed her husband, her marriage, her children, and herself. She spoke of her financial desperation, the humiliation of her new job with a boss who berated her Spanish accent in front of customers, and her guilt at not being able to make a better life, pick a better partner, or make a bad marriage better. "I can hardly get up in the morning. It's just no use. I'm no good to anyone. I really have nothing to live for, to look forward to. If I had the guts, I'd just crash my car into a tree and be done with it." Her tears, her anguish, her despair were so palpable during the session that her therapist found herself having to fight her own feelings of hopelessness and fear for Alina.

Such riveting situations are, if not routine, expected fare in our line of business. It is the "burned out" therapist, indeed, who cannot resonate with the suffering and seemingly inescapable dilemmas our clients present. And it is this resonance that permits the connection and, therefore, the possibility that we can be part of some kind of change. It is also this resonance that makes us vulnerable to finding ourselves, like our clients, in the land of no alternatives. And when, in that place, a voice appears speaking of the miraculous wonders of a biological cure, the superiority of "modern science" over primitive "talk" or "self-help," the sky brightens and a gleam of hope shatters the darkness. With no other equally attractive, powerful voice around, it's not difficult to see that, when facing the hard issues (like life or death), therapists with a heart naturally, inevitably reach for something they believe can give their clients (and themselves) hope and relief.

Our culture, our "mental health" mythology, speaks the following: "It's fine to go to self-help groups, talk to a therapist, try yoga, or take St. John's wort when you're just having a down time—the 'blues'. We're talking about a different animal; we're talking about the can't eat, can't sleep, can't not sleep, can't think, can't work, can't love kind of debilitation that threatens one's livelihood, indeed, one's very life. We're talking *major* depression—MD." How has such a climate flourished, where one option shines out above all others in such a compelling and irresistible way, virtually assuring its prominence in the lives of people in severe distress? How is it that forty years of research that confirms the preeminence of client resourcefulness, resiliency, and the healing capacity of the therapeutic relationship is dwarfed by a pill? How has it come to be that therapists, when put to the test, so readily abandon their belief in hard-won, professional skills, and instincts in favor of a medical solution?

Just to set the record straight, these are the very situations we must challenge therapists and clients to reexamine and to question the knee-jerk reaction to seek prescription. We challenge the belief that such depressive conditions, while undoubtedly fraught with pain, despair, and fear, universally require medication. In fact, we challenge therapists and clients to consider personal and social options on at least an equal footing—and to rebuild a faith in themselves and the inevitability of change.

Sitting there, facing Alina, the therapist found herself wondering about the best way to be of help. She began to think about medication, and the implications of the fact that 70% of all antidepressants are prescribed to women. Would medication augment Alina's sense of failure or provide the boost she needed to find hope and pleasure in her life once again? One path was predictable—referral to someone who could prescribe would inevitably focus on Alina's mental state, her fragility, and potential suicide. Other paths were far more uncertain. As the therapist struggled with the uncertainty, Alina talked about her past relationships, sharing some sad, and even some humorous, memories. As the conversation unfolded, Alina mentioned that she didn't like pills, and wanted "to do it on her own." Knowing that various plans, including medication, could be introduced at any time, the therapist trusted in Alina's direction and in the power of two people inhabiting an intimate moment of the tragedies and triumphs of Alina's life. It seemed natural, at the end of the visit, for the therapist to comment on what Alina had done to extricate herself and her children in the past from unbearable situations. Alina ended the discussion by emphatically stating that she had no plans to hurt herself. Three weeks later, after weekly meetings, the worst seemed to be over. Alina had managed to hang in with her new job and was quietly putting money away as her "escape plan" for an independent future. The therapist and Alina had weathered the storm together, with Alina, not medication (or the therapist), at the helm.

To be trigger-happy to bring medication into the discussion automatically in "scary" sessions is to be under the influence of bad science and great marketing. When clients are stuck or desperate, the medication solution is easy to whip up—like ready-made dinners, it takes the work and anxiety out of "What's for supper?" However, consider also that in most therapy, therapists hold more power than clients. Consequently, the therapist's suggestions, for better or worse, immediately garner a particular status in the client's mind. The introduction of medication at a particular point in the therapy conversation carries with it numerous messages, none of which is "Here's just one of many options to consider." Instead, the uninvited introduction of medication into the therapy conversation, even when framed as an option, is likely to communicate "Your problem is so severe, we have to look at something other than what we are doing here, or something other than what you can do to deal with it"; or "Medication is the best thing for what you are telling me." These messages serve to abort the natural search for answers that is the heart of change.

In a moment of crisis, of wanting to help or seeking help, if the option to try something different is not at least as attractive, doable, and potentially effective as the medical option, the magic pill will win. What is required is a shift, or, more likely, a reconnection, to what therapists know and have experienced over and over, both in their clients and in themselves—that most people can and will develop solutions to even the most daunting dilemmas given support and encouragement, that the impetus to health has many avenues and sometimes takes unorthodox routes, and that change will and does occur naturally and universally. This is not a "just snap out of it" or "grin and bear it" approach to either "character weakness" or moodiness. It is an effective, all-out assault on the sometimes terrifying and almost always destructive experience of depression. At its core is a faith in change and the human tendency to find a way even out of the heart of darkness.

We privilege this stance as a way to "level the playing field," to compete with the powerful and boisterous medical ideologies promoted by profiteers and championed by factions within our own professions. When we can hang on to these beliefs in our hearts, emboldened by personal, anecdotal, and empirical evidence, we, and our clients, can hear, loud and clear, other possibilities in times of crisis where once there was only the seductive chant to medicate. Recall, once again, the NIMH Treatment of Depression Collaborative Research Project; it found that clinical improvement was unrelated to the type of treatment received (e.g., psychotherapy, drug treatment). Researcher Janice Krupnick and colleagues, using the same data, reported in *The Journal of Consulting and Clinical Psychology*

(Krupnick, et al, 1996), have shown that the quality and strength of the therapeutic relationship was the *primary* determinant of successful outcome across treatments—including medication! The type of treatment administered didn't matter. The type of relationship formed mattered most. Indeed, the massive size of the NIMH study means that the best treatment for depression, the treatment having most empirical support, is a good relationship with a therapist.

For most of the history of the field, therapists have been trained and research conducted "as if" treatment models and their associated techniques explained and caused change. Like the anesthetic before surgery, "building an alliance" or "establishing rapport" has routinely been thought of as the procedure therapists must do *prior* to the "real" treatment (e.g., confronting dysfunctional thinking, prescribing drugs). In contrast to common perception, the therapeutic relationship is not another vague, unquantifiable, feel-good technique from the field of therapy. Neither is it the latest in a long line of miraculous technique to be hyped on the lecture circuit. Rather, the consistent finding in a virtual mountain of studies conducted over the last 40 years is that therapies that focus on the *client's* goals and ideas about the problem and change process and use the perceptions of a helpful therapeutic interaction are the most successful. Note the emphasis on the client's.

Here is where we differ from those who would apply the aggregate data about drugs and psychotherapy without considering the client's own views of what could be helpful. It is true that the data suggest that psychotherapy should be the first line of treatment for people with experiences of depression; then, if change is not forthcoming, medication can be considered. However, such an assumption does not integrate the unique aspects of what our work entails, nor does it include the most potent contributors to change in the decision-making process—our clients. Listening to and exploring their stories, experiences, and interpretations of the problem and the change process, what we have come to call the client's theory of change, over time, evolves to an approach that is tailored to the unique qualities of the individual client. In short, treatment is client-directed. Depending on the client's views of what effectively produces change, this could include anything from physical exercise and dietary changes to assertiveness training, cognitive-behavioral therapy, volunteering, St. John's Wort, restructuring family hierarchies, or learning how to get along better with others— all of which have been shown to sometimes have a positive impact on depression. We would, for example, never stand in the way of clients considering medication if they believed their problems were of biological origin and thought the drugs might be helpful. It is up to therapists to privilege clients' wishes in the therapy conversation, including their trains of thought, their brainstorming, and their talk. When clients put medication on the table, then therapists can naturally help them explore it as an option. When clients believe medication will help and feel more hopeful at the possibility of trying medication when they are "in the driver's seat" in making an informed choice (including information about side effects, length of treatment, and possibilities of relapse), then medication can be beneficial. To follow the client's lead is to maximize client participation, strengthen the therapeutic bond, and enhance therapeutic outcomes.

In a country that has come to expect, even demand, miracles from the pharmaceutical companies, it is little wonder that the chronic problems of drug therapy and the excesses of corporate marketing have been largely ignored. We hope against hope that some pill, some simple and painless solution, will be the cure-all for our emotional and familial woes. Finally realizing that psychiatric drug therapy is a profit-driven industry, built on a flimsy science, may be the bad-tasting medicine we've needed. Although it may be hard to swallow, it is time for therapists to learn the data, reinvigorate their belief in therapy, and offer clients real choices for addressing their concerns. Ultimately, therapists and consumers need to just sit back, take a deep breath, and accept the truth about depression and other human travails: there is no better medicine than enlisting your own strengths in a good therapeutic relationship.

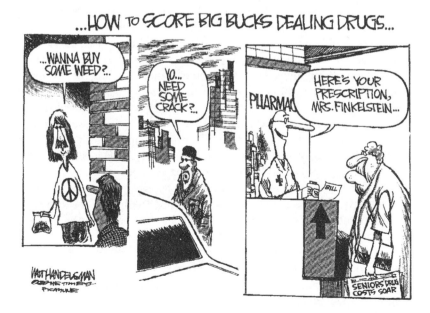

The development of political agenda-setting through the use of sophisticated public relations techniques is threatening to undermine the delicate balance of representative democracy. This has important ramifications for policies aimed at providing mental health services and the implementation of mental health laws. The principal agenda setters in this area are the pharmaceutical companies that have commercial reasons to promote public policies that expand the sales of their products. They have manufactured highly effective advocacy coalitions that incorporate front groups in order to set the policy agenda for mental health. However, policies tailored to their commercial purpose are not necessarily beneficial either for patients or the society at large.

## REFERENCES

American Association of Marriage and Family Therapy. (1998). *Intimacy and depression: the silent epidemic [Brochure]. Washington, D.C.: AAMFT.*

Blatt, S. J., Zuroff, D. C., Quinlan, D. M., and Pilkonis, P. (1996). Interpersonal factors in brief treatment of depression: Further analyses of the NIMH treatment of depression collaborative research program. *Journal of Consulting and Clinical Psychology,* 64, 162–171.

Breggin, P. (1999). *Your drug may be your problem.* Reading, MA: Perseus Books.

Day, K. (1995, January 18). Depression awareness—or a Prozac pitch? *The Washington Post,* C6.

Elkin, I., Shea, T., Watkins, J. T., Imber, S. D., Sotsky, S. M., Collins, J. F., Glass, D. R., Pilkonis, P. A., Leber, W. R., Docherty, J. P., Fiester, S. J., & Parloff, M. B. (1989). National institute of mental health treatment of depression collaborative research program: General effectiveness of treatments. *Archives of General Psychiatry,* 46, 971–982.

Emslie, G. J., Rush, A. J., Weinberg, W. A., Kowatch, R. A., Hughes, C. W., Carmody, T., Rintelmann, J. (1997). A double-blind, randomized, placebo-controlled trial of fluoxetien in children and adolescents with depression. *Archives of General Psychiatry,* 54 (1), 1031–1037.

Fisher, S., & Greenberg, R. R. (Eds). (1997b). *From Placebo to panacea: Putting psychiatric drugs to the test.* New York: Wiley.

Friedberg, M., Saffran, B., Stinson, T., Nelson, W., & Bennet, M. (1999). Evaluation of conflict of interest in economic analyses of new drugs used in oncology. *Journal of the American Medical Association,* 282, 1453–1457.

Greenberg, R. P., Bornstein, R. F., Greenberg, M. D., & Fisher, S. (1992). A meta-analysis of antidepressant outcome under "blinder" conditions. *Journal of Consulting and Clinical Psychology,* 60, 664–669.

Greenberg, R., Bornstein, R., Zborowski, M., Fisher, S., & Greenberg, M. (1994). A meta-analysis of fluoxetine outcome in the treatment of depression. *Journal of Nervous and Mental Disease,* 182, 547–551.

Gurin, R. (1992, February). Pushing drugs to doctors. *Consumer Reports,* 87–94.

Huffington, A. (1999, June 10). The dangers of the White House mental health conference. Arianna Online. (www.ariannaonline.com)

Johnson, J., & Bootman (1995). Drug-related morbidity and mortality. *Archives of Internal Medicine,* 155, 1949–1956.

Kirsch, I., & Sapirstein, G. (1998). Listening to Prozac but hearing placebo: A meta-analysis of antidepressant medication. *Prevention & Treatment,* Article 0002a. Available at http://journals.apa.org/prevention/volume1/pre0010002ahtml.

Krupnick, J. L., Sotsky, S. M., Simmens, S., Moyher, J., Elkin, I., Watkins, J., & Pilkonis, P. A. (1996). The role of the therapeutic alliance in psychotherapy and pharmacotherapy outcome: Findings in the National Institute of Mental Health Treatment of Depression Collaborative Research Project." *Journal of Consulting and Clinical Psychology,* 64, 532–539.

Lambert, M., Hatch, D., Kingston, M., & Edwards, B. (1986). Zung, Beck, and Hamilton rating scales as measures of treatment outcome: A met-analytic comparison. *Journal of Consulting and Clinical Psychology,* 54, 54–59.

Monmaney, T. (1999, October 21). Medical journal may have flouted own ethics eight times. *The Los Angeles Times,* 1.

Mosher, L. (1999, September). I want no part of it anymore. *Psychology Today,* 40–41, 80.

Seligman, M. E. P. (1995). The effectiveness of psychotherapy: The Consumer Reports Survey," *American Psychologist,* 50, 965–974.

Shea, M., Elkin, I., Imber, S., Sotsky, S., Watkins, J., Collins, J., Pilkonis, P., Beckham, R., Glass, D., Dolan, C., & Parloff, M. (1992). Course of depressive symptoms over follow up: The NIMH TDCRP. *Archives of General Psychiatry,* 49(10), 782–87.

Tanouye, E. (1998, January 8). Does corporate funding influence research? *The Wall Street Journal,* B1, B6.

Tracy, A. (1994). *Prozac: Panacea or Pandora?* West Jordan, UT: Cassica Publications.

Valenstein, E. (1998). *Blaming the Brain.* New York: Free Press.

Chapter 10

# Pig Pharma:
# Psychiatric Agenda Setting
# by Drug Companies*

Sharon Beder, PhD, MSCSoc, Richard Gosden, PhD,
and Loren Mosher, MD

*I passed by his garden, and marked, with one eye,*
*How the Owl and the Panther were sharing a pie:*
*The Panther took pie-crust, and gravy, and meat,*
*While the Owl had the dish as its share of the treat.*
*When the pie was all finished, the Owl, as a boon,*
*Was kindly permitted to pocket the spoon:*
*White the Panther received knife and fork with a growl,*
*And concluded the banquet by——*
                    Lewis Carroll, *Alice's Adventures in Wonderland*

This paper uses the theory of agenda setting to examine how pharmaceutical companies are using public relations techniques to manipulate psychiatric thinking and public policy-making in the mental health field in the

*A shorter version of this chapter was originally published as Gosden, R. & Beder, S., Pharmaceutical Industry Agenda Setting in Mental Health Policies. *Ethical Human Sciences and Services,* Vol. 3, No. 3, Fall/Winter 2001, pp. 147–159. Adapted with permission from Springer Publishing Company.

United States and Australia. Biologically based theories of mental disorders, and the accompanying imperatives to use drugs in treatments, have come to be accepted by most of the major players in the mental health policy arena, including advocacy groups purporting to represent "consumers." Mental health policies have been extensively studied from the point of view of their effectiveness in achieving desirable mental health outcomes, but the political basis of their formulation and adoption—the agenda-setting process—has been neglected.

The theory of agenda setting is common to the academic fields of mass communications, policy studies, and politics. The mass communications literature tends to concentrate on the role of the media in setting the "public" agenda while the political literature tends to concentrate more on how particular issues reach the governmental "policy" agenda. Of course, the two points of focus are interrelated, since the public agenda affects the governmental policy agenda, and vice versa. In regard to the mental health policy arena, pubic relations companies have played a major role in both using the media to set the "public" agenda while at the same time directly lobbying to get particular policies onto the "formal" agenda. The formal agenda can be described as the "set of items explicitly up for active and serious consideration of authoritative decision-makers" (Cobb & Elder, 1983, p. 86).

Although policy setting in Australia and the United States are very different (with a congressional and regionally based system in the United States and a Westminster style of government in Australia), both countries have federal systems of government, and both countries make mental health policies at state and federal levels of government. Drug-based mental health policies have become dominant in both countries. In most cases U.S. policy entrepreneurs have influenced Australian policies. However, in at least one area—preventive drug treatment for schizophrenia—it is Australian policy entrepreneurs who are influencing the development of U.S. policy. (Gosden, 1999).

## ADVOCACY COALITIONS

Most agenda-setting theory encapsulates the idea of the need for advocates to expand interest in a particular issue or policy. This is usually done by policy entrepreneurs (Kingdon, 1984) who build up advocacy coalitions (Sabatier, 1988) to push policies onto the agenda. What is unusual in the arena of mental health policy is the large role played by public relations in creating the relevant advocacy coalitions. These advocacy coalitions often have at their core purpose-built consumer groups that are little more than front groups for the psychiatric industry.

Front groups enable corporations, such as pharmaceutical companies, to take part in public debates and government hearings behind a cover of community concern. Corporations could do this openly and in their own names, but it is far more effective to have a group of citizens or a group of experts—preferably a coalition of such groups—which can publicly promote the outcomes desired by the corporation while claiming to represent the public interest. When such groups do not already exist, the modern corporation can pay a public relations firm to create them (Beder, 1997, ch. 2).

The use of front groups to represent industry interests in the name of concerned citizens is a relatively recent phenomenon and one that pharmaceutical companies have heavily utilized (See for example, O'Harrow, 2000; Picard, 2001; Menendez, 1998). Previously, businesses lobbied governments directly and put out press releases in their own name or that of their trade associations (Megalli & Friedman, 1991, p. 2). However the rise of citizen and public interest groups has been accompanied by a growing skepticism among the public about statements made by businesses:

> Thus, if Burger King were to report that a Whopper is nutritious, informed consumers would probably shrug in disbelief. . . . And if the Nutrasweet Company were to insist that the artificial sweetener aspartame has no side effects, consumers might not be inclined to believe them, either.
>
> But if the "American Council on Science and Health" and its panel of 200 "expert" scientists reported that Whoppers were not so bad, consumers might actually listen. . . . And if the "Calorie Control Council" reported that aspartame is not really dangerous, weight-conscious consumers might continue dumping the artificial sweetener in their coffee every morning without concern (Megalli & Friedman, 1991, p. 3).

These front groups lobby governments to legislate in the corporate interest, to oppose undesirable regulations and to introduce policies that enhance corporate profitability. Front groups also campaign to change public opinion so that the markets for corporate goods, for example, psychiatric drugs, are not threatened and are even enhanced. Merrill Rose, executive vice president of the public relations firm Porter/Novelli, advises companies:

> Put your words in someone else's mouth. . . . There will be times when the position you advocate, no matter how well framed and supported, will not be accepted by the public simply because you are who you are. Any institution with a vested commercial interest in the outcome of an issue has a natural credibility barrier to overcome with the public, and often, with the media (Rose, 1991, p. 28).

The public relations industry often refers to front groups euphemistically as "partners." Steve Rabin, a former executive vice president and general manager of Porter/Novelli, is an expert on the art of forming advocacy partnerships. According to Rabin, advocacy partnerships are all about "the joining together of organizations commonly regarded as adversaries, the establishment of brand loyalty, the enhancement of product sales, the maintenance of a company's reputation and image in the community" (Rabin, 1992, p. 32). More recently Rabin has been applying his skills in partnership formation with the giant PR conglomerate Nelson Communications World-wide. Nelson's client list includes Abbott Laboratories, AstraZeneca, Bayer, Bristol-Myers Squibb, Eli Lilly, GlaxoWellcome, Hoffman-La Roche, Janssen-Cilag, Lundbeck, Novartis, Pfizer, SmithKline Beecham, Wyeth-Ayerst International, together with the National Alliance for the Mentally Ill (NAMI). (Nelson Communications Worldwide, 2001).

Some of NAMI's funding sources were exposed in a *Mother Jones* article. All of the pharmaceutical companies identified as funding NAMI, together with NAMI itself, are on the above client list of Nelson Communications.

> According to internal documents obtained by *Mother Jones,* 18 drug firms gave NAMI a total of $11.72 million between 1996 and mid-1999. These include Janssen ($2.08 million), Novartis ($1.87 million), Pfizer ($1.3 million), Abbott Laboratories ($1.24 million), Wyeth-Ayerst Pharmaceuticals ($658,000), and Bristol-Myers Squibb ($613,505). NAMI's leading donor is Eli Lilly and Company, maker of Prozac, which gave $2.87 million during that period. In 1999 alone, Lilly will have delivered $1.1 million in quarterly installments, with the lion's share going to help fund NAMI's "Campaign to End Discrimination" against the mentally ill.
>
> In the case of Lilly, at least, "funding" takes more than one form. Jerry Radke, a Lilly executive, is "on loan" to NAMI, working out of the organization's headquarters (Silverstein, 1999).

The names of corporate front groups are carefully chosen to mask the real interests behind them, but they can usually be identified by their funding sources, membership, and who controls them (Megalli & Friedman, 1991, p. 4). Some front groups are quite blatant, working out of the offices of public relations firms and having staff of those firms on their boards of directors. The best-researched examples are in the environmental area. Here it has been observed that the Council for Solid Waste Solutions shares office space with the Society of the Plastic Industry, Inc., and the Oregon Lands Coalition works out of the offices of the Association of Oregon Industries (Stapleton, 1992, p. 35).

Corporate front groups have flourished in the United States. Several large companies donate money to more than one front group. For example, in 1991 Dow Chemical was contributing to ten front groups, including the Alliance to Keep Americans Working, the Alliance for Responsible CFC Policy, the American Council on Science and Health, Citizens for a Sound Economy, and the Council for Solid Waste Solutions. According to Mark Megalli and Andy Friedman, in their report on corporate front groups in America, oil companies Chevron and Exxon were each contributing to nine such groups. Other companies which donate to multiple groups include ExxonMobil, Du Pont, Amoco, Ford, Philip Morris, Pfizer, Monsanto, and Procter and Gamble (Megalli & Friedman, 1991, pp. 184–85). These large corporations "stand to profit handsomely by linking their goals with what they hope to define as a grassroots populist movement" (Poole, 1992, p. 61).

Front groups are not the only way in which corporate interests can be portrayed as coinciding with a greater public interest. Public relations firms are becoming proficient at helping their corporate clients convince key politicians that there is wide public support for their policy agendas. Using specially tailored mailing lists, field officers, telephone banks, and the latest in information technology, these firms are able to generate hundreds of telephone calls and thousands of pieces of mail to key politicians, creating the impression that there is wide public support for their client's position (Beder, 1997, ch. 2).

This sort of operation was almost unheard of fifteen years ago, yet in the United States today, where "technology makes building volunteer organizations as simple as writing a check," it has become "one of the hottest trends in politics" and an $800 million industry (Faucheux, 1995, p. 20). Grassroots campaigning became "the most popular political strategy in the 1990s" (Keim, 1996, p. 17). It is now a part of normal business for corporations and trade associations to employ one of the dozens of companies that specialize in these strategies, to run grassroots campaigns for them. Firms and associations utilizing such services include Philip Morris, Georgia Pacific, the Chemical Manufacturers Association, General Electric, American Forest & Paper Association, Chevron, Union Carbide, Procter & Gamble, American Chemical Society, American Plastics Association, Motor Vehicle Manufacturers Association, WMX Technologies, Browning Ferris Industries, and the Nuclear Energy Institute (Faucheux, 1995, pp. 21, 26–30).

The public relations industry itself refers to artificially created grassroots coalitions as "Astroturf" (after a synthetic grass product). Astroturf is a "grassroots program that involves the instant manufacturing of public support for a point of view in which either uninformed activists are recruited or means of deception are used to recruit them" (Stauber & Rampton, 1995/96, p. 23). According to *Consumer Reports* magazine, those engaging in this sort of work can earn up to $500 "for every citizen they mobilize for a corporate client's cause" (Anon., 1994, p. 318).

Mario Cooper, senior vice president of PR firm Porter/Novelli, says that the challenge for a grassroots specialist is to create the impression that millions of people support their client's view of a particular issue so a politician can't ignore it, and this means targeting potential supporters and targeting "persuadable" politicians. He advises: "Database management companies can provide you with incredibly detailed mailing lists segmented by almost any factor you can imagine" (Cooper, 1993/94, p. 14). Once identified, potential supporters are persuaded to agree to endorse the corporate view being promoted.

Specialists in this form of organizing use opinion research data to "identify the kinds of themes most likely to arouse key constituent groups, then gear their telemarketing pitches around those themes" (Anon., 1994, p. 317). Telephone polls in particular enable rapid feedback so that the pitch can be refined: "With phones you're on the phones today, you analyze your results, you can change your script and try a new thing tomorrow. In a three-day program you can make four or five different changes, find out what's really working, what messages really motivate people, and improve your response rates" (Stauber & Rampton, 1995, p. 84). Focus groups also help with targeting messages (Cooper, 1993/94, p. 15).

Demographic information, election results, polling results, and lifestyle clusters can all be combined to identify potential supporters by giving information about people's age, income, marital status, gender, ethnic background, the type of car they drive, and the type of music they like. These techniques, which were originally developed for marketing products to selected audiences, are now used to identify likely political attitudes and opinions. In this way the coalition builders don't have to waste their time on people who are unlikely to be persuaded and at the same time different arguments can be used for different types of people (Grefe & Linsky, 1995, pp. 216–220).

When President Clinton attempted to impose price controls on pharmaceuticals, seven pharmaceutical giants hired PR firm Powell Tate to repair their public image and to counter public demands for price controls on pharmaceuticals.

> To counter public support for price controls on drugs, the firm drummed up "white hats"—citizens and respectable-sounding groups with no known ties to the industry—to "deliver the industry's message." Then, to create the appearance of broad-based support for the companies' agenda, Powell Tate undertook a "targeted grassroots effort to influence decisions of key lawmakers." A massive letter-writing campaign recruited pro-business citizens and eventually generated over 50,000 form letters and messages, sent to dozens of congresspersons (Levine, 1993).

The pharmaceutical industry umbrella organization, the Pharmaceutical Research and Manufacturers of America, uses the specialized public relations services of Bonner & Associates. Bonner is thought to be one of the leading specialists in grassroots support for clients (Greider, 1993, p. 8), and boasts on its Web site that it is variously the "pioneer," "guru," and "king of grassroots" (Bonner & Associates, 2001).

## AGENDA SETTING IN THE MENTAL HEALTH ARENA

The central thrust of agenda setting in mental health policy-making over the last 20 years in both the United States and Australia has resulted in the triumph of biological interpretations of mental disorders—together with drug-based treatment regimes—over theories and policies associated with forms of "talking therapy" like psychotherapy and family therapy. This dramatic shift of policy has largely come about as the result of pharmaceutical industry-funded public relations activity, which has provided policy entrepreneurs and organized advocacy coalitions to promote drug treatments for what are often claimed to be imbalances in brain chemistry.

It is abundantly clear to any thoughtful observer of the American psychiatric scene that drug company influence is present at all levels. If expenditure levels are any indication, their power and control is expanding. A few facts are illustrative: between 1993 and 2001 prescription drug spending tripled—from $50 billion to $150 billion (Szegely-Marzak, 2001). In 2000, psychotropic drug sales in the U.S totaled $23 billion and will rise to $42 billion by 2005. Of the $23 billion, just over $10 billion was spent on antidepressants. Between 1990 and 2000 spending on antidepressant drugs rose 800% (Tanouye, 2001), due principally to the introduction of the SSRIs. Over the same period, the availability of the new "atypical" antipsychotic drugs caused spending on neuroleptics to rise 600 percent (Moukheiber, 2001).

The large pharmaceutical companies averaged between 30–40% of revenues spent on marketing and administration, 15–20% profit, and 12–15% on research and development. In the United States they paid an average of 16% of revenues in taxes, whereas all other industries averaged 27% (Angell and Relman, 2001). They have 625 paid lobbyists in Washington, DC—one per congressperson (Public Citizen, 2001)!

The industry's tentacles are everywhere. It spent $5.8 billion on direct-to-consumer (TV and magazine) advertising in 1999. Roughly a third of the American Psychiatric Association's budget is derived from various drug sources (*Psychiatric News,* 15/8/97, p. 4). APA meetings are dominated by drug company–sponsored exhibits and symposia that provide attendees with a variety of enticements—music, food, drink, disc players, and so on. Drug companies provide substantial support to nearly all of the mental health advocacy organizations, including the National Alliance for the Mentally Ill (NAMI), the National Mental Health Association (NMHA), the National Alliance for Research on Schizophrenia and Depression (NARSAD), National Depressive Disorder Screening Day (O'Harrow, 2000). The only groups they don't support are the true consumer advocacy organizations such as the Support Coalition International (SCI), the National Empowerment Center (NEC), and the National Association for Rights Protection and Advocacy (NARPA).

Perhaps the industry's most successful marketing tool is direct contact with doctors—long known as "detailers," recently reframed as "sales representatives." These representatives portray themselves as "conduits of information." Actually, they supply well-sanitized (adverse effects are either omitted or muted) information, promotional materials and samples about their company's newest silver bullets. In 2001 there were, industrywide, 83,000 such persons—twice the 1996 number. These "conduits of information" cost about $8 billion a year and their samples an equivalent amount (Angell and Relman, 2001).

The drug industry supports clinical trial research at universities to the extent that it is doubtful that many departments of psychiatry could survive without it (Angell, 2000). The pharmaceutical industry owns the data from clinical trials it supports, decides which studies will be published, chooses the authors, ghostwrites the articles, and revises them to present the best possible interpretation of the data (*Lancet,* 2001). They wine and dine and provide continuing medical education (with their very well paid speakers) to "grand rounds," local psychiatric societies, hospitals, and clinics. Psychiatric trainees are deluged with drug company goodies, including conference travel. Drug companies underwrite "education" for medical students during their psychiatric clerkships (Wazana, 2000).

The pharmaceutical companies also drive theory in psychiatry. Because the drugs are sold as "correcting chemical imbalances in the brain," they lend credibility to the unproven hypothesis that psychiatric disorders are in fact no-fault "brain diseases." So, today's psychiatrists prescribe the drugs *as if* they were addressing the cause of the person's problem(s). In the face of the ease of pill taking, psychosocial interventions have been relegated to an ancillary role—or dropped altogether by health insurers who are concerned about cost saving. The potential downside hazards of these powerful substances, especially in the long term, are given little attention in the calculation of cost effectiveness.

In the flowchart that follows, various pharmaceutical companies that manufacture drugs used for treating mental disorders are located at the top. These are mostly powerful transnational corporations. Agenda-setting lines flow from these individual companies to pharmaceutical industry organizations. The industry organizations are set up and funded by the pharmaceutical industry for the specific purpose of lobbying governments and setting agendas. In the United States the main industry representative body is the Pharmaceutical Research and Manufacturers of America (PhRMA). In Australia it is the Australian Pharmaceutical Manufacturers Association (APMA).

Downstream from the industry organizations are public relations and advertising consultants, on the one hand, and the psychiatric profession and psychiatric researchers, on the other. The commissioning of agenda-setting activity can reach these two entities directly from individual companies or through the industry organizations. Individual companies retain public relations and advertising consultants, and they also fund the psychiatric professional bodies by advertising in their journals. Pharmaceutical companies also set the agenda by selectively funding psychiatric research aimed at propagating the belief that mental disorders are caused by brain defects.

The propagation of brain-based theories provides the necessary foundation for claims that drugs are suitable forms of treatment. A good example of this strategy at work in Australia is the funding of the prestigious Neuroscience Institute of Schizophrenia and Allied Disorders (NISAD) by six drug companies, all of which manufacture new schizophrenia drugs: Janssen Cilag, Eli Lilly, Pfizer, Novartis, Lundbeck, AstraZeneca (Neuroscience Institute of Schizophrenia and Allied Disorders, 2001).

Similarly, the pharmaceutical industry organizations often front for sections of the pharmaceutical industry by retaining public relations consultants and sometimes by coordinating the funding of psychiatric research. An important line of agenda-setting communication is by means of a two-way exchange between PR/advertising and the psychiatric profession/researchers. Public relations firms are often used to disguise the sources of drug company funding for psychiatric research, and there is also a constant barrage of drug company advertising in psychiatric journals aimed at persuading psychiatrists to use specific drugs. The reverse flow, from psychiatry to PR, involves the utilization of psychiatric research, and psychiatric expertise, in public relations campaigning.

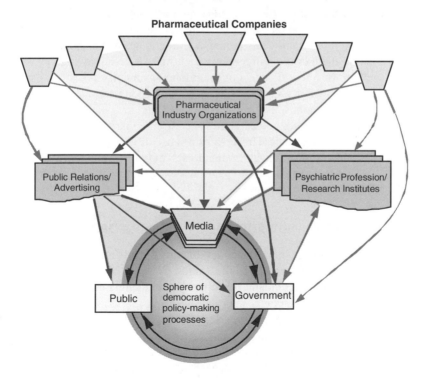

Flow of pharmaceutical agenda setting.

At the bottom of the flowchart is the sphere of democratic policy-making processes. These democratic policy-making processes largely involve a two-way circular flow of opinion and information and power between three entities: the public, the media, and the government. As in the game of paper, stone, scissors, each of these entities sometimes has power over the other two, depending on the sequence in a chain of events. The public can have power over specific media outlets by exercising consumer choices. It can also have power over government by exercising electoral choices. At the same time, the media can have power over the public by controlling the type and quality of information it receives. The media can also have power over the government by manipulating public opinion and electoral choices. The government, on the other hand, can have power over the media through regulation and the selective release of information. The government can also exercise power over the public through legislation and law enforcement.

The whole key to agenda setting in this democratic policy arena is to insinuate the right idea, at the right point in the chain, and have it flow around the circle in the right direction. Mastery of this skill is what public relations is all about. Although there are agenda-setting lines flowing into the sphere of policy-making from other entities, in regard to setting the agenda in mental health policy, it is the input coming from public relations consultants that is most relevant.

Public relations campaigns aimed at influencing mental health policy can target all three of the policy-making entities. A common strategy in a PR campaign is to use elements of the public as an entry point for a spin going in one direction and the media as an entry point for a spin going in the opposite direction. The purpose is to catch the government in a pincer movement and make it the focal point for complimentary imperatives spinning in opposite directions. This creates a sense of urgency in government circles and makes mental health bureaucrats and politicians vulnerable to direct and indirect approaches by pharmaceutical industry-sponsored consultants offering policy solutions.

## SETTING THE AGENDA FOR POLICY ON SCHIZOPHRENIA

An extended campaign to set the policy-making agenda in regard to schizophrenia offers a particularly good illustration of how these tactics work. All of the pharmaceutical companies involved in this agenda-setting campaign have introduced new atypical neuroleptic drugs for schizophrenia treatment onto the market over the past decade. These new drugs had been developed for two main reasons: (1) patents for the older generation of drugs were expiring and cheap generics were coming onto the market; and (2) the older generation of schizophrenia drugs had fallen into disrepute for being both ineffective and dangerous. However, in introducing the new drugs the pharmaceutical companies were confronted by two difficult public relations problems: (a) the new drugs are many times more expensive than the older drugs and (b) according to critics, they are not any more effective or safer than the old drugs they replace (Breggin & Cohen, 1999, pp. 76–82).

The pharmaceutical companies wanted to maximize their profits in what appeared to be a potentially critical environment and a tight market. They decided the best approach would be to find ways to expand the size of the market. Hitherto the market for schizophrenia drugs had been restricted by diagnostic conventions, on the one hand, and civil liberties protections on the other. Until recently diagnostic conventions generally limited the recognition of schizophrenia, and therefore the application of neuroleptic drug treatment, to symptoms that indicate psychosis. The agenda setters determined to expand the market by breaking this convention and promoting the concept of an additional prepsychotic phase of schizophrenia, which requires preventive treatment with their new drugs. To further expand the market they also decided to wage campaigns to weaken civil liberties protections and thereby increase the number of people who could be treated involuntarily.

The overall solution was the development of a twofold public relations campaign that is still in progress. The first part involves harnessing support groups for relatives of people suffering from schizophrenia as the driving force for an advocacy coalition. This has been achieved by carefully focused funding of these organizations (Gosden, 2001, pp. 94–97). Once they were made dependent on drug company "sponsorship" they could then be used as public relations front groups to assist with planting stories in the media about the efficacy and safety of the new drugs and about claims that schizophrenia has supposedly been scientifically proven to be a brain disease requiring urgent drug treatment at the earliest signs. A ready example of this practice can found at schizophrenia.com (schizophrenia.com, 2001a), which purports to be "A Not-for-Profit Information, Support and Education Center" representing consumers. However, schizophrenia.com acknowledges on its Web site that it is funded by Janssen Pharmaceuticals. (schizophrenia.com, 2001b). The slant on schizophrenia being promoted by drug company–funded organizations like schizophrenia.com is intended to impact on governments as expressions of public interest advocacy and to position the new drugs as preferred methods of treatment by government mental health services.

An aspect of the campaign involves funding selected psychiatric researchers to promote the doubtful belief that schizophrenia must be detected and treated in a prepsychotic stage to avoid brain deterioration (Gosden, 2001, pp. 224–247). This line of argument has the potential to vastly expand the market for schizophrenia drugs and has already led to the development in Australia of government-sponsored preventive treatment programs for schizophrenia, which utilize the new drugs.

A key element of the PR strategy involves funding from the drug company Eli Lilly that is channeled through both the World Psychiatric Association (Rosen et al., 2000) and NAMI (Silverstein, 1999; Oaks, 2000, p. 14) to mount an antistigma campaign. The thrust of the antistigma campaign is to advocate for the elimination of discrimination against people diagnosed with schizophrenia, *as long as they are taking medication.*

Meanwhile, in what appears to be a coordinated strategy, the Treatment Advocacy Center (TAC), which was originally established as branch of NAMI, has been feeding a very different, but complimentary, line to the media and the public about the dangerousness of *untreated* schizophrenia. This line involves associating untreated schizophrenia with news stories about violent behavior (Torrey & Zdanowicz, 1999, p. 27A) and promoting wild hyperbole about the murderous intentions of untreated schizophrenics: "Violent episodes by individuals with untreated schizophrenia and bipolar disorder have risen dramatically, now accounting for an estimated 1,000 homicides annually in the United States" (Treatment Advocacy Center, 2001a). This approach is intended to send an agenda-setting spin in the opposite direction by scaring the public and impacting on governments as a law-and-order imperative. The policy intention with this counterspin is to weaken civil liberties protections in mental health laws in order to increase the number of people eligible for involuntary treatment.

Involuntary treatment is an essential part of the market for schizophrenia drugs. Without involuntary treatment there would be virtually no market at all because most people diagnosed with schizophrenia initially have to be force-treated with neuroleptic drugs. A central objective of this hyperstigmatizing, law-and-order part of the campaign is the introduction of community treatment orders, or outpatient commitment. Outpatient commitment involves a court order that allows the forced treatment of people living in their own homes. Until the introduction of outpatient commitment, people could only be force-treated if they were patients in hospitals. This limited the number of involuntary patients at any one time to the number of beds available. However, considering the doubtful nature of diagnostic methods used for identifying schizophrenia, outpatient commitment promises to provide an open-ended expansion of the market for the new schizophrenia drugs. Outpatient commitment is already well established in most states of Australia and is being progressively introduced, state by state, in the United States.

As an offshoot of NAMI, the Treatment Advocacy Center is dedicated to playing its complimentary role of associating schizophrenia with violence and the urgent need for forced treatment, which they euphemistically call "assisted treatment."

Assisted treatment (also known as involuntary outpatient commitment, substituted judgment, or guardianship) must be provided before individuals become a danger to themselves or others, particularly for individuals who lack awareness of their illness—a common side effect of these devastating disorders.

Current federal and state policies hinder treatment for psychiatrically ill individuals. The Center is working on the national, state, and local levels to educate civic, legal, criminal justice, and legislative communities on the benefits of assisted treatment legislation.

The Treatment Advocacy Center serves as a catalyst to achieve proper balance in judicial, legislative, and policy decisions that affect the lives of individuals with serious brain disorders, such as schizophrenia and manic-depressive illness (Treatment Advocacy Center, 2001b).

In the middle 1990s, as a number of the new schizophrenia drugs were passing through their final stages of approval, and these public relations campaigns were gaining momentum, one analyst of the pharmaceutical market argued that the $1 billion a year U.S. market for schizophrenia drugs could be expanded to $4.5 billion a year. Annual sales of Eli Lilly's drug Zyprexa alone were projected "at $1 billion after five years on the market." But the analyst argued that the market expansion depended on the removal of two barriers. The first barrier was that currently only half of the 2.5 million Americans with schizophrenic symptoms were then receiving treatment. The implication was that ways would have to be found to ensure treatment reached this other half of the schizophrenic population. The second barrier was that a cheap generic drug was then dominating the market (Reuter Information Service, 1996).

As things have turned out, this analyst underestimated the potential for a PR-driven expansion of the market for schizophrenia drugs. A *Wall Street Journal* report in May 2001 described the market for schizophrenia drugs as a "fast-growing, $5 billion-a-year market" in which Eli Lilly's Zyprexa has already gained a $2.35 billion share and is "on course to surpass $2.5 billion this year" (Hensley & Burton, 2001).

## CONCLUSION

Cobb et al. (1976) proposed three models of agenda building: an outside-initiative model where citizen groups gain broad public support and get an issue onto the formal agenda; a second model in which the issues are initiatives that come from government and may need to be placed on the public agenda for successful implementation; and an inside-access model where the policy proposals come from policy communities with easy access to government, usually with support from particular interest groups, but little public involvement.

It is clear that the types of campaigns that have been run by public relations consultants to set the mental health agenda for the pharmaceutical industry utilize all three of these models. They run coordinated campaigns that involve funding consumer advocacy groups to simulate outside initiatives; they plant stories in the media that are designed to gain public acceptance of policies that are already on the government agenda; and they use the insider-access model when they utilize pharmaceutical industry lobbying organizations to gain easy access to government. This access is facilitated by the millions of dollars pharmaceutical companies and associations donate to politicians and political parties (See, for example, Mintz, 2000, p. A26; Public Citizen, 2000).

The use of sophisticated public relations techniques for setting political agendas has become a standard practice in most advanced democracies. The consequences are slowly becoming apparent. The system of representative democracy is being reshaped into a new kind of "managed corporatocracy" in which public opinion and government policy are custom-made products that can be shaped, packaged, and sold by skilled public relations experts.

The cynical way in which this shaping, packaging, and selling has been carried out in regard to mental health policy-making over the last couple of decades should serve as a warning to anyone who believes that the public good should come before corporate profits. Policies tailored to this commercial purpose are not necessarily beneficial either for patients or the society at large. The acute vulnerability of mental patients to exploitation, and the existence of mental health laws that provide for involuntary detention and treatment of certain classes of mentally disordered people, create conditions that require vigilant protection of civil liberties and human rights.

## REFERENCES

Angell, M. (2000). Is academic medicine for sale? *New England Journal of Medicine* May 18.

Angell, M., & Relman, A. (2001). Prescription for Profit. *Washington Post,* 20 June.

Anonymous. (1994). Public interest pretenders. *Consumer Reports, 59*(5), 316–320.

Beder, S. (1997). *Global spin: The corporate assault on environmentalism*, White River Junction, VT: Chelsea Green Publishing.

Bonner & Associates. (2001). *Strategic grassroots/grasstops to help you win.* Available: http://www.bonnerandassociates.com

Breggin, P. R., & Cohen, D. (1999). *Your drug may be your problem: How and why to stop taking psychiatric drugs*. Reading, Mass.: Perseus Books.

Cobb, R. W., & Elder, C. D. (1983). *Participation in American politics: The dynamics of agenda-building* (2nd ed.). Boston: Allyn & Bacon.

Cobb, R. W., Keith-Ross, J., & Ross, M. H. (1976). Agenda building as a comparative political process. *American Political Science Review, 70*(1), 126–38.

Cooper, M. H. (1993/94). Winning in Washington: From grasstops to grassroots. *Public Relations Quarterly, 38*(4), 13–15.

Faucheux, R. (1995). The Grassroots explosion, *Campaigns and Elections, 16*(1), 20–30.

Gosden, R. (1999). Prepsychotic treatment for schizophrenia: Preventive medicine, social control, or drug marketing strategy. *Ethical Human Sciences and Services, 1*(2), 165–177.

Gosden, R. (2001). *Punishing the patient: How psychiatrists misunderstand and mistreat schizophrenia.* Melbourne: Scribe.

Grefe, E. A., & Linsky, M. (1995). *The new corporate activism: Harnessing the power of grassroots tactics for your organization.* New York: McGraw-Hill.

Greider, W. (1993). Grassroots organizing, PR-style: Democracy for hire. *PR Watch 1*(1), 8–9.

Hensley, S., & Burton, T. M. (2001). Pfizer, Eli Lilly battle for share of growing schizophrenia market: high stakes lead to heated allegations against competing drugs Geodon, Zyprexa. *The Wall Street Journal, 84*, May 8.

Keim, G. D. (1996). Strategic grassroots: Developing influence. *Electric Perspectives, 21*(2), 16–23.

Kingdon, J. W. (1984). *Agendas, alternatives and public policies,* Boston: Little Brown.

*Lancet* (2001). The tightening grip of big pharma. April 14.

Levine, A. (1993). Grassroots or Astroturf? *Mother Jones,* Summer. Available: http://www.motherjones.com/mother_jones/SO93/levine.html

Megalli, M., & Friedman, A. (1991). *Masks of deception: Corporate front groups in America.* Washington, DC: Essential Information.

Menendez, P. (1998). The disease of childhood. *Eat the State! 2*(44). Available: http://eatthestate.org/02–44/DiseaseChildhood.htm

Mintz, J. (2000). Drug firms, unions funnel millions to parties. *Washington Post,* October 26, A26.

Moukheiber, Z. (2001). Health. *Forbes Magazine,* May 14, 267–268.

Nelson Communications Worldwide. (2001). *Client List.* Available: http://www.nelsoncommunications.com/about/clients.html and http://www.nelsoncommunications.com/about/clients2.html

Neuroscience Institute of Schizophrenia and Allied Disorders. (2001). *History.* Available: http://www.nisad.org.au/about/index.html

Oaks, D. (2000). NAMI: The story behind the story. *Dendron, 43,* 14–15.

O'Harrow, Robert, Jr. (2000, September 12). Grass roots seeded by drugmaker. *Washington Post.* Available: http://fdncenter.org/pnd/20000912/003633.html

Picard, A. (2001, January 4). Charities "thank God" for drug firms' money. *Globe & Mail,* Toronto. January 4. Available: http://www.health.bcit.ca/CRP/charity.htm

Poole, W. (1992). Neither wise nor well. *Sierra,* Nov./Dec., 88–93.

Public Citizen. (2000). *Addicting congress: Drug companies' campaign cash & lobbying expenses.* Available: http://www.citizen.org/congress/reform/addicting2.htm.

Public Citizen. (2001). The other drug war: Big pharma's 625 Washington lobbyists, *Public Citizen Congress Watch Report*, July 23.

Rabin, S. (1992). Pooling resources builds public/private partnerships. *Public Relations Journal, 48*(10), 32–33.

Reuter Information Service. (1996). Drugmakers look for home-runs with schizophrenia drugs. Available: http://somerset.nando.net/newsroom/ntn/health/032496/health3 14068.html

Rose, M. (1991). Activism in the 90s: changing roles for public relations. *Public Relations Quarterly, 36*(3), 28–32.

Rosen, A., Walter, G., Casey, D., & Hocking, B. (2000). Combating psychiatric stigma: An overview of contemporary initiatives. *Australian Psychiatry, 8*(1), 19–26.

Sabatier, P. (1988). An advocacy coalition framework of policy change and the role of policy-oriented learning therein. *Policy Sciences, 21*, 129–68.

Schizophrenia.com. (2001a). Legitimating brain disease: The case against "mental illness." Originally published in *Journal of the California AMI*. Posted on web site by D. J. Jaffe of the Alliance for the Mentally Ill/Friends and Advocates of the Mentally Ill in NYC. Available: http://www.schizophrenia.com/family/Braindisease.html

Schizophrenia.com. (2001b). A Not-for-Profit Information, Support and Education Center. Available: http://www.schizophrenia.com/

Silverstein, K. (1999). Prozac.org: An influential mental health nonprofit finds its "grassroots" watered by pharmaceutical millions. *Mother Jones*, November/December. Available: http://www.motherjones.com/mother_jones/ND99/nami.html.

Stapleton, R. (1992). Green vs. green. *National Parks*, November/December, 32–37.

Stauber, J., & Rampton, S. (1995). *Toxic sludge is good for you! Lies, damn lies and the public relations industry.* Monroe, ME: Common Courage Press.

Stauber, J., & Rampton, S. (1995/96). Deforming consent: The public relations industry's secret war on activists. *CovertAction Quarterly, 55*, 18–25.

Szegely-Marzak, M. (2001, August 8). The career of a celebrity pill. *US News.* www.usnews.com/usnewsissue/010806/ideas/prozac.htm

Tanouye, E. (2001). Marketplace. *Wall Street Journal*, June 13. Data from IMS Health Inc.

Torrey, E. F., & Zdanowicz, M. T. (1999, June 7). How freedom punishes the severely mentally ill. *USA Today*, 27A.

Treatment Advocacy Center. (2001a). *Violence: Unfortunate and all too often tragic side-effect of untreated severe mental illness.* Available: http://www.psych-laws.org/GeneralResources/Fact4.htm

Treatment Advocacy Center. (2001b). *Catalyst.* Available: http://www.psychlaws.org/default.htm

Wazana, A. (2000). Physicians and the pharmaceutical industry: Is a gift ever just a gift? *Journal of the American Medical Association, 283*, 373–380.

## GALLERY

J. Jules Vitali

... therefore, to restate in diametric occlusion the hypothesis as previously mundaned, it is the psychotropics that continually meander in the selfsame aforementioned that contraindicate a linkage to the systemic rather than to the plurality of singular outward modalities that become painfully self-indicative through the unsustained inclusion of unwanted research neutrinos linked by a bonding cellular triangulation found of late to be omnipresent and passive resistive in the isolated subject effluents emoted by diurnal hallucination and other misplaced thought patternings that spontaneously regenerate kindred pheromones and cause latent subjectivity to "rear it's ugly head" and show itself omniscient once the mastication has ceased its benevolence and started down the path of conducive exclusivity deemed only evident by the sole characteristic of windowbox parlancing in, and of which, the recipient cannot justify his or her own verifiable net income on a sustained equilibrium as was thought before the voracious onslaught of nonpsychotropic retrospectives that became, over time, expendable and more apt to reciprocate the lesser emotions in a noncombative purview and a program of regular preventative dental care and oral hygiene mostly considered by some to be the bane of all.

"George on Prozac." © Original design by Game Plan. All rights reserved. Recycled Paper Greetings, Inc. Reprinted with permission.

Part 4

# Seeking Health: Clients Describe Their Experiences with Family Therapy and Psychopharmacological Treatment

# Introduction to Part 4

> We have moved from what Leon Eisenberg called the "brainless psychiatry" of the '60s—everything taking place in the virtual space of the psychosocial world—to a "mindless psychiatry" of the '90s—with its assumption that our knowledge of the brain functions will provide us with the golden key to understanding the world of behavior, cognition, emotions and well-being."[1]

A recent television commercial for a phamaceutical product declares, "These symptoms of depression *may be* caused by a chemical imbalance in your brain. Xygott works to correct *this imbalance*." The question hanging in the air unasked is "What if these symptoms *aren't* the result of a chemical imbalance? What will this psychotropic drug do to your brain *then*?"

Modern psychiatry together with the pharmaceutical industry would like us to accept at face value the claim that all forms of emotional distress are purely and basically biological illnesses. Indeed, many in our contemporary society have accepted this idea uncritically and are making their way regularly to their psychiatrists and medical doctors for a check-in on the "meds" that alter the biology of their brains. However, as you can read elsewhere in this book, the jury is far from in about just how conclusively it has been established that "brain chemistry" is basically responsible for all that goes wrong in our minds. While there is surely a chemical reaction associated with all mental and emotional events, this fact is far from establishing that the chemical reaction is *causing* the events. In fact, there is a chemical reaction corresponding to every state we experience. If someone gives us a much-desired gift and we feel happy, that happiness corresponds to a certain shift in our brain chemistry. But does that mean that the shift in our brain chemistry *causes* the happiness? Wasn't it the gift? Or if, while walking in the woods or attending a service for worship, we experience a sense of ecstasy that rocks our chemical balance, is this *caused* by that same chemical imbalance? Wasn't there an interaction with the larger world at play?

Because we are interactive beings, our brain chemistry is constantly responding to the dynamic interplay between the world inside and the world outside of us. For this reason it is impossible to say that mental and emotional states are purely biologically based. Correspondingly, it is impossible to say, as modern psychiatry and the pharmaceutical industry would have us believe, that forms of mental and emotional distress are purely chemical imbalances. Why these two groups, and to some extent the managed-care industry, would be interested in making such a narrow claim is the subject of the political section of this book, to which we refer the interested reader.

How did the pharmaceutical industry and managed care get so involved with the intimate definitions and procedures of health care? In his book *The Turning Point,* Fritjof Capra traces the link of medicine with big business:

> American medical education was cast into its present form at the beginning of the century, when the American Medical Association commissioned a national survey of medical schools with the aim of putting medical education on a sound scientific basis. A related purpose of the survey was to channel the huge funds of newly formed foundations—especially those of the Carnegie and Rockefeller foundations—into a few carefully chosen medical institutions. . . . This established the link between medicine and big business that has dominated the entire health care system ever since.[2]

Evidence that commercialism has crept onto center stage in matters of health care is easy to find. In one three-hour stretch of daytime television there were twenty-nine commercials; eleven, or more than one-third, were for pharmaceuticals. Beyond the sheer amount of time the pharmaceutical industry purchases in attempts to get our attention, the most striking thing about the prescription drug advertising is that the people at whom it is aimed, the general public, cannot legally go out and *buy* the product. This is perhaps an unprecedented turn in advertising (with the exception of promoting products to children). Instead, the public is urged to consult their physicians in order to access these products. With this development the pharmaceutical industry has found a way to market physicians without doctors having to get into the messy business of promoting themselves, an activity once considered unethical for healing professionals. This creates a symbiotic relationship, tending to predispose physicians toward the use of their sponsors' products.

Further evidence appears unbidden on our computers. A typical promotional E-mail, whose subject line reads "This is the result of your feedback form," states:

> The future of Lifetime Pharmaceuticals has arrived. Now you can obtain the highest quality (insert drug X, Y, or Z) and more in just a few clicks of your mouse. Want to lose weight or stop smoking? Our compassionate and caring staff of licensed physicians are specially trained to be prompt, courteous and discreet. Click on LIFETIME PHARMACEUTICALS right now and see how easy it is to improve your quality of life.

Here we can see the healer-patient relationship practically disappeared, as it rests insubstantially between the computer user and the pharmaceutical company. In these situations medical practice has become a medicine show.

In the glare of the pharmaceutical industry's pressure to define mental health as a chemical balance in the brain arrived at through the use of its psychotropic medications, the obvious contribution of the forces surrounding a person—the context of relationship and emotion—to that person's state of mind is practically invisible; under intense lobbying pressure, these salient factors are either ignored or given lip service by those who determine mental health policy and disseminate mental health information. The field of family therapy that has grown so dynamically and offered so much promise to people struggling emotionally over the past fifty years has been all but eclipsed by the current emphasis on chemical imbalance and psychopharmacology. This essentially leaves the person who is suffering discomfort to suffer alone, diagnosed with a brain disease for which he or she daily takes a psychotropic medicine. Those around such a person, to whom family therapy would turn for further understanding of the complex systemic functioning of a human being, have been disqualified to lend a hand—except in the sense of "coping"—by this emphasis on brain chemistry. They generally have little medical expertise. Furthermore, they rarely have the opportunity to experience firsthand what their medicated family member experiences. A brief anecdote brings this point into focus.

A father approached a family therapist about his adult son, who had been in and out of a state mental hospital and halfway houses for ten years and was on high doses of medication, asking if something could be done to help him. Seven family therapy sessions with the larger family and six months later, the father, following a work opportunity, relocated to another country and his son was strong enough to accompany him. As they were about to depart from one of their occasional trips back to visit family, the father, a diabetic, reached into his suitcase and took his diabetes medication. He suggested to his son that it would be a good time to take his psychotropic medication, which by now was reduced to one-tenth the dosage he had been on when the father first called. The son reached into the same suitcase and took a pill from the same bottle. His father tried to stop him, only to discover it was *he* who had made an error: he had taken his son's psychotropic medication.

The two proceeded to the airport for the first leg of their connecting flight. The father remembers placing their tickets on the counter; then he passed out. When he regained consciousness, he was in a wheelchair boarding the plane for the second flight out of the country, surrounded by attendants and his son. He recalled being very confused and drooling. His son had finished the paperwork for the international flight at the ticket counter, gotten his father a wheelchair, and seen them onto the first plane. He then had arranged for the transfer of his father on to the connecting flight.

The father reported feeling disoriented for the following two days on arrival at his home. He could not get over the experience he had had with the psychotropic medication and was incredulous that his son had originally been taking ten times the dosage he had accidentally ingested. He said he had developed a new respect for his son.

For someone who has never experienced psychotropic drugs, it may be difficult, as it had been for this father, to appreciate the alienation from self that can occur with their use. Commercials coo to us, in the voices of actors portraying happy users, "I'm myself again" and "I've got myself back." But for many people the experience is quite the reverse.

In summary, with the current emphasis on brain chemistry and psychotropic medication, the elaborate network of relationship that holds us all and constitutes our outer world has been placed outside of the domain of mental health. In ignoring the people around us in defining and approaching emotional distress, we have allowed the loss of some of the richest soil for the nurturing and healing of the human psyche.

In the section that follows, we will hear from some people who sought help for difficulties they were experiencing.

In the first chapter, Patty Dyer describes encounters she and members of her family have had with the current medical establishment and the way it is using psychotropic and other medications.

The second and third chapters are by a wife and husband, respectively, who sought psychiatric help for severe turbulence expressed by the husband in their relationship. Their accounts of their experiences reveal some of the difficulties in the brain chemistry approach of modern psychiatry and point up the importance and healing potential of therapeutic work with the family.

## NOTES

1. Sluzki, Carlos. (1999) "The evolving context of the family therapy field: An overview," in the *Newsletter of the American Family Therapy Academy*, Fall, 9–10.
2. Capra, Fritzof. (1983). *The turning point.* New York: Bantam, 159.

# Chapter 11

# The Headache

Patricia M. Dyer, MSW

*The Hatter was the first to break the silence.*
*"What day of the month is it?" he said, turning to Alice: he had taken*
*his watch out of his pocket, and was looking at it uneasily, shaking it every*
*now and then, and holding it to her ear.*
*Alice considered a little, and then said, "The fourth."*
*"Two days wrong!" sighed the Hatter. "I told you butter wouldn't suit*
*the works!" he added, looking angrily at the March Hare.*
*"It was the best butter," the March Hare meekly replied.*
                    Lewis Carroll, *Alice's Adventures in Wonderland*

This is the story of a headache and the treatment I received for it. I tell it not because it is my story, but because it is typical of treatment today.

By the end of December 1997, after I had had a headache for three months, I decided it was time to go to the doctor. She took some fluid out of my spine and said the pressure and symptoms sound like pseudotumor cerebri. She said, "This is way out of my league; I'm sending you to a neurologist." I went to the neurologist a week later.

I was in constant pain. It was getting hard to concentrate on the coursework for my MSW. Driving was getting unbearable: trucks and cars were coming at me sideways. People were distorted. I was beginning to get depressed. I didn't feel the depression was anything mysterious: I knew it was the product of worrying about school and my headache.

When I got to the neurologist, he wasn't sure it was a pseudotumor cerebri. He said, "You seem to be depressed." He put me on Paxil and recommended bedrest. A week later, when I went back, he didn't see any improvement. So he put me on Prozac. Each week I went he had something different for me to try. In the four months this neurologist worked with me, he had prescribed Darvocet-n, phenobarbital, Zarontin, Ultram, Neurontin, Valium, Zoloft, Prozac, Paxil, Luvox, and hydrochlorothiazide. Ironically, these medications create adverse reactions identical to the symptoms I already had. Adverse reactions to Darvocet are headache and dizziness; to Ultram, headache, dizziness, and vertigo; to Zarontin, headache and dizziness; and to Valium headache, anxiety, and drowsiness. These prescribed *cures* actually had properties that could make my symptoms *worse.*

It seemed natural to me to feel depressed because I couldn't do much because of my headache. The doctor seemed to want to disregard the fact that the headache was causing the depression (he wasn't having much success with the headache problem) and treat the depression—cover up the symptoms with psychotropic drugs, all of which had headaches as potential side effects.

In East Indian folklore a figure named Nasrudin doubles as both a wise man and a fool. One of the many stories about him captures the essence of this medical sleight-of-hand. A friend encountered Nasruden late one evening on his hands and knees feeling around on the ground in the light of a streetlamp. The friend inquired of Nasrudin what he was doing. Nasrudin answered that he was looking for his watch. The friend asked where he last saw it. Nasrudin answered, "In the house." Puzzled, the friend asked, "Then why are you searching out here in the street?" Nasrudin responded, "There is more light here." The doctor here acted like Nasrudin: when he was unable to solve the presenting problem, he shifted the focus to a problem he *could* solve.

Each time I went to the doctor he had a new miracle drug for my headache. I was given drugs for epilepsy and depression, but the drugs did not touch the headache. It was interesting to me that a sales rep for a drug company was always leaving as I was going in.

The neurologist also gave me many diagnoses in that four-month period. I was diagnosed with depression, epilepsy, fibromyalgia, occipital neuralgia, and pseudotumor cerebri. When I asked the doctor about this, he said, " I'm not sure what the insurance company will cover, and I want to find out which one will get the best reimbursement."

By the fifth month of seeing this neurologist, I was beginning to wonder if I was losing my mind. I decided to write down what I wanted to know so I wouldn't forget, and he wouldn't be able to just write another prescription without giving me some answers. I wanted to know what was wrong with my head and what could be done to ease the pain. Two days before my appointment, I was informed that my doctor had taken his own life. He shot himself in the head.

I found a new neurologist. I had hopes that the headache would be treated. This doctor ordered expensive tests: CAT scan, EEG, MRI, computed tomography scan, skull X rays, cerebral angiography, and a lumbar puncture.

He also prescribed psychotropic medications while running the tests: Neuronton again.

His final diagnosis was pseudotumor cerebri, which the medical profession acknowledges it doesn't know how to treat. The doctors I saw started out by experimenting, but when they weren't succeeding, they changed the diagnosis to depression and gave me medication for depression. They seemed to be trying to convince me that the problem was depression and attempted to intoxicate me with psychotropics so I didn't know what was happening. Fortunately, I woke up to the fact that the real problem—the headache—was still there and stopped the psychotropic medication. Otherwise I could have become seduced into drug dependency in addition to my original problem. The headache persists today, more on than off, and I am not on any medication for it. I go every six months for follow-up. The doctor usually prescribes medications at these visits, but I have stopped filling the prescriptions. I have gone on with my life.

My older sister was diagnosed with postpartum depression two years after her third child was born. She was 27 years old at the time. She was put on psychotropic medications. Over the years she has been put on many different drugs. The result? Today she is 52 years old and is addicted to prescription drugs. Further, when she was first diagnosed, she weighed 96 pounds; today she weighs 368 pounds. Because of this weight gain, she is severely limited in her life and has developed heart trouble. Twenty-five years later, she still has her postpartum depression and is still on medication for it. She believes that the doctors know what is good for her. She also believes she needs a medication for any and every uncomfortable feeling she has.

So we now have the experiences of two people from the same family to compare: my sister, who listened to all the doctors said and took everything prescribed; and I, who attempted to be very discriminating about what to accept and what to reject and took little of what was prescribed. My sister is debilitated by being overweight and is in the hospital many times a year with pneumonia because she can't move around; and the antidepressants may help promote the pneumonia by slowing her body down. I am leading an active life, rarely incapacitated by illness, living with pain—but living.

I've found that doctors don't take responsibility for the illnesses they cause by their treatment. In the case of my sister, they preach to her about eating less instead of saying, "I caused this by my treatment," and setting about trying to help her out of the iatrogenic illnesses she has. The doctor is generally part of the healing process in his relationship to the patient and assumes he is helpful, but, in this instance, he is part of the problem.

People should not just accept the diagnosis and treatment of doctors because the doctor says so. There are so many life changes once a person gets a diagnosis. For example, if I had done what the doctor said—bed-rest—I would never have finished social work school three years ago and would still be in bed today, possibly weighing 400 pounds.

Then there is the story of what happened to my mother. When she was 70, she had high blood pressure and because she was poor, she had to go to a clinic to be treated. The doctors there said she had a heart condition. They had her coming in every week. For reasons she was not clear about, they put her on anxiety medication. She took one pill and felt very upset by it. She said, "If this is how drunks feel all the time, I don't understand why they drink." She refused to take them thereafter. But she was beginning to believe everything the doctors were telling her about her physical condition, and she was becoming afraid to move. She questioned whether she should even go shopping or do her regular household chores. She seemed frail. She was discouraged and becoming depressed, losing faith in her perceptions of her own body.

I found a new doctor for her. He examined her and said she was in good health for her age. He instructed her to continue her heart medication and blood pressure medication and come back in six months. Her mood changed. She began to think of herself as in good health again and resumed her normal routines including her household chores. Her sense of herself was revitalized.

The physicians at the clinic were attempting to be helpful, but she was demoralized by their perceptions. The more she went to see them, the more they thought she needed to see them, and the more demoralized she became. They viewed her demoralization as depression and treated it with medication, which demoralized her further. The process deepened her sense of herself as someone who was sick. The doctors had no idea that their treatment was the source of her depression. Once the second doctor gave her a positive report, she perked right up and no psychotropic medication was needed.

It had been strange to see her going to the doctor so often, since she always had felt it was not necessary to go to the doctor except in a critical situation. She came out of this situation believing that doctors today try to find things wrong with you, and if they can't, they invent an illness and prescribe a pill. She is from the old time when doctors were scarce and home remedies did the job. And the doctor's treatment did not include pills.

For the patient the question hangs daily in the air: Do I listen to the doctor and believe I am depressed, take drugs and have my life changed; or do I pick and choose with discrimination from what I am being told in order to maintain the preferred patterns of my life? If I listen to the doctor, chances are I will lose just about everything I enjoy. If I listen to myself, I will keep to my path and change a little to accommodate my physical state.

I may be a unique person, willing and able to handle my pain. Perhaps most people don't want that struggle. But then, in a sense, they give away their own healing power to illness and medication. Has our culture perhaps become unable to support us in developing the strengths necessary to activate our own healing? Does it promote illness? Are we being sold an illness so we will buy a cure? We need to question the medical treatment we receive, analyzing it to determine which of its aspects is beneficial and which may be destructive to our own well-being.

This is a photograph of the actual pills prescribed to this patient for this difficulty, prescriptions filled but not taken.

Chapter 12

# Love of a Lifetime*

Noralyn Masselink, PhD

*"Things flow about so here!"* she said at last in a plaintive tone, after she had spent a minute or so in vainly pursuing a large bright thing, that looked sometimes like a doll and sometimes like a work-box, and was always in the shelf next above the one she was looking at.

Lewis Carroll, *Alice's Adventures in Wonderland*

My husband and I celebrated our fifteenth anniversary on June 9, 2002. I write this essay as a tribute to our love and to the few social workers and single psychiatrist and nurse-practitioner who somehow understood that despite our emotional and mental disarray and the number of problems that stemmed from the marriage itself, nevertheless, we were worth working with *as a couple,* and eventually as a family. As I begin, I'm acutely aware of the fact that though I tell *our* story, I am really only telling *my* story. Were my husband to tell our tale, conceivably because we have different last names, readers might see no connection whatsoever between his ac-

---

*The following three chapters consist of two parts and a commentary. Noralyn Masselink and Oscar Davis are married and have three children. Noralyn and Oscar have each contributed a report about their travels in Pharmland in an effort to get help for themselves and their marriage. Along the way they encountered David Keith, a psychiatrist who is a family therapist. The therapy with Keith included eleven sessions between June and October 1995. The therapy ended abruptly in what seemed to be a failure. A chance event nearly a year later resulted in a reunion between the couple and the therapists.

count and mine. How I experience him and our relationship often has absolutely no correlation with how he perceives himself or the relationship, and vice versa. Perhaps the only thing we might agree on is that we have both loved deeply, and that while at times that love has been costly, ultimately, the rewards have surpassed the costs.

My own mental health story starts in July 1987 at the age of twenty-eight. My six-year marriage to my high school sweetheart had recently ended after slowly disintegrating during the five years we had both pursued graduate studies, he in physics and I in English literature. I had met Oscar, my current husband, at Interboro Institute, a junior college where I was teaching while finishing my dissertation and at which Oscar was completing an associate's degree in security management. As Oscar explained it to me, he had gone back to school in order to try "normal" life after having spent the previous fifteen years in show biz, touring the world as a successful and generally well-paid pop singer rubbing shoulders with celebrities like Mick Jagger, Ike Turner, and Donna Summer. If it's true that men are from Mars and women from Venus, then Oscar and I were probably from different galaxies. I'd been raised in a middle-class, Midwestern Dutch Christian Reformed community by two educators; he'd been raised in poverty in Brooklyn and on Long Island by his mother (and later an uncle and an upstate children's home) with his alcoholic father generally absent. I'd pursued a formal education for twenty-three of my twenty-eight years, but I lived in a bubble; he'd dropped out of high school and the army, but had acquired a wealth of worldly wisdom. I was white; he was black. But none of these differences mattered to me. Oscar had a sensitivity, depth, and sweetness I'd not found in others. He could keep up with me intellectually, and he made me laugh. In our forty days of formal courtship, we'd spent three full days together, I'd written Oscar over forty letters, and we'd talked endlessly on the phone. As we strolled through Central Park, we dreamed dreams of building bridges between our worlds by bringing together the best of both. I also welcomed the idea of having a child with Oscar, a prospect I'd dreaded in my first marriage. We were as crazily in love as we could be, and that crazy love has sustained us through the years.

While Oscar was moody at times during our courtship, we had been married only thirty hours when I discovered that his moods could "turn on a dime." He would shift mysteriously from blissful happiness to incredible irritation in what seemed the space of a few minutes. Unfortunately, the return to contentment often took much longer. I dismissed such fluctuations initially as the result of his having quit smoking. Nevertheless, the mood swings continued, and Oscar and I had been married for about six weeks when one night, after we had spent a joyful hour or two together, he suddenly abandoned me in our vehicle in the middle of the night in God-knows-where, the Bronx. We had stopped on a street of empty buildings to kill time in between our night classes and his 11–7 shift at a children's home. When he simply got out of the car and walked off after a "flash flood" argument, I realized that I needed help, that the behavior of my husband was inexplicable, that my life had been endangered by his actions (since I had absolutely *no* idea where we were in the Bronx and hadn't a clue as to how to return to our home in North White Plains). Though I was in shock, I managed to catch up with him and convince him to give me directions out of the area, but I barely slept that night because I knew that as much as I loved my husband, I didn't love him so much as to endanger my life.

The next morning I made an appointment with a social worker who referred me to a psychiatrist after our first meeting "to rule out the possibility that [I] might have a chemical imbalance that would need to be addressed via medication." I met with this psychiatrist twice for an hour each time. I was very candid about the major life changes I had experienced within the last half year, but to this day I wonder what it was about me that prompted her to prescribe lithium. Apart from my recent divorce (which was not yet finalized) and hasty remarriage (which was no less legitimate to Oscar or me despite our not yet having a license), I had no history of rash or unstable behavior, and though I'd been told I was intense, I certainly didn't feel mentally unstable or depressed. Nevertheless, after spending 120 minutes with me, she had somehow determined that I should try lithium and gave me a prescription with the instructions that I was to begin taking it immediately unless it turned out that I was pregnant.

Since Oscar was ten years older than I and I had been told I might have difficulty getting pregnant, we had decided not to postpone the possibility. As the preprescription bloodwork indicated, I was, in fact, pregnant—about two weeks so. As I was no longer a good candidate for lithium, the psychiatrist suggested that I continue the sessions with the social worker I'd initially sought out. I did. The primary topic I discussed with my counselor was what seemed to me Oscar's bizarre behavior. I'd grown up in an orderly home governed by logical rules; voices were rarely if ever raised. Oscar's lack of clearly defined boundaries confused me. At times, he seemed to speak in a foreign tongue. I would try to follow the logic of what he was saying, but when I couldn't follow his train of thought and pressed him to clarify or sort out contradictions, his exasperation was obvious. "You're the one with the PhD," he would shout. Having never before been confronted with something I couldn't somehow make sense of, I at times doubted my own sanity. The image I developed of our relationship was him as a helium balloon, me as the ground, and our love as the tether between us. Though there seemed little indication that he might become grounded, I somehow sensed that I might become unmoored; either prospect was dangerous, both to us as individuals and to our relationship.

What I didn't know at this time was that during the first years of our marriage, Oscar was dabbling in various street drugs. He agrees now that his drug use may have been some form of self-medication, a way of regulating the highs and lows he habitually experienced. Apart from the drugs, was there a chemical imbalance? I don't know, but I do know that frequently he would leave the house in one mental space and come home later in a totally different frame of mind—for no apparent external reason, including drug use. I experienced these changes as extremely threatening to me and to the health of our relationship since I could not predict them, account for them, or respond to them in ways Oscar found acceptable. To me his behavior was simply "abnormal" and "illogical."

When his erratic emotional states showed no signs of abating, I finally gave Oscar an ultimatum in February 1988. Either he needed to "seek help" or I would take the baby (due in April) and raise her on my own. I had come to believe I was married to a Dr. Jekyll and Mr. Hyde, except that my appellation for Oscar's split personality was "Chocolate Face" and "Nasty Face." These faces were actual physical manifestations: "Chocolate Face" appearing as a carefree, loving, hope-filled Oscar with a light in his eyes and a song in his heart, and "Nasty Face" being a dark, vitriolic stranger who seemed convinced I was out to destroy him. I viewed "Chocolate Face" as the "real" Oscar and "Nasty Face" as the unwelcome intruder. While I believed that as an adult I *might* be able to tolerate the extremes (wholehearted happiness and delight in our relationship one moment followed by unmitigated hopelessness toward life in general and our future in particular), I certainly couldn't see how a baby or child would benefit from being exposed to such an emotional roller coaster. Emotional stability—the implicit key to my upbringing—seemed like a good foundation for child rearing, and Oscar was anything but emotionally stable.

Some time that spring Oscar agreed to an intake interview at White Plains Hospital. During the fifty-minute appointment, a brief history was taken, and we were told that the waiting period to be assigned to a doctor was between six and eight weeks—an eternity from my perspective. We reveled in the birth of our daughter Emmalon Mika on April 1, and life was sweet until mid-May, when the bottom fell out. For lack of a better term, I'll say that Oscar had a nervous breakdown; perhaps he was experiencing an empathetic postpartum depression. For hours, he lay on the bed crying and begging me not to "let them take me away." He made oblique references to killing himself and just seemed to have reached the end of whatever emotional stores he'd been drawing from to keep our marriage going. Looking back, I'm amazed that he didn't fall apart sooner. In less than a year, he'd gone from being footloose and fancy free to being married and gaining a child, not to mention the fact that he'd been working two full-time jobs for the past five months so that we could pay the $825 a month rent on our three-room house. In the meantime, I'd been applying and interviewing for tenure-track positions throughout Pennsylvania and New York since my contract with Hofstra University (where I'd been a visiting professor for the year) would end in May; our future was highly uncertain. In retrospect, a breakdown seems in some ways a reasonable response to an extremely stressful situation.

Because he was only on a waiting list at the hospital, however, no help was available when I called the psychiatric unit. I was told that unless he would check himself in or I called the police and could prove that he was self-destructive or a danger to others, there was nothing anyone could do. Never mind the fact that he was terrified of "being locked up." Never mind the fact that police officers are not a symbol of "help" to many African-American men, let alone those in a state of mental disarray. Never mind the fact that neither of us had family or friends nearby who were capable of stepping in to help. In total desperation I called an emergency hot line and begged the counselor to contact the psychiatrist who had taken Oscar's history. Though I do not remember that doctor's name, I will be eternally grateful that when he was called, he agreed to see Oscar on Monday. We limped through the weekend with Oscar spending most of his time in bed.

On Monday, after one session with the doctor, Oscar was diagnosed with bipolar disorder and prescribed lithium. I was warned that it might take weeks for the drug to level things out, and another doctor suggested that I had best look after myself and Emmalon and forget about Oscar for the time being, advice that struck me as reasonable, but somehow very cold and callous at the same time. Having battled to hang on to my marriage for a full year, I would have welcomed some words of hope for our family along with the advice for self-preservation. The drug *did* take a long time to work, and we spent the next seven weeks apart, with Oscar moving back to the room he'd rented before we married. His parting words before moving out were "Good-bye, and good luck making a life for yourself without me."

Meanwhile, I'd accepted a tenure-track position in the English Department of SUNY–College at Cortland in March and planned to move upstate in July. By mid-June, the lithium had at least alleviated Oscar's depression, but I was very unsure as to whether or not Oscar would move with me to rural central New York. It had become very clear to me during the past year that while he'd officially "retired" from show business, he still dreamed of performing again one day. Thus, while I hoped he would move upstate with me, I was also fully prepared to set up some kind of commuter marriage if he felt the need to stay in the city with its access to a greater talent pool. When Oscar decided to join me in Cortland, I saw the choice as an amazing testimony of his love for and desire to be with me and our little girl. (In fact, every day that he stays in Cortland with its limited musical resources, I am aware of the fact that he is choosing his identity as father and husband above his identity as successful pop singer.)

Shortly after moving, we made an appointment for him at the Cortland County Mental Health Department so that a psychiatrist there could monitor the lithium levels,* and we found counselors who would work with us, albeit separately. After twice meeting with us together, Oscar's social worker said there was too much personal pathology involved for him to try to work with both of us, and mine said that she worked only with individuals because she could physically touch an individual, whereas a couple was merely a social construct. I'm sure we overwhelmed them. My counselor suggested that I read the book *Women Who Love Too Much* and that I envision a future without Oscar. I found then, and still find, the idea of "loving too much" an impossible contradiction: one cannot love too much; one can only love *with* healthy boundaries or without. I started my new job in August, with Oscar as "house husband" taking care of Emmalon. After a month or two, however, Oscar felt that he needed to be employed outside the home, if for no other reason than to increase our income. He found a job working nights at a group home for mentally handicapped adults.

By October Oscar had decided he'd learned the lesson lithium needed to teach him—it gave him a sense of boundaries and normality that he'd never known—and took himself off the drug without telling me. He had gained thirty pounds while on lithium and complained of numbness in his limbs, but his primary concern was that he had absolutely no creative impulses. So, without informing me, he just stopped taking the medication. By November, however, he didn't have to tell me, because his emotional state was as unpredictable as it had ever been. One day Chocolate Face would declare joyfully, "If it gets any better than this, I'm not interested," while the next Nasty Face would threaten to leave me or drive off the road and end it all. His mantra during the next few months was that he *never* wanted to become normal. Of course, having read all kinds of literature on bipolar disorder, I saw his behavior as confirming the original diagnosis.

While the relationship deteriorated, Oscar's creativity soared. He performed locally in his own band called Oscar, Oscar, Oscar and wrote over ten songs—among them "House Husband Blues," a funny but bittersweet account of what it felt like to be a stay-at-home dad. Finally, after I'd called the police in response to one of his more threatening bouts of behavior (he'd torn up the tour jacket I'd bought him and smashed a mug against the wall), we agreed that if we wanted to preserve the possibility of a future together, we could not continue to live together in our current state. The most

---

*We would not have received assistance if Oscar had not already been on medication.

troubling thing for me was that Nasty Face seemed to have absolutely *no* recollection of any of the good times we had shared or any bright periods in the relationship. Likewise, Chocolate Face seemed to have no recollection of the dark times or threatening behavior accompanying them.

Oscar left in February and eventually moved forty-five minutes away to Ithaca, where he took a job as a school bus driver. While I stopped seeing my counselor in March, Oscar continued his sessions throughout the next year, visited Emmalon and me most weekends, and joined us for our first family vacation, a camping trip in the Pocono Mountains in August. Meanwhile, I started saving to buy a house. Oscar joined me as I looked at places, and we agreed on a barn out in the country that was being re-fashioned as a two-bedroom dwelling. On the closing date in July 1990, after having lived apart for almost a year and a half, Oscar moved with Emmalon and me into our new home and applied to drive a school bus in Cortland.

By the fall of that year, though our problems were less severe than formerly, Oscar's attitudes toward our future were still variable, and my reactions seemed always to make things worse. I now see in retrospect that my attempts to help, the suggestions I made in response to his periods of emotional disarray, felt to him as though I were trying to dominate, manipulate, and control him. At the same time, when I chose silence out of fear of making things worse, he believed that I didn't care. I felt damned no matter what I did. Having just finished nearly two years of individual counseling, Oscar at first resisted the idea of additional counseling. If our marriage needed so much help in order to work, he argued, maybe it simply wasn't meant to be. For me, however, we'd come too far and worked too hard to give up now. Furthermore, Oscar had shown himself capable of being a fantastic father, and having benefited immensely from my own father's involvement in my life, I wanted Emmalon to have the same advantage. This time, we managed to find a counselor who was willing to work with both of us, and it felt exciting to be able finally to deal with "couple" issues. This counselor helped us see the extent to which our troubles had their roots in our different cultural backgrounds. He helped me to be more sensitive to Oscar's experience as a black man in the nearly all-white community we lived in. He helped Oscar see the extent to which childhood memories of his relationship with his mother were being superimposed on his relationship with me. He also gave us a visual image of how unbalanced the relationship would be if both of us "stood on only one leg," and he talked about our need to take turns leaning on each other. Up to this point in the relationship, it felt to me as though I had *always* needed to stand on both legs because Oscar rarely had both feet on the floor. We worked with this counselor for about a year and returned after a year's respite for a refresher course of another six months or so. During that time, we weathered the miscarriage of an unexpected pregnancy together. When we finally stopped seeing the counselor, we felt that we had gone as far as we could go with him.

In 1993, we welcomed a second daughter Eena Mae to our family, and our relationship seemed to me to have fallen into a fairly predictable pattern. The really dangerous times seemed to be from March through May and then again from November until January. Summer months were generally quite placid with only minor blips on the emotional screen, but Christmas was always iffy (one Christmas Oscar spent the entire day scrubbing the kitchen down from ceiling to floor), and almost without fail March brought major depression and irritability to Oscar. We'd go for weeks with me walking on eggshells until, as mysteriously as the bad times had come, they would leave.

That pattern continued until the spring of 1995. This time the depression seemed unusually severe. At an employees' training workshop of some sort, Oscar came across a list of the indicators for depression and realized that he experienced seven out of ten of the symptoms. After weeks of listening to him express his beliefs that our marriage was the primary source of his unhappiness, I suggested that he ask our family doctor about taking an antidepressant. He did, and for the first four weeks that he was on Prozac, I thought I was in heaven. Oscar was cheerful, full of energy, and most wonderful of all, for the first time in the eight years we'd been married, he seemed to have a "normal" interest in sex. Our Prozac-induced bliss lasted only six weeks. One day, Oscar just announced that he had again decided to take himself off the medication. He stated his reasons in the following terms: "That person on Prozac is not me. I can see what the drug does—it makes me not care about things that I usually care about. But all along I know that if it weren't for the drug, I *would* be caring. If I'm not going to care anyway, then I might as well be off the drug and do 'careless' things like having an affair or getting high." While I understood his desire to hang on to himself—the person he'd lived with for forty-some years—at the same time, I felt sad because part of that person seemed bent on destroying our family. And now there were two children as well as me who would lose out if that part of Oscar won the day.

Mother's Day seemed to have been a trigger for bad episodes in the past, and this year was no exception. I came home the Monday after Mother's Day to find the plant Oscar had given me the day before sitting out in our driveway. When I walked in the house and asked why he'd moved the plant outside, he just blew up. Thankfully, I've forgotten most of the wild things Oscar shouted during the next hour, but it ended with him threatening to burn the house down as he left to drive his afternoon bus run. Though things had been rough over the past few weeks, I had not foreseen his totally losing his mind. As he ranted and raved, he really seemed to me delusional, and nothing I said made a difference. His threats in the past had generally been limited to taking himself out or leaving me, and while he'd been physically threatening on one or two occasions, he'd never proposed something as bizarre as burning our house down.

I was at the end of my rope and also frightened, as I'd been the time I'd called the police in 1988. When the police had arrived that time, however, one officer had threatened to break Oscar's arm if he ever hurt me, and because of this, I certainly didn't want to call the police again. But I also didn't think I could go on. With two children to care for and be concerned about, juggling Oscar's mood swings had simply become more than I could handle. I called an older man whom we both knew from church and asked him if he would come to the house and ask Oscar to leave when he got back from work. I explained that I was scared—and, in fact, I truly was terrified. In the eight years we'd been married, I'd never feared for my life, but this time the cumulative effect of living with Oscar's roller coaster emotions overwhelmed me. Our good times were beyond anything I'd ever dreamed of, but when negative attitudes threatened to cross over into abusive behavior, I had to draw the line.

Oscar left and for the next three weeks, when I saw him, I barely recognized him. Though he managed to carry out his job responsibilities, when we were together there was a total lack of affect. He seemed to have turned completely inward. Though he could put on a cheerful face for the time he spent with the children each week, he had absolutely nothing to say to me. I believe now that he felt betrayed and had given up. In his mind, I had all the power; hence, he had absolutely no understanding of how threatened I'd felt, and, in fact, my fear affronted him. He also wondered why in the world I would want to stay married to him if I believed (as he thought I did) that he was the source of our problems. I never had believed that, however. What I believed is that "something" repeatedly came over him and robbed both of us of our joy. I didn't know what that something was, but I was absolutely convinced that he neither consciously desired it nor did anything to purposely bring it on himself. And that to me seemed consummately unfair. While I had certainly proven to myself that I could live a fulfilling life without him, I knew that my heart's desire was to live a fulfilling life *with* him. I definitely wasn't ready to give my husband, my lover, my friend over to the unnamed "something" without putting up the fight of my life.

Immediately after he left, I had made an appointment with yet another counselor, both for myself and for Emmalon, who at 7 years old saw her world cracking apart before her eyes. The counselor, who didn't know Oscar from Adam and, hence, could respond only to my account of things, insisted after hearing from me about Oscar's past diagnosis and emotional history, that unless he was willing to get back into counseling and get back on medication, we would probably never be able to live together again. At the same time, when Oscar did speak to me, he was adamant that he would *never* again take drugs for mental illness. While he readily admitted that something was definitely wrong, because he had coped with "it" all his life as a single person without the aid of prescription medication, he felt he would rather continue life unmarried than take medication just to make a marriage possible. While I believe that I would choose drugs if they were necessary in order for me to live with my children and husband, I also understood that for Oscar that choice represented too big a sacrifice to make. To make a life with me in "my" world, he'd already cut loose many of his old anchors: his freedom, his career, even to some degree his racial identity as a black man. He felt if he gave up anything else, he would no longer have any personhood at all. So though I wished he felt differently about medication, I did understand.

I would not, however, accept either my counselor's prognosis or Oscar's transitorily hopeless views of our future together. While I secretly hoped that some psychiatrist would finally convince Oscar that drugs would not be end of the world, my primary goal at this point was simply to find someone who would be willing to work with both of us. I also needed to find a psychiatrist who would accept the university's insurance since I knew from past experiences of working with nonparticipating providers that we probably wouldn't be able to afford any kind of sustained treatment plan without insurance. Oscar had not yet agreed to seek additional counseling, believing that we had "tried everything and, obviously, nothing helps." He absolutely refused to see anyone for individual counseling, something I wouldn't have asked him to do anyway, and my own individual counseling seemed to be yielding only suggestions that I obtain restraining orders, child support, and eventually a divorce.

At moments I was tempted to share Oscar's despair concerning our future because I too had been deeply disappointed that despite all of our individual and couple's therapy, we hadn't yet found a "cure." Each time we'd sought help, I'd been looking for a definitive solution—some shift in our relational dance that would result in a permanent change for the better. When things would improve, I'd feel hopeful, but then, when we'd go through a bad time, it seemed as though all of the therapy had been for nothing. What continued to be especially devastating for me was the way Oscar's "dark" states totally wiped out his memory of good times. During these times we might as well have been back in North White Plains prior to lithium.

All of the dozen or so psychiatrists I called refused point-blank to work with anyone other than the diagnosed patient, although a few offered "consultations" with a spouse at the patient's request. Of course, in order to get insurance coverage for psychiatric treatment at all, we had to identify an individual patient with a diagnosed mental illness. I was thankful for Oscar's initial diagnosis of bipolar disorder in that it afforded us insurance coverage, but at the same time I had grown increasingly dubious about the diagnosis. After all, it had been made eight years earlier after a one-hour appointment following an emotional meltdown. Furthermore, because of our move, the psychiatrist who had made the diagnosis had been able to see Oscar only two times thereafter. Early on, I'd clung to the diagnosis and read all kinds of books and articles on the illness, hoping that if I understood it, I'd be able to work around it. I'd believed that a diagnosis was the first step toward a cure or at least an amelioration of the condition. Initially, at any rate, naming "it," having a label for Oscar's weird behavior, somehow made it less scary. When neither a cure nor a permanent improvement followed the diagnosis, however, and in light of Oscar's refusal to treat himself with drugs (whether legal or illegal at this point), the diagnosis seemed less and less important or useful. I've since come to view it as a smokescreen that may have hindered, and certainly, delayed our healing.

Finally, a social worker friend gave me the name of a psychiatrist "who works with families and who is doing some really neat things using nontraditional approaches." This sounded like exactly the person we were looking for. We were certainly a nontraditional family, so perhaps nontraditional approaches would work where the mainstream methods had not. When I first called David Keith, I do clearly remember asking if he was opposed to medication. The message I received during that initial phone conversation was that he wasn't opposed to drug therapy if a patient felt that drugs were warranted. The focus of his therapy, however, was on family dynamics. At this point, I was hanging on to the idea that drugs were the panacea our marriage needed and that if only Oscar could be convinced to go back on them and stay on them, everything would be fine. At the same time, I had always been willing to accept my own part in the dysfunctional dance that made up the seasons of our marriage, so I looked forward to learning some new dance steps myself. David later asked me if I felt he'd misled me on the medication question, and I assured him that he had not.

How exciting, how creative, how refreshing for me—finally, someone who seemed to share my understanding that there is something sacred, inherently worthwhile, about the family. While I had obviously left a marriage when I'd felt I was spiritually dying, and would understand Oscar's need to leave if his sense of self could not withstand the pressures of marriage, I also knew that the family was the source of our greatest joys as well as our greatest frustrations. Thus, while permanent separation would bring relief for both of us from some of our misery, such a severing would bring with it different, but perhaps equally if not more excruciating pain. Oscar was attracted to the idea that David was doing things nontraditionally because that fit in with his own desire to steer clear of the "normal." And since David would work with all of us, children included, Oscar would not be the designated patient, the source of the problems. We would all be in this together.*

To be honest, at the time of our sessions, both Oscar and I agreed that David wasn't doing anything for us (one of the few things we agreed on at that point!). In fact, I had no sense of what he was trying to do, until, serendipitously, I saw his name in the footnote of a book *The Family Crucible* (Napier and Whitaker) which a friend had lent to me. The book, cowritten by former colleagues of David's, explained the basic tenets of family therapy. I work best with a concrete game plan, so reading the book helped give some shape to what otherwise felt to me like fairly goal-less, formless sessions with David.

David did have some great ground rules. We were not to talk to each other about the session afterward for at least twenty-four hours, and initially, at any rate, we were to talk to him, not to each other, a rule that was crucial, since at this point we couldn't hear each other anyway. Though we were still living apart, we generally rode up to our appointments together, and our two girls joined us at least half the time. All I remember of the first session is Oscar's yelling, "I'm not crazy; I'm just an angry black man!" As David described it later, the first few sessions were definitely "hot." After the second or third session, David asked us if we would mind if he invited a female colleague of his, Anne Marie Higgins, a nurse-practitioner/family therapist, to join us in the sessions. I certainly didn't mind and neither did Oscar. In fact, Oscar interpreted this move as David's admission that our problems were serious (a view that fed into his feelings that our situation might be hopeless).

In retrospect, we agree that what David did primarily was to validate both our individual experiences *and* the importance of our family. He also encouraged us to think about how our experiences in our families of origin had shaped our experiences within our current family. I remember very little of what actually happened during our sessions, but the defining moments were seminal and afforded what I can only describe as a paradigm shift that shook something loose for me. Whatever Oscar got out of our sessions, for me the therapy redefined my entire experience of him and our relationship.

At one point, David asked me if I'd ever felt crazy before. I remember that my immediate reaction was to say, "Of course not." I'd been playing the

---

*Since one of my biggest fears was the effect of Oscar's and my clashes on our children, I found it extremely comforting that David was not afraid they would be permanently damaged by witnessing their parents "go at it" during our hour with him. That fact alone made me feel as though perhaps our problems weren't as terrible as they seemed. And actually, our children enjoyed their trips to see Dr. Keith, and the oldest felt left out the few times we met without her.

role of sane, stable anchor of the marriage for so long that the very notion of
my feeling crazy was inconceivable. But later I gave the question more
thought, and I remembered two times in my life when I *had* felt crazy. The
first time was when, as an adolescent I'd read *I Never Promised You a Rose
Garden*, *The Bell Jar*, and *Lisa, Bright and Dark*. I remember being petrified
and confiding to my mother my fear that because I felt an affinity with the
female protagonists, all of whom had emotionally collapsed, one day I, too,
would go insane. My mother had assured me that I was mentally stable, and
I'd forgotten about the incident ever since. The only other time I had felt I
might be losing my mind was during the initial weeks of my marriage to
Oscar when, as I have already explained, I simply could not make sense of
what he was saying. What struck me as so remarkable is that my primary
feeling both times was overwhelming *fear*. I had never before considered
the possibility that during Oscar's times of mental disarray he might be feeling terrified. Feelings of terror might certainly lead to bizarre behavior;
I've read of animals that gnaw off limbs to free themselves from traps. Perhaps Oscar's repeated response of wanting to leave the marriage during
times of duress sprang more from fear of what might happen if he stayed
than from an articulated desire to leave. Another time when I was feeling
misunderstood by Oscar, David startled me by asking, "Have you ever
thought about how you could get even with him?" Again, my initial reaction
was that I never had. And, in fact, that was truthful. Having been raised in a
Christian home, I knew well that as Satan in Milton's *Paradise Lost* eventually discovers, "Vengeance ere long back on itself recoils." I am also grateful
to the Lord whose love empowered and sustained me through all my difficulties with Oscar and kept at bay bitterness, anger, and revenge. At the same
time, David's question got me to thinking about how I *could* get "even" with
Oscar for all the difficulties he had put me through.* I was amazed at what I
discovered. My greatest fantasy was to fall apart on him, to leave *him*
stranded with the responsibility of raising our two daughters as he had so frequently left me. I also had to admit that one of the reasons I would never have
done this is that I wasn't sure he was equal to the task. Perhaps he'd been living up to my low expectations of him in this regard. Still, it suddenly seemed
unfair to me that I was always left holding the bag, while Oscar had the "luxury" of insanity to excuse him. Though the insight didn't have any immediate effect at the time of our counseling, it would later bear fruit.

A third pivotal moment occurred for me when David proposed that craziness might in some ways be controlled without medication. He gave examples of patients who could function very well in one setting, but then at home
their behavior might be quite off the wall. This point really resonated with

---

*Of course, one could argue that he didn't put me through anything. I chose to be put
through it by staying with him.

me. How, otherwise, could Oscar have managed to stay employed and fool so many people into thinking that he was "normal" when he and I both knew that wasn't the case? And if Oscar was somehow saving his "crazy" (or more honest?) self for home because that seemed like the safest place to be crazy, I could understand that, too. At the same time, that choice seemed unfair to the girls and me. The rest of the world, in essence, was getting to see Chocolate Face while we who loved him most were still being visited too frequently by Nasty Face. But at least this view of craziness gave us new options.

Above all, David conveyed that message that "craziness" need not be eliminated at all costs. Since it seemed unlikely in our case that the mental disequilibrium would ever be eliminated, this message was good news to me. It was extremely liberating to feel that we could stop looking for the magical "cure." David also suggested that we look for new ways to live with craziness—ways that would accommodate the family as well as the individuals within the family. David explored with Oscar the life and friendships he had outside our home—only to discover that they really didn't amount to much. The primary outlet or life Oscar had outside our relationship was his musical endeavors. While I had two very close girlfriends who supported me well in my times of trouble, Oscar had only an unheated studio and his own creative flow to help him through bad times. David talked to Oscar about keeping these "escape valves" open. David's suggestion that families might need to cultivate nonconventional responses to periods of difficulty seemed to validate our own self-generated separations over the course of our marriage. Instead of being badges of defeat, our self-imposed separations could instead be interpreted as an attestation of our love—both for ourselves and for the family.

A final key insight came to me when Anne Marie asked me one day what our original dream of the relationship had been. Over the years of trying to hold our relationship together, I'd lost sight of the person I'd been when I met Oscar and what I'd been looking for from our relationship. I *did* know that I'd wanted someone who would tap the depths of my love (which Oscar had certainly done), but I had also believed I was marrying someone who could take care of himself, who wouldn't need a mother to take care of him. Because he'd lived independently for so long, I'd thought Oscar fit that description. *His* independence was necessary in order for me to be everything I knew *I* could be—a fantastic wife who loved him with heart, mind, and spirit; a devoted mother to whatever children resulted from the overflow of our love; and an effective professor of seventeenth-century literature—in that order of priority. It's quite possible, however, that Oscar interpreted my desire for his independence as my not *needing* him. And in a sense, that was true; I could live without him. Nevertheless, I believed (and still do) that when I was not being drained by his proclivity for leaving (the ultimate independence), I lived so very,

very much better *with* him. In short, while I may not have needed him,* I very much desired him.

Perhaps also in the process of trying to build a family, I'd forgotten about the woman who had been willing to risk everything for love. Over the years of being married to Oscar I'd become less and less free and spontaneous and more and more stable and grounded. While my groundedness had been part of what originally attracted Oscar to me, I also recognized, this time more clearly, that too much ground was deadly to his spirit (and ultimately to the health of our family), just as too much helium in his balloon tore at the family foundation. Perhaps as I'd gotten increasingly practical and logical and stable, Oscar's response had been to get increasingly impractical, illogical, and unstable to balance us out.

At any rate, I found in the weeks following our therapy that I gave myself permission more frequently to "lose control" even to the point of allowing hysteria to surface. In the past, I'd rarely raised my voice, believing from my own family's method of operation that maintaining a calm demeanor was the key to a "safe" outcome. Several times in the marriage when it had seemed Oscar was leaving for good, I'd broken down in tears and fallen apart in that way, but never had I shouted, ranted, or raved. I'd been too afraid, and besides, those behaviors had always been Oscar's prerogative. In fact, before I *allowed* myself to do so, I didn't even know that I was capable of such "wild" behavior. But I was, and exercising that side of my emotions was therapeutic for me, and I believe also for Oscar, who may have thought up to this point that I was somehow emotionally stunted.[†]

I remember very well our last session with David, a session that ended disastrously. I should have known what was going to happen because Oscar had made a special point of taking separate vehicles. I do not remember what prompted his exit from the session, but I remember very vividly his getting up and making it clear that he was leaving. David responded to Oscar's grandstanding with the statement, "You'd better take her with you." Oscar gave a dismissive wave of his hand, said "You take her," and walked out. Since I had not yet gained all of the insight that I eventually would from the therapy that had already occurred, I started to cry. It had been only five months since Oscar had threatened to burn the house down, and while I'd felt we'd made some important discoveries, our

---

*The notion of "needing" someone seems to me very complicated. Obviously, if Oscar died or left tomorrow, I'd carry on without him. At the same time, I cannot conceive of the loss of my soul mate as being anything other than severely debilitating. Would I survive and eventually flourish? Of course, but nothing would ever replace such loss.

†During one session, in response to Oscar's declaring that he didn't think I could change, I leapt out of my chair and threw myself onto his lap. He was startled by the force and suddenness of my reaction which spoke volumes in answer to his concern. My actions also bore silent testimony to the changes I was undergoing in response to the therapy.

sessions had been "all over the map." David didn't think we should continue the session without Oscar being present, but I felt completely incapable of just getting up and going about my business. Oscar and I were still living apart at this point, but with his storming out of what I knew was our "last hope" for help, I felt at a loss as to how to proceed. I remember asking David, "So what do I do now? Check myself in to a safe house?" I should also probably have mentioned that the O. J. Simpson trial of the previous summer was still a fairly fresh memory.

In response to my question, David and Anne Marie said that I needed to do whatever I felt that I needed to do. But I needed more to go on than that. I pressed them for their "reading" of Oscar. In the nine previous sessions, they had seen him and us at our worst as well as at our best, something I felt no other therapists had ever done. Therefore, I trusted their judgment. Had they responded only to my fears, as had my previous counselor, who had never even met Oscar, I'm quite sure our marriage would have ended in divorce. But what they said is that Oscar seemed to them like a "dog with a very big bark," but not one with a vicious bite. Since I've been startled by but never afraid of barking dogs, that statement changed my life.*

Before I left, they also encouraged me to do whatever it was that I had done in the past that seemed to work for me. On the ride home from Syracuse, I asked myself what exactly *had* worked, and I realized that I functioned best, and Oscar responded most positively, when I assured him of my love but then went about my business. I'd always been good at seeing the best in people, at believing the best of them until absolutely proven wrong. I was a born cheerleader, urging people to make the most of themselves.† So I determined to carry on in this mode—for better or for worse. Thus, on the way home, I stopped at the store, bought Oscar a card, delivered it to him as he pulled out of the bus garage on a run, and went home. The following weekend, when he called to suggest that we bring this whole thing to its inevitable conclusion and that I file for a divorce, I just calmly told him I had no plans to divorce him and wondered when he thought he

---

*I'm aware that David and Anne Marie could have been wrong in their assessment. Many feminists would argue that when it comes to male violence, zero tolerance is the only acceptable response and "bark" is as dangerous as "bite." I say that while threats are intolerable (hence, I asked Oscar to leave when he made them), they are not equivalent to actions. Might a bark lead to a bite in some instances? Of course, but as with all of life, you weigh the odds and take your chances.

†Years later Anne Marie reminded me of a session I'd wholly forgotten. Oscar had been particularly gloomy during the previous week about our prospects of ever getting back together. In response, I'd outfitted the girls and myself in matching red dresses for the next session, and we'd sung the Barney song for Oscar changing the words slightly: "I love you; you love me; we can be a happy family." Oscar was visibly moved.

might be able to come back home. We had started our sessions with David on July 25, 1995, and they ended on October 4 that same year. Oscar returned home on October 7, and we have not been separated since.

David and Anne Marie *were* concerned for me, and David called me a day or two after the last session just to check in. Then, several months later, he sent us a newspaper clipping about an interracial church in Syracuse, a gesture that touched us. When we called to thank him, he told us that after the final session, he had really felt he had somehow let us down; in fact, he had also thought we were probably no longer together. Far from feeling as though he let us down, however, Oscar and I feel we owe our very continued existence as a family to the grace of God and David and Anne Marie's work with us. David had invited us during one of our sessions to go on for our "Master's degree" by inviting our parents to participate in the sessions. I'd frequently "interviewed" my parents during the course of Oscar's and my therapy in order to gain insight on the dynamics of their relationship, and Oscar's mother had agreed to join us in a session over the phone. When we tried to call her from David's office at the prearranged time, however, she wasn't home. Nevertheless, though we didn't mine this field as deeply as we might have, an unexpected outgrowth of our therapy sessions has been an improved relationship with our parents. The web of my own relationship with my parents had felt very constrictive to me from childhood until my early thirties, and what had not been a close relationship had grown even more strained during the first years of my marriage to Oscar. Over the years, however, not only have my parents grown to be one of the chief supporters of our marriage, but I have come to respect them immensely and, in fact, now think of them as valued friends to whom I readily turn for advise.

In conclusion, while Oscar and I are, indeed, living happily ever after,* that does not mean our path has always been smooth. Oscar is still overcome periodically by intense feelings of despair as to the viability of our marriage, and when those times come, he still says some of the same hopeless things he's always said. But now, instead of feeling defeated because such feelings have not been eliminated, I remind myself that eventually they will pass. I do still feel extreme sadness as I witness Oscar's discontent and am tempted now and then to suggest that he try an antidepressant, but I also acknowledge that the pain he experiences during these times might in some mysterious way be part of what makes him who he is. Perhaps he wouldn't treasure our life together as much as he does if he didn't periodically revisit and contemplate the alternatives.

---

*Oscar and I have been blessed by the addition of a final daughter to our family, Endira Madre, who joined us in 1998.

In the absence of medication, when the "crazy times" strike in our home, I remind myself that they will pass. Occasionally, if bearing with Oscar's negative attitude seems too painful for me, I suggest (if he hasn't already beaten me to it, which is rare) that it might be best for him to leave for a little bit. Somehow, since our sessions with David, he's never felt the need to leave for longer than a few hours. I also see Oscar working to communicate his feelings of growing despair *before* they have gotten to the point of overwhelming him, and occasionally he'll say, "You'd better make an appointment with David." Actually, just the *thought* that we can make an appointment with David is therapeutic (which seems ironic, considering we were both so convinced that he wasn't doing anything for us!). In all but one instance, by the time we were ready to make an appointment, we discovered we no longer needed one. As a result of Oscar's better communication of what is going on for him (or perhaps I just am a better listener now than I was in the past), the "mood swings" no longer seem to materialize out of the blue.

Some day my daughters will have their own tales to tell, which like all good stories will begin "Once upon a time." My prayer for them is that they, too, will one day find husbands who bring them as much joy as Oscar has brought into my life. At the same time, I hope that their parents' work in family therapy (particularly David's "fairy tale" version, where dragons are to be dealt with directly rather than drugged into submission) will afford them insights that neither Oscar nor I had available to us as we set out to build a life together. If I cannot protect my children from emotional pain or even from mental illness (and I'm no longer convinced that such protection is necessarily healthy even if it were possible), I certainly hope that I have equipped them to face whatever joys and pains life sends them with honesty, integrity, and above all, love.

Chapter 13

# The Therapy That Almost Wasn't, or Imaginary Therapy

Oscar Davis

*"I'm afraid I can't put it more clearly," Alice replied very politely, "for I can't understand it myself to begin with; and being so many different sizes in a day is very confusing."*
Lewis Carroll, *Alice's Adventures in Wonderland*

Once upon a time, there lived two separate people going their merry way as they knew it. But wait, let's back up and start closer to the beginning. When I was around eight or ten, I would look at my family and say, "Something is wrong with this family; something is wrong with this family." Not "something is wrong with me." I could not accept the fact that there actually might be more wrong with me than there was with my family. When I finally saw that I could not deal with my home life, I took myself out of the family—first by running away, and later, after marrying when I was nineteen, by joining the army. Each time I left "family," however, I was forced to see that I couldn't be myself out in the world either and fit in. I found ways to fit in but discovered that *not* being myself brought on despair. I knew that I had caused the despair by removing myself from my familiar (but not wholly comfortable) world and then not being able to handle the new situation, but I covered up the despair with drugs, alcohol, women, you name it. Singing had been my thing, but being a performer, an entertainer, had its drawbacks. The lifestyle led me to the abuse of drugs and a warped way of thinking about others. Basically, I bought into the hype that goes along with being a celebrity and thought more highly of myself than was probably warranted.

So now, let's flash forward to 1987. There I was in college, midtown Manhattan, and there she was, fresh out of grad school. We met at the junior college where I was trying to figure out if the world had left me any portion of a brain after twenty years of show business. One of the highlights of the experience was this English teacher. Boy, was she something! Still is. I said, "I'm going to get that girl," but then I thought to myself, "Am I crazy?" I told a friend and he believed that I was definitely crazy. If you've read Noralyn's side of the story, you have a pretty good idea of what kind of a woman she is. But Noralyn was also very naive about life. Sure, she had spent a lot of years acquiring her education, but I had spent those years plus ten more experiencing the world. So naturally we approached life differently. One of my friends said, "What does she want with Oscar? We all know what he wants with her, but what does she want with him?" Whatever our reasons, we both wanted each other, so when the opportunity arose, we took it. The day we got married, June 9, was a beautiful day. Noralyn picked me up from the train station and our lives together began. She had given me a one-way ticket into her life, making it very clear that if I accepted this ticket, there was no way out—it was a one-way ticket. I thought about that for a minute, but that was all. I just knew that I wanted to take the ride.

The first challenge of the marriage was my decision to quit smoking—three days of hell while she tried to figure out what was happening. I think that the best and worst of us came out at that time. But the longer we were married, the more I knew Noralyn was seeing some of the less desirable sides of me and the more of that she saw, the more her defensive mechanisms kicked in. There were some times when it got pretty ugly, and Noralyn, to her credit, kept her ground and got us from one point to the next. I tried to help occasionally, but I think I hurt more than I helped through sabotage, destruction, even jealousy of her.

I don't remember most of the events of our early years because I was dazed or someplace else mentally, but one thing I do remember is the day I looked at her face and it said to me, "What are you talking about?" I realized then and there that my game of trying to fit in wasn't working. I figured I might as well give this up because I knew I couldn't make it. But the best thing she did was to hang on to my leg one time as I was going out the door. She held on, and I was dragging her along thinking to myself, "This is great!" Here is someone who cares enough not to let me go. I was so used to "Go! Do us a favor! Go!" But this was completely different. She made me think. She took me out of this sick place. Here was someone who thought me worth something, who wanted me to stay—who not only *wanted* me to stay, but was *making* me stay. It gave me a whole different approach to life. Not just to our marriage but to life. At certain times, I really couldn't help myself, but when I was able to, I tried to communicate to her, "Maybe if you help me along a little, I might be able to beat this thing."

And she did help—until she bought into the fear of the therapists and counselors. After we'd been married for a couple of months, we'd established that there was some mental illness going on. I'd thought there was mental illness involved long before this, but I'd always thought that the whole world was crazy. I knew that the mental illness was detrimental to my own well-being; it made me feel suicidal and depressed with unexplained anxiety. She knew that the mental illness was not helping our marriage. I knew that I needed help. This woman had given me everything she had to keep the marriage going—her love, her understanding. I was accepting this, all the while knowing that I wasn't returning it or giving her what she needed from a man or a husband, and that disturbed me further. She was the breadwinner and the anchor; she was the clear-minded one and who knows what else she was. And there I was—just a guy, praying that now that my dream had come true, I could live to enjoy it.

So I decided that I'd let Noralyn help me. I wanted to be in her world, but in order to fit into her world, I had to find out some methods I didn't possess. I really didn't have much faith in the mental health system to begin with, but I agreed to try to medicate myself out of my mess. I gave in to her, submitted myself—not completely—but way more than I was used to and way more than I was comfortable with. But I felt relieved about it, as though there might be hope. So I finally sought medical help. Sure enough, the doctors said, "He's crazy." What I heard them saying to her was "Go find a new man; get rid of him." But they didn't know Noralyn.

On the positive side, the lithium that was prescribed (and later the Prozac) gave me parameters that life hadn't given me. The drugs wouldn't allow me to go outside the boundaries. But the downside was that I felt helpless—like a big nothing. It felt like the drugs "un-leveled" the playing field. And my wife changed to accommodate the change that was made in me. And I didn't like that. I remember thinking, "This isn't the woman I married, and I'm not the man she married. Are we just going to settle for this?" Another problem with drugs is that they neutralize, and, therefore, certain information that might shed light on the problem lies dormant. The drugs tapped into a source that told me, "Forget about the problem," so I would communicate everything else that bothered me, but the real problem was still there, and I knew it. The drugs also interfered with my creative processes, and I'm an entertainer, so that just doesn't work. After five months on the lithium, I took myself off.

Noralyn had already decided, "This guy is crazy, but I love him, and I'm still going to try to help him." But it was tough love. It had to be because the more she fought for me the more I fought against it. Finally, the level of tension was so high that we had to separate. We had to separate because I no longer felt that I could control myself. Now I began fighting a battle between good and evil. One side of my shoulder was telling me, "You know what you're doing. Go ahead and do your thing. Forget that bitch. Don't let her control you. You're the man!" The other side was telling me, "Give in; she can help you. Sure it's going to cost, but she can help guide you to where you want to be."

After a year and a half of separation, I realized that I still loved my wife and wanted the dream. In the time we'd been separated, I was learning control and regimentation and organization. I'd learned that one of the things I needed to do was to listen to the people who were trying to help me. One of those people was Noralyn's father, Dewey. One day the two of us were taking a drive amidst a crisis between Noralyn and me. He told me "Don't fight, don't flee, just float," and that advice got me through some rough times.

It was the time of the O. J. Simpson trial, and on the surface we fit the profile. That didn't help matters, because as far removed as that whole scene was, it was still in the forefront of my mind; I still had this wife, my soul mate, that I was trying to live with, and it wasn't really working. Sure, the ties that bind were in place and life was going on, but it was rough. The next time we ran into a really bad time, I agreed to try Prozac. That just felt like I was getting high like crazy all the time. Now, trying to negotiate a marriage and family with a *clear* mind is difficult; being able to remember circumstances that caused problems in the past, being able to think back and retrieve information and facts that will help you approach situations in a repairing way—these are necessary tools. Drugs—both prescribed and otherwise—can interfere with the process. Obviously nonprescription drugs like cocaine, marijuana, and heroin had interfered with my ability to negotiate a family; such drugs are designed to have the user enjoy the high of the moment, not to consider the past or to dream about the future. But the same is true of prescribed drugs to a certain extent. I found it quite impossible to see how I could work into reality a dream such as building a family when I couldn't remember what the dream was. But that is what the Prozac did. As with the lithium, Prozac took away my ability to dream.

By this time I was thinking to myself, "There's something strange about this whole process. I take the lithium, I take the counseling, I take the therapy, I take the marriage counseling, I take the Prozac—and I keep getting to the very same place that upsets me—when I cannot be understood. How am I still misunderstood on the lithium and the Prozac?" I kept telling Noralyn not to listen to other people who kept pushing the drugs because I did know that if she continued to follow their path, our marriage would be over. When Noralyn would read the diagnostic descriptions of me, I knew I was what she was describing, but at the same time I would think, "What good is this information?" My only antidote to her insistence that I was manic-depressive or bipolar or whatever was "You don't *want* me to be those things. The world doesn't need another asshole." I wasn't willing to lose the best thing that had ever happened to me to a system that I didn't have much faith in anyway; but I couldn't battle it alone. All I remember thinking is "There's something wrong with this picture. Maybe the picture is wrong. Maybe we need to find someone who sees the picture another way."

That's when we found David Keith, and soon after, Anne Marie Higgins, his associate. Somehow I immediately knew that David understood the plight. He knew that we were dealing with the unknown. What we needed was *not* what my wife had read about in some book (and she reads all the time). It was also *not* anything I had yet experienced (and I've experienced everything from out-of-body experiences to drug habits). I was very relieved during the first session by his suggestion that we might need to consider divorce. If I was as bad as the picture that was being painted, then I didn't deserve a family and I shouldn't have been in one. Having the kids there was good because we had to be forthright. We couldn't pretend.

I also felt satisfaction or relief in knowing that during our sessions Anne Marie was with us. This reassured me because I knew that if something was to go on in our session that David did not understand, maybe Anne Marie could relate. It also made it feel as though each of us had our own individual therapist in the room. Neither therapist would have to compromise his or her devotion to one of us as an individual at a given moment, because the other counselor could take up the slack if the other person felt left out. Also, neither therapist would have to divide his or her attention or work to make sure that their viewpoint was equally understood by two people who did not *want* to be packaged into one. To put it another way, a single counselor might have to act as a stereo with a right and a left side directed out to the two people who've come for help. To hear the whole piece, the two people would each have to be listening to both channels, the right and the left. With the two therapists, it felt like two mono signals, one individual side for the right and the other for the left, as opposed to one stereo signal cut in half. This procedure was so important to me that on the occasions when Anne Marie wasn't present, I wondered if we would accomplish as much. It just felt incomplete with her missing— which isn't to take away from David's ability to handle the session solo. My fear was born perhaps from working with a marriage counselor prior to David who we both knew couldn't go any further with us. Somehow I felt that Anne Marie and David together could go further than either alone. I felt that there was a better chance of success with both of them working with us than there would be with just one.

The main thing that David did was to get us to speak the same language. We'd have to speak to him instead of to each other, and he would repeat what we said. When he repeated what my wife had just said, I'd think to myself, "Is that what she said? Because that's not what I heard at all!" We were able to say things to him that we couldn't have said to each other. But as we said them to him, we still knew that the other person was listening, though perhaps not understanding. I found particularly beneficial his rule that we could not discuss the session for a twenty-four-hour period afterward. This cool-off period gave me time to think about what had been said and how it could be used to move forward in the relationship. Normally, I would have been ready to go at it as soon as we walked out the door, but his rule gave us the chance to process some small tidbit of information instead of reacting immediately in the same old way.

When we first started therapy I was close to wanting to beat up the world. But somehow I knew that I had contributed to my despair by removing myself from my world in the first place and then not being able to handle my situation. I had covered up my despair for so long, but somehow through the therapy I got the message, "Now I have to be the real man, the man I'd left my family all those years ago in order to avoid becoming." I needed to take responsibility for my own part of the illness. In a follow-up interview, eighteen months after our last session, David asked how they had failed us. I was surprised by the question, but we had complained about him not being helpful. Then I thought that all of the other therapists before David and Anne Marie were failures in a sense because they were working toward a cure "out there" which we never did find. David knew that healing has to come from within us, this man, this woman.

For the therapy to work, I realized that it was going to take a lot of sacrificing, a lot of soul searching, a lot of being honest, and a lot of perseverance and sheer endurance. Lithium and Prozac had bridged the gap between where I was and where I wanted to be. But for the life of me, I cannot possibly see how anyone could do any kind of serious soul searching, any kind of serious reflection on their life—this kind of heartbreaking dialogue and life-altering work—under the influence of mind-altering or mood-altering drugs like these. Some of the things that I had to say hurt *me* to say, so I know that it hurt people to hear them. In the same way some of the things that were said hurt me. But such honesty was necessary in order for us to accomplish our objectives. What were those objectives? Number one, to find out whether or not we were compatible enough to be together and stay together. Number two, to find out if the other person was prepared and equipped to do the work that would make staying together possible. In order to handle this process, a great degree of vulnerability along with a high level of commitment are required in order to get from one place to another. For example, revisiting old hurts (both those a person has caused in another's life and those that have been done to the person) is extremely painful. Such a process is absolutely necessary if people are going to gain insight as to what caused the pain in the first place and figure out different ways to approach situations. But people aren't likely to dig around in old wounds involving others unless they have some reason to believe that doing so will end up with a different outcome. It's hard enough to face one's own pain with a therapist. Family therapy forces participants to face the entire family's pain. Therefore, partners must have an equal desire to succeed in the relationship as well as an equal level of commitment to do the work and make the necessary changes. For this reason, I don't think that family therapy is for everyone.

One especially interesting aspect of the sessions was how they began—with quiet waiting for an issue to present itself. Normally when you go to a counselor or a therapist you expect that they are going to ask you all kinds of questions, give you great advice, all this great direction, psychoanalyze you, but with David none of that happened. He almost seemed to sit in defiance. By allowing times of silence, by not filling in the gaps with his expert opinion, he conveyed the message that he wasn't there to tell us what was wrong with us, that if we simply reflected on what was taking place, we'd see things from a new perspective. At times it seemed as though he just wanted to make sure that *we* told him what we thought was wrong with us. That way, if we knew what was really wrong, we would have a better chance of knowing how to fix the problem. It amazed me how I would go there week after week and have David say maybe one or two key things in the whole session that would spark either Noralyn or me to embark on a new path that helped us experience life and each other in a new way.

In summary, while medication I'm sure has its place in this field of mental illness, I'm not so sure how it fits into repairing damage that has already been done in a family because of mental illness. My main reason for doubting its usefulness is the simple fact that mind-altering or mood-altering medications alter one's mind or mood. If my wife for some reason or another were to be prescribed one of these medications, she would no longer be the person I chose to marry or be involved with. That's not to say that a medication might not help a person get better or deal with their illness better. But I would strongly suggest that before medication is used, not only the person for whom the medication is prescribed but also the person who is going to be living with the person on medication give serious thought as to whether they are prepared to deal with the altered mind or mood. For myself, when I was on lithium and Prozac, I no longer felt like the person I had been before I'd taken the medication. Therefore, I could not possibly expect my wife to relate to me, or communicate with me, or even associate with me as she had in the past. Marriage requires commitment, determination, sacrifice, respect, and love for each other, not to mention hard work, patience, mutual admiration, and unselfish behavior. These things require a mind able to reflect on and grow through both the good *and* the bad, the positive *and* the negative, the health *and* the sickness, the pleasure *and* the pain.

Chapter 14

# The Therapist Replies: Observations from the Therapist Who Didn't Do Anything in the Therapy That Almost Wasn't While Attempting to Salvage the Love of a Lifetime

David V. Keith, MD

*"Hold your tongue!" said the Queen, turning purple.*
*"I won't!" said Alice.*
*"Off with her head!" the Queen shouted at the top of her voice. No-*
*body moved.*
*"Who cares for you?" said Alice, (she had grown to her full size by*
*this time) "You're nothing but a pack of cards!"*
Lewis Carroll, *Alice's Adventures in Wonderland*

The foregoing two essays describing a complex marriage and its interdigitation with mental health professionals, including myself, are moving to me. Even though Noralyn and Oscar express gratitude to me, I have a desire to say how they looked to me and what I thought I did within my symbolic experiential family therapy pattern. In the way I work with families, medication seems less necessary. I want to give an idea of what I do that makes medication seem less necessary. The first and most fundamental thing is to pressure the whole family to come in. The second is that no person is allowed to be more important than any other in the family. When Noralyn and Oscar came to see us, they found it impossible to agree on anything. In a follow-up interview, a year and a half after the last therapy interview (I will say more about this later), they mentioned that midway through the series of interviews, when they were talking about what they were getting out of therapy, they found something they could agree on. "David wasn't doing anything." Now, in their essays, both Noralyn and Oscar mention that David didn't do anything, so I want to say something about how this process of not doing anything can be therapeutic.

Noralyn arrived in the marriage and in the therapy with hopeful Protestant exuberance made more powerful by the fact that she is an accomplished scholar and professor with a PhD in seventeenth-century literature. She is a very appealing person, her inner world seems dominated by a sense of right and wrong, and she does not like to do it wrong. In our work she was kind, understanding, and forgiving, but at times her logic and self-sacrifice cornered Oscar. What she does not say about herself, because I think it is incongruous with the view of herself she values most, is that she has a high capacity for being a slightly outrageous, sexy, and lovable nut. Their marriage has not only lasted, but stayed alive because she also has a high capacity to go for a ride in someone else's reality. Because she has such a firmly rooted sense of self, she can take this ride and not lose her self or her identity. In this case she fell in love with Oscar because he catalyzed her departure from the secure, logical, preplanned living style that she sensed was leading to the early demise of her soul through suffocation. But inevitably there were crisis points where she would lock up and try to explain herself linearly. This is her burden from being a white scholar with her taproot in the Midwest.

By comparison to Noralyn, Oscar may seem boundaryless. My observation would be that he does not have white Midwestern boundaries. He is a black man who grew up in Brooklyn who has traceable roots that go back to slavery, and who has spent twenty years on the road of professional entertainment. "Boundaries" is an intellectual idea about people, and I have never liked or understood it. "Boundaries" is too static as a way to think about the living. I prefer concepts like self-awareness or self-ownership. Oscar was an impressive, if enigmatic, person. He has an abundance of personhood and integrity. While on the one hand he trusted me, on the other there was a caution that never disappeared. His is the language of the poet and songwriter. His descriptions of events are usually spontaneous, engaging, and lucid. Oscar by his beingness challenged and threatened Noralynn's reality structure, her reality attachments. His style insists on "I"; it collapses, confuses, enriches, and forces individuation. Hers is the language of the critic and scholar. While she could be nourished by interaction with Oscar, at other times she would instinctively separate herself. What would it be like if Oscar went back on the road for a year and took Noralyn with him? How would she handle living in his world? Come to think of it, I wonder what three months of living in that world would do for an old square like me.

I saw them eleven times. As Noralyn noted, the therapy ended when Oscar said, "I've had enough of this bullshit!" Then he walked out and slammed the door. I should note that he became very fierce when he felt cornered, but I never experienced him as dangerous. "Don't tread on me," he seemed to say. I considered my work with them a failure. I felt disappointed. In Noralyn's essay she describes how eight months later we had a communication in which I learned that, in fact, they were reunited and feeling healthier about the relationship than ever. Then, a year later, I asked them to participate in a seminar where they were interviewed by a colleague of mine about their experience as patients.

At the beginning of the therapy my instincts told me to beware of Noralyn's exuberant hopefulness about the marriage. That included her hopefulness about Oscar, which cornered him, interfered with his alternatives, made it necessary for him either to leave the field or stay and attempt to conquer her. Both alternatives made him a misfit in the white Protestant suburban world he was trying to fit into. The therapy began with high conflict, and in my mind the couple appeared to be headed for divorce. Later, I learned this opinion was a relief to Oscar, who felt pressured by her exuberance that created a feeling he needed to live in her world. This carried the implication he must not be himself, quite. Oscar liked that I was willing and able to deal with what he referred to as "the unknown," that certain something with no name. Awareness of, and respect for, this "unknown" is important, though perplexing. Michael Polanyi referred to it as the world we know we do not know. It is not accessible by questionnaire. If I was willing to deal with the unknown, then Oscar did not feel cornered and reactive.

It was during my work with this couple that I came to see that mania was a by-product of a failing effort to fit in and that depression was a way to recover from the despair, confusion, and exhaustion of this failed effort. One of the central issues in their marriage was the fact that Oscar wanted to fit into Noralyn's world. He sensed the health it offered would be healing, but he also found that it cornered and suffocated him and he fought against it.

They had been through a lot by the time they got to us. They learned from their experiences with professionals that Oscar had bipolar disorder. While it affected relationships, this bipolarness would not be affected by relationship or relationship therapy. This is an example of the odd logic of modern psychiatry, and it is one of the points where I depart from some of my psychiatric colleagues.

When the disturbance is more severe (high-conflict marriage, psychosis, biological depression), therapy is likely to lapse back to a framework based on the linear and the logical. My therapeutic motto, which comes from working with people with schizophrenia or other chronic illness is "Don't just do something, stand there." The reason they felt like "David wasn't doing anything" was that unlike their other therapists, we didn't *tell* them what to *do* or give them a how-to-list or a bag of tricks to fix the marriage. There was no task-oriented homework defined with each session. As noted, my only advice was not to talk about the therapy for 24 hours. This is not a paradoxical instruction. It is a way to keep the therapeutic experience separate from real life.

However, it is important the reader get some sense of how just standing there can lead to something. The following interview excerpt is from a paper that I prepared for a book of cognitive behavioral case studies (Dattilio, 1998). This segment comes from the fifth interview. It gives a sense of how I go about "not doing anything."

> The fifth appointment was at 10 A.M. Oscar said he awoke at four in the morning from a dream he could not quite remember. He woke up feeling very sad, then began to cry. "I couldn't stop crying. I cried until seven o'-clock. I don't know what it was. I didn't understand it, but for some reason, I didn't want to stop. There was something purifying in it. When Noralyn and the kids came to pick me up, I was glad to see them. But I felt sort of defensive, I suppose, like I wanted to be alone. But I do love them. When they came, my crying stopped. But before that it was just overwhelming. This has never happened to me before."
>
> DVK: Were you talking to yourself when you were crying?
> Oscar: I suppose. But Doc, I have no words for it. This has never happened to me before. You haven't known me for long, but can you imagine me speechless?
>
> Noralyn started to say she was glad to hear of his crying. I gently told her to be quiet, he wasn't crying to make her feel glad. This was an important experience for him. She should let it be, let him be alone with it. He did not know what to do next.
>
> My remark to her may sound rude. Disrupting the marital symbiosis can seem harsh. When a marriage is in therapy, there is a tendency for the partners to link all to the marital dynamics. This impulse is related to the marital symbiosis, and it is important to allow that condition to be disrupted. Then, each can have experiences (self-to-self, or self-to-therapist) and the other does not need to do anything about it.

I was impressed by Oscar's protracted crying experience. It came as a surprise. It gave me the feeling he had entered therapy, despite his early reservations. He had become a patient, a symbolic child (Whitaker & Malone, 1953). He was questioning himself in a deep way. . . . He was into therapy, and that was a surprise. We had gone through the zone of "lets define our problems, you give us advice and we will go on from here," to "we are on a journey together and we don't know exactly where we are going."

Noralyn said she was jealous. She wished she could cry like Oscar.

DVK: I think you may be too preoccupied with him to cry like that.
Noralyn: How do I get over it?
DVK: What comes to mind is you need to go crazy.
Noralyn: What? *I* need to go crazy? I thought we came here so *he* would *stop* being crazy, but now you are telling me *I* need to be crazy? I thought I was the sane one, "the good lady" who would lead him into the heaven of Protestant mental health. Now you tell me I'm supposed to be crazy.

She was outraged and a little surprised, but she was also mocking herself. This capacity for self-mocking and their pleasure in double entendre is a sign of health, a hint they can tolerate the pain of getting lost in this process we call experiential psychotherapy.

Noralyn: Oscar's always had this kind of emotion or passion about him. I know that's why I fell in love with him and I know despite the hard times we've had, this is why our relationship has continued. Sometimes I have to say that I *am* jealous of how open he can be emotionally, but me, I always feel, "I don't know how to do this," like I got, like I can only get it wrong. I don't even know how to be *crazy* the right way.

There is a switch here. Both have entered into the therapy process, have become what I refer to as "patients." They have detached from each other ever so slightly. They are *allowing the process* to take them over. Some families never leave the first interview stage of therapy, which, I am implying, can go on for five interviews. They stay safe, sane, controlled. We call it "in-sanity"—trapped inside of sanity.

From a psychiatric point of view, Oscar's uncontrolled crying episode following anger could be viewed as symptomatic, evidence of bipolar "rapid cycling." But we thought of his crying episode as a therapeutic regression, induced by the therapeutic process. In this context, "regression" refers to a non-rational, out-of-the-head experience, an openness to change is the usual implication, but pain, feeling lonely and confused are common concomitants.

Noralyn and Oscar are detached from one another as the symbiosis is disrupted, and he is in pain, which she did not cause, nor can she repair. The structure of her fantasy world, with him (as her patient) at the center, crumbles a bit. As we came to the end of the interview, both said in their own ways that they were feeling better, unburdened, but confused.

> DVK: If you are confused, then we must be getting somewhere. . . . But don't worry, the feeling better won't last. Enjoy it while you can.

This was an important interview for both.

In this situation I suggested she needed to be crazy; she who was the guardian angel of what would be considered normal and healthy. She was wise enough and felt sufficiently embraced by our caring to be able to take this seemingly absurd idea in. At first she rejected that idea as something preposterous, but as she noted in her essay, it had a delayed effect.

My hope is that these paragraphs give some sense of how we went about doing nothing. In effect, we met this couple where they were. We viewed what was happening as movement toward health rather than using these events as evidence of pathology. We pushed them toward individuation from the marital symbiosis by being parental and by being playful. I would like to say how much I got out of working with Noralyn and Oscar and how much I appreciated them.

## REFERENCES

Keith, D. V. (1998). Symbolic-experiential family therapy for chemical imbalance. In F. M. Dattilio (ed.) *Case studies in couple and family therapy*. New York: Guilford Press.

Whitaker, C. & Malone, T. (1953). *The roots of psychotherapy*. New York: The Blakiston Company (Republished in 1981, New York: Brunner/Mazel).

# An Afterword to the Client Essays

Our various emotions—even the unpleasant ones—have functions in our lives. If we are too quick to try to eliminate emotional pain through medication, we may lose important tools that help us find our way. Take, for example, depression. The *New York Times Magazine* (2002) published an article called "Viewing Depression as Tool for Survival" in which several researchers and professionals are quoted as describing the sorts of purposes depression can serve in our lives. Dr. Randolph Nesse, director of the Evolution and Human Adaptation program at the University of Michigan's Institute for Social Research, protests the idea that depression is simply a matter of disordered brain chemicals. He suggests that depression may have developed as a useful response to situations in which a desired goal is unattainable or "when one of life's paths peters out in the woods." Depression may help a person disengage from what has proved a hopeless effort or protect a person from jumping ship too rashly. Says Dr. Nesse, "If I had to put my position in a nutshell, I'd say that mood exists to regulate investment strategies, so that we spend more time on things that work, and less time on things that don't."

In her book *Productive and Unproductive Depression* (1989), Dr. Amy Gut describes the experience of a biochemist who frequently became depressed when a research strategy he was pursuing went nowhere. When the feelings of despair passed, he said, he saw "an entirely different way to tackle the problem, or else I have recognized that the project was unrealistic." Dr. Gut states, "I think that depression is a normal mechanism. It's an attempt toward adaptation to a problem."

Other thinkers on the subject have cited depression as a way to conserve energy and resources in hard times. Dr. Nesse believes there are many varieties of depression, not all of them captured by official diagnostic categories. He feels if depression is a useful defense, it may not always make sense to block its defensive properties with medication, and he encourages a broader, more nuanced search for treatments.

A poem by Kahlil Gibran from *The Madman* may speak to this idea the most eloquently:

### When My Sorrow Was Born

When my Sorrow was born I nursed it with care, and watched over it with loving tenderness.

And my Sorrow grew like all living things, strong and beautiful and full of wondrous delights.

And we loved one another, my Sorrow and I, and we loved the world about us; for Sorrow had a kindly heart and mine was kindly with sorrow.

And when we conversed, my Sorrow and I, our days were winged and our nights were girdled with dreams; for Sorrow had an eloquent tongue, and mine was eloquent with sorrow.

And when we sang together, my Sorrow and I, our neighbors sat at their windows and listened; for our songs were deep as the sea and our melodies were full of strange memories.

And when we walked together, my Sorrow and I, people gazed at us with gentle eyes and whispered in words of exceeding sweetness. And there were those who looked with envy upon us, for Sorrow was a noble thing and I was proud with sorrow.

But my Sorrow died, like all living things, and alone I am left to muse and ponder.

And now when I speak, my words fall heavily upon my ears.

And when I sing, my neighbors come not to listen. And when I walk the streets no one looks at me.

Only in my sleep I hear voices saying in pity, "See, there lies the man whose Sorrow is dead."

### REFERENCES

Gibran, Kahil. (2001). *The madman: his parables & poems.* Mineola, New York: Dover Publications.

Goode, Erica. *The New York Times Magazine,* Feb. 1, 2000, issue 5/285, vol. 149 F-7.

Gut, E. (1989). *Productive and unproductive depression.* New York: Basic Books.

# Part 5

# Clinical Illustrations: Systems-Based Practices as Alternatives to the Use of Medication

# Introduction to Part 5

The only war that matters is the war against imagination. All other wars are subsumed.
> —Diane Di Prima, from "Rant," in *Pieces of a Song*

Psychotherapy is a work of the practitioner's imagination. The imagination is what shapes and gives meaning to our experiences. Psychotherapy is a countercultural process. It is a process that is defined by whoever is looking at and thinking about it. It pays attention to enriching the human spirit—the only war that matters (Auerswald, 1995). It balances the complexities of freedom and responsibility, helps negotiate the dialectic of individuation and belonging. Psychotherapy depends upon creative emotional investment by the therapeutic practitioner. Much of what society does to "protect" "consumers" interferes with fundamental therapeutic processes. Psychotherapy, by disrupting the patient's relation to the culture, adds alertness and enriches relationships. It has an obvious relation to morality, insisting upon our taking responsibility for what we do. But it is further informed by a sense of beauty, which manifests in our own organization and relations, our own completeness and growth. Psychotherapy is a process of constant learning and innovation by practitioners, as is demonstrated in the following articles. They describe experiences and methods, ways of looking at therapy, that deepen our awareness of what therapy can do. Psychotherapy is not a scientific enterprise but has much in common with performance art—like music or theater.

We are presenting this diverse series of papers in the interest of stimulating your thinking about family psychotherapy. The processes outlined in other sections of the book emphasize that psychotherapy has been diluted by standardization of practice methods and the bureaucratization of mental health care. Psychotherapists are dumbed down by the promotion of drugs, the simplistic thinking of managed care, by what Pakman refers to as "globalization" of mental health practices. The most prevalent form of psychotherapy usually represents a pattern of guided social adaptation and accommodation. All therapists' offices have glass walls, which allows their work to be scrutinized by a variety of eyes from the community. If therapists' work moves outside of this realm of adaptation and accommodation, the watchers begin to question. Any defense by therapists of the idiosyncracies of their work is viewed only as further evidence of their incompetence and camouflaged chicanery.

John Flynn gives an example of the perceptions of the healer. The open mind of the beginner is perceptive in ways that the expert mind is not. This is an interesting view because in working with novice therapists in their first years, it is clear that they can be perceptive of family dynamics. Once they have had some clinical training, and been indoctrinated into the use of *DSM* and psychotropic medications, the new system provides explanations that interfere with the freshness of their perceptions.

Amy Begel is a family therapist and a musician. Her musical self began intruding on the work her therapist self was doing. She allowed both selves to collaborate in an interesting consultative model for expanding creativity in therapy. The musician self insisted on innovation, and the therapist self followed. Her paper, written with David Keith, demonstrates the process and progress of innovation in family therapy and gives the therapist clues about how to think about the nonverbal components of interpersonal experience.

Fred Ford's short piece is a retelling of a classic family story. You may be amused.

John Benda is a family therapist who describes his work with an autistic child in a children's playgroup. While working with an individual, he is guided by some in-the-head version of an ecosystemic holodigm. During his work with this young girl, she is taken for a follow-up visit to see the psychiatrist who had diagnosed her with autism and treated her with an antipsychotic medication for emotional-behavioral control. The psychiatrist either does not trust or does not notice any change and prescribes another medication that has a harmful effect. John's work depends upon identifying pathology in himself. It is interesting that in this essay the difference in roles between therapist and patient collapses several times, with therapeutic benefit. Part of a description of an intimate relationship is the ability to switch roles with the partner. This phenomenon can be seen in the therapist/patient, teacher/student, parent/child, mother/father and marital relationships.

Yaroshevsky and Bekiaris have written a paper that gives a fresh way of looking at a diagnosis *du jour,* attention deficit disorder. They develop the idea that deficit of attention disorder is a problem related to ways of gaining and giving energy in relationships. Their description is itself energetic and well outside the framework of conventional language about psychotherapy. Their views are portrayed in a way that affects experience in the same way poetry might.

The final piece in this section, and indeed our own amen for this book, is Dick Auerswald's paper, another rich sample of the body of ideas that were the germ of family therapy. This paper is a complement to his article on Planetary Healing that occurs earlier in the book. In an extended clinical illustration he applies these ideas, an example of his work in Hawaii. The illustration is a community level intervention, which changes the perception of what appeared to be a psychotic disorder in a woman.

## REFERENCE

Auerswald, E. H. (1995) *Ecovision, the only war that matters*. Self-published.

Chapter 15

# Expert Therapist—
# Beginning Therapist

John Flynn, PhD, MSW and Phoebe S. Prosky, MSW

*"Curiouser and curiouser!" cried Alice (she was so much surprised, that for the moment she quite forgot how to speak good English). . . .*
Lewis Carroll, *Alice's Adventures in Wonderland*

*In the beginner's mind there are many possibilities, but in the expert's there are few.*
—S. Suzuki

The singular importance of these words for the Zen perspective is signaled by the fact that this is the opening sentence of the prologue of S. Suzuki's *Zen Mind, Beginner's Mind* (1994). The statement startles because it runs against the current of our usual thinking about beginners and experts. Suzuki is saying that the beginner's mind *is* something that the expert mind *is not*. The beginner is ready for fresh possibilities, whereas the expert lacks this sort of readiness; the expert has the sense that things are more finished.

In our usual way of thinking, the beginner's openness to possibility is a sign of ignorance, of not knowing, of inexperience. The expert, on the other hand, knows how to read the situation and what to do about it. The expert's skill is honed over a wide variety of situations. The decisive and quick narrowing of possibilities is the very sign of what is valuable about the expert's contribution. So maybe Suzuki is right that in the expert's mind there are few possibilities, but isn't that a good thing about expertise?

An expert-centered paradigm is part of the traditional culture of psychotherapy, the culture that grew up with psychiatry. In graduate schools, clinics, and agencies novice therapists are trained in the discourses and practice protocols of the medical model. We are encouraged to develop our expertise more and more. We learn the *DSM* system of differential diagnosis; we study selected theories and practice maxims and study with experts to learn how to apply them; we want to become expert therapists ourselves.

The medical model is the dominant strain in the culture of psychotherapy. It is second nature for our developing practice to move along the lines already laid down by this established model of differential diagnosis, etiological history, treatment plan, and treatment interventions to remove symptoms and their causes. To learn how to do these skilled tasks well is to move along the continuum from beginner to expert therapist.

I [J.F.]* imagine that the general picture I've just painted of therapeutic career development goes down pretty easily. We find it useful to think and act as if there were a relatively progressive learning curve that runs from beginner to expert. But is this really accurate? Does this picture reflect or express our primary experiencing of doing and learning psychotherapy? Or is this picture not more like Magritte's painting of a pipe on which he inscribed, "This is not a pipe."

Shift from my words to your accumulated felt body sense of the field of experiencing what we are discussing. Recall just a few of the aspects of therapeutic practice that my depiction has left out or glossed over. What about the importance of being in tune with the client system's experience as it is actually experienced in your presence? What about the difficulty of maintaining accurate empathy in this regard because of our egos, our ideas, or strategic agendas? What about the ability to develop and maintain a therapeutic relationship? And what about the intricate mutual sensing that moves us toward and through a readiness for change.

Lack of the distinguishable aspects of therapeutic practice I've mentioned *could* be mapped on the usual continuum of beginner to expert. An "experienced" person could be good at learning theoretical concepts, but relatively unable to sustain a therapeutic relationship. To realize that this sort of scatter is common is to move away from the limitation of thinking that there is a relatively progressive learning curve across the range of therapy practice; it is to move away a little bit from the attachments of the expert mind.

---

*This essay is written in the first person by John Flynn. Phoebe Prosky is his sidekick.

If you reflect on these considerations for a moment and check my picture of the culture of expertise against your accumulated felt sense of participation in both the medical model and in psychotherapy generally, you might feel a number of different things. You might sense that my picture does not come close to doing justice to the subtlety of actual medical model–oriented practice in psychotherapy. And, recalling some of the relationship aspects of therapy, you might also be developing a sense that the expert-centered medical model itself is an inadequate developmental picture of how psychotherapy is learned and practiced.

On both counts you would be connecting with something you implicitly sense, something you could bring into focus and explicate further. What I've given you in my medical model picture is a conceptual account, an account that directs your attention to certain aspects of the practice of therapy and to a certain way (the expert-centered medical model way) of ordering those aspects. Yet this practice has, as I have begun to suggest, infinitely many distinguishable aspects. Insofar as my picture (or the medical model) proposes to be "the way it is" or "the way it should be" both are exemplifying more of the limitations and attachments of "expert mind."

The expert, in Suzuki's sense, tends to make two mistakes simultaneously. He confuses his map with the territory and he closes himself off from fresh possibilities of experiencing. The Zen version of "the map is not the territory" is "the finger pointing at the moon is not the moon."

I'm not saying that formulations cannot be useful. They obviously are. But the interplay between formulation and experiencing is not yet widely studied or understood. Rather than taking formulations as "corresponding to" or "picturing" some prearranged territory, we might find it more useful to take these formulations as more or less coherent and elaborately arranged jigsaw puzzle pieces that "lift out" some aspect of a fluid and responsive process. "Beginner's mind" and "expert mind" can be considered two such pieces. But each relates to the fluid responsive process differently. Expert's mind tends to obscure it by limiting it, while beginner's mind tends to open to its ungraspability.

## EXPERT'S AND BEGINNER'S MINDS IN ACTION

We need some clarification of Suzuki's use of "mind" in the phrase "expert's mind." The term for *mind* in Chinese and Japanese Zen has to be understood as quite different from the Western tendency to equate mind with intellect. *The Shambhala Dictionary of Buddhism and Zen* (1991) defines *hsin* (Chinese) and *kokoro* (Japanese) as ordinarily referring to "heart, spirit, consciousness, soul, mind, outlook, interiority and thought" (p. 188). The sense of this is to broaden the concept of *mind* to include all the powers of awareness and consciousness rooted in our bodily living. "Mind" is a whole orientation toward living.

In this sense, "jealousy" would be a manifestation of mind. Jealously is felt strongly as a bodily experiencing. I want to have *that*. I feel the lack of having *that*. I grasp viscerally that someone else has the *that* I want and I don't want someone else to have *that*.

In a twisty way, jealousy is an example of expert mind in action, an example of mind limiting itself by its attachments. The experiencing of jealousy, will, in fact, be much more implicitly complex than what I have suggested above. If we were to focus on any of the avenues immediately opened up (as we do in psychotherapy), if we were to follow the felt sense of the wanting or the sense of lack, or of the belief that someone else has what is wanted and so on, the experiencing would probably open up in surprising ways. For now I just want to underline that it is just this fact of implicit interactional intricacy that can be located in all our experiencing. Any action that closes to this intricacy is an example of expert mind.

By writing this essay I am acting as if it could be useful for psychotherapists to develop an experiential felt sense of the difference between the attitudes and the energies referred to by these terms. How pervasive and damaging to therapeutic process is what he calls "expert's mind"? And how enlivening and supportive of the process is "beginner's mind"?

Let me provide more of the context of Suzuki's statement so that we can address these questions: "The goal of practice is always to keep our beginner's mind. . . . You might easily lose your original attitude towards [something]. . . . [Beginner's mind] does not mean a closed mind, but actually an empty mind and a ready mind. If your mind is empty, it is always ready for anything. . ." (Suzuki, 1994, p. 21).

"If you discriminate too much, you limit yourself . . . in the beginner's mind there is no thought. . . . When we have no thought of achievement, no thought of self, we are true beginners, then we can really learn something. The beginner's mind is the mind of compassion. It is [important] to resume our boundless original mind. Then we are always true to ourselves in sympathy with all beings, and can actually practice" (Suzuki, 1994, p. 22).

What would be a good example of resuming our boundless original or beginner's mind in psychotherapy? The best intuitively available example I can think of is the therapeutic interaction. The quality of this concrete bodily interaction affects everything that happens in therapy moment to moment, because whatever happens happens in the context of *this* momentary interaction.

What kind of interaction is happening when the therapist has an expert's mind? The leading energy of the expert orientation is the expert's know-what and know-how. The expert "takes in" the "client system" according to some conceptual grid, technical, theoretical, or self-invented. Clients are seen as "behaving organisms," perhaps. Or as "having cognitive problems to be located." Or, more ordinarily, as "having problems." Clients will need "restoring," "new metaphors," "to find their strengths" or "desensitization." Clients are "difficult," "resistant," or "cooperative." They are surely "diagnosable by *DSM* categories."

Despite all the theoretical and practical variability of these examples, they have one thing in common. The therapist determines through his own "expert mind" *who* "clients" will be, *how* their experiencing will be interpreted, and *what* is to be done. The authority in the therapeutic interaction rests with the expert.

Now what might the interaction be like from the orientation of beginner's mind? Here is Gendlin's take on this.

> When I expect a client, I put my own feelings and concerns to one side. . . .
> I also put aside theories and procedures . . . in front of me the space is free, ready for the other person. . . . I keep nothing in front of me. . . . I don't [even] want the attitude of being ready to respond *between* me and the client. Because I keep nothing between, the client can look into my eyes and find me. (Gendlin, 1996, p. 286)

In this and related passages Gendlin describes his practice of "putting nothing between," and sitting down with "the person in there." Here authority rests with the experiencings of "the person in there." The therapist's expertise is given over to the service of the experiencing of the other, of "the person in there."

For example, one of the authors met with a couple for the first time about marital issues. As she sat looking at the couple in that first session, she was struck by the fact that the shape of the husband's beard did not seem to fit his face well. At the next pause in the exchange, she abruptly asked the husband how long he had had his beard. He answered that he had had it for many, many years—almost as long as he could remember. The person who was the therapist was moved to say, "Have you thought of shaving it off?" Husband and wife looked at each other, stunned by the sudden, unexpected, and rather personal turn the conversation had taken, and then began to laugh. They said then that they had recently discussed that very thing. The session continued about the various aspects of their relationship. The husband, on return to his house, immediately shaved his beard, at first to the shock, and then the increasing pleasure, of his wife. His new appearance also had an important impact on his work and on his sense of himself. The person who is the therapist here experiences her awareness as caught by something and brings that into the exchange, without rationally knowing why, for the family to respond and add to.

In another session the person who is the therapist suggests that an arguing couple find a symbol to bring out and place in a prominent spot when a certain kind of argument was taking place. "Perhaps a miniature seesaw" was the fantasy of the therapist. "Oh, I just made one in a toy playground I constructed for our child" came the answer. In these situations the therapist can see clearly from the inside that something has presented itself to her, but she does not know the meaning of it. She expresses this presentation as it has come to her to the others in the exchange, and it has special significance for them. These examples illustrate an internal experience of therapy when it draws on beginner's mind.

Who is "the person in there" beneath and at the edges of what feels problematical and stuck? Gendlin doesn't say so explicitly, but my sense is that "the person in there" is the implicit sense of our common inheritance of "beginner's mind." Saint Augustine says, "Love kindles love," and so beginner's mind kindles beginner's mind.

## HOW CAN BEGINNER'S MIND BE DEVELOPED?

The discipline of "putting aside" and "putting nothing between" and so interacting with "the person within" in this manner is quite demanding. Something like Carl Rogers's three necessary conditions for effective therapy—accurate empathy, unconditional positive regard, and genuineness would have to be cultivated and mastered. Without such mastery, ego, expert theories, and procedures would "put something between." To "put aside" expert's mind would be to be transform it into beginner's mind.

Gendlin's process of encouraging therapists to focus on the implicit felt body sense moment to moment shifts the authority to client experiencing. But his set of procedures does not show how to attenuate expert mind to transparency. Perhaps only ceaseless meditative practice can accomplish that.

If, at its heart, psychotherapeutic work is the skillful work of welcoming beginner's mind into our world, first here, then there, then ceaseless meditative practice must be the river bed supporting the flow of our expertise.

## REFERENCES

Gendlin, E. (1996). *Focusing oriented psychotherapy.* New York: Guilford Press.
*Shambala Dictionary of Buddhism and Zen.* (1991). Translated by Kohn, Michael. Boston: Shambala.
Suzuki, S. (1994). *Zen mind, beginner's mind.* New York: Weatherhill.

Chapter 16

# The Jazz Consultation: Improvisation in Family Therapy

Amy Begel, MSW, and David V. Keith, MD

*'Twas brillig, and the slithy toves*
*Did gyre and gimble in the wabe;*
*All mimsy were the borogoves,*
*And the mome raths outgrabe.*

Lewis Carroll, *Alice's Adventures in Wonderland*

## THE ORIGIN

The "jazz consultation", or the use of jazz musicians as consultants to family therapy sessions, began because of my [A.B.]* boredom. Actually, it was more a restlessness each time I attended a family therapy conference, and the format was typically the same: presenter, videotape of a family therapy session, comments, comments on comments. There was a yearning I could not quite articulate. Of course, part of me was envious that I didn't feel "expert" enough to show my work so confidently to large numbers of people. Was my discontent valid or was I simply jealous of my professional brothers and sisters? I love to feel confident of what I know, like I have a

*This essay is performed in the first person by Amy Begel. David Keith is her sideman.

professional body of knowledge that backs me up, that tells me what's "true," that soothes uncertainty and vulnerability. I know well the drug that protects my perfectionism.

I began to realize that my restlessness was related to feeling constrained by the parameters we family therapists had established for our work, and ourselves. I was tired of words and more words—including my own. Perhaps it reflects my somewhat short attention span regarding "content," but while watching one of those videotape presentations, I heard an inner murmur say, "I wonder what Barrry Harris would say about that family."

Though few outside the jazz world know Barry, he is widely recognized as a premier jazz pianist, educator, and so-called keeper of the flame in terms of preserving the bebop idiom of jazz. I had studied with Barry at his studio, the Jazz Cultural Theatre, and my work with him affected my way of seeing the world. I was quite certain it affected how I observed and responded to family therapy sessions. So when I wondered how Barry would comment musically about a family session, I was really trying to reach beyond words and logic and to look for ways to capture the rhythm, the phrasing, the harmonic patterns of families.

Initially, I thought about ways jazz music can expand consciousness in terms of a single musician. I later began to think that a jazz ensemble as an interactional, improvisational art form could potentially illuminate family interactional patterns in a new way. Also, since the nature of playing jazz involves spontaneity and the freedom to respond to the moment, the idea of using musicians as "consultants," much in the way family therapists use colleagues, seemed tantalizingly possible.

About ten years after my ruminations about Barry Harris, when I became a partner at the Minuchin Center, I was able to give birth to this idea in practice. During this long gestational period, I continued to deepen my experience, both as a jazz vocalist and pianist, and as a family therapist. My move to the Minuchin Center offered me the chance to apply my idea, with the help of óur one-way mirror and supportive colleagues. When I told my new colleagues of my plans to use jazz musicians as consultants in family therapy, they responded (as the reader might be responding) with what might be called a bemused tolerance. A couple of my more direct colleagues openly told me they thought I was nuts, but it was fine with them.

Before going further, I want to provide the reader with a frame for this essay. I am not writing this to promote a new clinical method. This is an essay exploring improvisation in family therapy. The article provides a way to look at and think about psychotherapy. In recent decades the dominant psychotherapy patterns tend to be based on what is most explicit and what is most teachable. In its carefulness this kind of psychotherapy tends to focus on social adaptation; it has a difficult time augmenting the creativity of a family or person. In this essay I am exploring the abstract understructure of psychotherapy.

## THE FIRST CONSULTATION

The first consultation took place in 1998 and was a highly anticipated event, with about 15 colleagues and friends gathered behind the one-way mirror. One overresponsible colleague told me she was so nervous she hadn't slept all night! Strangely, I wasn't nervous at all. My thinking was, What could be bad about this? We have some great musicians and an interesting family; the worst thing that will happen is that we'll hear some great music.

For this maiden voyage I chose consultants—a bass player and pianist—who were a combination of good friends and highly accomplished musicians. The portion of the family that presented itself was a newly married African American couple with a 14-year-old from the mother's first marriage. The husband was a very responsible, well-meaning, controlling kind of guy who could see his year-old marriage deteriorating because of his "rage problem."

I had seen the family four times and found they possessed a strong desire for health. Their wish to repair their marriage was palpable in their ability to transform some of their painful patterns in a short period of time. Despite the husband's tightness, I had a good therapeutic relationship to him. By the time they came for the jazz consultation, they were experiencing each other with a lot more care and tenderness.

Since this was the first jazz consultation, I could only ask the family to participate; I had no pattern for talking about this kind of consultation, and no way of explaining it. I just said I wanted to have a couple of jazz musicians come in, listen to the interview, then improvise some music from what they saw and heard. Strangely enough, they said yes.

Before the session I met with the musicians and therapist-observers and briefly outlined my work with the family. My instruction to the musicians was simple. I wanted them to play their "experience" of the family, to let the music reflect their reactions to the family interaction. I also asked them to let the music do the talking. They agreed to this, and, as creative artists, they were comfortable with this degree of ambiguity. It was more difficult for my friends to accept the uncertainty.

The therapists were more anxious than the musicians. This says something about the nature of the profession and is a partial explanation of my restless boredom when watching family therapy demonstrations. There is an overcautiousness in clinicians based on a belief that therapy needs to be done correctly. There is an uneasiness about engaging in an experience and trusting ourselves in the moment. There is an inability to trust this therapeutic capacity. In fairness this uneasiness is partly rooted in the responsibility we therapists have to our patients.

But musicians know that they are instruments of a larger music. The music comes through them. They use music to understand and express feelings and ideas. I hear writers talk about how they allow the writing to lead the writing. I'm sure this is true of painters and other artists. There is an unconscious component in both that is crucial to creativity, and we, of course, are extending this process to therapy.

The creative process for both musician and therapist is dependent on the practitioner's ability and willingness to give up control of the outcome. In his book *Free Play: Improvisation in Life and Art* (1990), the violinist author Stephen Nachmanovich writes, "As an improvising musician, I am not in the music business, I am not in the creativity business. I am in the surrender business" (p.21). "That mysterious factor of surrender, the creative surprise that releases us and opens us up, spontaneously allows something to arise. If we are transparent, with nothing to hide, the gap between language and Being disappears. Then the Muse can speak" (p. 30). That is, there is a therapeusis in the universe and the therapist is its instrument.

There is a body of research that shows that patients achieve similar results in therapy whatever the "school" or model of the practitioner. Though the family therapy chauvinist in me rebels at these findings, I think this relates to the importance of the personal qualities of the therapist. We all know practitioners in the field who exhibit a high degree of technical skill and conceptual knowledge but who are not at all therapeutic. Being therapeutic has something to do with the importance of letting go of control, of the therapists' ability to allow the patient or family to be who they are, and then challenge them to expand in some new ways.

It is impossible to capture the experience of that first consultation in words, except to say that, truly, for everyone involved, it felt like being witness to a birth. With the musicians and therapists behind the mirror I interviewed the family. They talked about some conflicts since the last interview and how they achieved a new understanding between them. Father had invented a "grudge day" where everyone gathered around the table to air annoyances, and this worked well.

Midway through the session, when I sensed a harmonious trend was clear, I invited the musicians in to hear their response. I didn't know if they saw, heard, or felt the family as I did. They came in, went to their instruments and, for the next ten minutes, launched into one of the sweetest blues I've ever heard. The family responded in ways which I later learned were typical: family members identified with particular instruments, and they focussed on the interaction as an extension or reflection of their own interaction. The son, who up until then had been rather quiet, reached into his book bag and pulled out some poetry that he had written entitled, "Blues in F." His sensitivity and penetrating perceptions were invited out by the music. He became an angel of health and healing.

One aspect I did not anticipate, and which I have learned more about since this first consultation, was the impact of the experience on the musicians. For this first meeting, the musicians remained in the room during the family response and the bass player was moved to tears as he heard the young son recite his poetry. As we were getting ready to close, the pianist spoke up, commenting on how "inspiring" this family was and how much he respected them for the effort they had shown. The pianist, who was recently and precipitously separated from his wife, was obviously fully engaged with this family.

In discussion with both the pianist and bassist a week later, they talked about the residue from this consultation. The pianist said he went home and found himself feeling more forgiving toward his wife, which shocked him, since he had been feeling badly burned and dismissed by her. And the bass player, who went on to play another gig that night, said he had "never played so well," that his music soared. It became clear that the therapy was not just for the family.

This comment highlights something about the restless boredom I described earlier. I am fascinated by the idea that the therapist is the real patient. (Whitaker, 1989). If the therapist is not getting something out of the therapy, it is unlikely that the patients are getting anything (and vice versa). I am a patient in the sense that I do not always know where I am going. I know this, and I believe the therapeutic process, not my intellect, is the guide. Modern family therapists rarely mention this component of therapy. We are armed with models and theories for working designed to foster certainty in the therapist. Musicians have a sureness about themselves as well, but there is also an edge of ambiguity and uncertainty. Therapy is for the patient in the therapist.

Nachmanovich addresses this theme in discussing blocks to creative openness: "It would be nice to have an easy set of recipes that we could apply: Seven Steps to Busting Our Blocks. Unfortunately the creative processes do not work that way. The only way out of complexity is through it. Ultimately the only techniques that can help us are those we invent ourselves" (1990, p. 10).

## THE FLOP: OR, MUSICIANS ARE PEOPLE TOO

Of course, after such a rousing experience, I was intoxicated with success and exhilaration and eager to do it again. In this inebriated state, full of confidence, I invited several out-of-town guests to come as observers. This time it flopped.

I invited a couple from my practice to come for the second consultation. They were a biracial couple, living together and not married. They came to therapy because the Russian-born girlfriend hadn't been able to tell her mother that she wanted to marry this man, whom she kept largely hidden from her family. This was the ostensible reason for therapy, though early interviews revealed a wounded relationship. The girlfriend had been honing her sniping skills on her boyfriend, who had gone into hiding, and she was taunting him to come out and play some more. Into this hostile scene, masked as "romance," stepped two well-meaning jazz musicians.

The consultants were, again, two friends of mine, both at the top of their craft; a male guitarist and a female tenor saxophonist. Since I was at the beginning of this exploration and was still defining the parameters, I changed the instructions to the musicians. I told them they could stay in the room following the music, and added, unlike the first time, the option of commenting if they chose.

As the musicians stood on the other side of the mirror, listening to the angry exchanges of this couple, they began to respond like inexperienced therapists, asking themselves how they could make this couple feel better? So they did it in the way they knew how, musically. When I invited them in, midway through the match, they opened up with the ballad "How Deep Is the Ocean?" The music was beautiful, but totally dissonant from the experience of this couple. The woman's first comments confirmed this: "That's not us," she said.

Following their musical response, the musicians sat down. The tenor player began trying to console the wife with tales of woe from her own marriage. The woman patient rejected the musician's efforts to make her feel better, insisted that her boyfriend was a hopeless case, and I, not wanting to undercut the musicians' fledgling career as consultants, felt any control I had over the session slipping away. After my initial intoxication with success, the sobering-up process began.

## THE JAZZ CONSULTATION NOW

After I recovered from the hangover, I realized, again, the truth in the cliché about failure being the best teacher. What I had failed to recognize was that musicians are not savvy about dealing with tensions in the therapy room that we take for granted, and that, generally, musicians play to make people feel good. The great trumpeter Louis Armstrong liked to describe himself as "The Minister of Happiness."

This new understanding helped shape my approach to working with the consultants. I learned that it is important to relieve musicians of the responsibility of reducing tension. Before introducing the family, I meet separately with the musicians and tell them they are not here to "treat" the family. They are there to help me, the therapist. I am responsible for the family and any reaction they have to the experience, including increase in tension. They help me most by musically reflecting what they hear, feel, and experience. This, I am pleased to say, has allowed the consultations to proceed in exciting and unpredictable ways—we had had our last "flop."

I have developed several criteria for selecting musical consultants. First, they must be at the top of their craft, able to play anything. Since I live in New York City, which has more talented jazz musicians per square inch than any city in the world, this is the easiest criterion to meet.

Second, and slightly more difficult, they must want and be able to play "free." After the failed consultation, I realized I wanted the musicians to walk into the room with the family without deciding what to play. I wanted the purest form of musical expression, with its tension and unpredictability, which would force the musicians to rely on their internal resources. Contrary to stereotype, even some jazz musicians have a difficult time being "free." Even though the music is improvisational in nature, and strives for unpredictability and novelty, there are musicians who are uncomfortable without the constraints of chord changes, and shy away from playing "free," with no script. (I have observed parallels among family therapists.)

Third, the musicians must be, or have been, in a long-term committed relationship. Of course, when it comes to jazz musicians this requirement drastically narrows the pool, since many full-time musicians are married to their instruments. But the subjective nature of the consultation means that musicians will be bringing their unconscious experiences to the meeting, and I want them to know what it means to be in a committed relationship to another human being.

## A JAZZ CONSULTATION WITH A DEFIANT ADOLESCENT

A musician friend of mine tells a story about a bass player, Michael Howell, who received a call at his home in New York one day from Dizzy Gillespie, the late great trumpeter. Diz told Michael, "We're recording in the studio and we need you. Get here!" He hung up. The bassist had no idea where Dizzy was, when, what studio, but after making a couple of phone calls he finally figured it out—Dizzy was in Los Angeles! The bassist got on a plane and made the session the next day.

This story captures the essence of the spontaneity offered by jazz musicians. The ability to tolerate and embrace ambiguity, the open pleasure in tension, then release, and the playful indirectness and ability to be "disrespectful" toward the official order makes each jazz consultation unique, unpredictable, and alive. A recent example illustrates this. The P. family came for therapy because their 13-year old son, V., a previously successful and obedient child, had been failing in school, playing hooky, "sassing" his mother with a broad repertoire of early adolescent rebellion. The family consisted of mother and father, both born in India, and three sons, ages 13, 11, and 8. The parents had been officially married about fifteen years. Much of their emotional gratification came from confusing and hurting each other. The threat of separation was always in the air. Recently they had in fact separated and reunited, though father continued to hold on to his own apartment.

After six or seven sessions I suggested a jazz consultation to which they eagerly agreed. Though a musical background in the family is by no means a prerequisite, in this case the idea appealed to them on both an intellectual level and a musical one. The mother and all of the children played instruments. In fact, the oldest "disobedient" son was an accomplished classical pianist. In addition, though the parents had been spectacularly unsuccessful as a couple, they were both quite concerned as parents and were willing to "try anything."

The consultants for this case were a pianist and a bass player, both highly creative and accomplished. This was the first family consultation for the pianist, though the bassist had participated as a consultant on several previous occasions. They had worked together regularly, but this was not a factor in the selection. On several occasions, musicians have met each other for the first time at the family consultation.

The session began with the mother expressing both worry and anger toward her son, who had turned the household upside-down with his defiance. Mother was clearly the stronger authority in the family, but she was obviously feeling defeated. Father, too, made some rather paltry attempts to talk his son into "picking up a book" to forestall academic failure. Both parents talked about how raising an American child contrasted with their own upbringing, where, "if your parents told you to do something, you did it!"

But of course the son's disobedience went beyond cultural issues and was a vivid and symbolic demonstration of his parents' inability to hear and listen to each other, despite their mutual concern for their son. And on some level, despite father's stated goals of obedience, he was signaling to his son that Mom's word was somewhat suspect. But he was unhappy with the results.

Enter the musicians. The piano began playing some rather haunting and abstract chords, suspended in air, and it appeared that the bass player was reluctant at first to "interrupt." Then he joined his voice to the piano, and for the next ten minutes they made musical conversation that oozed ambiguity, confusion, some anger, but mostly asked questions. Nothing definitive, nothing clear, with an agitated edge.

Listen to the bass player's comments: "Watching through the mirror I felt bad for the kid. . . . It seemed like a waste that a nice middle-class Indian kid with a lot going for him would throw it all over at so young an age and become one of the sad people with the deck stacked against him. When we went in the room, John [the pianist] started a harmonic sequence that I couldn't follow. Since I hadn't actually played a note I felt it better to not just do something but stand there . . . and eventually I started playing gently to see if we could hook up. The music was somewhat atonal with periods of convergence and confusion, but in this case we never achieved any kind of coherence. The more I played, the more John seemed to lose his train of thought, and then he seemed ready to stop, but it was in the middle of something I was doing, so I forced what I thought was a necessary ending."

In every jazz consultation, and this one was no exception, I am struck by how the musicians seem to capture the feeling in the room with penetrating accuracy. This is not through deliberate effort on their part, and it almost always feels to them like an "accident." This process takes place largely unconsciously. When the musicians finish playing, they often have no idea "what happened," until they hear the family react to their musical commentary.

The family response was immediate and striking, and, as usual, it gave form to the consultation. The mother and two oldest sons did what family members often do, which is to assign each instrument the role of a family member. Mother interpreted the bass as being "strong," "in charge," the archetypal male. She said, "But when the music ended, it was still a big question mark." Father responded by saying he knew nothing about music, but that he found the consultation agitating, disturbing, tense.

The son reacted strongly to the music and expanded on his father's theme. He said the musicians "weren't listening to each other"; they were playing separate tunes; they weren't harmonizing, an obvious, but unintentional, metaphor for his parents. He said he thought, while the instruments were fighting, *he* was the one controlling everything. He said with an anxious smile on his face, " No one I know can control their parents the way I do."

Now it was the therapist's turn to improvise. The therapist can learn much from listening and watching experienced jazz musicians, and many of these musical skills are applicable in terms of therapist creativity. Of course, the rudiments of any craft are necessary for creative freedom. The musician needs to learn the basics of scales and chords so they are built into the unconscious, allowing the musician the freedom to leave them and the freedom to return to them. Likewise, therapists need to know the basics of theory and technique.

Once the therapist knows the chord changes and scales of the therapeutic process, the challenge is to let the session evolve without his knowing where it is going. This means letting the tension build, not having any responses ready, allowing for a state of relaxed concentration, giving up control. For me it means paying attention to my inner therapeutic unconscious awareness and being responsive when I can. And one more thing, I try not to forget the possibility of having fun. Or, as musicians say, "to swing."

In my improvisations following the musical sequence I try to allow the family's responses to emerge in whatever form they take, and then it's my job to help give it meaning. I try to extend the musicians' improvisation into the session and to weave themes into the dynamic of family patterns. The music isn't an end in itself. It is a catalyst to break through some logical barriers the family has constructed in its well-honed dance.

In a way I am like the family in the consultation. I do not know what the musicians will play. I am not in control of that process, and I am not trying to achieve anything. And I, too, am generally moved by the music. I try to stay open to what the music reveals to me about the family and use my responses to enhance the therapeutic experience of the family. And when I am feeling tense or cautious, I try to remember the advice of the great jazz innovator Miles Davis, who said about improvisation, "There are no mistakes." I try not to interfere with the experience of the family following the musical consultation. In one recent consultation, the husband was weeping and the bond between husband and wife became deeper. In that case, I let the music do the work.

With this family, I told the son that one reason that the music sounded like it did was that the musicians had no idea what they were going to play, they had no script and no map, and they had to feel each other out. I said that if they had a plan and understood each other, the music would probably sound different.

Then I did something that I had not done in previous consultations. The whole family responded and reacted to the discord in the music, in their own way, and I wanted to hear how they would react to a different musical message. I asked the musicians to come in again and play. Again, hear what the bass player says: "It [the first playing] felt extremely inconclusive, so when Amy [the therapist] suggested that we play a blues just to show what happens when the musicians agree, I felt relieved to get a chance to pull it together. And we did."

When the musicians reentered the room I asked them to play " a blues" and to "swing it." In musical language, a blues gives musicians a chance for immediate shared language and understanding. There is a musical "map," and built into the form are endless possibilities for freedom and innovation.

They began to play, and the shift in mood in the room was dramatic and instantaneous. The tension lifted, the sun shone, and the littlest son had a ball playing "air bass." The music was syncopated, smart, accessible, sensible, clear, and fun.

The response of the family was thunderous. Mother reacted immediately by throwing a sexy look in her husband's direction and said, "Children, what children?" The implication was that if she and her husband were playing together like that she would feel much more like a lover, a woman, than a mother. She felt the power of the swing, of definition, of hearing the musicians so tuned in to each other, so free and having a great time. She immediately, and not totally consciously, saw herself and her husband in the musicians.

The son spoke up immediately, incredibly articulate in capturing what happened. He said that they were "listening to each other," the music was "well defined," and had punch and power. He said with a smile, "If my parents were like that, there'd be no way I could talk back or disobey."

If I had to write a short drama about this jazz consultation, I couldn't have done better than what spontaneously came out of the family when they listened to this blues that my consultants played. It says something about the therapeutic process that challenges the demand to conform to current cultural fantasies suggesting written records and diagnoses and measurable goals are crucial to adequate therapy. It is much like the fact that families know a lot about families, but something crucial is left out of the therapeutic experience when the therapist is too anxious and feels pressured to produce a concrete result. I think this pattern of consultation gives evidence of the fact that there is an abstract process in therapeutic work that we cannot put into words. I believe it comes from the freedom to play. D. Winnicott says that all psychotherapy is play. Part of the essence of play is that it is inherently, and by definition, purposeless.

This is perhaps the greatest gift of these consultations to the therapist. Being part of the process whereby jazz musicians spontaneously explore the meaning of a relationship gives the therapist immediate access to the creative part of the self. The therapist listens to the musical response and then "jams" with family. The therapist has no idea what the musicians will play—they themselves do not know—and has no idea how the family will respond. All this uncertainty forces the therapist into a position of heightened sensitivity and openness, a feeling of minimal control along with the exhilaration of something alive unfolding and taking shape. This combines with the experience of suffering that family members bring to the encounter. This truly forces the therapist into the position of patient or artist. They can be the same.

I am currently immersed in the world of improvisation. This extends to the playing of music, to doing psychotherapy, to being in relationships with family and friends. My acquaintance with the jazz idiom offers useful illustrations of the components of improvisation. A meaningful improvisation includes risk taking, the pleasure of pursuing an authentic relationship with oneself, empathy for others, and delight in the ambiguous and the illogical.

I realize that few readers will be likely to start doing jazz consultations. I am fortunate to have access to the world of jazz, both in friendship and as a budding musician. My closeness to the people and ideas of the jazz world make these consultations possible. My hope is that the readers will gain more access to that nonverbal creative component of psychotherapy through their own unique talents and insights. Psychotherapy is like music and the therapist and patients are the ensemble. If it doesn't swing, it's not therapeutic.

## REFERENCES

Nachmanovitch, S. (1990). *Free play: Improvisation in life and art.* New York: Jeremy P. Tarcher/Putnam.
Whitaker, C. (1989). *Midnight musings of a family therapist.* New York: Norton.

# Chapter 17

# Goldilocks and the Three Bears Revisited

Fred Ford, MD

*"Tell us a story!" said the March Hare.*
*"Yes, please do!" pleaded Alice.*
*"And be quick about it," added the Hatter . . ."*
Lewis Carroll, *Alice's Adventures in Wonderland*

Once upon a time there was a little girl named Goldilocks who lived in a big house by the woods. She was in the habit of taking exploratory walks in the woods but would go only as far as the light lasted. One day she decided to go beyond her usual limit and see what more was there. As she went deeper into the woods, she came across a well-lit clearing with a neat brown house in the center of it. Being something of an extrovert, as people with attention deficit hyperactivity disorder appear to be, she went right up and knocked on the door. The door swung open. She stepped inside the house. No one was there; the family had gone to town to pick up their medications at the pharmacy. She quickly discerned there was a pot of soup cooking on the stove. Naturally, what was a girl to do but taste the soup? As luck would have it, there were three bowls sitting on the counter. One bowl was very large, another was smaller, and the third was almost tiny. She took the tiny bowl and put a taste of soup in it. It was very good . She decided to have some more. She filled the middle-sized bowl and quickly swallowed it down. Then she filled the largest bowl and ate almost all of it. When she was finished, she yawned and felt sleepy. Looking around, she saw three chairs: one very large chair, one smaller chair, and one very small chair. She tried the biggest chair; it was too big. Then she tried the middle-sized chair, and it was too big and lumpy. So she tried the little chair, and it was too small.

Seized by another large yawn, Goldilocks went upstairs to find a bed. Since everything in this house came in threes, she was sure she would find three beds. Sure enough, she found a big bed which was much too big for her. She tried it anyway. And a middle-sized bed. But it was too hard. In the next room she found a little bed, which was just right. Lying down, she fell fast asleep.

While all this was going on, the Mama Bear, Poppa Bear and Baby Bear collected their pills and returned home. Seeing the door wide open, they rushed in to see what had happened. They found that someone had tried out all of the chairs. Then they looked at the dishes by the stove and were dismayed that someone had used each of the bowls. Wondering what else had happened, they went upstairs. First, Poppa Bear complained that someone had been sleeping in his bed. Then Mama Bear discovered that her carefully made bed was all messed up. But Baby Bear made the biggest discovery of all. *Someone was sleeping in his/her bed.*

End of story? No. Goldilocks did not run away as she was supposed to. Her Ritalin had started to take effect, and she didn't have the energy. Nor was she mauled and eaten by the bears; the bears did not behave like bears. Poppa Bear had taken his Haldol. Momma Bear had taken her Zoloft. And Baby Bear had snitched some Prozac.

So the three bears and Goldilocks sat down at the table together to finish the soup.

Moral: Bears and people can live together as long as they take the right pills.

Moral, take-two: Bears and people can live together as long as they aren't who they are.

Moral, take-three: With pills you don't need a moral.

# Chapter 18

# My Journey with Allison in Wonderland

John M. Benda, LCSW

*And here I wish I could tell you half the things Alice used to say, beginning with her favorite phrase, "Let's pretend." She had had quite a long argument with her sister only the day before—all because Alice had begun with "Let's pretend we're kings and queens;" and her sister, who liked being very exact, had argued that they couldn't, because there were only two of them, and Alice had been reduced at last to say, "Well, you can be one of them, then, and I'll be all the rest."*

Lewis Carroll, *Alice's Adventures in Wonderland*

This essay presents a personal and professional reflection about the author's one year therapeutic relationship with Allison, a 6-year-old girl diagnosed with autism. It is personal in that it is written from the therapist's emotional experience of the therapeutic relationship. It is professional as a case study of how a therapist-child relationship may evolve. It reveals how both child and therapist can be changed by their relationship. The author assumes a systemic, symbolic, attachment-focused, and corrective emotional experience approach to therapy. Allison was complex, relationally intense, and had a special affective presence. The author was aware while working with her that contemporary modern psychiatry trends toward asystemic, disembodied, and biochemical approaches to mental health care would fail and hinder the felt depth of the relationship. The author also presupposes without hesitation that the desired therapist-child, or therapist-family, relationship is toward healing, greater individuation, more playful and intimate belonging, increased life satisfaction, and not just functional coping.

I am a child and family therapist at a clinic that serves the emotional growth and needs of children and families. This essay recounts my therapeutic relationship with a child named Allison. I was moved to write it a week after the end of our daily time together, when Allison graduated from group play therapy. Putting our story into words turned out to be a way to integrate my feelings after Allison left. I also wrote about our relationship in order to honor, celebrate, and share our jointly created experiences and mutual growth.

I welcomed Allison, age 6, into a group play therapy room one early fall day about three years ago. She was dressed for play in her favorite black coveralls adorned with a vivid magenta heart. She inquisitively stared at me with her head tilted slightly back and to the side, her eyes peering through her thick wire-rimmed glasses. She looked at me silently for a long moment, then turned and walked into the room toward my cotherapist, Rachel.

After this beginning Allison and I were in a surrogate family group with two therapists as parents, two interns acting as aunts and uncles, and seven children for three hours every weekday afternoon for the next 11 months. If I were to write a book about us I would call it *Seven Desperate Children in Search of a Parent!* I had worked with children and adolescents in various settings for about 12 years. My early encounters with Allison told me she was going to be unique, but my first impressions clearly underestimated the kind and depth of relationship we would create together.

I had been informed that Allison would arrive with a diagnosis of "autism." Her biological mother's parental rights had been terminated several years earlier for extreme physical and emotional abuse, and Allison had bounced around the foster care system since then. She was now living in one of the better foster homes in the area. We knew she had probably been sexually molested in a day care center by an 8-year-old boy, and that she referred to her sexual experience by pointing to her stomach and talking about "boo-boo." During our first week together, Allison tested my capacity to respond concerning the boo boo taboo. Out of nowhere she asked me, "John, do you ever do boo-boo?" My response was, "No one ever does boo-boo here, and it's only okay for grown-ups to do boo-boo." That seemed to be enough for the time being as Allison pensively stared for a moment, said, "Oh," and went to play.

Early on, Allison's ways of being with us were at two extremes. On the one hand, she was focused inward and silent. At the opposite extreme, she would instantaneously and violently react to loud noises, accidental touch, and other children's expressions of rage or sadness. Allison's aggression erupted quite often because we had seven love-starved and voraciously needy children clamoring for the attention of too few adults in one play-room. Being in this room was like swimming in a turbulent sea of raw af-fect fed by the intergenerational tributaries of each child's ambivalent attachment. It was an anarchy of diverse emotions bordering on chaos, but somehow contained by the warm nurture and flexible strength of the adults in the room. Emotions ranged from acute pain to exuberant joy with every-thing in-between. The feeling tone in the room was intensely alive. If Shakespeare had written a play about us he would have called it *Much Ado About Everything.*

Allison was a major player in our wild room. We had to be vigilant of her whereabouts because she was attracted like a powerful magnet to any and every emotional outburst. She would reflexively move to kick, hit, or spit at any child who was angry or crying. Allison also came close to breaking one of our intern's cheekbones with a head butt to the face while she was being held from behind to prevent her from attacking another child. Her immediate response to even the slightest limit setting or frustra-tion was an in-your-face "I hate you," often accompanied by a strong kick at a leg or a shower of spit.

Allison was also capable of grand aggressive exhibitions of affection with greetings and hugs. She would sometimes welcome a new person into our room with an extended greeting I can only describe as strange and to-tally over-the-top verbal affirmations accompanied by volcanically explo-sive gesticulations. Allison could also be soothingly tender, even mushy, fawning over her favorite doll, "Baby Alex." She had immense generosity when feeling good within herself and safe in her surroundings. In the soft glow of a birthday candlelit room, she once unexpectedly broke into a gen-tle and moving solo of "Happy Birthday" to one of our staff that touched the hearts of everyone present.

During the first three months of our day-treatment year, I was often pre-occupied with attending to a boy in our group, Michael (age 6), who was as father-hungry a boy as I have ever worked with. Michael's starvation for a caring adult male in his life was satisfied only by complete and uninter-rupted one-to-one attention. When he did not get it, he beat up the toys in the room, aggressively went after the other kids, or just taunted in a rhyth-mic chant, "Suck my dick" or "You motherfucker." I was also therapeuti-cally attached with a scattered, sexually precocious, and emotionally famished 4-year-old girl, Taleasha, whose first response to our limit setting was to lay down and stroke herself while saying, "Lick my pussy." Taleasha also called Rachel my cotherapist a "bald-headed tramp." This was not to be confused with little 4-year-old David's creative "cocky ho bitch," though these were all defiantly expressed with smiling, wide-eyed snickering, and sashaying shoulders and hips. These extraordinary expressions "out of the mouths of babes" often sounded to me like the ghetto street version of "Nana nana boo boo." It was very difficult to keep from laughing, which would only encourage them to ever greater heights of off-color linguistic virtuosity. But they were not saying these things for laughs, and it was sad to realize that this was the language of their painfully deprived worlds of nurturing. In any case, working with these attachment-impoverished and demanding children left me much less time to get to know Allison.

Allison proved to be more difficult to connect with than any other child with whom I had worked. At first she did not readily respond to my enthusiastic or complimentary greetings or to invitations to play together with something she liked. When I had to occasionally separate from Michael or Taleasha to help settle down an angry and kicking Allison, she would always respond to my limit setting with her usual "I hate you." From previous experience, I was fairly adept at dodging her kicks and ducking her spit. Allison was also rigidly literal, even for a 6-year-old, with an aversion to pretending to the point of feeling that her sustaining world would crumble if anyone took her into the as-if world of play. For example, one day when I was pretending to be another child's dog on all fours, Allison came over and took a tight-fisted swing at me. Then she hysterically screamed, "It's not OK. You are not a dog! You are a man!" For the most part, Allison and I would get through the difficult situations, usually unscathed, and then go back to the usual cacophony of contained chaos that was our therapeutic world.

For about two and a half months I didn't connect much with Allison except to positively acknowledge her presence and actions, or assist others with her when she was in a fight with another child. I began to realize that I'd better learn something about how to relate with her or we would go through the whole year superficially pleasant, sometimes weathering a brief storm together, but rather distant. She was the first child I had worked with who was a perpetual mystery to me. She was unpredictable in unique ways. More than any other child I have met, she was a continual surprise, and her unpredictability was what I enjoyed most about her.

My approach to working more closely with Allison was both conscious and unconscious. I was increasingly aware that I wanted to know her better. I wanted to learn how to be a caring therapist to her. I began driving home some evenings wondering how Allison and I could come to matter to each other in a deeper way. It is interesting upon reflection that my unconscious then triggered what I had read elsewhere about connecting with what the patient brings in one's own experience. I intuitively found the "autism" in myself. I free associated and then fully recollected a time several years ago when I had a very short fuse, a blazing hot temper, and was mad or enraged at almost everyone. I didn't want to talk much with anybody except my therapist at the time, and was instantaneously angry whenever someone bugged me. I could even remember loud noises triggering strong reactions and being irritated if people inadvertently touched me. It helped to find some of Allison's sensitivities, feelings, and behaviors in my own past experience. I knew what it was like to have been socially withdrawn, stimulated primarily internally, and hypersensitive to any irritants, sensory or otherwise. On some level, I had something in common with Allison in my past personal experience.

Soon after this journey into my memory, around Thanksgiving, I dreamt about an article I once read. In my dream came the words of a metaphor used to describe how to join with autistic children. The words from my dream and the article were "In the beginning, always approach an autistic child by walking backward toward them." As I mentioned earlier in this essay, one of Allison's diagnoses was "autism." Michael and Taleasha were becoming more secure, so began to settle down. I was now able to work on connecting with Allison. I did this with a deeper shared feeling of how her pain and fear might be triggered internally and a more focused empathy for her hypersensitive bodily felt awareness of where her physical senses and skin met with others and the environment. I concentrated on working to get a more intense feel and conscious awareness of any deeper pain behind Allison's expressed pain (symptomatology). Still, all of this was at somewhat of a distance. I knew that without a solidly connected play relationship, we would have next to nothing with which to work and grow together, regardless of the depth and accuracy of my awareness.

At first I began to move nearer to Allison more often, taking care not to touch or startle her. I would parallel-play next to her with other children while softly talking out loud about what I was doing. I would sometimes start sentences to another child with "I'm going to pretend now that I am a . . . and it will be okay because I will stop if you tell me to." After a while, through the corner of my eye, I started to see her staring at me under her glasses. I began making short comments to her about how glad I was that she was in our room with the other children, what a fine girl she seemed to be, or how nicely her mother dressed her. I briefly complimented Allison, or commented on her positive social interactions, as a way to indirectly invite her to accept a new, playful relationship with me. After playing next to her awhile and making my short comments, I would wait a minute for some response and leave quietly if she didn't start a conversation. I was careful not to force any relating. It was like repeated practice in comfortable indirect joining and separating until Allison was used to my being in her more immediate space.

At first, Allison just quizzically looked at me and listened to my comments. A couple of times she told me I was silly. Then she gradually began asking me to play with her. We would do this for short periods of time with her in complete control, and I would always let her end the interaction if I could. This was often difficult as battles frequently broke out in various parts of the room. When Allison and I had a short period of play together, I would invite the same play the next day. Our interactions became more frequent and longer as time went on.

One day Allison surprised me by playing for a long time on our electric keyboard. I taught her to play "Doe, a Deer" (the extent of my piano repertoire beyond "Chopsticks"). I was amazed that Allison could follow and remember it in one sitting. Soon after this, Allison came to initiate play with me when I was off somewhere else. She also began to ask me to do circles on her back with my finger, something she often did with Rachel for sensory stimulation. As things progressed, Allison and I began taking turns initiating a few hugs a week.

Allison also began asking me, "Are you pretending now?" when I had not adequately introduced my play with her. The first pretend activity I can remember doing with Allison was when she wanted to be a doctor and I was her 6-year-old patient on the room couch. We had a white lab coat, pale green scrubs, and a miniature physician's bag with the general practitioner's common paraphernalia. Allison put on the white lab coat, took my temperature, did my blood pressure, gave me a shot, bandaged my arm, and told me to lie still and rest. She was very nurturing with a wonderful bedside manner. I got a rare rest in our room.

Another time, when Michael was out for several days with chicken pox, Allison got all the other kids to go along with her in putting red magic marker dots on their faces. She told them to do it so "Michael won't feel so lonely." Later on, when the movie *The Mummy* came out, Allison saw Michael imitating a mummy and slowly stalking me as I pretended to be terrified. She had us mummify her head to toe with toilet paper. Allison pretended to be a mummy for about an hour and wouldn't take off the toilet paper until it blew off like windblown streamers while she cruised by on a bike in our gym. Allison was becoming accomplished at as-if playing, also pretending to be a clown, various animals, a baby, a mother, our cook, and a cowgirl yelling "Yee-haa" while riding on my back as her beast of burden.

In addition to the increasing variety and extended time in parallel and interactive play, Allison's verbal responses began telling me we were growing together. When I had to set limits with her, she went from "I hate you" to "I'm mad" to "I'm frustrated." Her reaction time slowed down considerably, and she became much less volatile. The quality of flow and feeling tone between us was changing and becoming richer. It was increasingly less dissonant and fixed in rigid patterns and became surprisingly improvisational and more harmonious. An older therapist once told me to listen to the music I cocreate with my patients. Allison and I cocomposed at several different levels. The counterpoint play between us was spontaneous, increasingly more in synch, and growing in enjoyment and satisfaction.

Allison was extremely honest. She would tell me when my breath was less than what might be desirable ("John, your breath stinks") or sniff at my hair when we were reading together ("What's that yucky smell in your hair?"). In response to her mothering, I started chewing gum and seriously considered changing my shampoo. Giving and receiving gum also went on to become a ritual for a while. Allison noticed that I had started chewing it. I told her I was doing it to clean up my breath. She began to routinely demand to look under my tongue to see if I had gum when she would arrive each day. I would be examined by a dentistlike Allison, and then we would discuss the possibility of her getting a piece for herself. I often gave her one, as did her occupational and speech therapists. Unfortunately, the communal gum giving was administratively ended after the bus drivers informed officials that Allison was sticking large wads of stale Juicy Fruit under the car seats on the way home.

One day while I was spinning Taleasha on a large plastic spinner in our gym, Allison came over and asked if she could have a turn. I began giving her very fast rides that she loved. We would talk about her being in a spaceship and spinning to the stars and moon, or being a bird, or flying in a plane. The verbal content in this process was as if we were being characters in *Alice in Wonderland*. We consistently moved from seemingly absurd nonsense to coherent sense. Allison would often end the spinning play by asking to be held in my lap while she sucked her thumb and we continued to talk.

I increasingly enjoyed Allison's tricksterlike unconventionality and our completely unpredictable conversations (or maybe I was becoming more autistic). I once told Rachel that "Allison touches the autism in me." She laughed and nodded in acknowledgment. It helped that Rachel was the kind of coworker who would come up to me at the end of a particularly chaotic day and pretend to have facial ticks while commenting on the therapeutic gains we were making. We were playful coleaders and shared the view that almost anything that's fun is therapeutic. We also shared a mutual enjoyment of irony, the absurd, double entendres, silliness, and Allison's wild free associations. The two of us were a good match in responding to Allison's needs and ways of being with us.

Allison's spontaneously expressed free associations fascinated me, even when they seemed to worry others. She always started out our conversations sounding a bit bizarre and disconnected, but if I went with and expanded on them with her, they came to make sense. These playful conversations between Allison and me often started with some seemingly random and out-of-the-blue comment she would make, then moved into an improvised dialogue of bilaterally triggered free associations, and came to end in some shared feeling and coherent meaning of what Allison was initially wanting to express. There was an unconscious free play that guided our spontaneous and unpredictable dialogue, and it led to a surprising order and harmony. As time went on, the harmony our play brought about came to be more deeply felt as parent-child intimacy. By "intimacy" I mean the mutual satisfaction of being one's full self in the presence of another is being a full self.

Our spontaneous and unconsciously guided verbal play from random ambiguity to order and harmony went completely contrary to the current cultural system's expectation, fear, and persistent anxiety; that is, a lack of clear rational control or predefined purpose will lead to chaos and, ultimately, madness. Allison clearly lived in a countercultural world. Her proclivity for blurting out seemingly bizarre comments or metaphors was not irrational, but nonrational, until I was able to make the connections. She became highly anxious and aggressively reactive in the face of predetermined or anxiously pushed rational or behavioral control. Her selfhood was hypersensitive to getting squashed or externally molded, and she was more easily and intensely defiant than your average American adolescent. Put another way, you couldn't "do therapy" with Allison. The only thing that worked was to nonanxiously and playfully "be" with her. When I didn't have to set limits and be in charge of room safety control, my experience of *being with* Allison in our play activities and our conversations became more and more fun and sometimes surprisingly hilarious. At other times, Allison's symbolic expressions as a means of her own self-care were truly impressive.

Once, Allison's foster mother took her to a psychiatrist to check out her autism diagnosis and see if it needed to be changed. After only one hour of "observing" Allison, the psychiatrist told the foster mother that she should have the diagnosis of childhood schizophrenia. At the end of this conversation in front of her, Allison blurted out at the doctor, "Your glasses are ugly" and "You don't see right." The foster mother was uncomfortable with this doctor anyway and was afraid that these abrupt statements would confirm the childhood schizophrenia diagnosis to him. Later, when Rachel told me about the situation and the outburst, Allison's words made immediate poetic sense to me. I told Rachel that Allison's angry words were her only way of responding to her whole self reaction to being reduced to a thing by this doctor's objectification of her. While ignoring Allison's rich and complex subjectivity, this psychiatrist was acting as if he were the expert defining her from the outside. I am sure that this psychiatrist's diagnostic jargon, childhood schizophrenia, meant nothing to her. From his tone and nonverbal communication Allison sensed something literally coming at her that felt cold, tight, oppressive, and depersonalizing.

Allison was metaphorically right on. This doctor couldn't "see her right." His "ugly glasses" were Allison's angry symbol for his indoctrinated professional blindness to her unique and irreducible humanity. Allison felt and trusted what this doctor couldn't comprehend and obviously overlooked with all of his preconditioned "expertise." That is, Allison is too complex to reduce to behaviors and diagnostic categories as she lives, moves, feels, values, and has her being in the world much more deeply than anyone can ever think or name. I fantasize that under Allison's angry poetic response to this psychiatrist she was saying to him: "Stop what you are saying and the professional certitude with which you are speaking. I am not an object with the label 'child schizophrenic.' Definitions are not reality. Because you mistake diagnosis as such, you are trying to confine me to a lifeless prison of abstract descriptions and labels of fixed and permanent behaviors with predetermined prescriptions for control. I won't be controlled to relieve your panic about my unpredictability, or any anxiety about your own autistic fragments. Get me out of here!" (And the foster mother wisely did so.)

One very painful psychiatric response to Allison followed this incident. Her doctor decided to try her on Mellaril. I had refused to give any children psychotropic medications from the date of my employment in this agency, and though this was tolerated, others went ahead with any and all doctor's orders. Clinical social work since Freud's latter days has always had difficulty separating itself from being the dutiful servant of whatever current psychiatric or psychological theories are in vogue. It often even forgets its ecosystemic roots, or puts them aside, in the face of other professionals' epistemologies and presuppositions. My fantasy is that this is what happened when Allison received Mellaril for two weeks.

Allison had made great behavioral progress within day treatment concerning an initial symptom of hitting herself in the head when frustrated. She had pretty much stopped this by the time the Mellaril was given. She came into day treatment a few days after it was started and became extremely agitated over an interaction with another child. Allison immediately went to a building support beam in the room and began banging her head against it with full force. I had to stop her and then enlisted the help of my coleader. When we talked later that day, Rachel told me that Allison had been started on Mellaril and that was all she could think of in terms of Allison's renewed and intensified self-abusive behavior. We watched Allison closely. After a week or so of having to intervene several times to get her to stop banging her head, Rachel went and questioned the foster mother and the psychiatrist about the Mellaril prescription. Allison was taken off the Mellaril after two weeks and immediately stopped banging her head when frustrated. Needless to say I was relieved about Allison, and thankful I'd not participated in this modern psychiatric intervention that treated Allison in what was a harmful, reductive way. I wondered what had happened to the medical dictum, "First do no harm." Allison began to positively progress again when the Mellaril was discontinued.

After a while, Allison and Taleasha started going on the spinner together. We had moved to become a threesome, at least once in a while. Allison's social world was expanding beyond adults. We played a game in which, if I could get Allison and Taleasha off the spinner, I would win; if not, they would win. They would hold each other's arms to stay on. It was impossible for me to get them off even though I spun them dizzyingly fast. They would revel in remorseless laughter when I lost or acted devastated and sob dramatically in the humiliation and agony of defeat. Then they would giggle with delicious glee and clamor in unison to be spun again and again. Allison and Taleasha also began to be friends in other areas of play and, among other things, to pair off to tease me in our room. Much to their delight, I would always act appalled by their teasing. I would then chase and tickle them, accompanied by a chorus of coworkers: "John, you're stirring up the children."

All of this led up to an experience when I really knew Allison and I had deeply bonded. It happened around winter break in December. I had been complimenting Allison a lot in general. I was calling her "a very sweet girl" whenever she was generous, or when she used kinder and gentler words. One day I was helping her put on her winter coat at the end of the afternoon. Allison suddenly and unexpectedly held my face between her two hands, looked right into my eyes in her head-tilted kind of cross-eyed way, and said, "John, you are a very sweet boy, and I like you very much." I started to cry. My heart swelled, my eyes welled up, and tears rolled down my cheeks. After a few moments, I held back the tears and said, "I like you very much too, Allison, and you are a wonderful girl." She became at that moment a real life Alice to me. She was Allison helping to make our shared space more of a Wonderland; at least, it became more so for me that day.

My relationship with Allison kept growing at a more deeply bonded and attached level after this. One day in the early spring, Allison brought a live ladybug to the clinic. She laid on her back for an hour on the couch watching it crawl around on her stomach. Rachel was gone that day and I had to be more of a whole room referee. After the first hour of moving around the room like a perpetual pinball in order to handle various uprisings, things settled to a point where I could go over to talk with Allison about her ladybug. The first thing she said when I got there was, "John, do you think the ladybug does boo-boo?" I had to think about that for a minute, and then told Allison that I didn't think so. She said, "But it doesn't know the rules." I told her she could teach the ladybug our room safety rules. Allison looked at the ladybug on her stomach and rattled off two or three of them that she remembered. I told her that this was now a very smart ladybug and that we should let it go out into the world to teach the other ladybugs. Allison wouldn't let it go, but she did get up and put it in a cup with some leaves. I finished by complimenting her on being such a good mother to the ladybug, but was summarily dismissed for insisting that the ladybug was "born free" and ought to live that way.

Allison was also growing in her relationships with everyone in our room. Her increasing happiness and more secure and settled presence told us we were all doing our parts, including the parenting she was receiving in her foster home. Allison and I continued to expand our play. We learned to dance a little lindy and tango together, played on the trampoline, read, chased each other on little bikes, strummed and picked the guitar (she most liked one funky blues I remembered), and many other things. The content somehow seemed less and less important and the mutual enjoyment and appreciation of each other became what really mattered. I was increasingly aware that I had so much feeling about our relationship that could never be articulated. We grew together so much more deeply than I can think or say.

Before we parted 11 months after our first encounter, I did get a chance to tell Allison I would miss her very much, that I always enjoyed being with her, and that I would never forget her. I felt and meant these words from the bottom of my aching heart. We were able to have a very long hug good-bye, and I am tearing up again as I write this. I don't consider this a boundary problem. My "empty nest" feelings are bittersweet. They are, among other things, the real and accepted confirmation of the level of involvement I experienced in caring for Allison, mixed with what I took in of what she reciprocated so well by loving and trusting me in her life.

Allison changed me at least as much as I affected her. She moved me deeply with her open expression of pain and joy. She also invited and yanked me into places I hadn't been before in a therapeutic relationship. She has been so preciously valuable, surprising, unusual, unpredictable, irreducible, and unrepeatable in all of her particular and wonderfully strange ways of being. This article has been one way for me to grieve the loss of Allison in my everyday conscious life. It's also a way to celebrate and share our relationship while trying to show the extent that we were able to become part of each other's lives in our 11 months together. From experience with other children I have been close to, I know my tears of good-bye to Allison will pass. I already have a deeply felt sense that she has become a permanent part of who I am. My hope is that I will also be a felt part of Allison's growing self in the deep recesses of her being.

Like others who have become part of me, I know I will experience Allison inside of me as my memory of her floats up into my conscious awareness from time to time. I can immediately and clearly imagine her looking into my eyes, head tilted, and dressed in those black coveralls adorned with that, now so fitting, vivid magenta heart. I will always be thankful to Allison for helping me to become a better person and therapist by just being true to herself in the moment. I am thankful to her for showing me her joy and pain, for allowing me to care for and love her, and for being with me while I got better at it. I am grateful to have been loved back in the ways that only Allison could. I thank her for showing and teaching me about her world, for stretching me to find undeveloped parts of myself in order to meet and be with her. Though I was clearly the parent in our relationship,

Allison let me know when I was learning how to be with her in the ways she needed and wanted. What a gift she has been in helping me to grow as a person within and beyond my work. How alive our shared world has felt. Our space was truly a therapeutic wonderland.

Love exchanged never dies. It seeps deep into our being and remains a vital part of what constitutes our expanding and evolving sense of self, personal stature, or, if you like, soul. Yes, this is how Allison feels inside me. Her presence and ways of being have increased the volume and complexity of my soul. Meeting and being with others like Allison is why I am a therapist.

Chapter 19

# Deficit of Attention Disorder

Felix Yaroshevsky, MD, CRCPC, and Vivian Bakiaris

*"Speak roughly to your little boy,*
*And beat him when he sneezes;*
*He only does it to annoy,*
*Because he knows it teases."*
Lewis Carroll, *Alice's Adventures in Wonderland*

This paper questions the current practice of diagnosing children who are disruptive, using the label ADHD, and treating them with Ritalin, thus pathologizing and medicalizing common childhood behavior. The suggestion put forward is that these children experience a deficit of appropriate parental attention and love—this is the attention deficit. If it is perceived as "Blaming Parents," then so be it. Our goal, though, is not to blame, but to assign responsibility and, therefore, point out remedial direction. The authors propose a restructuring of parenting as the appropriate response to disruptive childhood behavior rather than using medication only. Their impression (and perhaps biased but sincere opinion) is that medication is warranted in less than 5% of cases. We include two case illustrations demonstrating these principles.

At first glance the scene around the swimming pool is quite typical of a spa in this part of Mexico. It promises its guests, the majority of whom are women between 30 and 80 years of age, a very tranquil, if not boring holiday. Remain more than 15 minutes at any one spot, however, and you are bound to encounter a phenomenon in the form of the spa's activity director, who leads daily exercises in the pool. She is a petite woman from Manhattan, ageless in her energetic presentation and her name is Esther. She has young eyes and a lot of teeth. Esther will turn 81 this year. Her group usually consists of people who, rather than go for local hikes, stay by the pool or go for massages. Esther is an enthusiastic entertainer and the people who gather around her are infected by her energy. To an imaginative and distant observer, however, it is understood that she only appears to be providing them with energy. In fact, she actually gathers, processes, and reorganizes their energy, subsequently acquiring a lot of it for herself. This formulation can be compared to a bank, which is in the business of giving people money for "only a small service charge and a little bit of interest." In fact, wherever Esther goes, she seeks attention in a way that is not imposing but rather appealing, thus hiding the fact that the attention she seeks is a source of energy for her.

Esther is an excellent example of an "attention-seeker." Traditionally, attention-seekers are believed to be looking for reassurance, but we contend that attention is also a way for them to obtain energy. If they do not get the attention they need, they will do whatever it takes to get as much as they can. This is particularly true of children. Although Esther has found an acceptable way to recharge, children often do not. Within the last decade, physiologically healthy children who "act up" and are described as "uncontrollable" or "disruptive" are labeled as having attention deficit hyperactivity disorder (ADHD) or have been labeled in the past as "hyperkinetic." Most often what these children really need is to be shown plenty of attention and love, which they simply are not receiving. They do not have ADHD. They cannot "pay" attention because they themselves have not been paid. The children may be busy from morning until night with horseback riding, hockey practice or music lessons, but they usually have parents who are extremely preoccupied with their own personal feelings and experiences, relational problems, responsibilities, and so forth.

## THE CASE OF FAY

For as long as she can remember, 9-year-old Fay has been taken care of by her nanny, Salina. Both her parents are functioning, structure-oriented people with stressful jobs. Mom manages a restaurant and Dad is a vice president of a financial investment firm. They had promised each other to never deprive their child (nor themselves, for that matter) of the little luxuries they had been deprived of as children. As Fay grew older, her parents felt guilty about spending increasingly less time with her, so they decided to sign her up for some extracurricular activities.

On Tuesdays Dad takes her to piano lessons and on Saturdays to ballet. On Thursdays Mom takes her to swimming lessons. They are proud of her when she does well; when she does not perform satisfactorily, they express their concern and worry. Though Fay finds this schedule demanding, she neither complains nor ever considers cutting any of these lessons because they provide her with some of the emotional and physical contact she lacks from her parents. If not for these activities, Fay would only see them late at night when she is in bed, for she refuses to fall asleep until at least one of them tucks her in. Sometimes this may be an hour or two after her usual bedtime so that, come morning, she is as grumpy as a bear and battles with Salina all the way to school.

As a result of her having too much on her plate, Fay's ability to function well at school slowly deteriorates. Fay had always been evaluated as an average student with a pleasant personality until she entered grade four. Since then, she cannot seem to concentrate, to focus on her studies. Her teacher is under the strong impression that her pupil has a learning disorder (which until now had mysteriously remained dormant).

Fay's irritability causes her to fidget in her seat, to overreact to her friends' good-natured teasing, or to impatiently speak out of turn. The teacher interprets this as Fay "disrupting the class." She decides to contact Fay's parents and suggests to them that they have her assessed for possible ADHD and need for medication. Fay's interpretation is that there is something wrong with her.

## THE CASE OF BILLY

Billy is a 7-year-old boy who always seems to get himself into trouble. He has two older sisters, both in their mid-teens, who consider him to be a pest. Needless to say, they avoid him as much as possible. Their father, a construction worker for the past six years, prefers to stay at home, relax, and watch television at the end of the day. He takes his son to karate lessons Saturday mornings, talks to the other fathers and then takes him back home. Mom calls Dad "a bump on the log." She is in her forties and is quite anxious about her looks, so she keeps herself busy with a part-time job, exercise clubs, and spas, privately doing her best to look as she did when she was her daughters' age. She packs her "wild" little Billy a nutritious lunch, takes him to school, and picks him up every day. She also tends to yell at him a lot.

For the past couple of years, Billy has found it difficult to connect with members of his family. From Billy's perspective, everyone seems to be busy doing their own thing, having their own life. A child his age requires a lot of attention, something he does not seem to be receiving. So he unconsciously devises some nonconventional methods to attract it.

He learned that when he barges into his sisters' rooms and teases them about how ugly they are or jumps on their bed until the frame breaks, they acknowledge his existence. If he pretends to be Rambo and leaps from the bookcase onto the coffee table during the football game, Dad will have a talk with him. When he runs about the house, howling like the storm which brews eternally between his parents, he may eventually break a crystal vase or a porcelain pot. Occasionally he may trip over the Persian rug and hurt himself. Then Mom stops dyeing her hair or reading her book to scold him for playing in the living room when she has told him a hundred times not to do so. When Mom yells out to Dad for assistance in dealing with their son, that is even better, for then Billy gets the undivided attention of both.

This boy has learned that by wreaking havoc, people will notice him and give him the reassurance (such as it is) that they care.

If they attract enough negative attention, children form a negative identity. They come to believe that they actually are slow or stupid or just plain bad. When they are regularly dealt with by critical or angry adults and peers, their poor self-image may be reconfirmed, but they have still been given energy—although it is negative energy. When you are terminally thirsty, you will even drink from a muddy puddle. Children need reassurance and energy; therefore, those who are emotionally fed stay put, pay attention, concentrate, get busy by themselves. The others have to fly from flower to flower, gathering drops of nectar where they can. Esther is a perfect example of an attention-seeker who was lucky enough to escape being labeled through the industrious, and in many ways constructive, application of a character. She found a way to apply herself and lead a successful, useful, and positive lifestyle. The people who finish exercising with her may go to the *el comedor* and stuff their faces with an additional portion of food or go for another massage to replenish themselves. For the time that she has them going, Esther does not have to fly from one flower to another, for they have all gathered around her, faces open toward her. They all feel that they are getting attention from her and never notice that they are actually paying her with a substantial amount of their own energy.

On the other hand, there are people unlike Esther, who do not actively seek attention. Some of them are content and do not wish to spend their energy; nor do they seek anyone else's, because they are capable of generating their own. They do this by meditating, listening to music, through hobbies, taking nature walks, and so on. Then there are those who are afraid that, should they speak, someone will begin to drain them of their energy. Their vulnerability probably developed from the early training they received from their families during very specific types of interactional processes. They were expected to give energy, not to receive much in exchange and certainly not to try to get any from the adults or even from some siblings who, for whatever reason, were receiving preferential treatment from the adults. When, in early childhood, people are not taught to

exchange energy freely and fairly, it leads to the inability to develop satisfactory social skills and relational harmony.

Family therapy can be extremely helpful in improving relational processes among members of a household. Interestingly, this avenue is rarely
pursued by the more neglectful or overwhelmed parents who are inclined
to go for a "quick fix," to get their children on medication and off their
backs. Whatever the theoretical position, one cannot deny the usefulness of
paying attention to the context and quality of relationships. However, those
parents would refuse to participate in family assessments and therapy.

They would hold onto their energy, reluctant to share it with the professionals and, ultimately, with their child. They would always prefer to pay intense attention to the child's pathology. When the professionals (often being
coerced by the parents) conduct only a "child psychiatric evaluation," they
have great freedom to comment at length about the child, but there is little
freedom to comment on the parents' behavior. In family therapy the parents
can become patients, which means they have the freedom to question themselves in a situation that can attend to their emotional hunger.

And, unfortunately, there are times when family therapy can become
part of the problem, that is, by endless pathologizing of the family. Sometimes the child, because of genetic or other individual problems (organic
brain syndrome, specific learning disability, etc.) needs to be the "identified patient." In these much rarer cases, the caring, loving, and attention-
paying family will attend endless family therapy sessions. The focus then
is on the "dysfunctional patterns of the families" when it should actually
be oriented toward psychological and social remedial help for the individual child as well as support for the family.

It is through their scattered behavior that the children get into the cycle
of negative attention and the reaffirmation of their negative self-image.
Before they know it, they are labeled by the vicious circle of delegated responsibilities: the teachers complain to the parents (who are very often surprised, because in the family they do not notice or are used to the child's
behavior); the parents tell the child's doctor who prescribes a stimulant,
usually Ritalin. While on the powerful drug, the child's performance and
concentration may dramatically improve for a period of time—"confirming" the "diagnosis" and "treatment." Thus the responsibility is delegated
by the teachers to the parents, by the parents to the doctor, from the doctor
back to the parents, and from the parents back to the teachers, who, in turn,
point out that they are only following the doctor's orders.

All of the above is yet another attempt at illustrating the absurdity of
our culture's pattern of jostling, conniving, and hustling behaviors that is
directed at acquiring resources and energies. The unconscious motivations
are camouflaged by the ideological declaration of good intentions.

Parents constantly exploit their children in so many different ways. The more they do it, the more incensed they become when someone points out to them their conflicts of interests.

People who know how to *exchange* energy, can do so with their kids. In an intentionally oversimplified way, we can say that takers, who do not know how to give, are more apt to raise children who are givers; and givers, who do not know how to take, produce children who are takers.

To be able to show the givers and the takers their behavior in a stark, realistic light is quite a tricky job, as we all know; but that's what we do. We call our method DEBULLSHITIZATION ©.

Chapter 20

# Thinking about Thinking in Family Therapy*

Edgar H. Auerswald, MD

*"What is it you want to buy?"* the Sheep said at last, looking up for a moment from her knitting.

*"I don't quite know yet,"* Alice said very gently. *"I should like to look all round me first, if I might."*

*"You may look in front of you, and on both sides, if you like,"* said the Sheep; *"but you can't look all round you—unless you've got eyes at the back of your head."*

Lewis Carroll, *Alice's Adventures in Wonderland*

A dictionary (*Webster's New Collegiate Dictionary*, 1981) definition of epistemology is: "The study or a theory of the nature and grounds of knowledge." Contemplation in study or theorizing is cognitive, and, too, it is fair to say that the nature and grounds of knowledge are expressed in language, and that language is the expression of cognition. Thus, another way of defining epistemology could be "thinking about thinking."

Yet another, more concrete, but closely related definition of the word was used by Gregory Bateson and has been appearing in many places in

*This essay was published in *Family Process,* 10: 263–280, 1972. Also in *Evolving Models for Family Change,* H. Charles Fishman and Bernice Rossman, Eds., Guilford Press, 1986. Presented at Ackerman Family Institute International Conference on Family Therapy, 1980.

recent years. In this definition the word is preceded by a definite or indefinite article: "an epistemology" or "the epistemology."† Some of us in the family therapy field, mostly those who knew or read Bateson, have used it this way. The definition of this usage could be: "A set of immanent rules used in thought by large groups of people to define reality." Also, I have used the word "paradigm" to denote a subset of rules used to define a particular segment of reality.

It is my assertion that a new epistemology, a new set of rules governing thought, is immanent in "new science," which is profoundly different from the predominant thought system of the Western world, and, furthermore, that these two thought systems are separate and discontinuous (Auerswald, 1968, 1971, 1975). It is also my belief that the ecological systems epistemology as identified in the family therapy literature is congruent with the new science epistemology, and that the ecosystemic epistemology provides the basis for a technology of transformation.

In the late nineteenth century most physicists believed that the formal basis for understanding the micro- and macro-universe forevermore had been virtually completed. They believed that the rules of thought, the epistemology, for establishing the boundaries and nature of physical reality had been revealed through the work they had done on the foundation provided by the genius of Isaac Newton. There were, they recognized, a few unfilled cracks in their epistemological edifice, but the assumption was that, with time, these cracks would undoubtedly be filled.

One of these cracks was a phenomenon which the physicists, perhaps with some prescience, had playfully nicknamed "the Ultraviolet Catastrophe." Classical Newtonian physics demanded that the electrons of heated objects oscillate at a rate proportional to the heat energy absorbed and that this oscillation emit energy in the form of light waves at a frequency proportional to the rate of oscillation. This meant that as an object was heated, the light emitted should run through the red end of the light spectrum quickly, and that moderately heated objects should emit more high frequency blue-white light than low frequency red light. Furthermore, it meant that highly heated objects, if heating continued, should emit infinite amounts of high frequency blue-white light. It also meant that the frequency of emitted light should rise smoothly as the object heated and drop smoothly as the object cooled.

Experimental evidence (experience), however, met none of these demands. Moderately hot objects emit primarily low frequency red light; highly heated objects emit a finite amount of high frequency blue-white light; and the transition from red to blue-white light occurs abruptly, not smoothly.

---

†Retrospective note: This definition turned out to be unfortunate, as it caused a great deal of confusion in usage of the word. Although I use it in this essay, I later opted for the word *holodigm* to denote "a set of rules or principles used in the cognitive construction of a complete reality system," and the word *paradigm* to denote a "set of rules or principles used in the cognitive construction of a segment or subsystem of a complete reality system."

In 1900, in Germany, Max Planck was working in an effort to seal off this crack in the Newtonian edifice. To his surprise, he discovered experimentally that the oscillating electrons both absorbed and emitted energy in chunks— discrete packets, which he called quanta. The chunks of low frequency red light are smaller than the chunks of high frequency blue-white light. When an object is heated, it will emit red-sized chunks until a point when the quantity of heat energy is sufficient to shake loose larger-sized blue-white chunks.

While his experiment "explained" the behavior of radiation emitted by a heated object, Planck did not fill the crack in the Newtonian edifice. As it turned out, his experimental results demanded a whole new structuring of physics, a whole new set of rules governing reality, a whole new epistemology. Instead of sealing up the crack in the Newtonian edifice, Max Planck had stepped through it.

Planck took this step with great reluctance. He was a respected established physicist, a professor with a high regard for his colleagues and his field of endeavor. He recognized that his findings could transform his field and destroy the certainties painfully acquired in classical physics over centuries. He did not want this to happen. However, he had too much integrity not to report his findings (Planck, 1900).

Albert Einstein, unlike Planck, was a young man working in obscurity. He had no professorships. He had no history in the field. He had nothing to lose. He was a theorist, not an experimenter like Planck. He could let his thoughts soar, and soar they did. In one year, beginning in 1905, Einstein literally burst through the cracks in the Newtonian edifice. He published five papers, three of which established the epistemological base for what is now known as "New Physics."

In the first of these papers, Einstein took Planck's discovery a giant step further. Planck's experiment had shown that light energy was emitted in quanta. Einstein (1905a) argued that light *existed* in quanta, which he called photons. He supported this idea by using it to explain another phenomenon that comprised a crack in the Newtonian edifice, namely, the photoelectric effect. The inference in this paper was that *all* energy was quantized. Einstein went on in another of these three papers to describe the nature of molecular motion in a non-Newtonian way.

These first forays outside of the Newtonian epistemology by Planck and Einstein were grounded in the physics of the microsphere. Up until this point in the story, the writings of classical physicists still contained some hope that the certainties of Newtonian physics could be saved. Several attempts were made to cram the quantum notions into classical concepts. Einstein's third paper, which concerned the macrosphere, blew up any such hopes.

The crack in classical physics confronted by Einstein in this third paper was the finding that the speed of light measured the same regardless of the motion of the measuring instrument with respect to the light source. That is to say, the measuring instrument registered the same when stationary, when moving away from the light source, and when moving toward the light source. According to Newtonian physics, this finding was crazy. The classical rules for thinking about time, space, and motion demanded that the instrument should record the velocity of light minus the velocity with which the measuring instrument was moving away from the light source or plus the velocity with which the measuring instrument was moving toward the light source. What Einstein did was quite literally mind-blowing. Instead of trying to figure out how to fit the incongruous findings into the established rules thinking about time, space, and motion, he changed the rules. In his special theory of relativity, Einstein (1905b ) suggested new ways to think about time, space, and motion.

In a few short years Planck and Einstein created the epistemological skeleton upon which a new non-Newtonian physics could be constructed. The point of retelling this story here is that a reluctant Planck and an aggressive Einstein, by stepping through the cracks into the contextual space outside the realm of classical Newtonian physics, and by seeding that space with ideas, created a transformation of the entire world of physics. Neither of them made any attempt to attack frontally the basic tenets of classical theory. In fact, by creating a new epistemology and expanding the context, they saved classical physics from ultimate disintegration. While Newtonian physics is no longer looked to as a source of universal truth, or as a way of thinking that provides a final definition of reality, it is still viewed as a heuristically useful paradigm.

These events in the realm of physics have been followed by similar transformations in other realms of thought. Most relevant to the topic herein is a transformation occurring elsewhere in natural science. Darwin's theory of evolution evolved within the same mechanistic epistemology as Newtonian physics. The most glaring crack in Darwin's theory has always been that it led inevitably to the mindless notion of "survival of the fittest," a notion that satisfied only the most concrete of thinkers. By synthesizing ideas found in the work of Lamarck and Wallace with the information cybernetics of Weiner and McCollough and with evolving general systems theory following von Bertalanffy, Bateson (1979) stepped through this crack in Darwin's theory and created a paradigm of evolution that included mind. I believe, by so doing, he stepped into the universe of the "new science" epistemology. Bateson's evolutionary paradigm has been published only recently, and the transformation of thinking, which I believe it will inevitably produce, is just getting under way.

"New science" emerged from the study of the "inanimate" universe; Batesonian evolution emerged from the study of the "living" universe, and; the ecosystemic epistemology emerged from the study of a segment of the "living" universe: namely, families in the context of sociocultural systems. It is my contention that these three idea sets share the same rules for defining reality, the same epistemology.

The linkage between Batesonian evolution and the ecological systems epistemology is readily apparent, since Batesonian evolution is ecological. In his usual Socratic style, Bateson makes this argument repeatedly and convincingly. If one constructs a four-dimensional holographic thought model of Batesonian evolution, any segment of any size of that model turns out to be an ecosystem. A randomly selected segment will be an open system, most likely nonviable, but a segment selected on the basis of an identifiable boundary can show varying degrees of openness/closedness and viability. The awareness that such a system is a segment of a larger field, however, precludes treating it permanently as a closed system. The family is such an ecosystem. An individual is such an ecosystem. A community is such an ecosystem. A nation is such an ecosystem. You name it.

The epistemological links between Batesonian evolution and new science are equally apparent in my opinion, but Bateson in his writing alluded to them only in passing, and, to my knowledge, they have not been argued elsewhere. The contention that such links exist deserves more detailed examination than is possible here, but I can begin by pointing out some basic ideas relating to space and time and truth in each idea set that are epistemologically congruent, and by contrasting them with the epistemological congruencies that connect Newtonian physics and Darwinian evolution (See Table 20–1).

The epistemological differences between the two thought systems as represented in the two columns of the table below are profound, and the list is

## Table 20–1. Epistemological Congruencies between New Science and Batesonian Evolution and between Newtonian Physics and Darwinian Evolution

| Concepts Common to New Science and Batesonian Evolution | Concepts Common to Newtonian Physics and Darwinian Evolution |
|---|---|
| 1. Both assume a monistic universe (both/and). | 1. Both assume a dualistic universe. |
| 2. Both use concept of 4-dimensional timespace. | 2. In both, space and time are treated separately. |
| 3. Both view linear clocktime as a heuristically useful concept which does not, however, establish causative relations between events. | 3. Both view linear clocktime as real time in which one event is causative in relation to the next event. |
| 4. Both include abstract ideas or mind as part of the field of study. | 4. In both, the field of study is mechanistic and separate from the study of mind. |
| 5. Primary focus of both is patterned events in a 4-dimensional context. | 5. Primary focus of both is atomistic examination of entities in space and progression of events in linear time. |
| 6. Both discard certainty. Truth is seen as heuristic. | 6. Both accept certainty. Truth, therefore, is seen as absolute. |

open to indefinite expansion. What is important for the topic of this paper, however, is the congruence between new science and Batesonian evolution. The common epistemology they share not only represents a transformation in thought, but also points the way for a technology of transformation.

The behavioral sciences, like Newtonian physics and Darwinian evolution, evolved within the old Western epistemology. The issues confronted in the behavioral sciences are so complex that no single discipline or no single thought paradigm could encompass them, the result being that no paradigmatic consensus has emerged. The behavioral sciences are fragmented, and epistemological "cracks" abound, not only in the form of unexplained phenomena, but also among the plethora of paradigms.

In the realm of unexplained phenomena one glaring crack is the phenomenon of "schizophrenia." Most of the pioneers in the family therapy movement began by studying this phenomenon (or, more appropriately, these phenomena). Some of them "stepped through the crack" in a significant way with the assertion that the behavior of an individual could be viewed as family behavior with the individual as carrier. This assertion and the accompanying expansion of a definition of mind violate the thought rules of the old epistemology. The implied movement from the predominant Western epistemology to a new epistemology was, I believe, what gave the quality of a "movement" to family therapy as a body of ideas and a therapeutic action system.

But unlike the quantum-relativity physicists and unlike Bateson and his followers in the natural sciences, family theorists, researchers, and therapists as a general group do not seem to have recognized fully the discontinuity of the two thought systems. Like the physicists who tried to cram Planck's experimental findings into the Newtonian view of reality, most familiologists unwittingly seek ways to ignore the split.

In brief, I think it is fair to say that as of this writing only a handful of people in the field have thought seriously enough about epistemological issues to transform their thinking into print. Most of those who have done so have, for the most part, leaned heavily on Bateson—correctly, I think—but Gregory is no longer with us, and the work has just begun. Happily, he left us a legacy, which links us through ecosystem to evolution to new science.

To date, I know of no writings that present research done on families avowedly in the context of the new epistemology, although there is some research in which data have accumulated and concepts have been developed that will be usable in the new epistemological context. There are also techniques developed by a number of therapists that are usable in the context of a therapy rooted in the new epistemology. In fact, most family therapy techniques developed by those who view the family as a system, closed or open, are congruent. The trend, however, has been toward the usual Western atomization. Each technique has acquired a label, and a separate therapeutic paradigm has been built around it that makes it usable only in the static environment of the therapy room, out of which only a handful of therapists or writers have moved. Most unfortunate is the current trend to treat each of these technique-based paradigms as separate therapeutic modalities and to argue in and out of print about which is the most effective. For example, it is clearly not an accident that, among others, the techniques that have acquired the labels of "structural family therapy" and "strategic family therapy" have attracted more interest. Both identify cracks in the old epistemology. However, they generally have been discussed in terms congruent with the old thought system, which requires an either-or contrasting of the two techniques. In the "new" epistemology, the approach is both-and.

For some years I have been experimenting with ways of responding to families in distress which I think are congruent with the new epistemology and can provide a unifying context for the use of the variety of techniques now available.

What I have been doing and teaching and advocating casts the "therapist" (or preferably the cotherapists, since the presence of two thinkers and actors is synergistic) in the initial role of a nonblaming ecological detective. The initial task, in this context, is to seek out and identify the ecological event-shape in time-space that includes the situation that led the family to issue a distress call. Most of the events contributing to this shape will be found outside the constricted time-space of the office appointment. Once identified, a plan of action can be constructed to alter the evolution of the event-shape by adding a therapeutic event (or events) in a way that alleviates the distress. Each event-shape, of course, is different, and what techniques are used in the exploratory process and in the plan of action will depend on a combination of the nature of the event-shape and what techniques the therapist(s) are comfortable with. The intent is to transform the family as ecosystem, not to produce linear change within the family system.

I can illustrate this by a story in which, for reasons I will explain, I did not initially follow the above procedure. What happened, I believe, demonstrates the usefulness of this way of thinking.

One weekend in 1972 I was on crisis call for the mental health center in which I had recently begun working. On Sunday morning I received a call from a police officer who wanted to alert me that he was bringing a woman to the local hospital emergency room for admission to the psychiatric service. In his words, the woman had "cracked up" in church.

My routine response to such calls was to request that the caller remain where he or she was and ask all other persons involved to stay in place until I arrived. The police officer, in this situation, agreed.

Twenty minutes later, I arrived at the site, which turned out to be the priest's chamber of a Roman Catholic church. The police officer, whose name was Manuel, was waiting outside. When he led me inside, I found a silent and somber group made up of Rose, the "identified patient," a well-preserved and fairly attractive woman who looked about 40, her husband, Joe, her son, Warren, her daughter, Geri, Geri's husband, Paul, and the priest, Father John. Joe, Warren, and Paul were seated on one end of the room on a couch. Rose was across the room leaning against a desk staring out the window. She was barefoot and wrapped in a blanket. She was flanked by Geri and Father John. On the desk was a pile of woman's clothes.

After introductions, I invited Rose, Father John, and Geri to be seated on the chairs near the couch. Geri and Father John responded, but Rose did not. I then asked what had happened. The silence exploded. Everyone, except Rose and Paul, spoke at once, and then stopped. Manuel, who apparently considered himself in charge, then spoke up. He reported that Rose had disrupted the morning mass by removing her clothes in the middle of it. Hoping, I guess, to establish that her act was clearly that of a madwoman, and to turn the situation over to me, he ended his report with "and she did it for no reason."

I asked Rose, for whom I had developed some admiration by this time, if she could tell me her reason. After a pause, she answered softly, "I just couldn't stand it anymore." I asked her what it was she couldn't stand. She turned, seemed about to answer, but apparently thought better of it, and again fell silent, turning back to the window. The tension was again rising in the room.

I then decided to get more information, hoping that by this process I could defuse the situation somewhat. Most of the information I collected came from Geri, the daughter. I discovered that the family was of Portuguese background, that Rose was actually 45, Joe was 48, Warren, 22, Geri, 19, and Paul, 21. All were lifelong residents of the area except for Rose, who had been brought up in a rural area on another island.

Rose and Joe had married when she was 18. They had fought for four years following their marriage. Then they had stopped fighting, and, so it seemed, came together after the birth of their son. Rose was known as a good and dedicated mother, overly possessive of her children, but in the end willing to let them grow up and leave the nest. She was also known as a lively, though somewhat complaining, person.

Warren, the son, had moved out of the parent's household two years before the present incident. When Geri announced that she was planning marriage a year later, active fighting had broken out once again between Rose and Joe. Rose wanted a better house to live in. Joe's answer was that the house they lived in had always been his family home, and he didn't want to leave it. They couldn't afford to buy a new house, and he didn't want to live in somebody else's house and pay rent. Once, their arguing had reached the point of violence, with the husband belting his wife after she threw a breadboard at him.

About a week after this incident, Rose had stopped talking and had been hospitalized at the psychiatric service of the local general hospital.

She had been treated with medication. Rose's explanation of this episode, according to her daughter, was that she needed a good rest, which she got.

Geri had now been out of the home, too, for four months since her marriage. Having pieced together this much of the story, I was about to pursue more detailed information on the morning's events when I was interrupted by Manuel, the policeman. He wanted to know if I was willing to transport Rose to the hospital, since he had to get back on the road. I can recall a feeling of annoyance at this interruption, but I can recall no conscious intent to do what I then did.

Addressing Rose, I said, "I think I have a way for you to get out of this situation. All you have to do is change your religion. If you join the Holy Roller church down the road, taking off your clothes in church would make you a star."

There was a shocked silence, the shock of which I shared somewhat.

Manuel and Father John looked aghast. Husband and son looked increasingly angry. Geri and her husband looked bemused, and, finally, Rose, turning to look at me, broke into laughter.

With Rose's laughter, in a matter of seconds, the whole scene broke up. The police officer arose and announced he was leaving. The daughter said, "Come on, Ma, I'll take you home." She picked up the pile of clothes off the desk, took her mother's hand, and they walked out the door. Joe and Warren followed. The priest and I were left staring at each other. Father John was clearly speechless, and I felt I had to say something. I made some lame comment that his mass this morning must have been really something, and that I thought Rose would be all right, and then beat a hasty retreat.

Driving home, I felt a strong sense of conflict. On one hand, I was bemused and slightly elated. On the other hand, however, I felt I really did not know what had happened. My comment to Rose had been made with such spontaneity that I had literally shocked myself. With a little thought, however, it was easy to trace its origin.

I had been working in my job as the director of the mental health center which served the island on which I was living for only four months. During this short time I had become enormously impressed with the degree to which families on the island had been conditioned to dump their aberrant members on the doorstep of the center. The message they seemed to bring with them was "Here, he's crazy. You take him and fix him. Call us when he's fixed." It was clear that to get community support in its early days, the mental health center had promised to do just that, and was now busy trying to deliver on its promise. Sixty % of the center staff was taking care of hospitalized "patients" and the rest were busy passing out psychotropic medications. In this context, I was also impressed by the need to train the staff in the use of techniques that would involve families and social networks and that would be effective with a minimum of time expenditure because of the volume of demands. I did not have enough workers yet to staff the kind of ecological intervention unit I had developed.in previous jobs. Also, I had learned that the culture of the island was heavily influenced by the Oriental concept of "face." Direct confrontation could not be used in work with most families. The person confronted lost face and would not come back. It seemed to me that paradoxical prescriptions, if used with care, might be a useful technique to emphasize.

So what I had done in my session with Rose and her family, without conscious intent, was to come up with a paradoxical prescription that came from my overall mind-set and also expressed my annoyance with the police officer's impatient comment. He had wanted me to cut short the conversational nonsense and get on with the task, which he considered my assignment, that of hospitalizing Rose.

I remained uneasy, however, about the outcome of my intervention. I had certainly succeeded in some of my intents. I had prevented Rose's admission to the hospital. I had also lessened the possibility that Rose would take off her clothes in church again. And I knew that it was to Rose's advantage not to become imbedded in a "mental patient" career. Beyond these effects, however, I did not know whether my intervention would be useful to the family, or whether I had simply driven them away. In other words, I did not know whether my intervention had been therapeutic. The meeting had broken up so rapidly that there had been no time to schedule another. I decided to see the family again.

The next day, Monday, I looked for a telephone number for Rose and Joe in the phone book. There was none. Paul and Geri were listed, however. I called and got Geri. When I told her I wanted to arrange another meeting, she said she did not think it was necessary. It turned out that after the happenings in the priest's office, the entire family had gone to Geri's house and held a family meeting. Rose had said that now that the children were gone she was afraid to be home alone, especially on weekends, which Joe routinely spent fishing on the beach with his cronies. Both Geri and Warren had sympathized and had insisted that Joe change his ways and stay home with Rose on weekends. Reluctantly, Joe had agreed to do so.

I decided that my intervention of the day before had been useful and that for the time being I would leave well enough alone. Occasionally, in the ensuing months, I would think of Rose and Joe and wonder how they were doing. But as time passed, I forgot about them.

About four years later, I was at a party one Saturday night when I was summoned to the telephone. The caller turned out to be a nurse working at the hospital emergency room who had somehow traced my whereabouts. I was not on call, and my first response was annoyance that her efforts had resulted in an intrusion on my private time. My annoyance was joined by curiosity, however, when she told me that Rose had appeared in the emergency room and was asking to see me. Now ambivalent, I gave the nurse a time the following Monday to give to Rose with instructions that I would see her then in my office. The nurse left the phone, returning in a short time to say that Rose wanted to see me now, and that in her judgment, I should come. So I left the party and drove to the hospital.

I found Rose sitting, head bowed, on an examining table. She could barely talk. What she did say was barely audible and was delivered in a droning, affectless way. I asked her to speak louder and she did, but the droning quality of her voice grew more apparent. I commented that her voice sounded like that of a computerized robot. She fell silent, and I feared I had put her off with my comment, so I said, "That's okay. We have to talk anyway." When she spoke, affective overtones had returned to her speech, and she said, "Nobody hears me, anyway." So I said, "Well, let me try." She remained silent.

Trying to find out more about her, I asked her about the family she grew up in. She talked mostly about her mother, who it turned out was Hawaiian, not Portuguese. Her mother and her relatives on her mother's side had spent long hours telling her about her Hawaiian heritage. She had learned much about Hawaiian mythology, about spirits, about Pele, the goddess of the volcano, about Hawaiian taboos. She also told me how she had been taught to obey her husband. At first, as she spoke of her childhood, her voice became stronger, but after a time it again became faint and, finally, she fell silent once again. I tried changing the topic. I asked her, "What were you trying to accomplish by taking off your clothes in church?" She answered, "Joe was there." But I was not to get the complete answer to this question until later. Rose stood up, turned her head to the heavens, and threw up her arms. Then she looked me straight in the eye and said in a belligerent tone, "You come my house?"

By this time, it was nearing midnight. I had no wish to make the journey to Rose's house that night. I asked if it would be all right if I came to see her in the morning. Her answer was that she wanted to stay in the hospital, and that I should pick her up from the hospital in the morning and go to her house with her. I agreed, and arranged for her admission overnight.

The following morning, having collected Rose from the hospital, I drove to where she lived. When we arrived, Rose directed me to park my car in a small clearing on the edge of a pineapple field. I could see no house. We got out of the car and Rose led me across the pineapple field for several hundred yards to the edge of a gulch. I still could see no house. Rose led me down a steep and rocky path to the bottom of the gulch, through the gulch, and up on the other side. When we emerged over the lip of the gulch, I saw Rose's house. It was an old and ramshackle affair. Not more than a few feet beyond the house as we approached it I could see the lip of another gulch. It turned out to be, however, not another gulch, but rather the same gulch. Rose's house was situated on a mound created when eroding waters had split apart into channels, joining again further down the mountain from Rose's home. She lived, in a sense, on an island on an island. I noticed, piled up on the edge of the gulch, the remnants of a rope bridge that apparently at one time had provided passage across the gulch to the pathway leading to the road. I asked Rose about the bridge, and she told me that it had been intact when she moved into the house as a young woman, but that within a few years it had fallen apart. Joe had explored building a more substantial bridge, but the cost had always been too great for them.

I was amazed when I entered the house. First of all, there was much more room than one would have guessed by looking at the outside. Second, it was furnished with old but tasteful furniture, arranged in a very artistic way. Most startling, however, were the walls. They were covered with colorful and beautiful crayon drawings of flowers and fruits, all shapes and sizes. As I walked around the house, exclaiming at the beauty of the drawings, I made a comment about one particular drawing of a plumeria plant. Rose promptly took it off the wall and gave it to me. It turned out that the walls exhibited what Rose did with her weekends. While Joe was away, she drew flowers, and plants, and fruits. I learned later that all the homes of people who knew Rose had her pictures on their walls.

But Rose had not brought me there for an art show. What she wanted to show me was the isolation of the place. She led me to the upper tip of her island in the gulch. She pointed to where she had seen the goddess Pele many times while home alone. She spoke of sounds of marching she heard from the gulch which came from the spirits that dwelt there. According to Hawaiian legend, if the marching spirits of the dead touched a living person, that person would die. She was terrified of them. She was especially terrified during the times when the rains came. The water would come tumbling down the gulch on both sides of her island, totally isolating her from the outside. She could not cross the gulch to get away. She was alone with the spirits, and terrified.

Thinking back to my phone conversation with Geri following the meeting at the church, I asked her if she was still terrified, since Joe had decided to forego his weekends on the beach and stay home with her. She told me that that arrangement had lasted only a few weeks. Joe had come to her and, almost in tears, pleaded with her not to take away from him his days with his cronies on the beach. Protesting that he loved her and that he did not wish to have her so upset, he confessed that he missed the time with his friends desperately. He had been too long on the beach with them. It was very, very hard for him to give that up. Compassionately, Rose had released him from his promise.

I then asked Rose the question that had been lurking in the back of my mind since the night before. "What did you think would happen when you took off your clothes in church?" Rose answered, "I thought he would be ashamed of me. I wanted him to take me away to another part of the island. I cannot stand it in this house anymore." From a drawer in a remote corner of the kitchen, Rose drew another stack of crayon drawings. They were drawings of a house in the sunshine surrounded by flowers and by other houses. There were figures of people everywhere. There were dogs and cats and children.

I took Rose to her daughter's house and arranged for a meeting with all family members the next day. Rose's daughter agreed to go to Rose's house that evening to let Joe know where she was.

Before going back for the family meeting the next day, I went to the hospital and looked up the record of Rose's first hospitalization. She had been diagnosed as a catatonic schizophrenic. The nurses' notes showed that while she had been speechless on admission, she had begun talking shortly after her arrival. She had spent a week in the hospital, on antipsychotic medication, spending most of her time drawing flowers and houses.

At the family meeting the next day, I did what I could have done four years earlier if I had taken the time to tease out the event-shape in time-space that contained Rose's distress. I proposed a trade-off. I told Joe that I thought Rose had been very understanding when she had released him from his promise to stay home and allowed him to continue to enjoy his friends, and that I thought he needed to make an effort to find Rose a place where she could be among people on the weekends. Joe protested that he did not want to leave the house of his family. But both of the couple's children came to her defense. They agreed with what I said, and came on strongly in support of the idea. By the time I left, the decision had been made that Joe and Rose would move to town.

A week later I held another meeting with the family. Rose had not gone back to the house in the gulch. The family was actively looking for a place for Rose and Joe to live in town. Between meetings, Rose had decided to get a job, to help with the added expense of a new place to live.

Two months later I called Rose's daughter, not knowing where Rose and Joe were. Geri told me that they had found a house in the central valley of the island in one of the two towns there. Rose was working in a supermarket. I got the address of the new house, and two days later I paid the family a visit.

As it turned out, Joe had not been too happy during the first few days of their move into town. He was, however, willing to admit grudgingly that there were some advantages. He did not have to take Rose on long shopping trips anymore. And now he was living closer to some of his friends who lived in town. He thought he could get used to it.

Rose, on the other hand, was bouncing. Full of smiles and talk, she told me of her new friends in the houses that surrounded their new home. On her walls were her drawings. They were arranged so that the drawings of flowers and plants and fruits surrounded a central arrangement, which consisted of the drawings she had pulled from the kitchen drawer. Houses and people and dogs and cats were everywhere.

The point of this story is that resolution of this family's distress was attempted on three occasions using three thought paradigms.

The first response used the medical-psychopathological paradigm. Rose was diagnosed and treated accordingly. Her improvement was attributed to her treatment. It was not possible for those "helping" her to come to the conclusion that her improvement was due to the respite she experienced from the fear she felt when alone in her home. These helpers did not think that way. Even if they had had the necessary information, they would have come to the same conclusion. This way of thinking is firmly rooted in the old Western Newtonian epistemology.

In the second response, the session in the priest's office, the thought system immanent in my paradoxical intervention was the communications paradigm, which evolved this technique. My intervention "cured" Rose's symptomatic behavior (which probably would not have recurred, anyway) and forced the family to act on its own behalf. A promise was extracted from Joe, which he could not keep. No structural change took place in the family. Joe simply promised to change his ways. What was needed was a quid pro quo agreement between Joe and Rose. This agreement did not occur because I did not complete my exploration of the event-shape in timespace. I did not "see" the need. While this thought paradigm fits into the new epistemology, the ecosystem I was looking at was too constricted. I looked only at the family.

It was not until four years later that Rose forced me to do what I could have done in the first place; that is, to complete my exploration of the event-shape in time-space in an ecosystem just expansive enough to let me "see" it. The event-shape that emerged contained the following elements:

1. Rose's Hawaiian upbringing, which taught her the Hawaiian mythology of Pele and the marching dead, and that she must obey her husband.
2. Rose's marriage to Joe and their move into Joe's family home in the gulch.
3. Joe's lifelong lifestyle, which included his pleasure at spending his weekends fishing with his friends, and his attachment to the family home.
4. The breakdown of the rope bridge that resulted in Rose's entrapment on her island in the gulch when it rained.
5. Warren's departure from the family home.
6. Geri's departure from the family home.
7. Rose's fear and symptoms.

Only when I had done enough detective work to "see" this event-shape was I able to "see" the quid pro quo solution.

It is probable that the medical helpers at the time of Rose's first hospitalization concluded that their treatment had produced "change" in Rose. My paradoxical prescription did produce "change" in the family and in Rose's behavior—albeit limited and temporary. But not until I had completed my ecological exploration did I find the intervention that produced a transform, not a change. It was necessary for me to think this way, and then to act accordingly. I had to step through the crack in the family system, as marked by Rose's "crazy" behavior, into the surrounding contextual time-space.

There is a postscript to Rose's story. Only a couple of months before I sat down to write this article, I saw a number of Rose's drawings displayed in a gift shop at a shopping center near the tourist hotels on our island. They were as beautiful as I remembered them.

A well-dressed tourist was admiring them, and decided to purchase one. As I watched the clerk wrap the drawing lovingly and hand it to the tourist, I wanted to tell them Rose's story. But, of course, I did not.

## REFERENCES

Auerswald, E. H. (1968). Interdisciplinary versus ecological approach. *Family Process, 7,* 202–215.

Auerswald, E. H. (1971). Families, change, and the ecological perspective. *Family Process, 10,* 263–280.

Auerswald, E. H. (1975). Thinking about thinking about health and mental health. In G. Caplan (ed.), *American handbook of psychiatry* (Vol. 2). New York: Basic Books.

Bateson, G. (1979). *Mind and nature: A necessary unity.* New York: E. P. Dutton.

Einstein, A. (1905a). Concerning an heuristic point of view toward the emission and transport of light. *Annalen der Physik, 17,* 132.

Einstein, A. (1905b). On the electrodynamics of moving bodies. *Annalen der Physik, 17,* 891.

Einstein, A. & Infeld, L. (1938). *The evolution of physics.* New York: Simon & Shuster.

Planck, M. (1900). Distribution of energy in the normal spectrum. *Deutsche Physiologischen Gesellschaft,* Verlag Lungen, *2*(17), 245–257.

Planck, M. (1936). *The philosophy of physics* (W. H. Johnston, Trans.). New York: W. W. Norton.

# Afterword

We can't imagine a more fitting juncture at which to leave you, the reader. The global nature of Dick's work and thought epitomize the worldview of systemic consciousness.

Whatever path you have followed with us through this book, we hope it has opened new vistas on pharmland and family therapy, stimulating creativity in your own approach to working with the emotional and psychological textures of life.

# Contributors

David V. Keith, MD, is Professor of Psychiatry, Family Medicine and Pediatrics, SUNY Upstate Medical University, Syracuse, New York.

Phoebe S. Prosky, MSW, is founder and director of training at A Center for the Awareness of Pattern in Freeport Maine, consultant to several institutions, and in private practice in Freeport.

Edgar H. Auerswald, MD (deceased), was founder and Director of the Center for Applied Epistemology in San Francisco, California.

Larry Freeman, MD, is in private practice in Bellingham, Washington.

Marcelo Pakman, MD, is director of Psychiatric Services, Behavioral Health Network, Springfield, Massachusetts.

Catherine Ducommun-Nagy, MD, is president of The Institute for Contextual Growth, Inc; adjunct assistant professor in the Graduate Program in Marriage and Family Therapy at MCP/Hahnemann University/Drexel University, Philadelphia, Pennsylvania; consultant to several institutions; and in private practice in the Philadelphia area.

Paul Schaefer, MD, is a consultant to Northern Home Children and Family Services in Philadelphia, Pennsylvania, and is in private practice in Philadelphia.

Zhao Mei, MD, is founder and Director of the Chinese Healing Arts Center in Portland, Maine.

Barry Duncan, PsyD, is cofounder and Codirector of the Institute for the Study of Therapeutic Change; author of ten books, among them *The Heroic Client* (Jossey-Bass, 2000), *The Heart and Soul of Change: What Works* (APA, 1999), *Escape from Babel: Toward a Unifying Language for Psychotherapy Practice* (Norton, 1997), *Psychotherapy with "Impossible" Cases:* (Norton, 1997), *Handbook of Solution-Focused Brief Therapy* (Jossey-Bass, 1996), *Changing the Rules: A Client-Directed Approach to Therapy, and Brief Intervention for School Problems* (Guilford, 1992), and *Heroic Clients, Heroic Agencies: Partners for Change* (ISTC Press, 2002).

Scott Miller, PhD, is cofounder and Codirector of the Institute for the Study of Therapeutic Change; author of seven books, including *The Heroic Client* (Jossey-Bass, 2000), *The Heart and Soul of Change: What Works* (APA, 1999), *Escape from Babel: Toward a Unifying Language for Psychotherapy Practice* (Norton, 1997), *Psychotherapy with "Impossible" Cases* (Norton, 1997), *Handbook of*

*Solution-Focused Brief Therapy* (Jossey-Bass, 1996), *The Miracle Method: A Radically New Approach to Problem Drinking* (Norton, 1995), and *Working with the Problem Drinker: A Solution-Focused Approach* (Norton, 1992).

Jacqueline Sparks, PhD, is an adjunct faculty member at the Graduate School of Humanities and Social Sciences, Nova Southeastern University and an associate of The Institute for the Study of Therapeutic Change, and coauthor of *Heroic Clients, Heroic Agencies: Partners for Change* (ISTC Press, 200). She practices psychotherapy at Partners for Change in South Florida.

Sharon Beder, PhD, MscSoc, is Professor of Science and Technology Studies at the University of Wollongong, Australia, and author of *Global Spin* (2nd Ed., 2002), Chelsea Green, Vermont.

Richard Gosden, PhD, is the author of *Punishing the Patient* (Scribe, Melbourne, Australia, 2001).

Loren Mosher, MD, is Director of Soteria Associates in San Diego, California; Clinical Professor of Psychiatry at the University of California at San Diego, School of Medicine; Adjunct Professor of Psychiatry at the Uniformed Services University of the Health Sciences, Bethesda, Maryland; and coauthor of Mosher and Burti, *Community Mental Health: A Practical Guide* (Norton, 1994).

J. Jules Vitali is a sculptor in Freeport, Maine.

Patricia Dyer, MSW, is Clinical Director of A Center for the Awareness of Pattern in Freeport, Maine.

Noralyn Masselink, PhD, is a graciously participating patient.

Oscar Davis is a graciously participating patient.

John Flynn, PhD, MSW (deceased), was Associate Professor of Human Services, Philosophy, and Comparative Religion at the State University of New York Empire State College.

Amy Begel, CSW, is on the faculty of the Department of Family Practice, Lutheran Medical Center and in private practice in New York City.

Fred Ford, MD, is in private practice in Kensington, California.

John Benda, LCSW, is in private practice in Minneapolis, Minnesota.

Felix Yaroshevsky, MD, CRCPC, is Medical Director at Satyr Enterprises Incorporated, Toronto, Canada.

Vivian Bekiaris is President of Satyr Enterprises Incorporated, Toronto, Canada.

# Index